And the Winner Is . . .

Of Related Interest
from Continuum

American History/American Film—New Expanded Edition, John E. O'Connor and Martin A. Jackson, eds.

American History/American Television, John E. O'Connor, ed.

The Cinema of Stanley Kubrick—New Expanded Edition, Norman Kagan

The Dead That Walk: Dracula, Frankenstein, the Mummy, and Other Favorite Movie Monsters, Leslie Halliwell

Fellini the Artist, Edward Murray

Film Noir: Reflections in a Dark Mirror, Bruce Crowther

Framework: A History of Screenwriting in the American Film, Tom Stempel

The French Through Their Films, Robin Buss

Hitchcock: The First Forty-Four Films, Eric Rohmer and Claude Chabrol

Italian Cinema: From Neorealism to the Present—New Expanded Edition, Peter Bondanella

A Project for the Theatre, Ingmar Bergman

The Screening of America: Movies and Values from "Rocky" to "Rain Man," Tom O'Brien

Screening Space: The American Science Fiction Film, Vivian Sobchack

Silent Magic: Rediscovering the Silent Film Era, Ivan Butler

Toms, Coons, Mulattoes, Mammies, and Bucks: An Interpretive History of Blacks in American Films—New Expanded Edition, Donald Bogle

World Cinema Since 1945: An Encyclopedic History, William Luhr, ed.

And the Winner Is . . .

The History and Politics of the Oscar® Awards

New Expanded Edition

EMANUEL LEVY

A Frederick Ungar Book

CONTINUUM • NEW YORK

1990
The Continuum Publishing Company
370 Lexington Avenue, New York, NY 10017

Printed in the United States of America

Library of Congress Cataloging-in-Publication Data

Levy, Emanuel, 1946-
And the winner is—.

Bibliography: p.
Includes index.
1. Academy awards (Moving-pictures) I. Title.
PN1993.92.L48   1987   791.43'079   86-30824
ISBN 0-8264-0450-2 (pbk.)

All photographs courtesy of The Museum of Modern Art/Film Stills
Archive, 11 West 53rd Street, New York City

This book is dedicated to
Rob Remley and
Nathan Waterman

Contents

Acknowledgments   xi

Introduction to the New Expanded Edition   xiii

Introduction   xvi

Chapter 1.   The Academy of Motion Picture Arts and Sciences
and the Oscar Awards   1

The Academy's Structure and Membership   5
Procedures for Nomination   8
Award Categories and Nominees   14
The Academy Awards   17
The Awards Ceremonies   19
The Oscar Television Show   24

Chapter 2.   The Extraordinary Preeminence of the Oscar
Award   31

The Preeminence of the Oscar in the Film
World   31
Film Academies and Institutes   31
International Film Festivals   33
Film Critics   37
Popularity and Other Awards   39
The Preeminence of the Oscar in the Entertainment
World   41

Chapter 3.   The Nomination System   49

The First Nomination   49
Early and Late Recognition by the Academy   53
Nominations for Lead and Supporting Roles   59
Single and Multiple Nominations   63
Effects of the Nomination   69

Chapter 4. The Oscar as an International Award 73

The International Dimension of the Oscar 73
The British Dominance 75
Other Foreign Films and Artists 85
Nationalism and Film Awards 91

Chapter 5. The Winning Process 95

The Winners' Age 95
The Oscar as an Instant Reward 98
Nomination and Winning 104
Ties and Multiple Awards 107
The Nominees as a Social and Artistic
Community 111

Chapter 6. The Oscar-Winning Films 119

Biographical and Fictional Films 119
The Serious-Problem Film 122
The Serious Woman's Film 124
The Problem-Message Film—Race, Politics, and
Crime 127
The Problem-Message Film—Individual and
Family 135
Comedy Films 141
Lack of Respect for Comedy Players 148

Chapter 7. The Oscar-Winning Films: Other Genres 151

Musical Films 151
Historical-Epic Films 156
War Films 163
Action-Adventure Films 167
Suspense Films 171
Western Films 173
Conclusion 175

Chapter 8. The Oscar-Winning Roles 181

The Oscar Roles and Film Genre 181
Gender and the Oscar Role: The American Hero
and Heroine 183
Prevalent Male Oscar Roles 186
Enduring Female Screen Stereotypes 191

Suffering and Victimization 197
The Oscar Roles, Hollywood, and Male
    Dominance 201
Recent Changes in Oscar-Winning Roles 204

Chapter 9. The Oscar as a Reward System 209

The Error of Omission 210
The Oscar as a Popularity Contest 212
The Oscar as a Reward for Mediocrity 217
The Oscar as a Reward for Eccentricity 219
The Oscar as a Compensation 221
The Career Oscars 225

Chapter 10. The Meanings of the Oscar Award 231

Total Embracement: Oscar and Peer
    Recognition 231
Ambivalence and Rejection of the Oscar 238
Reaction to Winning 243
I Would Like to Thank . . . The Acceptance
    Speech 249
Losing the Award: Defeat in the Public Eye 254

Chapter 11. The Multiple Effects of the Oscar 259

The Oscar's Effects on Films 259
Effects on the Winners' Careers 264
    Skyrocketing Salaries 264
    International Stardom 266
The Oscar and Cumulative Advantage in Film 269
The Triple Crown: Oscar-Tony-Emmy 273
Negative Effects of the Oscar 276
    Quality of Film Work 276
    The Curse of Typecasting 279
Oscar Anxiety 284

Chapter 12. Politics and the Oscar Award 289

Studio Politics 289
Advertisement Campaigns 294
Societal Politics 303
Politics and the Careers of Oscar Artists 311
The Use of the Oscar Show for Political
    Propaganda 317

Conclusion   The Oscar Award, Film, and American Culture   329

                    The Preeminence of the Oscar in American Culture   333

Appendices   339
Notes   353
Selected Bibliography   367

Index   373

Photographs may be found following pages 150 and 207

Acknowledgments

My initial interest in studying and writing about the Oscar Award began in 1979, when I was asked to teach a course on popular culture at Hunter College. I had just completed a book on the Jewish and Israeli theater and was looking for a new and different research site, preferably a symbol that would capture the essence of American popular culture. I could not have found a more appropriate topic for my concerns than the Oscar Award, established by the Academy of Motion Picture Arts and Sciences in 1927. I have always been amazed by the immense popularity of the annual Oscar ceremonies and thought that exploring this subject from a social-historical perspective would be of great interest—and tremendous fun, too. And it was.

I began to collect systematic data on the Academy Awards in 1981, not realizing then the amount of work involved. But I wanted to be comprehensive and to start from the very beginning of the Oscar, from the establishment of the Academy of Motion Picture Arts and Sciences, sixty years ago. I also knew that, for limitations of time, budget, and space, the book would have to focus on few award categories, thus choosing the Best Picture, Best Director, and the four acting awards.

During the collection of materials, the scope of the research expanded and various comparisons between the Oscar Award and other film and cultural awards were included—to place the Academy and its prestigious prize in broader cultural and historical settings. The present book, however, is not a chronological, year by year, history of the Academy Awards. Rather, it provides a sociological view of the historical, cultural, and political contexts within which films and film artists have been nominated for and have won the Oscar Award over the last sixty-one years.

Many friends and colleagues have read and commented on earlier drafts of this book and papers presented in various conferences. I would like to thank Judith Blau, Herman Enzer, Gary Alan Fine, Wendy Griswold, Edward Johnson, Rob Remley, Pamela J. Riley, Yaffa Schlesinger, Bill Shepard, Gabriella Taylor, and Andrea Walsh for providing helpful comments. I have benefited immensely from conversations about film and popular culture with two of my professors and friends at Columbia University, Sigmund Diamond and Allan Silver. This book owes an intellectual debt to my teacher and friend Harriet A. Zuckerman, whose excellent study of the Nobel Prize contributed to my earlier attempts to formulate significant research problems. The use of and attempt to apply the theory of cumulative advantage in science to the film world is based on Professor Robert K. Merton's influential ideas in the sociology of science. My students at Columbia University have also contributed to this book by challenging my ideas about film and society.

I spent a most pleasant sabbatical at the University of New Hampshire, where I worked on the final draft of the manuscript and my secretary Kerry typed some of it. Finally I would like to thank my friend Eli Meron, whose gracious hospitality I enjoyed in my extensive trips to Los Angeles.

The collection of data took place in many libraries and I would like to thank the personnel of the Margaret Herrick Library of the Academy of Motion Picture Arts and Sciences, the Lincoln Center Library for the Performing Arts, and the libraries of the American Film Institute, the Museum of Modern Art, the University of California at Los Angeles, and the University of Southern California. My special thanks to Mr. Bruce Davis, the Executive Administrator of the Academy, for the useful information he provided, and to Mary Corliss and Terry Geesken of the Museum of Modern Art's Stills Archive, for their patient guidance in selecting pictures for this book. It gives great pleasure to thank Mr. Michael Leach and Mr. Evander Lomke, of The Ungar Publishing Company, for the interest they have shown in my work and for improving the manuscript.

Finally, I would like to stress again that this book could not have been completed without the assistance and moral support of my friend Rob Remley at every phase of the process. No writer could hope for better assistance or more supportive encouragement.

Introduction to the
New Expanded Edition

It gives me great pleasure to write an introduction to the second, expanded edition, though, because of brevity of space, I can only indicate general trends of the recent Oscar Awards. As the decade is coming to its end, the Oscar seems to be gaining in tradition and acceptability. No other award in American culture has sustained its popularity and prestige in the same way that the Oscar award has. The legitimacy of the award is now almost universally accepted as a symbol of achievement and success. The 1980s have been marked by the absence of criticism (by the likes of Marlon Brando, Dustin Hoffman, and George C. Scott), concerning the structure and operations of the Oscar process. Even advertising is now regarded (and practiced) as a valid means of calling the attention of peers to the existence of a film and/or a good performance. Though fluctuating in length, interest, and production values, recent Oscar ceremonies have run smoothly; no more political statements from the Oscar platform on the order of Vanessa Redgrave's. Like the artists themselves, the general public continues to embrace the Oscar Award (and the annual show) as an obligatory ceremony to be watched. As such, the Oscar Award is one of the few unifying collective symbols in an increasingly stratified and heterogeneous American culture.

That politics plays a part in the Oscar Award is beyond doubt; this is the nature of awards determined by majority vote. However, the fact that most film artists regard the winning of an Oscar as the highest accolade in their career is probably related to changes in the structure of the film industry. The award is no longer manipulated by the moguls and the major studios, and there is no more pressure to vote for one's studio since the traditional studios do not exist anymore. The fact that every branch consists of the best artists in the field makes the award all the more desirable. For instance, the Acting Branch is composed of artists of the caliber of Jack Nicholson, William Hurt, Meryl Streep, Sigourney Weaver, and Christine Lahti. If *they* single out performances, their votes are meaningful and carry a good deal of prestige.

The tendency to nominate foreign artists in major categories has become even stronger, attesting to the outstanding internationality of the Oscar, extending its visibility as much more than an American award. In recent years, Max Von Sydow *(Pelle the Conqueror)* was nominated for Best Actor, and Hector Babenco *(Kiss of the Spider Woman)*, Akira Kurosawa *(Ran)*, Peter Weir *(Witness)*, and James Ivory *(A Room with a View)* for Best Director. Indeed, in 1987, for the first time in the Academy history, all five nominees for the directorial achievement award were foreign filmmakers: Bernardo Bertolucci *(The Last Emperor)*, John Boorman *(Hope and Glory)*, Lasse Hallstrom *(My Life as a Dog)*, Norman Jewison *(Moonstruck)*, and Adrian Lyne *(Fatal Attraction)*.

Compared with the days of the studio system, it has become a rarer phenomenon for one major film to sweep most nominations and awards. Winning nine awards, in every category it was nominated, *The Last Emperor* has been the exception. There has been only one other film, *Gigi* (1958), to receive awards in each and every of its nine nominated categories. In recent years, more films have been nominated, and subsequently there has been a more egalitarian or even distribution of awards. The Academy's different branches have displayed varying degrees of independence in their judgments. It is possible that Steven Spielberg is not "popular" among his peers at the Directors Branch, a claim that is made by his defenders in explaining his failure to win a nomination for *The Color Purple* (not a good movie) and *Empire of the Sun*, even though both movies were nominated for many awards. At the same time, it is encouraging that David Lynch was nominated for *Blue Velvet* (1986) and Martin Scorsese for *The Last Temptation of Christ*, even though the material of both was controversial and far from the typical "Oscar stuff."

Another positive development in the 1980s has been the greater attention paid to comedy films and performances, a genre underestimated in previous Oscar contests. Though none won, in recent years the country's best comedians have finally received the praise and attention they deserved: Kathleen Turner *(Peggy Sue Got Married)*, Robin Williams *(Good Morning Vietnam)*, and Tom Hanks *(Big)*. Of the fifteen films nominated for Best Picture over the last three years, six have been comedies, an unusually high proportion compared with previous years. To be sure, "social problem" *(Children of a Lesser God)* and "sensitive" films *(Rain Man)* still have better chances to be nominated for the top award, but "frivolous" comedies *(Moonstruck, Working Girl)* have increased their visibility in the Oscar competition—provided they are well made and well acted.

The range and quality of screen roles nominated for Oscars, particularly among the women, have become more diverse. For example, Sigourney Weaver's Best Actress nomination in *Aliens* makes her the first woman to be nominated for a lead award in an action-adventure film, in the past an exclusively "male" genre. Glenn Close's two Best Actress nominations *(Fatal Attraction* and *Dangerous Liaisons)* were also for atypical, villainous roles, the kind of roles that, at best, would win supporting nomination. To be sure, these roles prevail side by side with the more conventional, *typical* Oscar roles, such as Jane Fonda's great performance as an alcoholic, has-been actress in *The Morning After.* Eccentricity has also continued to pay off, as the awards of Cher *(Moonstruck)*, Kevin Kline *(A Fish Called Wanda)*, and Geena Davis *(The Accidental Tourist)* demonstrated. Finally, British performers still dominate the acting categories (Bob Hoskins, Denholm Elliott, Alec Guinness), but, as in the past, they tend to win in the supporting leagues (Michael Caine, Sean Connery), and in American-made films *(Hannah and Her Sisters* and *The Untouchables*, respectively).

I am delighted to report that most of these trends were pointed out and discussed in the first edition of the book, and that this expanded edition includes new information, which brings the Oscar Award up to date.

Emanuel Levy
New York City, January 1990

Introduction

The Oscar Award, bestowed by the Academy of Motion Picture Arts and Sciences for the best achievements in film, is the most important award in the film world. Moreover, the annual Oscar ceremonies are watched on television by people who are neither American nor moviegoers. It would not be an exaggeration to claim that the Oscar is the most visible prize in the world. The Oscar television show has become an international *media event* of the utmost importance, watched live or on tape by one billion viewers in over seventy countries. It is one of the few events, along with the Olympic Games, to lend credibility to the notion of the world as one supranational community.

The Oscar's longevity and amazing international popularity are in many respects ironic as well as paradoxical. This prize has continued to capture the public's attention despite the steady decline of film as the dominant cultural medium in America, and despite the decline of Hollywood as the world's film center. The Oscar has continued to fascinate millions of Americans despite the immense decline in film production and in the size of movie audiences. How did it happen? How did the Oscar Award acquire such outstanding dimensions of preeminence? Is it just a nostalgic tribute to films' glorious past, or is there more to it? Using a sociohistorical perspective, *And the Winner Is: The History and Politics of the Oscar Awards* provides answers to these queries by examining the Oscar from its inception in 1927 to the present.

Every year there are heated debates not only about the "fairness" of the Academy's choices but also about the quality of the television show itself. In 1983, film critic Vincent Canby raised the question: "Why do we watch this nonsense with such rapt attention?" In his answer, he suggested that "more than any other program of its kind, the annual Oscar telecast epitomizes American show-business and where show-business happens to be at that particular moment." In Canby's view, the show "has to do not only with movies, but also with television, with business and especially with the American civilization, as it is and as it wants to see itself."[1] Canby's statement offers interesting insights but it is too general to serve as satisfactory explanation for the Oscar's phenomenal popularity.

Interestingly enough, the production values of the Oscar show have almost no impact on its popularity with viewers: it seems to be beyond criticism. Watching the annual ceremonies has become an obligatory ritual for many people. But the interesting questions are: why is the show beyond criticism? and why is it an obligation to watch? These are the two central issues that this book attempts to answer. Clearly, if the Oscar has survived for over half a century with such striking popularity, it probably continues to fulfill some important functions that go beyond honoring excellence in film —functions that are probably relevant outside the film world.

And the Winner Is documents the process through which the Oscar and its show have become important cultural symbols of achievement and success all over the world. It shows that the Oscar is one of the few symbols that still epitomize "the American Dream." After all, there have been numerous awards, in and outside the film world, but none has acquired such outstanding dimensions. The Nobel Prize, the most prestigious award in science, is also important and visible, but it has never achieved the preeminence of the Oscar Award.

This book analyzes the unique place occupied by the Oscar in American culture by describing its distinctive history, characteristics, and multiple functions for the film industry, film artists, moviegoers, and television viewers. The Oscar's remarkable preeminence is seen as related to film's double nature as an art form and as a commercial product. A mass, audiovisual medium, film can cross geographic and national boundaries more effectively than other arts. Its mass, commercial nature also allows large and diverse audiences to relate to it in a highly emotional and personal way. Movies depend on the immediate response of audiences much more than other arts, and this dependency gives the viewing public tremendous power. By going to see a particular movie, for example, the public affects not only its standing at the box office but also the very chances of the artists who made it to work in the future.

Film, like other art forms, does not operate in a social or political void. Meant for the enjoyment of contemporary audiences, it is inevitably subject to the stimulative and disruptive influences of the sociohistorical contexts in which it operates. Thus, demographic changes (size and age structure of the population), historical events (World War II), political circumstances (the McCarthy era), and the prevailing dominant culture (conservatism versus liberalism, patriotism versus self-criticism) have been some of the most basic factors to affect the kinds of movies made and their reception by audiences. More specifically, these social forces have also influenced the kinds of movies nominated for or winning the Oscar Award. On another level, *And the Winner Is* attempts to shed some light on the place of movies in our lives and on the ways in which we relate to them.

Examination of the Oscar Award in its entire fifty-nine-year history can serve as an effective demonstration of the complex interplay between films and their specific social, political, and cultural settings. The Oscar-winning and Oscar-nominated films are therefore analyzed in relation to two systems—the state of the film industry and the state of American society at large.

The book deals with six specific issues:

1. The preeminence of the Oscar Award in film and entertainment.
2. The nomination system.
3. The winning process.
4. The winning and nominated movies and performances.
5. The meanings and effects of the Oscar Award.
6. The functions of the Oscar in American popular culture.

Through the systematic exploration of these themes, *And the Winner Is* provides an overall understanding of the Oscar Award's operations. For that purpose, the Oscar is placed in three broader contexts: the film world, in and outside the United States; show business, or the world of entertainment; and American culture in general. Extensive comparisons are made between:

1. The Oscar and other film awards (by critics associations, film institutes, and international film festivals)
2. The Oscar and other entertainment awards (the Tony, the Emmy, and the Grammy).

Recently, it has become fashionable to condemn and to poke fun at the Oscar and the television show. The uniqueness of *And the Winner Is* is that it neither condones nor condemns the Oscar Award. Rather, the book attempts to provide an objective evaluation of the award and the show by placing them in a broader perspective.[2]

One of the book's strongest assets is its comparative, cross-cultural approach, making seven valuable comparisons, between:

1. Actors and actresses, to determine the impact of gender on careers, film roles, screen images, and prize-winning performances.
2. American and foreign artists, to evaluate the role of nationality in the nomination and winning processes.
3. The four acting categories, to assess the differences between the lead and supporting awards.
4. Winners and losers, to evaluate the effects of winning on the artists' careers.
5. The careers of players and other film artists, particularly directors.
6. The nominated and winning films, to estimate the relative importance of artistic (film quality) and extra-artistic (politics, ideology) considerations in the nomination and in the winning.

The Oscar Award is conferred at present in twenty-three categories and in the past in a larger number. Some selection was required, because it was impossible to do justice to all areas honored by the Oscar. This book focuses on four areas—films, directors, players, and writers—consisting of eight award categories: Best Film, Best Director, Best Actor, Best Actress, Best Supporting Actor, Best Supporting Actress, Best Original Screenplay, and Best Adapted Screenplay. The other categories, such as cinematography, editing, and music, are mentioned, though not discussed in great detail. The selection of the four areas is by no means a reflection of their higher ranking or greater prestige. Rather, it is based on necessity and on the idea that most moviegoers relate to films in terms of their narratives and acting performances. However, as a film scholar, I am aware of the fact that the look and sound of films are just as important as their subject matter and acting quality to their overall effectiveness. I hope that these important categories will be analyzed in the future, perhaps by me in another book. . . .

And the Winner Is draws on a variety of sources and data. First, analysis of the careers of all 645 players in the four categories,[1] and 147 directors nominated for an Oscar, in terms of age at first nomination, age at first winning, number of nominations, number of awards, etc. Then over three hundred biographies and autobiographies of film artists were read for the chapters dealing with the subjective meanings and effects of the Oscar Award. Film reviews of all Oscar-winning pictures and performances were examined in various newspapers and magazines for the comparisons between their critical reception and their commercial appeal. The 367 films nominated for Best Picture, from 1927/28 to 1989, were classified according to genre, themes, critical response, and box-office popularity. In addition, each of the 233 Oscar-winning roles in the four acting categories, was viewed and content-analyzed with special attention to differences between the male and female roles. The data also include a large number of archival documents of the Academy of Motion Picture Arts and Sciences, the Screen Actors Guild, the various film critics associations, film festivals, etc.

In writing about the Oscar films and performances, I faced a problem of how much and in what detail to describe their themes and contents. I decided to describe briefly the narratives of most Oscar-winning and nominated films, even of such popular features as *All About Eve* and *Grand Hotel*, which most readers have probably seen many times. At the same time, because the research deals with hundreds of films, performances, and players, I could not do justice to many of them. And because I did not want to limit myself to the winning films, I often had to be extremely brief in covering a large number of films. As mentioned, this book stresses the *nominated* films and performers as much as the winning ones. I therefore ask the readers' forebearance if descriptions are at times too short.

The information gathering for this book lasted four years and took place in many libraries: the Museum of Modern Art Film Archives, the Performing Arts Library at Lincoln Center, the Margaret Herrick Library of the Academy of Motion Picture Arts and Sciences, the Charles K. Feldman Library of the American Film Institute, the Film Library of the University of California at Los Angeles, and Library of the University of Southern California.

CHAPTER 1

The Academy of Motion Picture Arts and Sciences and the Oscar Awards

*T*he idea for an Academy of Motion Picture emerged in the 1920s under the leadership of Louis B. Mayer, head of Metro-Goldwyn-Mayer (MGM). On January 11, 1927, Mayer and a group of thirty-six directors and actors met at the Ambassador Hotel in Los Angeles and decided to establish an Academy of Motion Picture Arts and Sciences (AMPAS).[1] On March 19, the AMPAS was founded as a nonprofit association, and shortly after its goals were determined, the most important of which were:

> The Academy will take aggressive action in meeting outside attacks that are unjust.
> It will promote harmony and solidarity among the membership and among the different branches.
> It will reconcile internal differences that may exist or arise.
> It will adopt such ways and means as are proper to further the welfare and protect the honor and good repute of the profession.
> It will encourage the improvement and advancement of the arts and sciences of the profession by the interchange of constructive ideas and by awards of merit for distinctive achievements.
> It will take steps to develop greater power and influence of the screen.
> In a word, the Academy proposes to do for the motion picture profession in all its branches what other great national and international bodies have done for other arts and sciences and industries.[2]

It is noteworthy that the bestowal of merit awards was only one, not the most important, goal of the Academy when it was established.

A prime motive for the foundation of the Academy was the 1926 unionization of the motion picture industry, when nine major studios and five unions signed the Studio Basic Agreement. But this union Agreement applied only to technical workers; the creative groups—directors, writers, and actors—still lacked standardized contracts. Indeed, in its first years, the Academy regarded itself as a labor organization, representing the interests of the various talent groups. It therefore stressed that as an organization its membership was neither limited to the production studios nor to any particular creative group. Another goal was to create a forum in which artists of various expertise would meet and exchange ideas. However, because the studios, particularly MGM, were instrumental in creating the Academy, many artists feared that the Academy would become the studios' stronghold, thus controlling and restricting the interests of the other talent groups.

That the functions of the Academy were not entirely clear to its founders is also apparent from the power struggle between the Academy and the Actors Equity Association, founded in 1911, over the issue of which organization should have the authority to represent actors. This issue was unclear because many screen players came from the New York stage and thus were members of Equity. In the end, the Academy won the battle when it announced in 1929 a contract for free-lance players, the first such standardized contract. In 1932, the Academy announced another achievement, when it helped settle a labor dispute between James Cagney and his employer, Warner Brothers, demonstrating "the efficiency of the Academy in arbitrating disagreements."[3]

The Academy managed, as film historians have observed, "to forestall serious labor organizing among the Hollywood artists for over five years,"[4] up to the creation of the various screen guilds in the 1930s. It was a strange organization in this respect, because on the one hand it lacked a binding enforcement procedure for its labor code, but on the other it was clear that of all other talent groups it represented best the interests of the production companies. However, as a labor organization, the academy was innovative in both structure and ambition, for it gave equal representation to both employers (the studio executives) and employees (film artists and craftsmen).

The Academy was established as an honorary organization; membership is and always has been by invitation only. From the very start, the idea was to create an association of Hollywood's creative elite. Artists would be invited to join "when their services to the Motion Picture Industry have been prominent enough to make the Academy members feel they would like to have them as brother members."[5] Article II of Section I of the Constitution formalized the qualifications for membership: "Any person who has accomplished distinguished work or acquired distinguished standing in or made valuable contributions to the production branches of the motion picture industry, directly or indirectly, and who is of good moral and personal standing may become an active member of the Academy by vote of the Board of Directors or recommendation of the Committee on Membership."[6]

In 1931 the Academy distinguished between two classes of membership. One category, the Academy Member, "has all the privileges of membership, entitled to vote on all Academy matters, and may serve on the Board of Directors." The other, Associate Member, "has voting privileges limited to branch policies and action."[7] The new policy required that all invitees to membership be first admitted as associate members. And once a year the Board of Directors, on the recommendation of the Branch Committee, selected from the Associate Members those whom the Board felt were entitled to "special distinction" of Academy membership. In this way, the membership grew steadily, from the 270 artists who attended the second Academy banquet in 1929 to 1,200 members in 1932.

In 1933, the AMPAS faced another crisis when President Roosevelt signed the National Industry Recovery Act, which suspended antitrust laws and allowed industries to regulate themselves through "fair competition." The talent groups were concerned that the code would increase the studios' control over them, which indeed it did. The studios used the Recovery Act as an excuse to reduce the salaries of the talent groups. Attempting to mediate, the Academy intervened, but the resulting compromise, which stipulated that the reductions would be temporary, pleased no one. As a countermeasure, the various talent groups—writers, actors, directors—formed their own guilds. The Screen Actors Guild (SAG) was formed in October 1933, and within a year had gained tremendous power, with a membership of close to three thousand.

Moreover, large numbers of the talent groups left the Academy in protest, including prominent players like James Cagney, Gary

Cooper, Fredric March, and Paul Muni. The dispute over the authority to represent the talent groups in their labor negotiations with the studios was the main issue. The SAG accused the AMPAS of trying to jeopardize the possibility of an organization representing the interests of actors. The actors who left were angered at misrepresentation by the Academy and dissatisfied with the manner in which their interests were dealt with at code hearings in Washington, claiming that the Academy had become "a producer-ruled body."[8] Needless to say the membership of the Academy decreased dramatically, and its very existence was threatened. Those remaining were described by Frank Capra, then president of the AMPAS, as "very staunch Academy-oriented visionaries, dedicated to the cultural recognition and preservation that has become the Academy's strong card."[9]

On May 27, 1935, the Supreme Court declared Roosevelt's National Recovery Act unconstitutional. However, the SAG asked its members to boycott the eighth awards banquet, held on March 5, 1936, and subsequently only a few members attended the ceremonies. Labor strife continued for the next few years, but under Capra's leadership the Academy survived. In 1939 the Guilds won their fight, and Academy membership again began to grow under a newly structured Constitution that was "non-economic and non-political in theory and in fact."[10] From then on, the focus of the Academy became cultural and educational—though not by choice. There has always been a debate over the functional and historical importance of the AMPAS. Some critics still think it was a major force in industrial relations, because it helped artists obtain standard contracts. They stress that the AMPAS was not a labor union, as some had wanted it to be, but nevertheless it did introduce the principle of collective bargaining, later adopted by all the various guilds.

During World War II, the national political climate overrode industry concerns, and the strife between the Academy and the guilds subsided. And after the war, the membership increased dramatically: in 1939 there were 600 members; in 1947, 1,433; in 1952, 1,600; and in 1956, 1,770 members. In the 1960s the Academy saw a further increase in its ranks, from 2,084 members in 1959, to 3,030 in 1968. At present, there are 4,523 members in the Academy.

The Academy's Structure and Membership

Originally the Academy's structure consisted of five branches, each representing a different talent group: producers, writers, directors, actors, and technicians. However, the increasing division of labor in the film industry, based on specialized areas of expertise, resulted in a more complex organizational structure, composed at present of fourteen branches or areas of film craftsmanship. They include four of the original ones (producers, writers, directors, and actors), creation of an administrative unit (administrators, executives, public relations), and subdivisions within the technical unit (cinematographers, editors, sound men, art directors).

The Acting Branch has always been the largest in the Academy, amounting to one-fourth the membership. In 1928 there were 362 Academy members, of which ninety-one (25 percent) were players, seventy-eight directors, seventy writers, sixty-nine technicians, and fifty-four producers. And in 1988, the Academy is composed of 4,523 members including: 1,267 actors (28 percent), 378 writers, 349 producers, 320 executives, 317 sound technicians, 287 public-relations executives, 257 art directors and costume designers, 257 directors, 244 musicians, 203 short-subject artists, 181 editors, and 110 cinematographers. The rest (353) are members at large, who did not fit into any of the other categories, and associates (516).

Compared with the three major screen guilds, however, the Academy has always been small. The members of the Acting Branch, for example, amount to about 2 percent of the members of the Screen Actors Guild. And the Academy's Writers and Directors Branches are even smaller and more elitist than the Actors Branch in relation to their respective guilds. But the Academy's small size has contributed to its prestige. The defenders of such size claim that democratizing its structure, by opening it to a large number of workers of the film industry, will defeat its original purpose of being an elite organization consisting of the most accomplished film artists. They stress that the Academy was never meant to be an egalitarian organization representing all film artists. The elitist nature of the Academy makes membership a desirable goal for most film artists.

The policy and requirements for membership differ from branch to branch. The easiest and fastest way to become a member has been by winning a nomination: nominees are almost automatically invited to become members; the Academy has seldom used its right to withhold an invitation to a nominee. Beyond that, each branch has its own criteria of admission. In most branches, it is necessary to have at least two film credits, a number of years of professional experience, and sponsorship by two established members. The Actors Branch requires "a minimum of three theatrical feature film credits, in all of which the roles played were scripted roles, one of which was released in the past five years, and all of which are of a caliber that reflect the high standards of the Academy." But actors are also invited to join if "in the judgment of the Actors Branch Executive Committee, (they) otherwise achieved unique distinction, earned special merit or made an outstanding contribution as a motion picture actor."

Membership in the Academy is for life, although occasionally members are transferred from the status of active to that of associate members, which means they cannot vote for Academy Awards. Needless to say, very few members have relinquished membership voluntarily; the prestige of the Academy and the power to determine which films will be nominated and which will win Oscars are two important rewards for being members. The composition of membership has been a controversial issue, about which the Academy is still sensitive. Some critics feel that artists who have retired or are no longer active in the industry should not have the right to vote. However, one should distinguish between members who have retired from their screen careers to pursue other lines of work or to settle down into domestic life, and artists who have retired as a result of old age but have been involved in film for most of their lives. It is one thing to criticize the membership of people like Susan Kohner or Pat Boone, who are no longer involved in films, and another to criticize members like Irene Dunne, who is indeed very old but has spent most of her life and has had a distinguished career in film.

Because Academy membership is for life, it is plausible to assume the average age of members is rather old, which may pose some problems. First, the age difference between the older members and those actively involved in filmmaking (writers, directors, players) indicates a generation gap that, among other things, has implications in film aesthetics. One could argue that the older age of the average member makes him or her less competent or at least not as up-to-date in recent film development, thus impairing judgment of film quality that, after all, is the official purpose of the Oscar Awards. Secondly, because of the increasingly younger age of the frequent moviegoers in the US, the age gap between them and the Academy members is immense. Thus, at least a generation difference prevails between the average member and the active filmmakers (those nominated for awards), and two or more generations between the average member and the average filmgoer.

These differences in age and the generation gaps they imply inevitably make the Academy vote, in both nominations and final choices, quite conservative, lagging behind the aesthetic, thematic, and technological innovations in the film industry. The built-in conservative bias in the Academy vote is therefore almost inevitable.

The average age of Academy members has decreased in the last decade: many members have died or retired and younger generations of film artists and technicians have been admitted. However, as Vincent Canby observed, the younger members are probably more sophisticated than their veteran counterparts, but they are still more conservative in their tastes and values than the average moviegoer.[11] Note that the teenage movie, the dominant genre in the American cinema of the 1980s, has been conspicuously missing from the nominations. None of the commercially popular (*The Karate Kid*, 1984) or the more artistically acclaimed (John Hughes's *Sixteen Candles*, 1984; *The Breakfast Club*, 1985) has received a major nomination. And no member of the younger generation of performers, labeled by the media as "the brat pack," has been nominated for an acting award, though several have been praised for their work, most notably Emilio Estevez, Sean Penn, Ally Sheedy, and Molly Ringwald.

Another line of criticism concerns the gender structure of the Academy. With the exception of the Acting Branch, which consists of both men and women in equal proportions, all the other branches have been male-dominated. In the Directors Branch, for example, only five of the 257 members in 1988 were women: Martha Coolidge, Randa Haines, Elaine May, Joan Micklin Silver, and Claudia Weill. And there is only one woman, Brianne Murphy, among the 110 Academy cinematographers. An interesting question arises as to how this gender structure has affected the film achievements nominated for an Oscar. But unfortunately, because of the secrecy of the balloting, it is impossible to examine the differences between male and female voting patterns. Nonetheless, one can assume that because the Acting Branch consists of both male and female players, the nominated performance has been based on a more balanced voting.

Moreover, because of the disproportionate size of the Acting Branch in relation to the other branches, the films nominated for Best Picture are often those that contain strong acting achievements. For example, a movie like *The Dresser* would probably not have been nominated for Best Picture if one-fourth of the Academy members, all of whom nominate in this category, had not been players. It's not that the *The Dresser* was not a high-quality film (it was), but that its subject matter (backstage life, through the relationship between an aging and selfish actor and his dresser in World War II England) and the extraordinary performances by Albert Finney and Tom Courtenay made it a likely candidate for Best Picture in the opinion of the Acting Branch. Indeed, because of its large size, the Acting Branch has more of a say over the films nominated for the top award than other branches. And this is one of the reasons why many films dealing with the acting profession and show business have been nominated for Best Picture, such as *The Great Ziegfeld, Stage Door, A Star Is Born, All About Eve, Sunset Boulevard, The Country Girl, Cabaret, Lenny, Nashville, The Turning Point, All That Jazz, Coal Miner's Daughter*, and *Tootsie*.

By contrast, because of the small size of the other branches, it takes few votes to nominate achievements in their respective areas. Thus, twenty or thirty members of the Directors Branch, which consists of only 231 filmmakers, can nominate a directorial achievement. And amounting to 5 percent of the entire membership, the directors have less clout than players, who constitute 25 percent, in nominating films for Best Picture.

Procedures for Nomination

The procedures for selecting nominees and winners have undergone substantial changes over the years. For the first year of the awards (1927/28), the Academy asked the entire membership to nominate achievements. Indeed, by the August 15, 1928, deadline, about one thousand nominations were received. Five boards of judges, one from each branch, were appointed to consider the nominations. The list of ten nominees who received the highest number of votes was turned over to the board of judges, which narrowed it down to three in each category. A central board of judges, one from each branch, then examined the finalists and determined the winner and the two honorable mentions. The winners were announced immediately, though the ceremonies took place at the Academy's annual banquet.

For the next six years (1929–35), the selection process was broadened. The nominations were then made in primary elections by the branches, and the final voting by the entire membership. The regulations stated: "Each Branch will vote separately for nominations, like a primary election. The five highest persons, or achievements, for each award will be certified and placed on a ballot for submission to all members of the Academy. Academy members will then select from the submitted nominees, one for each award and those votes will govern the final selections."

These procedures for nomination came under severe attack in 1935, when Bette Davis's performance in *Of Human Bondage* failed to get a nomination. Consequently, in February 1935 the voting was thrown wide open and write-ins were permitted; members were allowed to name anyone they chose and could substitute a write-in on request. The substituted write-in votes were counted exactly as the votes for the regular nominations. However, the confusion and technical problems involved in write-ins eventually brought about a rule prohibiting them.

In 1936 the nominations were made again by a committee, consisting of fifty members and representing all branches. The final vote was retained by the entire membership. But the labor problems and the internal conflict that resulted in the resignation of many members led to other changes in the procedures. Frank Capra, then the Academy president, decided on a novel strategy: to open up the Academy and extend voting privileges to the Screen Actors, Writers, and Directors Guilds. Getting the guild members to vote was not easy, for they accused the Academy of being against labor unions, but Capra succeeded in convincing them that they should participate.

For the acting nominations, only members of the Senior Screen Actors Guild took part, but ballots for the final vote were also sent to the Junior Screen Actors Guild and the Writers and Directors Guilds. It is noteworthy that in 1936 the participation of the industry was very active: out of fifteen thousand ballots mailed, over 80 percent came back. The Academy wanted to prove that it kept abreast of the times by making the awards widely representative of the entire industry. In 1938 again the nominations for the acting awards were made by Class A members of the Screen Actors Guild, but about twelve thousand professionals of the various guilds took part in the final balloting. This practice continued into the 1940s.

The Academy publicized the fact that the Oscars "are awarded on the basis of ballots which receive industry-wide distribution," thus "representing the majority evaluation of those who work in the medium."[12] There were, however, two specific rules for the acting awards. The first stipulated that "only Class A members of the Screen Actors Guild shall be invited to take part in the nominations vote." And the second, that "ballots for the final awards shall be sent to both Class A and Class B members of the Screen Actors Guild, Writers, Senior and Junior Directors, Producers, Technicians, and other members of the Academy."[13] In this way, the nominations were made by peers: actors nominated actors, directors nominated directors, etc. But all groups were eligible to nominate movies for the Best Production (Picture) Award.

In 1943, for example, 3,800 nomination ballots and 8,000 final ballots were sent out. In 1944, only Class A, Junior members of the Screen Actors Guild, and members of the Academy Actors Branch (a total of 4,500) were invited to take part in the nominations, but final ballots were sent to all members of the Academy and Class B members of the Screen Actors Guild (9,000 persons). In 1946, however, nomination ballots were sent to all 11,669 creative workers in the movie industry, but final ballots were mailed only to the 1,600 members of the Academy. This practice continued throughout most of the 1950s. For example, in 1956 nomination ballots were sent to the 16,721 workers of the industry, but final ballots only to the 1,770 Academy members.

In 1957, the voting was restricted for the first time to active Academy members; the guilds and unions no longer participated. Director-writer George Seaton, then Academy president, was instrumental in bringing about this change, urging members "to exercise the privilege now reserved solely for Academy members." In a letter to the members Seaton wrote: "Since the number of eligible voters has been reduced, you can see how important it is that we get as nearly 100 percent return as possible, so that the nominations and final selections may truly reflect the majority choices of the Academy membership." The 1957 rules for nomination and final balloting are still in effect.

One of the few original practices that has always been in effect is the reminder list. From the first year, a list of productions, released in the eligible year, has been sent to all members for the purpose of refreshing their memories. The reminder list was first arranged according to studios; then alphabetically according to movie titles. It is not guaranteed to be complete or accurate, though each studio is asked to furnish its own list of movies. The list is intended to include the outstanding pictures, not every film released. The Academy's board suggests, "if any film you wish to nominate is not included here, or if you need any further information please telephone the Academy office."

At present, rule six of the nominations voting states: "The Academy shall prepare reminder lists of all eligible pictures, but before distribution to voters, studios must check and assume full responsibility for errors and omissions." The list refers "only to the motion picture in which the achievement was made, and not to any individual responsible, except in the case of nominations for acting which name both the individual and the one picture wherein the achievement occurred." The Academy also aids the members "in coming to intelligent decisions in their voting" by sending each one of them a list of booking dates of the nominated pictures, which they may see without admission charge.

In 1936, a preferential system of voting began by which

> Each member has one vote, which may be expressed in several alternate choices, in the order of his preference. If his first choice agrees with that of a sufficient majority, that achievement becomes one of the nominations. However, should this first choice be in the minority, his vote is applied to his second choice, or his third, and so on, until the voter has helped to select one of the achievements. In this way, the entire voting group has a choice in the ultimate selections. Voters are not obligated to list more choices than they really have, but if only one choice is expressed, and it is in the minority, the ballot becomes void and cannot help in the selection of another achievement.

Achievements are eligible for nomination if they have met the general rule of "The Awards Year":

Academy Awards of Merit shall be bestowed for achievements in connection with feature-length motion pictures (defined as motion-pictures over 30 minutes in running time) first publicly exhibited by means of 35mm or 70mm film for paid admission (previews excluded) in a commercial motion picture theater in the Los Angeles Area, defined as Los Angeles, West Los Angeles or Beverly Hills, between January 1, 1985 and midnight of December 31, such exhibition being for a consecutive run of no less than a week after an opening prior to midnight of December 31st, following normal exploitation and advertising utilized by the producer for this or other pictures within the dates specified.

Several categories allow exception to this rule. Documentaries and short films are entered by their producers, and music awards require the creator to file an official submission form. Foreign films are submitted by each country's equivalent of the Academy of Motion Picture; there is a limit of one picture per country. There are also exceptions to the location rule: documentaries need not play in the Los Angeles area, and foreign-language films need not have opened in the United States, but must have English subtitles.

The first Academy Awards were presented on May 16, 1929, for the years 1927 and 1928. The period of eligibility was a specific twelve-month period, from August 1, 1927 to July 31, 1928. This eligibility period remained in effect for the next four years. In 1934, however, the eligibility period was changed to cover the calendar year, from January 1, to December 31, which required the addition of five months to the previous awards year: the 1932/3 awards covered the period from August 1, 1932 to December 31, 1933.

At present, the voting timetable for the Annual Awards is as follows:

December	1, 1986	Deadline for official screen credits forms to qualify feature films
December	31	Awards year ends (at midnight)
January	16, 1987	Mail nomination ballots
January	30	Nominations polls close
February	11	Nominations announced
February	20	Screenings of nominated films begin
March	14	Mail final ballots
March	24	Final polls close
March	30	Awards presentation

Price, Waterhouse and Company, a firm of certified public accounts, began counting the Oscar ballots in 1936, and continues at present. During the first twelve years, the results of the final balloting were released to the press prior to the presentation to accommodate newspaper deadlines, but news was to be held back until 11 o'clock p.m. In 1940, however, when one newspaper revealed in its early edition the winning sweep of *Gone with the Wind*, the practice of advance notice was discontinued. Consequently in 1941 the Academy declined to give out any advance release, and the practice of sealed envelopes began. Indeed, the regulations of secrecy have been very strict. Votes are tabulated by a staff of no more than three at Price, Waterhouse, who are locked in a counting room. Votes are then counted in each category, but are totaled on the day of the Awards. The sealed envelopes are then prepared in duplicate. One set is held by the Price, Waterhouse official, who hands them to the presenters on the very Oscar telecast. The other is held by another official, seated in the audience, who functions as a back-up man, in case the first does not arrive to the show on time. So far, the reserve man has never been used.[14]

The winners' identities are really unknown until they are actually called to the platform to be handed the award. This is the reason why the winners receive a blank Oscar; after the show, their names are engraved on its base. Furthermore, no executive of the Academy sees the ballots, because they are destroyed at the end of the year. This secrecy undoubtedly contributes to the excitement, tension, and popularity of the ceremonies. The only exceptions to the rule of secrecy are the Honorary, Scientific-Technical, the Jean Hersholt, and the Irving Thalberg Awards, which, beginning in 1956, have been announced in advance.

The Academy awards differ in this respect from other prestigious awards. The Nobel Prize Nomination Committees, for instance, are silent about the names proposed for the awards and always abide by the rule of secrecy. However, the winners' names are made public weeks before the actual presentations to accommodate their arrival in Stockholm from all over the world. By contrast, the nominees for Academy Awards are announced publicly six weeks before the ceremonies, but the winners' identities are kept in utmost secrecy up to the very last moment. When the awards' presenters say, "May I have the envelope please," the nominees, the voters, and the public at large are really in a state of genuine suspense.

Award Categories and Nominees

The number of award categories has changed over the years, reflecting broader developments in the film industry, such as the advent of sound and color. All the nominees for the first Best Picture were silent films, and only one award was given to a "talkie." In the first year, there were eleven categories: Actor, Actress, Director of Drama, Director of Comedy, Outstanding Picture (Producer), Outstanding Quality (Production Company), Original Screenplay, Adaptation of Story, Cinematography, Art Direction, and Engineering Effects. The production awards distinguished between the Best Producer, "who produced the most outstanding motion picture, considering all elements that contribute to a picture's greatness," and Best Production Company, "which produced the most artistic, unique, and/or original motion picture without reference to cost or magnitude." Members were asked to choose the best performance, "with special reference to character portrayal and effectiveness of dramatic or comedy rendition."

In the second year (1928/29), however, awards were given in only seven categories. The distinction between the direction of a comedy and a drama was dropped as well as the distinction between original and adapted screenplay. And there was no longer differentiation between Best Producer and Best Production Company— the top award was named Best Picture. In the third year, two new categories were added: Sound Recording and Scientific-Technical Achievement. In the fourth year (1930/1), the writing award was divided again into two: Original Motion Picture Story and Adaptation. By 1934 the number of categories had increased to thirteen, with new areas for Editing, Short Subjects, and Music. And in the following year, due to the popularity of the musical film, a new category was created to honor Dance Direction.

Until 1935, there were only two acting categories: Best Actor and Best Actress. In 1936, the Academy decided to create two more acting divisions: Best Supporting Actor and Best Supporting Actress, which required new rules to distinguish between leading and supporting performances (see chapter 3). And in keeping abreast with the advent of color, the Cinematography and Art Direction Awards were subdivided in 1939 into black-and-white and color achievements. The first winners in these areas were Gregg Toland for his distinguished black-and-white cinematography in

Wuthering Heights, and Ernest Haller and Ray Rennahan for their color work in *Gone with the Wind*. In addition, the Music Awards honored Best Original Score, Best Scoring Achievement, and Best Song.

The highest number of awards bestowed by the Academy was in 1956, with no less than twenty-seven categories; there were many new fields, including some for documentary films. New categories were established and others dropped in accordance with developments within the industry. For example, in 1957, the Academy eliminated the category for Best Scoring of a Musical due to the decline in the production of musical pictures. The general tendency was toward compression of categories, to keep the number of awards to a minimum. A major change occurred in 1967, when the former duplicate awards in Art Direction, Set Decoration, and Cinematography, previously given for black-and-white and color, were discontinued. The members felt that these awards would be more prestigious and meaningful if there would be one system of technical awards. But it also made the competition in these categories more intense.

The most recent category has been that of Makeup, given for the first time in 1982, after a lengthy fight for it by makeup artists. In previous years, some honorary awards were given to makeup artists, such as William Tuttle for *Seven Faces of Dr. Lao* in 1964, and John Chambers for *Planet of the Apes* in 1968, but there was no regular award for it. A competitive category was established following the Academy's refusal to honor the makeup achievement in *The Elephant Man*.

At present, merit awards are conferred in twenty-three categories of achievement: Best Picture, Best Foreign Picture, Director, four acting awards (Actor, Actress, Supporting Actor, and Supporting Actress), two writing (Original Screenplay and Adaptation), two documentary (Feature and Short Subject), two music (Original Score and Original Song), two short-film awards (Animated and Live Action), Art Direction, Cinematography, Costume Design, Editing, Sound, Sound Effects, Visual Effects, and Makeup.

There have also been fluctuations in the number of nominees in each category. In the first year, three actors were nominated for Best Actor: Richard Barthelmess for two films, *The Noose* and *The Patent Leather Kid*; Emil Jannings also for two films, *The Last Command* and *The Way of All Flesh*; and Charlie Chaplin for *The Circus*.

In the same year, three actresses were nominated for five performances: Janet Gaynor for three films, *Seventh Heaven*, *Street Angel*, and *Sunrise*; Louise Dresser for *A Ship Comes In*; and Gloria Swanson for *Sadie Thompson*.

In the second year, five nominees were singled out in each acting category. But in the third year, four actors were nominated for six roles (George Arliss and Maurice Chevalier were each nominated for two different performances). And five actresses were nominated for seven roles (Greta Garbo was nominated for two, *Anna Christie* and *Romance*; and Norma Shearer also for two, *The Divorcee* and *Their Own Desire*). For three years (1932–4), the two acting categories contained three performers, each nominated for one role. But in 1935, there were four nominees in the Best Actor and six nominees in the Best Actress category. It wasn't until 1936 that the number of nominees was standardized to five players in each group.

In the first year, there were two directing awards, one for comedy and one for drama, and three directors competed for each. The first directorial winners were: Frank Borzage for the drama *Seventh Heaven*, and Lewis Milestone for the comedy *Two Arabian Nights*. This distinction, however, was dropped in the following year. For two years (1929–30), five nominees competed for Best Director, but in 1932, the number of contestants was reduced again to three. Nonetheless, from 1936 on, the number of directorial nominations was standardized to five every year.

The fluctuation in the number of films nominated for Best Picture has been even greater. In the first four years, five movies were nominated, but in 1931/2 it was decided to increase their number to eight. The Best Picture category continued to increase: in 1932/3, ten films were nominated and in 1934 and 1935, twelve. In the next seven years (1936–43), ten movies competed annually for Best Picture. The competition in these years was extremely fierce. Note, for example, the competition in 1939, one of the watershed years in Hollywood and the Academy's history, with so many excellent movies nominated for an Oscar: *Dark Victory*, *Gone with the Wind* (the winner), *Goodbye Mr. Chips*, *Love Affair*, *Mr. Smith Goes to Washington*, *Ninotchka*, *Of Mice and Men*, *Stagecoach*, *The Wizard of Oz*, and *Wuthering Heights*.

But the nomination of ten movies for Best Picture not only made the competition more intense but also split the votes into too many subgroups. Consequently, in 1944, the Academy decided to standardize the Best Picture category so that it contains the same number, five, of contestants as the other categories.[15]

The Academy Awards

The Academy Award is universally nicknamed the Oscar. Three persons have claimed credit for the nickname—Bette Davis, librarian Margaret Herrick, and columnist Sidney Skolsky—but the matter has never been resolved. Bette Davis reportedly nicknamed the Academy Award as Oscar because it looked like the backside of her then husband, Harmon Oscar Nelson. Librarian Margaret Herrick, later the Academy's Executive Secretary, reported to her first day of work in 1931. After having been formally introduced to the gold statuette, she looked it over carefully and said it reminded her of her uncle, Oscar Pierce. Columnist Sidney Skolsky was apparently on the scene and immediately seized on the name and printed it in his column: "Employees have affectionately dubbed their famous statuette 'Oscar.'" But according to Skolsky, he was the first to use the word Oscar, and for the following reason: "It wasn't a case of 'give our child a name.' I wasn't trying to make it legitimate. The snobbery of that particular Academy Award annoyed me. I wanted to make the gold statuette human." Skolsky wanted a "name that would erase the phony dignity," and he remembered vaudeville shows in which comedians, having fun with the orchestra leader in the pit, would say, "Will you have a cigar, Oscar?" The first time he used the term was when he reported that "Katharine Hepburn won the Oscar for her performance as Eve Lovelace in *Morning Glory*." In a few years, it became the accepted name, proving to be "the magic name."[16]

Whatever the source, the Academy Awards were universally called Oscars. The statuette was designed by MGM's chief art director, Cedric Gibbons, and created by sculptor George Stanley. The first Oscars were printed on scroll, but later cast in gold. Gibbons sketched a knight standing on a reel of film and holding a two-edged sword. Its base represented the five original branches of the Academy: producers, writers, directors, actors, and technicians. The only change, since the Oscar was first made, has been a minor streamlining of the base.

The Academy bestows various kinds of Oscars:

The Annual Merit Awards in twenty-three categories

The Scientific or Technical Achievement Awards

The Irving G. Thalberg Award "to a creative producer whose body of work reflects a consistently high quality of motion picture productions."

The Jean Hersholt Humanitarian Award "to an individual in the motion picture industry whose humanitarian efforts have brought credit to the industry."

The Gordon E. Sawyer Award "to an individual in the motion picture industry whose technological contributions have brought credit to the industry."

The Honorary Awards "for outstanding achievements not strictly within the other categories, for exceptionally distinguished service in the making of the motion pictures or for outstanding service to the Academy."

The awards themselves take different forms. The Annual Awards, Class I Scientific or Technical, Special Achievement, and Jean Hersholt Humanitarian Awards, take the form of the Oscar statuette. Class II Scientific winners receive a plaque, and Class III winners a certificate. The Irving G. Thalberg Award is a bronze head of the late distinguished producer. Honorary Awards may be a statuette, scroll, or any design ordered by the Board of Governors.

The Oscar statuette is thirteen and a half inches tall and weighs eight and a half pounds. It is gold-plated over a composition of 92.5 percent tin, and 7.5 percent copper. During World War II, plaster statuettes were awarded because every piece of metal was needed for the war effort, but after the war, the Academy went back to the original gold statuettes. The Oscars are awarded to the winners without charge; the Academy, however, makes some profit from the sale of duplicates (in case of loss or theft).

Every year the Academy orders fifty statuettes from Southern California Trophy, which began producing them in 1930 to make sure that there will be no shortage. While only twenty-three categories of achievements are honored, there have often been collaborations of two or three artists, particularly in the writing and technical classifications, and there are also Special and Honorary Oscars. Shortly after the announcement of nominees, a count is made of the maximum number of awards that can conceivably be given. In the first years, the statuettes were not numbered, but in 1949 it was decided to number them; 501 was chosen as a starting point, even though the estimate is that more than 500 statuettes were awarded in the first two decades.

The Awards Ceremonies

Judging by the extraordinary publicity and media coverage it generates, the Academy Awards show has become over the years an international event of the utmost importance. Furthermore, most people, in America and all over the world, relate to the Oscar and to the Academy interchangeably: for them the Academy's raison d'être is to bestow the annual merit awards. Few are aware of the Academy's other functions, such as preserving and restoring motion pictures. For most, the Academy lies "dormant" most of the time, then "comes alive" once a year for "the Oscar season."

Indeed, the Academy Awards were originally designed as a local gesture by Hollywood's artists to honor the best achievements in their respective fields. The Oscars were merely an afterthought on the Academy's agenda, barely mentioned in its 1927 statement of goals. Conferring awards was one of the seven functions, by no means the most important, described in the statement: "It (the Academy) will encourage the improvement and advancement of the arts and sciences of the profession by the interchange of constructive ideas and by awards of merit for distinctive achievements." Louis B. Mayer of MGM, the Academy's chief architect, explained: "The awards have a dual purpose. One is that we want to recognize fine achievements, and the other is that we want to inspire those others to give finer achievements tomorrow."[17]

The initial idea was to bestow the awards at the annual meeting of the Academy, in either an open meeting or a dinner. The board later decided in favor of a dinner, and this format lasted for seventeen years. In 1944, however, because of the war situation, the practice seemed too conspicuously luxurious and thus inappropriate; the Academy has always been extremely sensitive to public opinion, and the banquets stopped. But the reason was also pragmatic: the membership had expanded so much over the years that it was difficult to accommodate all of them for dinner.

Veteran members of the Academy are still shocked by the tremendous attention accorded to the awards. "It was just a small group getting together for a pat on the back," Janet Gaynor, the first winner, recalled. True, the banquet resembled an intimate "family affair."[18] In the first two years there was no radio or extensive press coverage, and subsequently the awards had no dramatic effects on the box-office popularity of the winning films.

Sidney Kent, then President of Fox Studios, was the first to make a suggestion "to use radio to sell our pictures," an idea that was immediately and wholeheartedly adopted by all the studios. Consequently, the third annual banquet, held on April 3, 1931, was broadcast on radio over station KNX in Los Angeles. However, for the next fifteen years, only a portion of the ceremonies was broadcast. The entire ceremonies were broadcast for the first time on March 15, 1945, over the ABC network and the Armed Forces Radio Service. This was the beginning of what some members describe as the awards getting out of the Academy's control.

The dramatic increase in public awareness of the awards really baffled the Academy. In 1940 the board of directors felt an urgent need to publish the following statement: "Somewhat to the embarrassment of the traditional dignity of the Academy, the words 'Oscar' and 'Academy Awards' have slipped into the popular language like 'Sterling' and 'Nobel,' as recognized symbols of quality."[19] The board was unaware that in a few years the Oscar would stand for something much more than "recognized symbols of quality."

The awards ceremonies have gradually received the endorsement and support of all segments of society, including the power elite. Vice President Charles Curtis pushed the Academy Awards into the national spotlight in 1932, when he attended the ceremonies to pay tribute to the film industry, which had boosted the country's morale during a year of depression. In 1941 Franklin D. Roosevelt became the first president to address the motion picture industry via radio. President Harry S. Truman followed in his footsteps when in 1949 he sent a congratulatory message to the Academy. And in 1982, president Ronald Reagan, a former Hollywood actor, participated even more actively in the proceedings via a pretaped, one-minute greeting.

The board continued to rationalize the purpose of the Oscar, reminding the public that the Academy was conceived as "an honorary association," whose "prime object is to advance the arts and sciences of motion pictures and to foster cooperation among the creative leadership of the industry for cultural, educational, and technological progress." The Academy would not let the public forget its "multi-aims and purposes," aside from "recognizing outstanding achievements." These functions included: "to conduct cooperative research; to provide a common meeting ground for the various arts and crafts of the cinema; to serve as an impartial clearing house of achievements, records and statistics; to cooperate in educational activities between the public and the motion picture industry."[20] Needless to say, the Academy did not fulfill all of these functions and it is doubtful that the awards contributed "to raising the standard of production," as they were officially meant to. However, the Academy was successful in elevating the status of film among the arts, which was one of its official goals, and in popularizing the Oscar, a function unintentional and unanticipated at the Academy's inception.

The organization continued to fight the accusation that it had become a commercial tool and a monetary spectacle, insisting that the Oscar was first and foremost "a merit award," designed to honor excellence, not to promote the popularity of films or of winners. However, at weak moments, members conceded that "some awards have been given to commercial successes," but they reminded that "awards have also been given to commercial failures." They claimed that "the winning films have always been achievements which represented worthy attainments," independently of how well they did at the box office.[21] But once the Academy had become aware of the tremendous influence of the Oscar, honoring average films with nominations and awards to boost their commercial appeal has become a practice. This is yet another example of a function that was originally latent but over the years has become manifest and is intended and recognized by the members.

The Academy's service orientation has continued to be stressed, especially its self-image as a standard setter, reminding the public "of worthy achievements" and calling "the attention of millions to the significance of motion pictures as a fine art as well as popular entertainment."[22] Members still like to believe that the Academy functions as "constant stimulus or incentive" for better work and "for hundreds of millions of people to think and to talk about the best in motion pictures."[23] Indeed, the fact that once a year the attention of a huge international community focuses on film and that people think and talk about the *same films* at the *same time* is an amazing achievement, whether intended or unintended by the Academy. There are very few events of such an international caliber!

In addition to bestowing annual awards, the Academy fulfills other functions which, less publicized than the Oscars, very few people are aware of. It publishes every three months "the Players Directory," which lists over 10,000 actors and actresses thus serving as a major casting tool. Another important publication has been "the Screen Achievement Records Bulletin," which serves as a current guide for individuals and organizations, and "Who Wrote the Movie," listing thousands of screenwriters and screenplays, prepared in collaboration with the Writers Guild of America. Affiliated to AMPAS is the Academy Foundation, which sponsors several educational and cultural activities, including a scholarship program, annual student film awards, and preservation of films.

The major funding source of the ceremonies initially came from the big studios which, for obvious reasons, had vested interests to support the awards. For example, the studios contributed over $80,000 to the 1948 ceremonies. A year later, however, some of the major companies refused to underwrite the costs of the event. The amount of money needed, about $20,000, shocked many because of its relatively small proportions. The decision to discontinue the support was delivered to the Academy in December 1948, before the announcement of the year's nominations, which favored several British movies, *Hamlet* and *The Red Shoes*, over American productions. Jean Hersholt, the Academy's president, explained that the moguls' decision was based on the notion that they don't want "Academy standards foisted upon them," preferring to make "commercial pictures, unhampered by consideration of artistic excellence." And while Hersholt saw in their criticism "the highest praise of our organization," he was upset that MGM, Paramount, Twentieth Century Fox, and Warners each gave $12,500 and that Universal, Columbia, and Republic "didn't support us at all."[24]

In their statement, the big studios claimed that their step "is not a commercialistic one but is in the interests of less commercialization," reminding that "the companies, as companies, were never members of the Academy," an organization designed to include the most accomplished individual artists. Furthermore, they declared, though few believed it, that they were "heartily in accord with the principle of individuals in the industry democratically selecting the best in artistic achievement,"[25] and that "it is in the interest of this principle," that they take this step "to remove any suspicion of company influence."[26]

The winning of *Hamlet* as Best Picture, and the multiple awards accorded *The Red Shoes* made it worse; as Bosley Crowther wrote, "prides had been wounded by the bombshell bestowal of the Academy upon *Hamlet*," making the timing of the studios' expose sound "like very sour grapes."[27] Moguls and top executives were indeed upset that the Academy voters favored British art films over what they considered distinguished American movies: John Huston's *The Treasure of the Sierra Madre*, nominated in four categories; Jean Negulesco's *Johnny Belinda*, nominated for twelve awards; and Anatole Litvak's *The Snake Pit*, predicted to receive Best Picture, but winning only one minor award (sound recording) out of its six nominations. The studios denied—to no avail—any connection between their decision and the prominence of British films. The British winners, by contrast, expressed shock and bewilderment. "I can't believe American companies would do such a thing," said producer-director Emeric Pressburger, and producer Alexander Korda is reported to have said, "I'm sure Americans are too generous for any ill-feeling to arise."[28]

But the studios' withdrawal of support and the subsequent separation of the Oscar from the major production companies was seen by many as a positive move, hoping that members would now feel freer to vote. In the past, the studios put tremendous pressure on their employees to choose their pictures and to select winners that worked for them (see chapter 12). Emmet Lavery expressed the feeling of many when he wrote in the *Saturday Review*:

So we come now, in the twenty-first year of the Academy's existence, to the parting of the ways between the major Hollywood studios and the Academy as co-sponsors of the annual awards program. And a happy parting it is. The only wonderment is that it did not happen sooner-preferably at the very beginning of the Academy's existence.

This does not mean the end of the Academy. On the contrary, it means an expansion and development on a completely independent level. There can now be little question that the annual awards are the free choice of the 1800 members who represent twelve general fields of work in film. This is the moment, and a very good moment, when

Oscar comes into his own. At the ripe old age of twenty one, Oscar has shown that he is free to vote as he chooses.[29]

For three years, radio commercials, increased annual dues, a fund drive and modest contributions from some studios helped finance the Oscar ceremonies, which were simple and modest. The new format of presenting the awards at the Academy's own theater was considered an "economy move" and described by one journalist as "the fastest and smallest" in the Academy's history, with awards handed out in "cafeteria style."[30] In 1952, however, there was a turning point: television, the movies' long-time enemy, came to the rescue, a move that was totally unexpected. This cooperation was mutually beneficial: television needed stars, as it had not developed yet its own performers, and the Academy was desperate for funds to cover the show's costs. It is noteworthy that in the past the studios either prohibited or restricted the appearances of their big stars on television, so intense was the animosity between the two media.

The Oscar Television Show

RCA Victor sponsored the 1953 awards ceremony and NBC televised it. The date, March 19, 1953, was quite appropriate: The Oscar was celebrating its twenty-fifth anniversary. A new significant era in the Academy's history began.

Simultaneous ceremonies took place in New York and Los Angeles from 1953 to 1957. Viewers were switched back and forth, according to the city where the winners were at the time. This practice was discontinued in 1957. The ceremonies were televised in black and white, but in 1967, the show was telecast in color, which contributed even more to its spectacular effects and to its popularity. American households that could not afford to buy a television set were not dropped. The simultaneous broadcast on radio and television continued as late as 1969, when the Academy realized that few people listened to the ceremonies on radio.

By then, television had become well established as the dominant medium in American culture. Indeed, the show's audiences grew rapidly. In 1948, an unprecedented audience of close to a hundred million listened to the proceedings, when ABC beamed the event to all its national affiliates and the Armed Forces Radio Service aired it to American soldiers overseas. But a decade later, in 1959, the audiences doubled: eighty million Americans watched on television or listened to the radio, and another hundred million people were reached overseas, also via radio.

The dramatic increase in the show's audiences had direct impact on the amount of money paid to purchase the television rights. In 1952, the rights were purchased for $100,000, but in 1964, it skyrocketed to a million dollars. At present, the exact amount of money is undisclosed, but it is estimated at over two million dollars. The ABC network, which has the TV contract for the Oscar show, takes advantage of this extraordinary exposure and charges an all-time record of $100,000 for a ten-second advertisement. This means that a commercial of thirty seconds costs $300,000. Despite periodic criticism and dreams to change the format of the show, most people realize that without television, which pays for all the preparation and work involved, the ceremonies would be impossible. For example, clips from the five nominated pictures and the sequences shown in the presentation of Honorary Oscars have to be prepared in advance. The Oscar ceremonies take place on a Monday night, but there is usually a dress rehearsal on the preceding Sunday.

Special attempts have been made to make the show a formally elegant event. The late Edith Head, Hollywood's best-known costume designer, herself a winner of numerous Oscars, served as the Academy's consultant for many years. This fashion aspect of the show has increased over the last decade: audiences have now come to expect to see the latest in fashions. Using its old competitor, the Academy has tried to put on an entertaining show, though with varying degrees of success. The ultimate goal is to have exciting ceremonies, which depend on the intensity of the competition and the selection of winners, as well as on having a well-staged, top-rated television show. It took several years for this twofold goal to materialize. In the late 1950s a reporter noted that for the first time "every word, every motion was designed for the camera this year. No more was the glittering festival a self-conscious performance with TV's cameras guiltily watching what they could. Oscar has broken the 25 year shroud of dignity, dullness, and routines for its sprightly marriage partner, TV."[31]

Popular figures such as Will Rogers, humorist Irving S. Cobb, and comedian Jack Benny were among the hosts of the show. But the emcee most closely identified with the ceremonies has been co-median Bob Hope, serving as host twenty-two times, nine as a solo. Hope was the perfect choice for the job: he was a popular movie star, especially in his "Road Movies" with Bing Crosby in the 1940s. But Bob Hope was much more than a comedian or film star; he was a genuinely American *institution*, particularly after enter-taining American soldiers during World War II. Critic Walter Kerr has appropriately described him as a "Constant Uncle" of the Oscar show.

Johnny Carson, the host of NBC's *The Tonight Show*, was a host for a few years. Unlike Bob Hope, Carson is a unique creation of television, a genuine star of the small screen, though his popularity extends beyond television. But Carson did not last long as host. In 1984 the Oscar show changed to a multihost format, which is still current. In the latest, the fifty-eighth ceremonies, there were three hosts: Jane Fonda, a genuine movie star, and two actors, Alan Alda and Robin Williams, who are familiar faces on television and film. The idea, of course, is to appeal to the audiences of the two media.

Interestingly enough, the show has continued to be popular with unprecedentedly large audiences, independent of its production values. Indeed, the Oscar Show has consistently been popular, with an average Nielson rating of 35.0, and in many years even higher. The most popular Oscar show was in 1970, with an alltime record of 43.4 rating, attributable to public anticipation that John Wayne would win the Best Actor Award, which he did. By con-trast, the 1969 show had an average rating of 31.8, ranking as the least popular ceremonies in the last two decades. In the 1970s, the rating of the Oscar show ranged from 38.7 in 1972 to 34.6 in 1979.[32]

Indeed, Johnny Carson described the not-very-interesting 1979 presentation as "two hours of sparkling entertainment spread over four hours." This was an understatement compared with the dull-ness of the 1983 show, which Vincent Canby compared to "taking an extremely slow Seventh Avenue Local to heaven," as it is "a very long ride, and over-crowded, and the arrival—by which time one is exhausted—is always a bit of an anticlimax."[33] The show's typi-cal atmosphere usually mixes "the solemnity of the annual Nobel ceremonies in Stockholm with the cheerful bad taste of the grand opening of a shopping center in Los Angeles."[34]

However, the 1984 Academy Awards show, broadcast on April

9, captured an impressive audience, drawing an average rating of 36.0. The other two networks did extremely poorly on that night: CBS got 7.3 ratings and NBC 7.2. The show itself was one of the longest, running three hours and forty-five minutes. This prompted Johnny Carson to compare the proceedings to a fund-raising gala on public television. "OK folks," he said, "we're into our fourth hour, let's check the tote boards and see how much money we've raised."

Nostalgia has seemed to be the key theme of recent Oscar shows. The 1985 show paid a tribute to film achievements from 1934 and audiences were treated to film clips of Shirley Temple, who later appeared in person, the spectacular dancing of Fred Astaire and Ginger Rogers, and clips from the 1934 Best Picture, Frank Capra's *It Happened One Night*. Director Capra also presented the Best Picture of the Year award. The show's homage to Hollywood's glorious past came as a response to the criticism that it had become too much of a television event. Indeed, in recent years, many of the awards presenters have been young performers who have nothing to do with movies, but whose popularity among television viewers was the only reason for their being on the Oscar platform.

The 1986 Oscar show also paid tribute to Hollywood's past, but was in many ways better than any show in recent memory. The choice of comedian Robin Williams was fortuitous, for he provided the funniest moments of the show, with his quirky sense of humor. Appearing with two Price and Waterhouse representatives, carrying the winners' names in briefcases, he suggested that they "open up the suckers right now," and, rejected, told the public, "I'm afraid we have to do this show." Williams's brilliant jokes and one-liners were so fast that there was no time to digest and be offended by them, as Jack Valenti could have been, when he was introduced as "the man you never heard of, but you have to listen to him anyway."

A tribute to MGM musicals, featuring eight of its female stars— Jane Powell, Cyd Charisse, June Allyson, Leslie Caron, Kathryn Grayson, Marge Champion, Ann Miller, and Esther Williams— was the nostalgic highlight of the show. Further, Gene Kelly, Debbie Reynolds, and Donald O'Connor, the presenters of the music award, reprised their classic number from *Singin' in the Rain*. And there was a nice gesture, when all the nominees were asked to stand up and were applauded as a group. Celebrating Hollywood was also the theme of "hymn to the losers," sung by Irene Cara and accompanied by clips from films that have been nominated but did not win Best Picture. An impressive group indeed, with such excellent movies as *The Wizard of Oz, Citizen Kane, Sunset Boulevard,* and *Tootsie.*

The Oscar show has been criticized on several accounts, particularly the presentation of the five nominated Best Songs, usually the most tedious part of the show. And winners have been reproached for "wasting" too much time, thanking their families in their acceptance speeches. But with all the criticism, a recent study found that 66 percent of the viewers enjoyed the show, 20 percent didn't, and 12 percent had no opinion. The prime motives for watching the show seemed to be "to find out the winners," and "to see the celebrities."[35]

The length of the 1986 show was over three hours, or, to be exact, 195 minutes. And its structure consisted of the following segments:

Commentary by show's hosts	23 minutes	11.8 percent
Introduction of presenters	20	10.3
Announcement of nominees and winners	67	34.4
Acceptance speeches	23	11.8
Production numbers	34	17.4
Commercials	28	14.3

Thus, contrary to popular opinion, the acceptance speeches amount to only 12 percent of the show's time, and considering the fact that awards were given in twenty-three competitive categories plus two Honorary Awards, the average duration of an acceptance speech was about one minute.

The attempt to prepare a show that would combine the best of film and television traditions, though understandable, is not easy. The producers feel that it should be much more than a tribute to film, that it should also be an interesting *television* program, because the ceremonies are watched by people who are not moviegoers. Indeed, the Oscar *show* is no less important than the awards presentation itself. It has become a special experience in its own right because, as John O'Connor observed, "The viewer gets not only the event, but also the overall television context."[36] The commercial breaks have been at times more interesting and more entertaining than parts of the ceremonies themselves.

Moreover, the viewer gets not only the overall television context, but also the overall culture context. The Oscar Award and the Oscar show have become part and parcel of American culture, a symbolic ritual that occurs every year at the same time. There have been annual ceremonies, in one form or another, for fifty-eight years, thus making the Oscar a deeply rooted tradition. On few occasions only, the ceremonies were postponed—though never canceled.

The first delay took place in 1938, when heavy floods held up the ceremonies for one week. And in 1967, a national network strike threatened the telecast of the ceremonies that, among other things, meant a substantial loss of money. However, the Academy decided to keep the ceremonies on schedule, with or without television. Fortunately, the strike was settled a few hours before the show, on April 10, was going to begin. The second delay, of two days, occurred in 1968 when Dr. Martin Luther King, Jr. was assassinated. Gregory Peck, the Academy president, felt that "postponement was the only appropriate gesture of respect," and there was a unanimous agreement over his assessment. And in 1981, the ceremonies were delayed by twenty-four hours because of the attempt to assassinate President Reagan on the day of the scheduled event, March 30. Ironically, the Oscar show was going to begin with a pretaped greeting from the President. Emcee Johnny Carson used the occasion for a joke: "Because of the incredible events of yesterday, that old adage, the show must go on, seemed relatively unimportant." But the show did go on—only one day late, indicating all the more the institutionalization of the Oscar Award as a sacred ritual in American culture.

CHAPTER 2

The Extraordinary Preeminence of the Oscar Award

The Oscar Award is the most popular and the most prestigious award in the film world. But the Oscar enjoys extraordinary preeminence in the entertainment world and in American popular culture, not just in the film industry. Its prestige and visibility have surpassed other entertainment awards, such as the Tony, the top award in the Broadway theater, the Emmy, honoring achievements in television, and the Grammy, the most prestigious award in the recording industry. How did it happen? How did the Oscar Award and the Oscar television show acquire such extraordinary dimension? To answer these questions, the unique characteristics and history of the Oscar are examined in relation to other film and entertainment awards. Indeed, the Oscar Award is better understood when placed in two broader contexts: that of the film world and of the entertainment world.

The Preeminence of the Oscar in the Film World

The Oscar is the most important award in the international film world: it is considered to be "the king of honors." However, it is not the only award honoring distinguished achievement in film. There is a wide variety of awards bestowed by national academies and film institutes, international film festivals, film critics' circles, and various film-oriented associations.[1]

Film Academies and Institutes

Most countries with established film industries have national academies or institutes of film that, among other activities, bestow merit awards. The Oscar is conferred by the American Academy of Motion Picture Arts and Sciences, which, founded in 1927, is the oldest academy in the world. Most people refer to it simply as *the Academy*—not the *American* Academy—attesting to its international status as the world's most famous film organization.

In England, the British Film Academy (BFA) was established in 1946 for the "advancement of film." After a series of mergers and reorganizations, the most recent of which was in 1975, it became the British Academy of Film and Television Arts (BAFTA). The annual award of this organization is the Stella, honoring achievement in both film and television. In the United States, by contrast, the separation between the Academy of Motion Picture and the National Academy of Television Arts and Sciences underlines both functional and symbolic differences. The Academy and its Oscar Award have always been more prestigious than television and its Emmy Award. Unlike many other countries, film and television in America are still considered to be different media, performing different functions in popular culture.

In France, the equivalent of the Oscar is the César, created in 1976 by publicist Georges Cravenne. It is voted on by the entire membership of the French Motion Picture Academy, consisting of about 2,200 members of the film industry. The French Academy and its César Awards are modeled after the Academy and its Oscar, honoring twenty-one categories of film achievement.

In Italy, the top film award is the David Di Donatello Award, which is now administered by the Italian film industry. The regulations of this award changed most recently, and its accent now is on European films. Indeed, the Italian, like other national academies but unlike the Oscar, distinguishes between achievements by local and foreign artists, which increases the number of awards and decreases the intensity of competition. For example, in 1983, the winner of the best Italian film was Paolo and Vittorio Taviani's *Night of the Shooting Stars*, and the winner of the best foreign picture was Richard Attenborough's *Gandhi*. The same distinction prevails in the acting, directorial, and writing awards.

Merit awards are also bestowed by various film institutes. The American Film Institute (AFI) was established in 1967 and consists of thirty thousand members from all over the country. Its Life Achievement Award, conferred since 1973, is highly respected in the film world. But it differs from most awards in its purpose, which is to honor "the total career contributions of a filmmaker, regardless of place of birth, whose talent has fundamentally advanced the art of American film or television, whose accomplishments have been acknowledged by scholars, critics, professional peers, and the general public, and whose work has withstood the test of time." The award is based on the collective judgment of the AFI's board of trustees, although in the last two years the entire membership has been asked to suggest candidates for the award. The annual ceremonies take place in early March and are televised, but not live. Of the thirteen winners, there have been seven directors (John Ford, Orson Welles, William Wyler, Alfred Hitchcock, Frank Capra, John Huston, and Billy Wilder), four actors (James Cagney, Henry Fonda, James Stewart, and Fred Astaire), and two actresses (Bette Davis and Lillian Gish).

In 1978, the John F. Kennedy Center for the Performing Arts started to honor achievements in the performing arts: theater, dance, film, and music. The annual awards are televised in the last week of December. Every year, five artists are honored with such awards. In 1983, for example, three of the five winners were from the film world: director Elia Kazan, James Stewart, and Frank Sinatra, as singer-actor. And in 1985, Bob Hope and Irene Dunne represented Hollywood in these awards.

The difference between the Oscar and the awards bestowed by other national film academies is that the former has been much more internationally visible. And the difference between the Oscar and the awards conferred by the American Film Institute or the Kennedy Center is that these two honor *careers* of achievement, which means that their recipients tend to be old. The Oscar, by contrast, honors, at least in theory, a performance-achievement in a single film. And because its winners tend to be younger, it has tremendous impact on their careers.

International Film Festivals

Most international film festivals bestow merit awards, which officially are based on a fair contest of films from all over the world. Of the various festivals, four are of special importance: the Venice, the Cannes, the Berlin, and the New York film festivals.

The Venice festival is the oldest of the international film festivals. It was first held in 1932, under the auspices of the Venice

Biennial, but in 1934 it became an independent event. At its inception, the festival served as a vehicle for Fascist propaganda, receiving the sponsorship of Mussolini, who was well aware of the effectiveness of film as a tool of political indoctrination. In the first years, no merit awards were conferred, but prizes, based on public referendum, were given to "the most touching," "the most amusing," and "the most original film." The awards for "the favorite actor and actress" went to Fredric March (*Dr. Jekyll and Mr. Hyde*) and Helen Hayes (*The Sin of Madelon Claudet*), both of whom won Oscars for these films. The Venice festival is held in late August or early September and its chief prize is the Golden Lion of St. Marks.

Because political favoritism was a crucial factor in the selection of winners, especially in the 1930s and 1940s, the festival's prestige was seriously damaged. However, in recent years, the festival has restored its credibility, honoring films that are highly respected, such as Krzystof Zanussi's *A Year of the Quiet Sun* in 1984, and Agnes Varda's *Vagabond* in 1985.

The Cannes festival, the best known of all international film festivals, emerged in opposition to the political nature of the Venice festival. It was originally scheduled to open in 1939, but because of the war the first festival was held in September 1946. The Cannes operation has always enjoyed tremendous publicity, and not just because of its cinematic functions. It has become over the years a highly commercial and international event, attended by celebrities from all over the world. The Cannes is also the biggest festival, screening hundreds of films, in and outside the official program. Until 1950, it took place in the fall but then it was decided to hold it in early May—some say in order to precede the Venice festival. The structure and number of awards have changed over the years. At present, the highest prize is the Golden Palm (Palme d'Or), honoring the best film from the twenty entries that are in official competition. But the festival also honors achievements by actors, directors, and cinematographers.

For two decades, the Cannes has been an extremely important operation, presenting the most recent developments in international cinema. However, as a result of the increasing number of festivals, the Cannes has gradually lost its uniqueness. In fact, some festivals, most notably the New York Film Festival, have been performing these functions more effectively. And as in the Venice festival, politics, in and outside the film world, has afflicted its operation. In 1968, political demonstrations forced the festival to close in midprogress, but it somehow recovered and managed to regain its former popularity. The choice of films for competition, particularly the winners, has at times been motivated by ideological rather than aesthetic considerations (see chapter 4).

The Berlin festival, founded in 1951, enjoyed immense publicity and official support in its first decade due to the city's special political status. As a festival, it is supposed to be less commercial than both the Venice and the Cannes festivals, and more committed to the exhibition of documentaries and independent productions. Until 1957 it was held in the summer, but at present, it is held in February so that it will come well in advance of the Cannes and Venice operations. In the first years, the bestowal of awards was quite democratic: a jury as well as lay audiences participated in the process. This practice was discontinued in 1957 due to growing criticism. The top prizes are the Golden Bear for best film and the Silver Bear for directorial and acting achievements.

The New York Film Festival has been one of the most recent, though highly prestigious, operations. It was established in 1963, under the auspices of the Lincoln Center Film Society, which also publishes the magazine *Film Comment*. From its beginning, it has functioned under the leadership of Richard Roud, a cineast and British film critic. The New York festival is undoubtedly the most important in the United States, where no less than twenty film festivals take place every year. Its duration is two and a half weeks, from late September to mid-October, during which about twenty-six features and some shorts are screened. The purpose of the festival has been "to bring the most interesting films with the greatest artistic merit from all over the world to the attention of the New York film community." The films, selected by a five-member committee, have tended to be either innovative and different from conventional films, or plain and solid achievements.

It is probably the only major festival that does not bestow merit awards, attempting to steer clear from the political favoritism and negative competitiveness of the other festivals. Mr. Roud is apparently appalled by "the shenanigans that go on at other festivals where there are prizes and pressures to win." "Prizes are for the one who wins," claims Roud, stressing instead that "all of the great filmmakers have won a prize by being in the festival."[2] There has been fierce competition to be included in the festival: the twenty-six final selections are drawn from a pool of over four hundred films, though about half of the films come from other festivals, predominantly Cannes.

Most international film festivals have been active arenas of aesthetic and political conflicts. The selection of films and the bestowal of awards have been criticized as inadequate or inappropriate, because they are based on many biases, in particular special-interest politics. On many occasions, prizes have been given to those national cinemas that the jury felt deserved attention and recognition for political reasons, thus ignoring the quality of the honored films (see chapter 4). The politics of these festivals, however, has also had positive results, calling the public's attention to the variety of yardsticks—aesthetic, moral, ideological—used in the evaluation of film as an art form.

In addition to their politics, the international festivals, particularly Cannes, have been accused of favoring big-budget and commercial over small art films, thus functioning as springboards for commercial releases. The 1986 Palme d'Or, for example, went to the British big-budget epic, *The Mission*. Another frequent claim, often raised against the New York festival, is that it has consistently sponsored a few favorite filmmakers, such as Truffaut, Godard, Fassbinder, and Wajda, while disregarding the work of innovative or young filmmakers. Godard and the late Fassbinder have been the most popular directors: fourteen of the former's films and eleven of the latter's have been shown in the festival.[3]

Furthermore, unlike the Academy, the festivals depend on the goodwill of studios and producers to send their films for competition. The availability of films through studio cooperation has indeed been a determining factor for their selection in the festivals' programs. Martin Scorsese's *After Hours* was not included in the 1985 New York festival, because its producers reportedly demanded that it be shown on opening or closing night. Furthermore, some producers fear that the inclusion of their films in festivals will label them as "art" or "esoteric" films and subsequently damage their commercial potential with the larger movie public. By contrast, every film released in the United States within the calendar year is considered eligible to compete for the Academy Awards, regardless of the studios' or filmmakers' wishes.

Film Critics

Film critics also honor achievements in film. The most influential associations of critics in the United States are: the New York Film Critics Circle, the Los Angeles Film Critics Association, and the National Society of Film Critics.

The New York Film Critics Circle was founded in 1935 with a twofold goal: to recognize the finest achievements in motion pictures and to maintain high standards of film criticism. For over three decades, the circle recognized achievements in four categories: picture, actor, actress, and director. In 1969, it created additional categories for acting (supporting actor and actress), screenplay, and cinematography. The New York Circle announces its winners at its annual meeting in late December and the certificates of honor are conferred in a modest gathering at Sardi's in late January.

The National Society of Film Critics was founded in 1968 as a "high-brow" association, to counter the "middle-brow" circles whose tastes were considered to be too similar to the Academy's. In the first years of its operation it was accused of being "too harsh" and "snobbish" toward Hollywood's commercial pictures, and too "avant-garde" in its preference for European art films. The National Society stressed that one of its major purposes was "to give annual recognition to the best works in films of the preceding year, without distinction of nationality." Unlike the other circles, in the first years, the votes of each critic and the complete tabulations were published in the Society's annual publication. In the 1970s, the Society broadened its base and included many new members (it is composed of forty critics), a democratic procedure that led to the departure of some of its more elitist founders.

The Los Angeles Film Critics Association consists of about twenty reviewers in the Los Angeles area. It is one of the most recent circles, presenting its first awards in 1975. It is believed that its proximity to the film industry makes its influence on the Academy more direct and more pervasive than the other critics' associations.

The critics' awards perform at least three functions in the film world. First, they confer tremendous prestige on the winning films and winning artists. The critics, unlike the mass public, are considered to be "experts," who use more matter-of-fact and rational yardsticks in their aesthetic evaluations. Second, film critics serve as tastemakers and guides for the general public. Because every year hundreds of films are released and the public could not possibly see all of them, moviegoers often rely on the critics' judgments.

But critics also have influence on the operations of the Oscar Award. All film circles announce their choices in late December— that is, two weeks prior to the beginning of the nomination process in early January, thus inevitably affecting the nomination ballots. The Academy members, like other moviegoers, cannot possibly see all films eligible for nominations. Hence, the critics' reviews and annual awards assist them in focusing their attention on a smaller number of films. Films that appear on the "ten best" lists of influential critics, such as Vincent Canby of the *New York Times* and Charles Champlin of the *Los Angeles Times*, tend to get special consideration by the Academy members.

But with all the critics' importance, their awards, unlike the Oscar, have little impact on the films' standing at the box office. Further, the critics' status is ambiguous. As Andrew Sarris put it, "At best movie reviewers are considered a necessary evil, at worst, a positive plague of locusts."[4] If their reviews are favorable, they are used as advertisements for the movies in the press, but if they are negative, they are not only ignored but also chastised for exerting a damaging influence on the industry, its artists, and the public.

The critics' awards have differential meaning and prestige in the film world. The National Society of Film Critics enjoys greater prestige than either the New York or the Los Angeles critics circle because it represents critics from all over the nation, not just from these two cities. And in some circles, the choices of the New York critics are considered to be less biased by commercial considerations than the choices of their counterparts in California. The choice of *Brazil* by the Los Angeles critics as the best film of 1985 was interpreted by many as influenced by the conflict between its director, Terry Gilliam, and Universal, over its running time and ending. Further, the selection of *Brazil* by the Los Angeles critics resulted in its earlier release in December so that it could be eligible for Academy nominations, though the film was not scheduled for distribution until the following year.

The solemnity of the California critics' televised ceremony is sometimes ridiculed in New York, as by Vincent Canby when he wrote: "This event always fascinates their Eastern colleagues, not one of whom has ever had the ineffable pleasure of hearing his own luminous prose—in praise of this or that film performance, special effect or junk tune—read at such sonorous length on national television."[5]

Film artists also attribute differential meaning to the critics' prizes. James Cagney, for example, was very appreciative of the New York critics' award when he learned that it took nine ballots before he was cited best actor in *Angels with Dirty Faces* (1938). And Susan Hayward, honored for her role in *I Want to Live!* (1958), is quoted as having said: "The big treat was winning the New York Film Critics Award. That's a tough one to win, not because they know so much, but because they're such rats and they don't like to give anyone a prize, especially anybody from Hollywood."[6] By contrast, one of the unique attributes of the Oscar Award, compared with the critics and international festivals' awards, is its almost *universal* acceptance as the most prestigious film award.

Popularity and Other Awards

The National Board of Review and the Hollywood Foreign Press Association, which also confer awards, are on the borderline: they neither consist of film critics nor of moviegoers.

The National Board of Review is the oldest film association in America. Established in New York in 1909 by a voluntary group of film-oriented citizens, it was first called the National Board of Censorship of Motion Pictures, serving as the country's first voluntary censorship body, and enjoying the full support of the film industry. In 1922, however, its powers were diminished when the industry established its own regulatory board under the leadership of Will H. Hays. Diminished in function, it changed its name to the National Board of Review and devoted its activities to the classification and evaluation of quality films. In its first years, it honored the best films (American and foreign), but since 1930, it selects "the ten best" films of the year, best performances by players, and other achievements.

Founded in 1940, the Hollywood Foreign Press Association consists of about eighty journalists representing some hundred million readers in over fifty countries. Its awards, the Golden Globes, were first presented in 1943. All members vote for the nominees in early January, and for the winners in late January. Because of its international nature, the occasion has enjoyed quite extensive media coverage. The Golden Globes were modeled on the Academy Awards, with three major exceptions. They distinguish between achievements in drama and in comedy/musical, thus doubling the number of awards and diminishing their relative significance. Second, the association honors achievements in television, not just in film. And third, it also celebrates impressive film debuts, life achievement careers, and the "world film favorite actor and actress." Established in 1951, this popularity award is determined by the results of a worldwide survey, excluding North America, conducted by the Reuters News Bureau.

The film critics' circles look down on the Golden Globes because they are selected by reporters, not critics, and because there are so many of them. Canby probably represented the opinion of many colleagues when he wrote that at the Golden Globe Awards ceremony "there seems to be a prize for anyone who shows up."[7] The studios use the Golden Globes as "free publicity," because they are given two months before the Oscars. "If the Golden Globes took place after the nominations closed," a press agent was quoted, "nobody would go."[8]

Meant to be based on merit, the Golden Globes are also influenced by the popularity and nationality of the nominees. In the 1984 awards ceremonies, for example, three of the winners were British: Tom Courtenay (*The Dresser*), Michael Caine, and Julie Walters (both for *Educating Rita*); all three were nominated for, but didn't win, the Oscar. Furthermore, Barbra Streisand, who is extremely popular overseas, won several awards for her one-woman endeavor *Yentl*, which she produced, wrote, directed, and starred in. But *Yentl* was almost ignored by the Academy, which nominated it for five minor awards. Despite their low prestige, the Golden Globes have been much more influential in foreign film markets, as far as box-office receipts are concerned, than any of the film critics' awards.

Popularity awards are also given by various associations and magazines. The oldest, most comprehensive, and most accurate poll of America's "top box-office stars" has been the Quigley Publications Poll, first conducted in 1932. There have been other polls, but the Quigley is regarded by the film industry as "the poll." From 1932 on, the poll has asked film exhibitors in the US to name the year's top ten box-office attractions, that is, the ten players whose names on the marquees have drawn the largest number of customers to their theaters. This popularity poll is based on film rentals paid to their distributors in the US and Canada.

For example, the ten box-office stars in America in 1985 were: Sylvester Stallone, Eddie Murphy, Clint Eastwood, Michael J. Fox, Chevy Chase, Arnold Schwarzenegger, Chuck Norris, Harrison Ford, Michael Douglas, and Meryl Streep. Note that only one of the ten stars is a woman, and that most male stars specialize in action-adventure or in comedy. Only three of the ten stars have been nominated for an Oscar: Streep, Stallone, and Ford. The disparity between the country's commercial stars and its acclaimed players, reflected in Oscar nominations and awards, has never been as great as at present. By contrast, in 1932, seven of the nation's top stars had been or would become Oscar winners and nominees, like Marie Dressler, Janet Gaynor, Joan Crawford, Greta Garbo, Norma Shearer, Wallace Beery, and Clark Gable; the three who were not were Charles Farrell, Will Rogers, and Joe E. Brown.

The National Association of Theater Owners also confers popularity awards on the year's top male and female star. In 1985, the two top stars cited by the Association were Michael J. Fox (*Back to the Future*) and Kathleen Turner (*Prizzi's Honor* and *Jewel of the Nile*). Neither was nominated, though some believed Turner deserved it for *Prizzi's Honor*. Turner's omission was particularly conspicuous, because all of her three costars received a nomination, Jack Nicholson, Anjelica Huston, and William Hickey.

In recent years there has been a proliferation of film awards. In 1975, the People's Choice Awards began to honor the public's favorite performers in film, television, and the recording industries. The annual ceremony takes place in Santa Monica, California, in March, a few weeks prior to the Academy ceremonies and there is a live coverage of the event. Another recent prize is The American Movie Awards, honoring the best players and films and based on a national sample of moviegoers. These awards have cashed in on the suspense and excitement that precede the Oscar ceremonies, and through television reach extremely large audiences.

The Preeminence of the Oscar in the Entertainment World

The importance of the Oscar Award goes beyond the film world: it has become a symbol of achievement firmly rooted in the entertainment world. A combination of factors has accounted for the preeminence of the award in show business.

First and foremost, there is its longevity. Conferred for the first time in 1929 (for achievements in 1927/8), the Oscar is the oldest prize in film history. The fifty-eight-year history of the Academy has made the Oscar a respectable symbol with historical heritage. The other entertainment awards are, agewise, children and grandchildren of the Oscar. The Antoinette (Tony) Perry Awards, given by the League of New York Theaters and Producers and the American Theater Wing, were first presented in April 1947, almost twenty years after the first Academy Awards. The Emmy, awarded by the National Academy of Television Arts and Sciences, were presented for the first time in January 1949. And the Grammy, the youngest entertainment award, was first bestowed by the National Academy of Recording Arts and Sciences in May 1959.

In addition to the Oscar's amazing longevity, there are also differences in the scope and nature of these awards. The Tony is essentially a local award, given for achievement in New York's Broadway theater. Consequently, most people cannot relate to this award because it is confined to shows produced in New York. There has also been a growing criticism of the Tonys for excluding achievements in the Off Broadway and the Off Off Broadway theater, where most of the original, innovative, and interesting stage work is now being done. The movies, by contrast, have the potential of reaching, sooner or later, everyone. Even people who don't live in the United States and don't speak English can relate to the Oscar show and to the honored movies and performers.

Much of the Oscar's prestige stems from the status of the Academy of Motion Picture within the film industry. The Academy has always been elitist in its orientation, constituting a very small percentage of the entire film industry. But despite its elitist nature, the Oscar's selection of nominees and winners has been more open and democratic than the prevailing practices at the other academies of entertainment. The Academy's structure, with its twelve branches, gives equal representation to all film artists, regardless of their speciality (writers, directors, players). And the nomination process is really democratic and based on peer evaluation. The Acting Branch selects nominees for the acting awards, the Directors Branch for the directing awards, etc. However, each Academy member proposes nominees for the top award, Best Picture of the year. And the entire membership participates in the final selection of winners—that is, each member votes for all the awards.

The procedure for nomination and voting is very different at the Tony Awards. The selection of nominees for each of the categories is done by a nomination committee of twelve members appointed by the Tony Awards Administration Committee. The final ballots are sent out to the 670 eligible Tony voters, composed of members of the governing boards of the Actors Equity Association, the Dramatists Guild, the Society of Stage Directors and Choreographers, the board of directors of the American Theater Wing, members of the League of the New York Theaters and Producers, and those on the first and second night press lists. Unlike the Oscar Award, which has always had a nomination system, during the first decade of the Tonys there were no prior nominations; the nomination process actually began in 1956.

The Oscar is awarded by peers, not by film critics or the public at large. Film artists, like other professionals, attribute the utmost importance to peer recognition because they consider them the only experts with the necessary knowledge to make a competent evaluation of their work. For most film artists, the significant reference group, the one that sets goals and standards to be emulated and also serves as a comparative frame for judging one's performance, consists of fellow-workers (see chapter 10). Film artists tend to compare the rewards of their work (money, power, and prestige) not with those of other professionals but with their peers.

The scarce number of awards also contributes to the Oscar's extraordinary prestige. In the entire Academy history, for instance, only 608 players have been nominated for and only 188 have actually won acting awards. Every year, only twenty players are nominated in the four acting categories, and only four win: Best Actor, Best Actress, Best Supporting Actor, and Best Supporting Actress. The performances nominated for acting awards are singled out of thousands of eligible performances. Indeed, only five films compete for Best Picture. These five are selected from a large pool of films: In 1985, 222 films were eligible to compete for Academy nominations. It is of interest to note that in the past the number of eligible films was twice as large because of the tremendous annual film output. In the 1940s, for instance, over four hundred films were released on an average year, and in the 1960s over three hundred.

Consequently, the Oscar Award has always been much more competitive than the Tony Award. In recent years, the Broadway theater has been in such a dismal state that the Tony Committee had problems to fill the categories with competent performers, particularly in the musical awards. But even in better times, no more than thirty new plays and ten musicals open in an average season— this in comparison to hundreds of movies and performances, American and foreign, eligible for Academy nominations in a given year.

Because many superlative performances by foreign players tend to be ignored or bypassed by the Academy, it has been suggested that an additional category be created: best performance by a foreign actor and actress in a foreign film. It has also been suggested that the categories be divided according to genre: that is, best achievement in straight (serious) drama, comedy, and musical film. The Tony Awards have two separate sets of categories: one for dramatic plays, the other for musicals. Those who defend the awarding of one prize only, regardless of genre or the artists' nationality, have claimed that increasing the number of awards will make them meaningless and decrease their prestige. Too many categories tend to belittle the award and its winner. In 1984, for example, Grammys were awarded in no less than sixty-five different categories, and some singers were nominated in three or four categories for the same song.

The Oscar has always been awarded to film artists of all nationalities. No less than one-fourth of the nominees have been foreign artists (see chapter 4). This international dimension has extended the Oscar's visibility and contributed to its immense prestige. And the Oscar's prestige in turn makes for intense international competition. This is probably one reason why no other award has matched the Oscar's in international significance. The cumulative effect of the scarcity of awards and the intense competition among artists of all nationalities has made the award all the more desirable. Most awards by national film academies or national industries, as has been shown, tend to distinguish between achievements by local and by foreign artists. The only Oscar category that was specifically designed to honor foreign achievements is the Best Foreign-Language Picture.

The Oscar's tremendous effects, symbolic as well as pragmatic, on winning films and artists, has been another unique feature. Unlike the prestigious Nobel Prize, there is no direct financial honorarium. But the Oscar's economic worth has been extraordinary: the winners' salaries skyrocket overnight! Moreover, winning an Oscar means not only prestige but hard cash at the box office. Winning the Best Picture award can add up to twenty or thirty million dollars in movie ticket sales. Winning the lead acting awards is less influential, but it can also amount to four million dollars in a film's profitability. Significantly, the Oscar's effects have been visible in both the domestic and international film markets: the box-office receipts of movies abroad at times amount to more than half of their overall profits. In addition to prestige and money, the winning artists also gain power in negotiating for better roles with better directors, and earn increased popularity outside the film industry and outside of the US.

No other entertainment award has effects comparable to the Oscar. The Emmys are the least influential in this respect, for the very reason that reruns of Emmy-winning programs, unlike re-releases of Oscar-winning films, cannot add more money. As for the Tonys, many of the winning shows are no longer running by the time of the award ceremonies. However, in recent years, winning a Tony for best play or best musical has affected their commercial appeal much more than winning the Pulitzer Prize for drama or the New York Drama Critics Award, especially in the case of musicals. For example, *The Wiz*, the all-black musical that opened to lukewarm reception, became a long-running show after it won the Tony for Best Musical. And plays that received nice reviews, such as *The Elephant Man* and *Children of a Lesser God*, became much more successful at the box office after winning the Best Play award in their respective years.[9]

Evidence is inconclusive concerning the precise impact of the Grammy Awards. Most critics agree that the Grammys have some impact on record sales. For instance, Quincy Jones' 1982 album *The Dude* hit the top ten after winning five Grammys. And the 1981 Grammy-winning album of songwriter-singer Christopher Cross leaped back up onto the charts and eventually sold more than four million copies, compared to the two million sale prior to winning.[10] Still, this impact is incomparable to the financial bonanza experienced by the Oscar-winning films.

The four major entertainment awards divide the calendar year with a big show-business event in every season: The Oscar show takes place in the spring; the Tony in the early summer; the Emmy in the fall; and the Grammy in the winter. However, the telecast of the Oscar's annual ceremonies has always been the most popular event. For instance, the 1980 Oscar show, telecast by ABC on April 14, was the sixth most watched program in the 1979–80 television season. It received 33.7 of the Nielson ratings and 55 percent of the audience share, compared with the telecast of the Emmy Awards, on September 9, which occupied the twenty-seventh place, with 27.3 of the rating and 45 percent of the audience share. The Grammy Awards, telecast on February 27, were the sixtieth most watched program, with 23.9 of the ratings and 30 points of the audience share. The popularity of the 1980 Oscar show was surpassed by only five programs that season, mostly sport events: Super Bowl XIV, NFC Football Conference Playoff, the screening of the adventure thriller *Jaws*, the World Series Game 7, and the Super Bowl Post-Game Show.[11] And the 1985 thirty-seventh Emmy ceremonies captured an average rating of 21.2 percent, compared with the 33.2 of the Oscar show.

The Oscar's outstanding preeminence in the entertainment world has also been enhanced through its extensive coverage in all the mass media: press and radio in its first decades, and television in the last thirty years. And this extensive coverage is not confined to the United States. The Oscar show has been one of the most popular television programs in the world, watched live or on tape by one billion people.

The variety of film awards attest to the uniquely complex nature of film as an industry, as an art form, and as a profession. Every profession is stratified, though some are more sharply stratified than others. The profession's stratification, or inequality between the elite and the rank-and-file in terms of rewards (money, prestige popularity, power), depends to a large extent on its significant audiences, that is, those who have the authority and power to evaluate the professional's performance. In film, there seem to be three relevant audiences and three corresponding evaluations: evaluation by peers, evaluation by film critics, and evaluation by the lay public. The first evaluation is internal, operating within the film world, whereas the other two are external, or outside of the entertainment industry. However, all three evaluations and audiences are important because they operate at the same time and, more significantly, each has some feedback impact on the films and their artists.

Most film artists, writers, directors, and particularly players, aim at achieving two different, at times contradictory, goals in their careers: professional attainment, as defined by fellow-artists and critics, and a broader, commercial popularity, as determined by the general public of consumers. Many film players are aware of the potential problems in fulfilling these goals. They know that to be accomplished players, respected by peers and critics, is one thing; and to be popular stars is quite another. And it seems that in film, more than in other arts, outsiders—that is, the moviegoers—exercise more power over artists' work and careers. For instance, by choosing to see a particular film or a particular film actor, the public determines not only the actor's present status but also his very chance to work in the future.

What makes the Oscar such an influential award is that it combines elements of the three evaluations and the three audiences. Through the Oscar Award, the Academy members function as peers, critics, and tastemakers. No other award combines so well these elements of critical and popular judgment of film artists. The Oscar is also the only award to exert such direct and pervasive influence on every element of the film world: the honored movies and artists, the moviegoers, and the television viewers of the awards ceremonies (see conclusion).

CHAPTER 3

The Nomination System

*E*arning a nomination for an Academy Award signifies recognition of talent by fellow-artists. Moreover, winning a nomination early on in one's career can make a big difference in its duration and viability. The first nomination often serves as a predictor of future careers because it places the nominated artist in a different class in terms of prestige and visibility, which is precisely the reason why artists make special efforts to earn a nomination as early as possible in their careers.

The First Nomination

There has been quite a variability in the age and specific career phase at which artists have won their first nomination. By and large, actresses have received their first nomination at a much younger age than actors: 20 percent of all actresses, but only 5 percent of actors, were younger than twenty-five when first nominated. And about half of the actresses received their first nomination prior to the age of thirty, compared to only one-tenth of the actors.

There are also differences between lead and supporting players. Supporting players have tended to win their first nomination either at a very young age or at a very old age, particularly among the women. Eleven percent of the supporting actresses earned their first nomination prior to the age of twenty, compared to only 1 percent of the lead actresses. And 10 percent of the supporting actresses, but only 3 percent of the lead actresses were older than sixty when first nominated. These age differences also prevail within the two male categories but to a lesser extent.

The youngest nominees in the Academy history have been in the supporting leagues. Justin Henry (*Kramer vs. Kramer*) was only eight when first nominated, and it was a remarkable achievement because he had never acted before. The youngest nominee among supporting actresses is Quinn Cummings (*The Goodbye Girl*) who at eleven earned a nomination for her first picture, though she had previously appeared on television. Earning a nomination at an early age has been more prevalent in the supporting categories, because supporting players tend to be cast in younger screen roles. But the Academy voters have also been less discriminating in their appraisal of performances by children or teenagers; sentimentality has always played a considerable role in Hollywood. Furthermore, the competition has usually been less intense in supporting than in lead leagues.

The tendency to nominate child players, particularly girls, has prevailed since the supporting awards were created in 1936. Bonita Granville was the first child actress to earn a nomination in 1936 for *These Three*, based on Lillian Hellman's first play, *The Children's Hour*. In some years, such as 1962, two child actresses competed for the supporting award: Patty Duke (*The Miracle Worker*) and Mary Badham (*To Kill a Mockingbird*); Duke won. The same situation occurred in 1973, when Tatum O'Neal (*Paper Moon*) and Linda Blair (*The Exorcist*) were up for Best Supporting Actress; O'Neal won. By comparison, fewer child actors have been nominated for a featured role. This group has included: Brandon De Wilde (*Shane*) in 1953, Sal Mineo (*Rebel Without a Cause*) in 1955, Jack Wilde (*Oliver!*) in 1968, and Justin Henry in 1979.

No child actress has ever been nominated for Best Actress, and Jackie Cooper, nominated at ten for *Skippy*, is the only boy to compete for Best Actor. However, the Academy has acknowledged the importance of star-children as money-makers with a number of Special (Junior) Awards. In 1939, for example, Deanna Durbin and Mickey Rooney were awarded miniature Oscar trophies. Durbin was honored for her performance in her first feature, *Three Smart Girls*, which made her a star and also saved Universal studio from bankruptcy. And Rooney received the award "for significant contribution in bringing to the screen the spirit and personification of youth and as a juvenile player setting a high standard of ability and achievement," in his Andy Hardy movies. In 1940, Judy Garland won a Special Oscar as "the best juvenile performer of the year," for her appearance in the musical *The Wizard of Oz*, one of the smash hits of the season. Other children were honored with a Special Oscar in the 1940s, but later, performances by children were nominated for the regular, legitimate awards.

The youngest nominee among the Best Actresses is French Isabelle Adjani, nominated for the title role in Francois Truffaut's *The Story of Adele H.* at the age of twenty-one. Adjani began her theatrical career in amateur productions at twelve, and made her film debut at fourteen. She was asked to join the noted Comédie Francaise, with no previous formal training, when she was seventeen. But later, she rejected a tempting twenty-year contract with that theater in order to appear in *The Story of Adele H.* It paid off: the movie, assisted by her nomination, put her at the forefront of the international film scene.

There have been consistent differences between the careers of female and male nominees. By and large, women have received their first nomination at a younger age than men: the median age[1] at first nomination is thirty-one for women and forty for men, a significant gap of nine years. Of the four groups, the Best Actresses have been the youngest at their first nomination. The median age at receiving the first nomination is twenty-nine for Best Actress, thirty-three for Supporting Actress, thirty-eight for Best Actor, and forty-three for Supporting Actor. Within each category, lead and supporting, women have had an advantage over men when it comes to getting early Academy recognition.

Supporting players have been either older or younger than their lead counterparts, a fact related to the kinds of screen roles they play. Character roles are typically younger or older in age than leading parts. This is especially true in the case of women: very few Best Actresses have been over forty at their first nomination. In the 1940s, for example, Joan Crawford (*Mildred Pierce*) was the only actress in this age category, and in the 1950s, there were only two, Shirley Booth (*Come Back Little Sheba*) and Anna Magnani (*The Rose Tattoo*). but all three performers have been the exception, particularly Magnani. Foreign players tend to receive their first nomination at an older age than their American counterparts (see chapter 4). In general, less than one-tenth of the Best Actresses, but over one-fourth of the Best Actors, were over forty years old when first nominated.

Indeed, many actresses have rightly complained that once they reached the age of forty they have either had to switch to supporting roles or to retire because of the dearth of screenplays with middle-aged heroines. The leading lady in the American cinema has typically been young (in her twenties) and attractive (see chapter 8). The position of middle-aged actresses in the film industry began to change in the 1970s. And the Academy has reflected these changes: in the last decade, there were more leading roles for middle-aged actresses than ever before. For example, Gena Rowlands (*A Woman Under the Influence*), Ellen Burstyn (*Same Time Next Year*), and Mary Tyler Moore (*Ordinary People*), were all middle-aged actresses nominated for playing middle-aged women. Another encouraging development has been the nomination of elderly actresses in the lead category for playing elderly characters, such as Katharine Hepburn (*On Golden Pond*), and most recently Geraldine Page (*The Trip to Bountiful*). In the past, elderly actresses were nominated in the supporting categories regardless of the nature or importance of their roles.

The tendency to nominate older players has also characterized the male categories in the last two decades. In the 1950s, only two supporting actors (Erich von Stroheim in *Sunset Boulevard*, and Sessue Hayakawa in *The Bridge on the River Kwai*) were in their sixties. But since 1970, over fifteen nominated players fall into this age group, including: John Mills (*Ryan's Daughter*), Lee Strasberg (*The Godfather, Part II*), Burgess Meredith (*Rocky*), and Robert Preston (*Victor/Victoria*). The recent awareness of the problems of aging and aged people in America has been reflected in the kinds of screenplays written, with many of their protagonists elderly men and women. And the Academy has expressed its concerns for elderly players with a large number of nominations.

Despite the fact that there have been established norms for the age of nominated men and women, it is possible to win a first nomination at a relatively old age. The oldest nominees are: George Arliss (*Disraeli*) at sixty-three, and Art Carney (*Harry and Tonto*) at fifty-seven among Best Actors; George Burns (*The Sunshine Boys*) at eighty, and Don Ameche (*Cocoon*) at seventy-seven among Supporting Actors; Dame May Robson (*Lady for a Night*) at seventy-six and Ida Kaminska (*The Shop on Main Street*) at sixty-eight among Best Actresses; and Eva Le Gallienne (*Resurrection*) at eighty, and Dame Edith Evans (*Tom Jones*) at seventy-six among Supporting Actresses.

The history of the Oscar Award shows that it is possible to win a nomination at any age, particularly in the supporting categories. The ages of supporting nominees have ranged from eight (Justin Henry) to eighty (George Burns) among the men, and from ten (Quinn Cummings) to eighty (Eva Le Gallienne) among the women. However, this has not been the case among the lead categories. In the two lead leagues, the norms have been more rigid concerning the dominant age of receiving the first nomination. In each lead category, there has been one particular age group in which most nominees were concentrated. Most Best Actresses were in their late twenties and most Best Actors in their late thirties when honored with the first nomination. This age difference, a full decade, between the Best Actresses and Best Actors, is quite significant in the careers of performing artists.

Early and Late Recognition by the Academy

At what phase of their careers do film artists win their first nomination? How long does it take to win a nomination once a film career has been launched? Surprisingly, quite a considerable proportion of players (16 percent) have received Academy nominations for their very first film. Particularly for supporting roles: one-fifth of the supporting, but less than one-tenth of the lead players, have been nominated for their first picture.

The time span between the film debut and the first nomination has been shorter for women than men: half of the actresses, but only one-third of the actors, were nominated within a period of five years after their first movie. Indeed, the acting talent of women has been certified by the Academy much faster than that of men. But this also means that the chances of lead actresses to get a first nomination in the second decade of their careers are rather small. The career "fate" of leading ladies in terms of Academy nominations is determined quite soon: actresses failing to impress the Academy in their first five or six movies have slim chances to be honored with a Best Actress nomination.

Once again, the careers of supporting players are different. Supporting players have received their first nomination either very early or very late in their careers. Eighteen percent of the supporting, but only 5 percent of the lead performers, have experienced two decades between their film debuts and their first nominations.

About one-tenth of the Best Actors have earned nominations for their *first* film or for their first *major* film, including: Paul Muni (*The Valiant*), Montgomery Clift (*The Search*), Anthony Franciosa (*A Hatful of Rain*), and Alan Arkin (*The Russians Are Coming, the Russians Are Coming*). A similar percentage of the Best Actresses were also nominated for their first film appearance, some for recreating successful stage roles, such as Julie Harris (*Member of the Wedding*), Maggie McNamara (*The Moon Is Blue*), and Jane Alexander (*The Great White Hope*). Other lucky actresses singled out by the Academy for a film debut include Carrie Snodgress (*Diary of a Mad Housewife*), Diana Ross (*Lady Sings the Blues*), and Bette Midler (*The Rose*).

Dustin Hoffman was also fortunate enough to win a nomination for his first major film, *The Graduate*, in 1967; his very first film, *The Tiger Makes Out*, was made the same year. But like many actors in this group, his career was not launched overnight. After graduating from the Pasadena Playhouse in Los Angeles he moved to New York, where he was forced to make his living as a typist and moving man. For a while he could not get any acting work and, at one point, even considered quitting. Then, after working as an assistant director Off Broadway, he was cast in *Journey of the Fifth Horse*, which enjoyed only a short life but won him an Obie Award. Director Mike Nichols was impressed with his performance and, looking for a young actor to play the title role in *The Graduate*, summoned Hoffman to Hollywood for a screen test. Hoffman became an instant star after this one film.

Indeed, in addition to talent, luck (or being the right player at the right time and place) also plays a considerable role in earning early recognition. Take Martha Scott, for example, who after a brief experience in stock scored a great triumph in her first Broadway play, Thornton Wilder's *Our Town*. This success led to a film career in Hollywood, marked by a nomination for her movie debut. There has been a considerable number of players who were cast in what later became their Oscar-nominated roles by sheer accident (see chapter 5).

The Academy has been even more generous in conferring nominations for film debuts on supporting players. Among the actors who immediately caught their colleagues' attention in the Academy were: John Garfield (*Four Daughters*), Robert Morley (*Marie Antionette*), Sidney Greenstreet (*The Maltese Falcon*), Richard Widmark (*Kiss of Death*), Don Murray (*Bus Stop*), Terence Stamp (*Billy Budd*), Brad Douriff (*One Flew Over the Cuckoo's Nest*), and Howard Rollins Jr. (*Ragtime*). And among the supporting actresses nominated for their very first film were: Maria Ouspenskaya (*Dodsworth*), Teresa Wright and Patricia Collinge (both for *Little Foxes*), Angela Lansbury (*Gaslight*), Lee Grant (*Detective Story*), Diana Varsi (*Peyton Place*), Maureen Stapleton (*Lonely Hearts*), Shirley Knight (*Dark at the Top of the Stairs*), Carol Channing (*Thoroughly Modern Millie*), Cathy Burns (*Last Summer*) and most recently Glenn Close (*The World According to Garp*).

Interestingly, some of the nominated performances were not delivered by professional actors. For example, Harold Russell won two Oscars, one legitimate and one Special, for recreating onscreen (*The Best Years of Our Lives*) his real-life experience as a paratroop sergeant, who lost both of his hands in World War II. It was Russell's first picture and for many years his only one.

A number of professional singers and dancers have also received nominations for their first pictures, especially if they were successful at the box office. Miliza Korjus, the Polish opera singer, was nominated for her first and only movie (*The Great Waltz*). And Mikhail Baryshnikov and Leslie Browne, both dancers of the American Ballet Theater, earned supporting nominations for playing dancers in *The Turning Point*.

A group of noted writers were also singled out for their acting debuts. Jason Miller, a successful Broadway playwright (*That Championship Season*) was nominated for portraying a priest in *The Exorcist*. And Michael V. Gazzo, a writer of plays and screenplays (*A Hatful of Rain*) earned a nomination for his first movie, *The Godfather, Part II*. Both Miller and Gazzo earned nominations, not so much for their distinguished acting but because their performances were contained in blockbuster movies. Commercial hits have quite often earned Oscar nominations, deservedly or undeservedly, in a disproportionately large number of categories.

Receiving a nomination for a first film, thus reaching the top in one's profession with only one screen credit, is quite unique to acting careers. In most professions, a lengthy period of formal training and some years of professional experience are required before one is thus honored. But in the performing arts, neither formal education nor training are prerequisites for entry into the profession or for occupying the top positions. One film, especially if it happens to be a commercial hit, can make or break a career. And many factors, in addition to talent or acting skills, are involved in making a particular performance (or particular film) worthy of recognition by the Academy.

In contrast to those who received an early recognition—through an Academy nomination—for their work, some players have received quite late recognition. These artists had to wait for a long time (over two decades) to earn their first nomination. This is particularly the case of foreign players, who had started to perform at a very young age but were much older by the time they received their first nomination, because it took a long time until they were cast in American movies or made foreign movies that were commercially successful in the American market. Anna Magnani, for example, received her first nomination and award (*The Rose Tattoo*) twenty-one years after her film debut in Italy. And if it had not been for Tennessee Williams's demand that she play the title role, she would probably never have been nominated for an Oscar, despite the fact that she was one of the greatest screen actresses in the world.

The crucial factor in the careers of foreign players is the age at which they were brought to Hollywood. Many of them showed promise in their countries but for a variety of reasons did not get the international recognition they deserved. Maximilian Schell, for instance, did not establish a reputation as a movie star in Europe, despite some good work early in his career. He arrived in Hollywood as Maria Schell's younger brother, but it took only one American film, *The Young Lions*, in which he was cast at the suggestion of Marlon Brando, to make him a player of international caliber. Indeed, three years later, Stanley Kramer assigned him the role of the German counselor in *Judgment at Nuremberg*, for which he received the 1961 Best Actor Award.

Many British players have become movie stars only after they moved to Hollywood and began to make American pictures. Rex Harrison began his film career in England when he was twenty-two, but his first American movie (*Anna and the King of Siam*) occurred sixteen years later, and he received his first nomination (*Cleopatra*) thirty-three years after his film debut, at the age of fifty-five. Peter Finch was another excellent actor who began his career in Australia in his late teens, and established himself as a prominent actor in the British film industry in the 1950s. However, he too received his first nomination (*Sunday Bloody Sunday*) thirty-six years after his first movie. Richard Burton's first five pictures in England failed to launch him as a major international star, despite acclaim for his acting. In America, however, it took only one Broadway play (Christopher Frye's *The Lady's Not for Burning*) and one movie (*My Cousin Rachel*), to earn him his first supporting nomination and make him a big star.

By contrast, American players who have received late recognition tended to be box-office stars who developed into *actors* later in their careers. For example, John Wayne made his film debut in his early twenties but received his first nomination (*Sands of Iwo Jima*) twenty-one years later, at the age of forty-two. In between Wayne made numerous B Westerns and went on to become a movie star after his breakthrough role as the Ringo Kid in John Ford's *Stagecoach*. Nonetheless, Wayne matured as a screen actor a decade later, after Howard Hawks cast him in his first character part in *Red River*. This performance and the Oscar nomination a year later certified his talent in Hollywood.

Late recognition by the Academy has also characterized popular performers who have appeared in many commercially successful films, but have failed to gain peer esteem. Later, however, for a reasonably good performance, preferably in a successful film, they have often been honored with a nomination, serving as both recognition of their acting and tribute to their endurance. Doris Day, for instance, made her film debut in 1948, appearing in musicals and romantic comedies. As a tribute to her popularity, the Academy conferred on her a nomination for a passable performance in the sex comedy *Pillow Talk*.

The most recent example of a player who was first a box-office champion and only later earned recognition as a gifted actor is Harrison Ford. Ford has appeared in more box-office hits than any other contemporary star: his movies have earned collectively more than one billion dollars at the box office. His screen credits include the role of Han Solo in George Lucas's *Star Wars* trilogy (1977–83) and of the archeological soldier of fortune in Steven Spielberg's *Raiders of the Lost Ark* and its sequel, *Indiana Jones and the Temple of Doom*. Some of these films were nominated in many categories, including Best Picture, but their stunning special effects have overshadowed his acting. In 1985 Ford had the chance to play a real character in Peter Weir's *Witness*, instead of his usual comic-strip roles, and the Academy rewarded him with his first Best Actor nomination when he was forty-three years old.

Actresses who have managed smooth transitions from child performers to ingenues and leading ladies have also been rewarded by the Academy. This group of talented actresses include: Carole Lombard, Mary Astor, Loretta Young, Natalie Wood, and Tuesday Weld. Elizabeth Taylor, another in this group, started taking dance lessons as soon as she could walk. A striking beauty, she made her first film at the age of ten for Universal: *There's One Born Every Minute*. In the following year, she was signed by MGM to a long-term contract. In the decade that followed, she matured into one of the most beautiful and most popular screen personalities of all times. She somehow skipped adolescence, moving almost directly from child roles to romantic leads.[2] Taylor received her first nomination for playing a troubled Southern belle in *Raintree County*, fifteen years after her debut.

There is also a small group of players who started their careers in the silent era, long before the Academy Awards, and made a successful transition to talking pictures. These actresses were usually nominated for featured roles, like Alice Brady, Jane Darwell, Ethel Barrymore, Marjorie Rambeau, and Billie Burke. Perhaps the most distinguished among them is Lillian Gish, one of the pioneers in the American cinema, joining D. W. Griffith in 1912 when she was sixteen. In the 1930s Gish retired temporarily from the screen but, a decade later, returned, this time as a character actress. In 1946, she received a supporting nomination for playing a wife driven to drink by her brutal cattle-baron husband in King Vidor's Western *Duel in the Sun*, a sweeping box-office success. This nomination was regarded as much a symbolic tribute to Gish's comeback and lengthy career as an honor to her performance.

The Academy, and Hollywood in general, has tremendous respect for comeback performances by distinguished players who after years of absence from the screen or after years of mediocre work can still surprise with an effective piece of acting. Take Gloria Swanson, for example, a major silent star who began performing in her early teens. Swanson was nominated for the silent movie *Sadie Thompson*, and for her first talkie, *The Trespasser*. However, her subsequent movies were unsuccessful and in 1934 she decided to retire. She did make an abortive comeback, though, in the comedy *Father Takes a Wife* (1941). Then, after close to a decade, she made a memorable comeback in *Sunset Boulevard*, in which she played a neurotic, fading movie queen. Hollywood could not deny her a nomination for her comeback as well as for her indelible portrayal.

The Academy history is replete with comeback stories, some successful, others less so. Rosalind Russell was an extremely popular star in the 1940s, receiving three Best Actress nominations, but in the 1950s her career seemed to be in decline. Instead of despairing, or waiting for the right role, Russell went back to the stage and bounced back with a triumphant performance in *Auntie Mame*, possibly the best performance of her career. She first played on Broadway, then repeated it on the screen. The Academy honored her with a fourth nomination, eleven years after her third (*Mourning Becomes Electra*, 1947).

Nominations for comeback performances show, among other things, that Hollywood is loyal to its previous champions and believes they should get a second chance. Moreover, these nominations have been extremely instrumental in providing second chapters to previously faltering careers.

Nominations for Lead and Supporting Roles

For eight years, there were two acting awards: Best Actor and Best Actress. In 1936, however, the Academy created two additional acting categories: Best Supporting Actor and Best Supporting Actress. This required new rules to clarify the distinction between lead and supporting roles. At first, the Academy asked the studios to designate leading and supporting roles in their annual reminder lists, which gave them tremendous power. For instance, Luise Rainer's role in *The Great Ziegfeld*, as the showman's first wife, was so small that by today's standards she would have been nominated for a feature role. Nonetheless, with the backing of MGM's publicity machine, Rainer was nominated (and won) the lead award.

There have been many controversies over the criteria of designation of lead and supporting roles. In 1942, Agnes Moorehead was nominated for a supporting role in Orson Welles's *The Magnificent Ambersons* because the studio (RKO) believed she had no chance to win the lead award. The competition that year was particularly fierce, and Greer Garson (*Mrs. Miniver*) was considered to be the favorite. But Moorehead's role as the neurotic, spinster aunt, was of considerable size and importance, and it convinced many that she deserved a nomination for Best Actress; she was cited as Best Actress for that performance by the New York Film Critics Circle.

The Academy instructed its members: "Actors marked in the Reminder List by a star are considered Leads and can be nominated only for the General Best Acting Awards." But members were given the option "to nominate any supporting player for both the Supporting Award and the General Best Performance Award." Consequently, in 1944, Barry Fitzgerald became the first (and last) player to be nominated for the same role (*Going My Way*) in both the lead and supporting leagues. A compromise was reached when Bing Crosby, also nominated for that film, won Best Actor and Fitzgerald the Supporting Award. Many members were disappointed because they believed his role was clearly a major one. And once again, the New York Film Critics cited Fitzgerald's work as Best Actor.

In the following year, the Academy changed the rules to avoid future unclarities. It was determined that "performance by an actor or actress in any leading role shall be eligible for nomination only for the General Awards for acting achievements." But "performance by an actor or actress in supporting role may be nominated for either in the General Best Performance or the Awards for Supporting Players."

The rules still allowed players to be nominated in both the lead and supporting categories, but for different screen roles. Nomination in both categories in the same year has occurred only three times in the history of the Academy. In 1938, Fay Bainter was nominated for Best Actress in *White Banners* and for supporting Actress in *Jezebel*. In 1942, Teresa Wright became the second actress to be nominated twice in the same year, for a lead role in *The Pride of the Yankees* and for a featured role in *Mrs. Miniver*. And in 1982, Jessica Lange won two nominations, both for portraying an actress: the fiery but doomed Frances Farmer in *Frances*, and a supporting role, as the submissive television actress, in *Tootsie*. Significantly, all three actresses lost the major but won the supporting Oscar. This tradition, however, was not followed last year, when Sigourney Weaver emerged as the greatest loser, failing to win the award for either the lead (*Gorillas in the Mist*) or supporting (*Working Girl*) categories.

In 1950, a further clarification was introduced: "If performances or a performance by an actor or actress should receive sufficient votes to be nominated for both the Best Actress Award and the Award for Supporting Player, only the achievement which, in the preferential tabulation process, first received the quota shall be placed on the ballot. The votes for the second achievement shall thereupon be redistributed."

The designation of the nomination continued to be made by the studios, regardless of the role's importance and billing considerations. Thus, in 1950, Anne Baxter persuaded Twentieth Century-Fox to back her nomination for the lead award in *All About Eve*, thereby running against Bette Davis, who clearly was the film's star and had the major role. Had Baxter been nominated for a featured role, as many believed she should have, Davis would have won Best Actress and she a second, supporting award. Baxter had already earned a supporting Oscar in 1946 for *The Razor's Edge*, which was precisely her reason to compete for the Best Actress Oscar. As it turned out, Davis and Baxter canceled each other out, leaving the award to the least expected nominee that year, Judy Holliday in *Born Yesterday*.

By contrast, Betsy Blair's 1955 performance in *Marty*, as the shy and lonely schoolteacher, was nominated for a supporting Oscar despite the fact that some considered it to be a lead role; Blair was honored with the Best Actress Award at the Cannes festival. However, the competition for Best Actress that year, headed by Anna Magnani (*The Rose Tattoo*) was very intense, and Blair had no chance of winning it. A serious dispute erupted the following year, when Dorothy Malone volunteered, under her studio's "suggestion," to lower her standing in *Written on the Wind*, to qualify for a supporting nomination. Malone initially received co-star billing, but Universal-International designated her performance as supporting because her chances to win were much better in this league, which turned out to be true. However, the switch in classification was seen as "grossly unjust" to performers who legitimately deserved recognition as supporting players.[3] This resulted in a new rule in 1957, according to which the Academy, not the studios, would make the final determination as to the appropriate classification of screen roles. The Academy would consider the information provided by the studios, but should any screen credit be questioned, the matter would be submitted to a special committee for final decision.[4]

But unexpected nominations continued to be made. In 1961,

Piper Laurie was nominated for Best Actress, as Paul Newman's alcoholic girlfriend in *The Hustler*, in which she received costar billing with George C. Scott and Jackie Gleason; it was a pleasant surprise because Scott and Gleason were nominated for featured roles.

A major change in the rules occurred in 1964, when the Academy decided that "the determination as to whether a role was a lead or supporting is made individually by members of the Acting Branch at the time of the balloting." Members in this branch could nominate any player, in either the lead or supporting league, regardless of studio billings and publicity. The Academy felt that each member should have the right to exercise his or her good judgment—without promotion or interference from other sources.

Nonetheless, politicking through ad campaigns and other irrelevant factors have continued to operate. At times, the chances to win have determined the designation of the performance. This became quite clear in 1966, when Walter Matthau was nominated for a supporting role in Billy Wilder's *The Fortune Cookie*, despite the fact that his role was major and the whole film was based on team acting by him and his costar, Jack Lemmon, who was not nominated. But Matthau's chances to win were much better in the supporting classification because there were two extremely strong lead performances: Paul Scofield in *A Man for All Seasons*, and Richard Burton in *Who's Afraid of Virginia Woolf?* When the results were announced at the Oscar show, the politics behind the designation turned out to be true: Scofield won Best Actor and Matthau Best Supporting Actor.

In 1980, Columbia Pictures campaigned for Meryl Streep for a supporting nomination in *Kramer vs. Kramer*. Streep's role, as the confused wife-mother, was small but constituted the center of the movie. The decision, however, to campaign for her in the supporting category had nothing to do with the role's size but with the realization that she had no chance beating Sally Field's performance in *Norma Rae*, particularly after Field had been honored with practically every critics award, including the New York, the Los Angeles, and the National Society of Film Critics.

That players attribute great importance to star billing and to lead roles is self-evident. But they also attribute greater importance to winning nominations in the lead categories because they are much more prestigious and have more influence on their future careers. Shelley Winters, for example, has not forgotten to this day that her two Oscars were for supporting roles. And Peter Finch was reportedly upset at the suggestion of his publicist that they try for the supporting award in *Network*, which Finch felt represented his best work. He was therefore determined "to go for the top award or be out of the competition altogether."[5]

The new rules, however, have sometimes had completely surprising results. Thus, Marlon Brando's role in *The Godfather* was considered by many to be suitable for a supporting nomination, but he was nominated (and won) the Best Actor Award. And Valerie Perrine would have had better chances to win, for playing Lenny Bruce's wife in *Lenny*, had she been nominated for a featured role. Perrine was cited as Best Supporting Actress by both the New York Critics and the National Board of Review, but the Acting Branch nominated her in the lead league.

In 1982, the biggest surprise of the acting nominations was the placement of Susan Sarandon for Best Actress in *Atlantic City*. Paramount had been pushing for her nomination in the supporting classification, and Sarandon herself admitted that she voted for her role in the supporting category.

The criteria used to distinguish between lead and supporting roles are far from clear, and the confusion prevails in other film organizations, not just at the Academy. For example, in 1985, Peggy Ashcroft's role, as Mrs. Moore, the bright elderly lady in David Lean's *A Passage to India*, received rave reviews and went on to win a number of important critical citations. But even the critics' circles were divided as to the appropriate category of her role. The New York Film Critics did not hesitate to cite Ashcroft as Best Actress of the year, but their California colleagues, the Los Angeles Critics, cited her as supporting actress. The Academy followed the California group and honored her with Best Supporting Actress. Judy Davis, her costar, playing the mysterious young woman, was nominated for Best Actress. The prevailing feeling was that had Ashcroft been nominated in the lead category, neither she nor Davis would have won because they would have canceled each other out in the final voting.

Single and Multiple Nominations

Is earning an Academy nomination a once-in-a-lifetime achievement? In other words, have different players been nominated every year? Apparently not, judging by the high percentage (one third) of players who have won multiple nominations. This generalization, however, conceals important differences among the four groups as well as differences between the winners and the losers.

To begin with, there are differences between lead and supporting players: the vast majority (82 percent) of supporting players have received a single nomination, compared with half (47 percent) of leads. Indeed, half of the Best Actor and Actress nominees have been nominated more than once—a considerable proportion. The difference in the number of nominations stems from the fact that the pool of lead players has always been smaller than that of supporting players. Consequently, the competition for lead roles is tougher, but it also increases the chances of those who get them to earn a nomination for their performances.

There are also differences between winners and losers. Winning an Oscar almost assures another nomination, usually in the near future. Three-fourths (76 percent) of the losers have received only one nomination, compared with two-fifths (41 percent) of the winners. The most dramatic differences prevail between male and female winners. The average number of nominations has been 3.5 for the women, but 2.9 for the men. More importantly, the women have tended to win their multiple nominations *after* their first Oscar, whereas the men have won them *prior* to winning the award. Consequently, the average number of nominations *after* getting the first award has been 0.9 for the men, but 2.0 for the women. This career difference stems from the fact that women tend to win the Oscar at their first nomination, whereas men tend to win at their second or third nomination (see chapter 5).

The vast majority (89 percent) of the Best Actress winners have won two or more nominations. In Oscar's entire history, only six women have received a single nomination: Mary Pickford, Ginger Rogers, Judy Holliday, Shirley Booth, Louise Fletcher, and Marlee Matlin, but they have been the exception. By contrast, no less than one third, or 19 of the Best Actors have received one nomination: Emil Jannings, Warner Baxter, George Arliss, Lionel Barrymore, Paul Lukas, Ray Milland, Broderick Crawford, Ernest Borgnine, Yul Brynner, David Niven, Charlton Heston, Lee Marvin, Paul Scofield, Cliff Robertson, Art Carney, Richard Dreyfuss, Ben Kingsley, F. Murray Abraham, and Michael Douglas. The elite of film actresses has been much smaller than that of actors. In every decade, a smaller number of women have dominated Hollywood —that is, were popular with the public, sought by the studios, and in relative control over their careers. The best screen roles in every decade have therefore circulated among a smaller group of women than men; there are more potential candidates for the lead male roles.

Multiple nominations have taken two forms: in one category (either lead *or* supporting) and in two categories (lead *and* supporting). Most of the multiple nominations, however, have been in the same category: either in the lead or in the supporting. For better or for worse, once players have been labeled by agents, producers, and directors, as leading or character players, these labels have been hard, at times impossible, to remove, a phenomenon known in Hollywood as "the curse of typecasting." Nonetheless, in the last decade it has become easier to cross over from one category to another, including the transition from character to lead roles. In the past, the direction was usually one-way, from leading to supporting roles. One of the positive developments within the film industry has been that the previously rigid concepts of lead and character players are not as clearly defined and religiously observed as they used to be.

About one-tenth of all players have been nominated in both leading and supporting categories. This group has included thirty-one actors and twenty-eight actresses, but there are differences between them. Most of the men first started in character roles, then earned nominations in the lead category. For many years, this was considered to be the natural evolution of acting careers. For example, John Garfield's first nomination (*Four Daughters*) was for a featured role, but his second (*Body and Soul*) was for a lead. And Rod Steiger's three nominations include one in the supporting (*On the Waterfront*), and two in the lead (*The Pawnbroker* and *In the Heat of the Night*) categories.

The other direction, from leading to character roles, characterizes the careers of elderly actors. For example, James Mason's first nomination (*A Star Is Born*) was for a lead role, but his two subsequent nominations (*Georgy Girl* and *The Verdict*) were for supporting roles.

By contrast, very few of the actresses who began in supporting roles were able to make the transition to leading ladies. As was mentioned, women have been much more limited than men by both biological and cultural restrictions concerning the range of their screen roles. Moreover, several actresses who began as leading ladies soon found themselves relegated to playing character roles. Take British actress Wendy Hiller, who won her first nomination for playing Eliza Doolittle in *Pygmalion*. Despite the fact that she always commanded leading roles on stage, in Hollywood she was soon classified as a supporting actress and subsequently her second (*Separate Tables*) and third (*A Man for All Seasons*) nominations were for featured roles. Shelley Winters also played leads early in her career, winning a Best Actress nomination for her portrayal of the pregnant factory girl in *A Place in the Sun*. However, shortly after this nomination producers and casting directors relegated her to supporting roles, and she remained in this classification for the rest of her career, winning three supporting nominations (*The Diary of Anne Frank, A Patch of Blue*, and *The Poseidon Adventure*).

Recently though, women in Hollywood have been much more flexible in their choice of roles, often beginning in one category and moving to another, or switching back and forth between lead and supporting roles. For instance, Ellen Burstyn, Meryl Streep, and Glenn Close have all begun their careers by playing supporting roles but later succeeded in becoming leading ladies. And for a good role in an interesting film, they would still be willing to play featured roles. It seems that the "stigma" of being supporting and therefore "second-class" players is much less in effect and has lesser impact on the course of acting careers than it had in the past.

The Academy nominations have been concentrated in a relatively small group of players. Indeed, one-fifth of the Best Actors and Actresses have earned more than four nominations. Among those nominated four times were: Barbara Stanwyck, Rosalind Russell, Jane Wyman, Charles Boyer, Mickey Rooney, and Anthony Quinn. A smaller group of artists, including Irene Dunne, Audrey Hepburn, Glenn Close, Fredric March, Paul Muni, and Arthur Kennedy, earned five nominations.

The top of the pyramid of Academy nominees is composed of players with six or more nominations. This distinguished elite is rather small, consisting of fifteen players (or 2.5 percent of all nominees):

6 nominations	3 players	Thelma Ritter, Deborah Kerr, and Dustin Hoffman
7 nominations	5	Marlon Brando, Richard Burton, Peter O'Toole, Paul Newman, and Jane Fonda
8 nominations	3	Jack Lemmon, Geraldine Page, and Meryl Streep
9 nominations	2	Spencer Tracy and Jack Nicholson
10 nominations	2	Bette Davis and Laurence Olivier
12 nominations	1	Katharine Hepburn

While the number of nominations reveals something about the structure of acting as a profession dominated by a small elite of players, the time span between the first and last nominations attests to the viability of acting careers as perceived by the Academy. In addition to providing peer recognition, the nomination also reflects the standing and popularity of the nominees in the movie colony.

Surprisingly, the viability of players' careers, as measured by the number of years between first and last nomination, is rather short. For half of the players the time span between first and last nomination is a decade, indicating that most players tend to receive their multiple nominations within a relatively short period of time. For only one-third of the multiple nominees, two decades elapse between their first and last nominations. And only one-sixth of the players receive their multiple nominations in a period extending over two decades.

Furthermore, the time span between first and last nominations has been much shorter for actresses than for actors. For two-thirds of the women, but only one-fourth of the men, this time span is shorter than a decade. And conversely, one-third of the men, but only one-tenth of the actresses, receive their nominations over a twenty-year period. Consequently, with a few exceptions, the longevity of actresses' careers tend to be fifteen to twenty years, mainly because they cannot find suitable screen roles when they reach middle age and subsequently are forced to retire. By contrast, the durability of men's careers can be three or four decades because their opportunities are better and their range of roles wider.

It is therefore possible to describe most actresses' careers in terms of the *decade* (or at most, two decades), in which they are popular and in demand. For example, Greta Garbo and Irene Dunne were stars of the 1930s, and Olivia de Havilland, Rosalind Russell, and Greer Garson of the 1940s. Audrey Hepburn, Susan Hayward, and Deborah Kerr did their best work in the 1950s, and Sophia Loren, Anne Bancroft, Patricia Neal, and Shirley MacLaine in the 1960s. The decade of the 1970s was dominated by Ellen Burstyn, Faye Dunaway, and Diane Keaton, but the 1980s saw the rise of Sally Field, Sissy Spacek, Meryl Streep, and Jessica Lange.

In comparison, the males' careers have tended to be active and viable for prolonged periods of time. Their careers have spanned three, four, and even five decades. A considerable number of actors did good work consistently, for which they were rewarded with multiple nominations. For example, Laurence Olivier's film career began in 1930 and continued to be viable for half a century. His ten nominations have spanned thirty-nine years, from *Wuthering Heights* in 1939 to *The Boys from Brazil* in 1978. Olivier's brilliant career was rewarded with one nomination in the 1930s, three in the 1940s, one in the 1950s, two in the 1960s, and three in the 1970s. Spencer Tracy, another Hollywood giant, began his career in 1930 and went on to make movies up to his death, in 1967. His thirty-seven-year career brought him nine nominations: three in the 1930s, three in the 1950s, and three in the 1960s, the first of which was for *San Francisco* in 1936 and the last for *Guess Who's Coming to Dinner?*, which was released after his death. Of the current generation of players, Jack Lemmon's spectacular career stands out because it has been distinguished by seven nominations (so far), from *Mister Roberts* in 1955 to *Missing* in 1982.

The time span between the first and last nominations of the supporting players has been shorter because most were older when they received their first nomination. Distinguished character players, such as Walter Brennan, Charles Coburn, Charles Bickford, and Gladys Cooper, have won multiple nominations, but usually within a short period of time because they were not young at their first nomination.

Claude Rains, for example, made his stage debut as a choir boy in London at the age of eleven. He went on to hold almost every possible position in the theater world, ranging from call boy and prompter to leading actor and stage manager. However, Rains's film debut, the impressive *The Invisible Man*, in which he appeared faceless, occurred when he was forty-four. He won his first nomination in 1939, for playing the corrupt senator in *Mr. Smith Goes to Washington*; he was then fifty. Rains soon established himself as one of Hollywood's finest character actors, winning four supporting nominations within seven years. His second nomination was for *Casablanca*, and his third for *Mr. Skeffington*. But perhaps most memorable of all was his role in Hitchcock's *Notorious*, playing the mother-ridden Nazi betrayed by the woman (Ingrid Bergman) he loves, for which he received his fourth and last supporting nomination. It is a shame that Rains, who distinguished himself in numerous films and worked almost consistently up to his death (in 1967) never won an Academy Award.

As Rains's and many other careers attest, the Academy has not hesitated to nominate the same players year after year. Over one-third of all nominees have won consecutive nominations at one time or other in their careers. Their numbers are, of course, much higher (about half) among the lead players. For example, the peak of Bette Davis's career was undoubtedly between 1938 and 1942, during which she received five successive nominations. And in the early 1940s, Greer Garson and Gary Cooper were perennial nominees; Garson was nominated four times from 1941 to 1944, and Cooper three times between 1941 and 1943. Marlon Brando won his first Oscar (*On the Waterfront*) in 1954, following three consecutive nominations. And of Elizabeth Taylor's five nominations, four were in successive years, from 1957 to 1960. At present, Meryl Streep and Jessica Lange are perennial Academy nominees: Streep was nominated in 1978, 1979, 1981, 1982, 1983, 1985, 1987, and 1988, and Lange in 1982, 1984, and 1985.

Effects of the Nomination

The very nomination for an Academy Award has pervasive impact on artists' careers, contributing to their visibility in the film industry through the immense exposure and publicity that follow the first nomination. Once artists have been nominated for an Oscar, their careers are watched carefully by producers, directors, and film critics. The nomination tends to place artists on a different level, carrying with it status, prestige, and popularity.

Many film artists have been unknown prior to their first nomination, but have leaped into stardom afterwards, particularly if their performances were contained in commercially successful pictures. For instance, Gregory Peck's first nomination in *The Keys of the Kingdom*, his second movie, made him a star. Kirk Douglas did not make much impression in the film world until he earned a nomination for *Champion*, and Joan Fontaine played small, undistinguished parts in several movies (*The Women*) until she won her first nomination for *Rebecca*. In recent years, *Midnight Cowboy* brought to Jon Voight the kind of instant stardom that *The Graduate* had brought to Dustin Hoffman. Voight and Hoffman would have become international stars without getting nominations for their respective film debuts, but the nomination expedited the process by making them more visible.

Ann-Margret's career not only benefited from her first nomination, but also got a tremendous boost when she appeared at the 1962 Oscar show, at which she sang "Bachelor in Paradise," one of the nominated songs. "In the space of three minutes," she reportedly became "the Hottest Name in Town."[6] This got her work, but not recognition as a serious actress; she had begun her career in night clubs and not in the legitimate theater. It took an imaginative director, Mike Nichols, and a good, though supporting, part, as Bobbie Templeton, Jack Nicholson's love-starved actress-girlfriend in *Carnal Knowledge* (1971), to change her screen image from a teenage sex kitten (*Bye Bye Birdie*, *Viva Las Vegas*). The supporting nomination brought critical acclaim and bolstered her self-confidence as an actress; in the last decade Ann-Margret has continued to grow and she is now one of the best actresses in America.

Several foreign players have become international stars only after their movies have been nominated for (or won) Academy Awards. Laurence Harvey established himself as a screen actor only after *Room at the Top*, which earned him a nomination, was released in the US. Albert Finney's nomination in *Tom Jones* and the commercial success of that movie made him a household word in America. Richard Harris's first starring role in *This Sporting Life* established him as an actor of the first rank because it won some acting nominations; it was the kind of movie that would have received limited release had it not been for the nominations. *Alfie* performed the same function for Michael Caine, and *Georgy Girl* for Lynn Redgrave; both Caine and Redgrave received nominations and later became international stars.

But perhaps equally important is the effect of the first nomination on the status and power of artists in Hollywood. Most film artists are anxious to receive their first nomination at a relatively young age because they know that it will bring them other nominations, usually in the near future. In some cases, players would not have received these other nominations, had it not been for the first one. In other words, only the first nomination was well deserved; subsequent nominations were conferred on these players because of their increased visibility and prestige *after* the first nomination.

Take Marsha Mason, a four-time Oscar nominee: of her four nominations, only the first (*Cinderella Liberty*) and possibly the fourth (*Only When I Laugh*) were well deserved. Mason received her second (*The Goodbye Girl*) and third (*Chapter Two*) nominations for lukewarm performances, because she had established herself as an Oscar-caliber performer. This status means that more attention is paid to *her* work than to the work of equally gifted performers because of her previous achievements.

The best and most recent example, illustrating the effects of the first nomination, is provided by the career of Glenn Close. Close won a supporting nomination for her film debut, *The World According to Garp*, playing the plum role of the eccentric, liberated mother. In the following year, she was the only actress from the gifted cast of *The Big Chill* to be singled out by the Academy. The success of *The Big Chill* was really based on its great ensemble acting by the best of America's players, including Kevin Kline, William Hurt, JoBeth Williams, and others. Yet only Close's performance was nominated, indicating that it was not the quality of her acting, which was superb but so was that of her colleagues, but the fact that she was considered to be an Oscar-caliber actress as a result of her first nomination. Furthermore, in 1984, Close earned her third consecutive nomination for *The Natural*, as Robert Redford's naive girlfriend. Neither the role nor her acting were extraordinary; had the same role been played by another actress, it would probably not have received a nomination. Yet while watching *The Natural*, her fellow-actors focused their attention on her acting *because* of her Academy status. Close has not only become a perennial nominee, but has also made a transition from supporting to leading parts. Ironically, it took a villainess role, that of the *other woman* in the suspenseful blockbuster *Fatal Attraction*, to put her at the forefront of leading ladies. She was rewarded with her fourth (and first Best Actress) nomination. Her new "sexy" look in this film convinced producers of her versatile talent and wide range. In 1988, she was cast by Stephen Frears in the sumptuous costume picture, *Dangerous Liaisons*, playing another unsympathetic role, a manipulative French aristocrat, for which she received her fifth nomination. Glenn Close is now a bankable star and one of Hollywood's busiest actresses.

CHAPTER 4

The Oscar as an International Award

Most countries with established film industries bestow awards for achievements in film, usually through their film academies. However, none of these film awards has been nearly so important or as prestigious as the Oscar. Established in 1927, it is the oldest film award in the world. But in addition to longevity, the Oscar has differed from other awards in being extraordinarily visible all over the world. The Oscar has always been regarded as more than a local or American prize. Indeed, compared with other countries that have two systems of awards, one for local and one for foreign achievements, the Oscar disregards the nationality of film artists, who can compete in any of the categories. With one exception: the Best Picture Oscar differentiates between English-speaking and foreign-language movies.

The Academy rules stated from the very beginning: "No national or Academy membership distinctions are to be considered."[1] Officially, the awards were going to be conferred without regard to nationality and citizenship. The Academy was therefore very proud that the first Best Actor, German player Emil Jannings, "was not even a citizen of our country," and that the first Best Actress, Janet Gaynor, "was not a member of the Academy."[2] Established as merit awards, the Oscars were based on the philosophy that true art knows no boundaries. But theory aside, the interesting question is: To what extent has the Oscar *actually* fulfilled its goal of being an international film award?

The International Dimension of the Oscar

Which nationalities have been represented in the Oscar contest and in what proportions? By and large, American players have dominated the Oscar race. The vast majority (74 percent) of Oscar nominees have been American, about one-fifth (18 percent) British, and about one-tenth (8 percent) players from other nationalities.[3] But the artists' nationality has played a differential role in the lead and supporting categories. The proportion of foreign players in the lead classifications (31 percent) has been bigger than that in the supporting (23 percent). Clearly, the chances of foreign players to get an Academy nomination have been better in the lead (male and female) leagues, mostly because leading players are more visible and consequently attract more attention than players cast in supporting roles.

However, a major difference between the male and female winners prevails in the lead category: there have been more British winners among Best Actors (25 percent) than among Best Actresses (17 percent). By contrast, female winners have represented a larger number of nationalities than their male counterparts.

Has the artists' nationality played a differential role in the nomination and the winning processes? Have foreign players had better chances to get a nomination than the actual award? A clear case of favoritism, or preferential treatment based on nationality, would have prevailed if there were significant differences between the nationality of the nominees and the winners.

Interestingly and contrary to popular belief, there have been no differences between the nationality of winners and nominees.[4] For example, 76 percent of the winners and 73 percent of the nominees have been American, 17 percent of the winners and 15 percent of the nominees have been British, and 7 percent of the winners and 9 percent of the nominees have been other foreign players. Despite accusations of favoring American over foreign artists, the nationality of the nominees has not had an impact on their chance to win. Moreover, the same proportion of foreign winners and nominees exists in all four acting categories. For instance, among the male lead players, 24 percent of the winners and 26 percent of the nominees have been British. And among the female supporting players, 7 percent of the winners and 7 percent of the nominees have been foreign, that is non-American and non-British.

The fact that over one-fourth of all Oscar winners and nominees have come from foreign countries attests to the outstanding internationality of the Oscar, extending its visibility beyond the borders of the United States. In its fifty-eight-year history, there have been only nineteen years in which all four acting awards were conferred on Americans. In the other years, at least one of the four winners has been of foreign nationality. This is yet another dimension of the international importance of the Oscar.

One out of every three foreign players has been British, indicating the English dominance of the Oscar contest. But there have been fluctuations in the British representation in different decades. Has it been the high quality of British films and British acting that contributed to their disproportionate preeminence in the Oscar competition? Or is it perhaps the fact that they have appeared in *English*-speaking movies?

The British Dominance

The British representation in the Oscar competition has ranged from 11 percent in the 1950s to an all-time high of 31 percent in the 1960s. The decade of the 1960s seems to have been the most hospitable to all foreign, not just British, artists: two-fifths (40 percent) of the acting nominees were foreign. British players also made a strong showing in the 1940s, commanding one-fifth (21 percent) of the acting nominations. In other decades, the British participation was between 13 and 17 percent of all acting nominees. The poorest British representation was in the 1950s, which, as will be shown, was the most conservative and the most "patriotic" (i.e., American) in the history of the award (see chapter 12).

Compared with the British representation, the share of other foreign artists in the Oscar contest has been more or less stable, ranging from 6 to 11 percent of all acting nominees. There was one notable exception: in the early 1980s, only 2 percent of the nominees in the acting categories were drawn from foreign countries. The 1980s resemble the 1950s in more ways than one.

There have also been interesting trends in the representation of British-made films in the Best Picture category. In the 1930s, the American market was accused by the British of being insular and of denying support to their products. Alexander Korda's *The Private Life of Henry VIII* (1933) was considered to be an exception, for it was the first British commercial hit in the US since the advent of sound. Very few British films were nominated for major awards in the 1930s, with a few notable exceptions. One such was Anthony

Asquith's *Pygmalion* (1938), which brought acting nominations to its two stars, Leslie Howard and Wendy Hiller, and two writing awards, one for writing adaptation, and one to playwright George Bernard Shaw for best screenplay. It was one of the high "literary" moments in the Academy's history, though the noted recipient greeted the award with irony and amusement.

In 1939, the two lead acting awards went to British players for the first time, though both Robert Donat (*Goodbye Mr. Chips*) and Vivien Leigh (*Gone with the Wind*) appeared in American movies. Ironically, Vivien Leigh won two Best Actress awards (the second was for *A Streetcar Named Desire*) for portraying two of the most famous Southern belles in American literature. The casting of *Gone with the Wind* received such extensive coverage in the press, that apparently some Southern women threatened to boycott the movie if Vivien Leigh did not measure up to their expectations of how Scarlett O'Hara should be portrayed.

This generosity to English performers was used by the Academy for public relations, promoting the notion of "objective," matter-of-fact voting, disregarding political or national considerations. At the same time, it prompted many speculations as to "would England have done the same to us?" to which patriotic columnist Louella Parsons answered unequivocally "I doubt it."[5]

In the early 1940s, two British movies were nominated for Best Picture, both dealing with the war. The first, Michael Powell's *The Invaders*, about the survival attempts of a group of Nazis, also earned Emeric Pressburger the 1942 Oscar for best original story. And the second, *In Which We Serve* (also 1942), codirected by David Lean and Noel Coward, won the latter a Special Award for his outstanding production; Coward also wrote the music and starred in the film. Prior to that, British movies had won a few technical awards. For example, in 1940, *The Thief of Bagdad*, also directed by Michael Powell, won for cinematography, color art direction, and special effects, and Alexander Korda's *That Hamilton Woman*, a huge success in the American market, starring Laurence Olivier and Vivien Leigh, won for best sound recordings.

But it was not until the late 1940s that British films began to make a real impact on both the Academy and the American movie market. The nominations for Laurence Olivier's screen version of Shakespeare's *Henry V* (1946), as Best Picture and Actor, annoyed the heads of the Hollywood studios who regarded them as acts of treason. And as if that was not enough, three other British pictures were nominated for important awards in 1946. David Lean's exquisite tale of an unconsummated adulterous affair, *Brief Encounter*, won acting as well as other nominations. Compton Bennett's *The Seventh Veil*, the film that made James Mason an international star, won best screenplay. And Gabriel Pascal's *Caesar and Cleopatra*, the most expensive film made in England, was nominated but didn't win any awards. The resentment against the Academy's seemingly preferential treatment of British movies increased in the following year, when David Lean's version of Charles Dickens's *Great Expectations* was nominated for Best Picture and Best Director, and most deservedly earned the best black-and-white cinematography and art direction. One journalist, who took the matter extremely seriously, wrote that the US helped the British win the war, but should not help them win "our Oscars."

The British were disappointed because they believed that *Great Expectations* should have won the 1947 Best Picture; the winner was *A Gentleman's Agreement*. "A certain amount of bias influences Hollywood's Oscar Awards," said J. Arthur Rank, the powerful British producer, in response to the 1947 awards, but at the same time he expressed hopes that the number of bookings for British films in the United States would double from 6,000 to 12,000 a year, the number that American films received in Britain. Curiously, Rank reported that many exhibitors complained to him about the difficulty American audiences apparently had in understanding the speech of British players, but he assured that "efforts are being made to correct this."[6]

The turning point in the relations between American and British pictures occurred in 1948, when, against all expectations, *Hamlet* was named Best Picture and earned Laurence Olivier the Best Actor award. The film also won black-and-white art direction and costume design. It was the first time that a British product won the top award, an act which, according to some reports, reinforced the moguls' earlier decision to withdraw their financial support from the awards ceremonies. In the same year, another British film, Michael Powell's *The Red Shoes*, a sentimental love story set in the ballet world, was also nominated for Best Picture and went on to become the top money-maker of the year, grossing in domestic rentals five million dollars. The British sweep of awards was a most pleasant surprise, as Olivier said, "It's incredibly generous of Hollywood to confer their honors upon the British film industry."

The *Hamlet* incident was remembered so well that in 1956, when

Mike Todd's *Around the World in 80 Days* won Best Picture, its British director Michael Anderson received a nomimation but not the directorial award; the winner was George Stevens for *Giant*. It was one of the few occasions in which the Academy split its vote for Best Picture and Best Director. In most years, there is a strong correlation between the two categories (see Table 1, pp. 341–47).

Indeed, in the 1950s, few British movies were nominated for or won important awards. Carol Reed's masterpiece, *The Third Man* (1950), based on Graham Greene's mystery novel, was singled out for its great black-and-white cinematography of postwar Vienna. And Charles Crichton's *The Lavendar Hill Mob* (1951), which made Alec Guinness a star in the US, won for best story and screenplay. Most of the nominations for British films in this decade were in the writing categories. In 1953, two British screenplays competed in the same category: *The Cruel Sea*, based on Nicholas Monsarrat's best-seller, and the comedy *Ladykillers*, featuring Alec Guinness as a sinister lodger plotting to kill his old landlady; neither won.

David Lean became the first British filmmaker ever to win Best Director in 1957, for the war epic *The Bridge on the River Kwai*, which was named Best Picture and also won for Best Actor (Alec Guinness), screenplay, editing, cinematography, and music scoring. Financed by Columbia Pictures, *The Bridge on the River Kwai* used many cast and crew members who were British.

The British representation in the Oscar contest improved dramatically in the 1960s, undoubtedly the best decade for British movies. A considerable number of movies were nominated for Best Picture: Jack Clayton's *Room at the Top* (1959), John Schlesinger's *Darling* (1965), Lewis Gilbert's sex farce *Alfie* (1966), and Anthony Harvey's historical melodrama *The Lion in Winter* (1968). Moreover, four British-made films won the top award: *Lawrence of Arabia* (1962), *Tom Jones* (1963), *A Man for All Seasons* (1966), and *Oliver!* (1968). And the directors of these movies (David Lean, Tony Richardson, Fred Zinnemann, and Carol Reed, respectively) were singled out by the Academy for their directorial achievements. A fifth British filmmaker, John Schlesinger, won the directorial award for *Midnight Cowboy* (1969), which was made in the US with American stars Dustin Hoffman and Jon Voight.

However, in the 1970s, few British products were nominated for important awards, reflecting the depression of the British industry in general. Two movies, *A Clockwork Orange* (1971) and *Barry Lyndon* (1975), both financed with American money but made in England by expatriate director Stanley Kubrick, were nominated for Best Picture; neither won. And *Midnight Express* (1978), a thriller about Billy Hayes, the American student arrested in Turkey for carrying hashish, was directed by Briton Alan Parker, and nominated for best film. The poor British representation in the Oscar competition was reflected in other film forums. For example, in 1980, for the first time in thirty-three years, not even one British movie competed in the Cannes Film Festival.

But in the early 1980s several movies, made in England and about distinctly British subjects, made their mark, artistically and commercially. *The Elephant Man* (1980), was not really a British film, it was financed by Paramount, produced by Mel Brooks, and directed by David Lynch. But it had a distinctly British "flavor," telling the story of John Merrick, the grossly deformed victim exploited by Victorian society, and was cast with mostly British actors, headed by John Hurt in the title role (who won a nomination) and Anthony Hopkins, as the doctor who took care of him. The Academy showed its appreciation with eight nominations, including Best Picture, though the film lost in every category. Roman Polanski's romantic historical epic, *Tess* (1980), beautifully made in England, was also nominated for six awards.

Nonetheless, it took thirteen years after *Oliver!* for another British film, *Chariots of Fire* (1981), to win the Best Picture award. Directed by Hugh Hudson and based on the true story of the two British runners in the 1924 Olympics, it was the "upset winner," competing against such big-scale movies as Steven Spielberg's *Raiders of the Lost Ark* and Warren Beatty's *Reds*. Made in England on a modest budget of six million dollars, it was turned down by every major studio in Hollywood. Its success, four Oscars, was attributed to its story, stressing the spiritual courage and passion of its two characters (played by unknown actors), who triumphed against great odds. And despite the fact that the movie was considered "too British" and "too specialized" (dealing with sports), it became a commercial hit, though only *after* winning the Oscar. Many filmmakers resented the fact that American money (Twentieth Century-Fox helped to finance it) was used to help a British product in a year in which *Reds*, an historical epic movie, failed at the box office despite critical acclaim.

The British had better reason to celebrate in the following year, when Sir Richard Attenborough's *Gandhi*, financed by Columbia Pictures, was nominated for eleven awards and swept most of them, including Best Picture, Director, and Actor. British movies continue to fare well at present. In 1983, Peter Yates's screen adaptation of *The Dresser* was nominated for five awards, including the top one. And in 1984, two British films were recognized by the Academy with multiple nominations. Roland Joffe's *The Killing Fields*, based on Sydney Schanberg's 1980 *New York Times Magazine* article, "The Death and Life of Dith Pran," and recounting the political situation in Cambodia during its civil war through the friendship between journalist Schanberg (Sam Waterston) and his Cambodian assistant (Dr. Haing S. Ngor), was nominated for seven awards. It won three: Supporting Actor to Ngor, a non-professional and the first Asian actor to win an Oscar; cinematography to Chris Menges's distinguished work; and editing to Jim Clark. David Lean's exciting epic *A Passage to India*, based on E. M. Forster's famous novel, was nominated for eleven awards, though won only two. The big winner was Milos Forman's *Amadeus*, sweeping eight out of its eleven nominations.

Trevor Nunn's 1982 Tony Award acceptance speech (for his adaptation of Charles Dickens's *Nicholas Nickleby*), in which he exclaimed, "The British Are Coming, the British Are Coming," turned out to be true.[7] In 1986, two of the Best Picture nominees were British. The production team of *Killing Fields* returned to the Oscar arena with the high-minded historical epic *The Mission*, which received seven nominations and one award, honoring Menges's cinematography. The other nominee, *A Room with a View*, Ismail Merchant's and James Ivory's adaptation of E. M. Forster's novel, won in three of its eight nominations: writing, art direction/set decoration, and costume design. John Boorman's charming autobiographical *Hope and Glory* (1987), which reconstructed his adolescents' memories of war-time London, was highly acclaimed by the critics and received five nominations, but no awards; another foreign-made film, *The Last Emperor*, won most of them.

The one category in which the British have excelled and fared even better than their movies or plays is acting. British acting has always enjoyed great prestige in the United States, to the point of becoming a most revered institution. The film work of British players has been admired for their versatile range and technical skills. Meryl Streep expressed the opinion of many American players when she stated: "I am vastly intimidated by English actors. We American actors think we're just a bunch of slobs compared to them, and that they can quote all of Shakespeare by heart."[8]

The great prestige of English players has been reflected in both the nominations and the winning. Thirteen of the Best Actors (24 percent), 14 of the Best Actresses (30 percent), eight of the Supporting Actors (18 percent), and five of the Supporting Actresses (11 percent) have been British. The first British player to win Best Actor was George Arliss, but he won for two American films (*Disraeli* and *The Green Goddess*). Charles Laughton was actually the first Briton to win for a British film (*The Private Life of Henry VIII*). The other British winners have been: Victor McLaglen, Robert Donat, Ray Milland, Ronald Colman, Laurence Olivier, Alec Guinness, David Niven, Rex Harrison, Paul Scofield, Peter Finch, and Ben Kingsley. Note that with the exception of Olivier (*Hamlet*), Scofield (*A Man for All Seasons*), and Kingsley (*Gandhi*), all the others have won for American-made pictures.

It has been much easier for British players to win the Oscar if they appeared in American movies. Most of the British winners of Best Actress, including Vivien Leigh, Greer Garson, Audrey Hepburn, Julie Andrews, Maggie Smith, and Glenda Jackson, have won for American movies. The only exceptions have been Julie Christie (*Darling*) and Glenda Jackson's first Oscar (*Women in Love*).

The same trend prevails among the British players who won supporting awards, with most winning for American films, like Donald Crisp (*How Green Was My Valley*), Edmund Gwenn (*Miracle on 47th Street*), Hugh Griffith (*Ben-Hur*), Peter Ustinov (*Spartacus* and *Topkapi*), John Gielgud (*Arthur*), Michael Caine (*Hannah and Her Sisters*), and Sean Connery (*The Untouchables*). The only supporting winner in a British-made film was John Mills in *Ryan's Daughter*, directed by David Lean. Among the British Supporting Actresses too, Dame Peggy Ashcroft was the only one to win for a British movie, *A Passage to India*. The other four British actresses won for American films: Wendy Hiller (*Separate Tables*), Margaret Rutherford (*The VIPs*), Vanessa Redgrave (*Julia*), and Maggie Smith (*California Suite*).

The list of Oscar-nominated British players is so illustrious that it reads like the Who's Who register, composed of distinguished performers honored with titles of Sirs and Dames. Sir Michael Redgrave, Sir Ralph Richardson, Dame Edith Evans, Dame May Whitty, Dame Judith Anderson, Dame Gladys Cooper, and Dame Flora Robson have all been nominated. The status of these players has contributed to the prestige of the Academy. Both the Academy and the British players have benefited from these nominations. The Academy made some of these players movie stars, and the British players in turn have contributed to the prestige of the Academy, making it a more reputable institution.

The largest number of British players were nominated in the 1960s, marking the high quality of British films in that decade. It included: Peter O'Toole, Michael Caine, Albert Finney, Ron Moody, Tom Courtenay, Alan Bates, Rachel Roberts, Deborah Kerr, Jean Simmons, and Janet Suzman. The prestige of these players goes beyond the film world because of the different structure of the performing arts in Britain, where there is a good deal of mutual fertilization among theater, film, and television. By contrast, until most recently, there has been quite a separation among these media in the United States. American players have tended to "specialize" in one medium, often to the exclusion of the other two, but British players have always "commuted" successfully between theater and film or film and television, to the appreciation of all three arts and audiences.

In addition to the high quality of acting, there were other reasons for the British dominance in the 1960s and for the favorable reception of their movies in the US. This decade, particularly in its early years, was not very good for the American cinema and its players. The American film industry, still suffering from fierce competition with television, had not yet adjusted to its new, inferior status as the second cultural medium, after being for close to half a century the most dominant form of entertainment in the national culture. The decline in American films was quantitative as well as qualitative. In 1963, for example, the industry reached an all-time production low, when only 141 American movies were released in the US. Compare this poor figure with over 400 movies released in a typical year in the 1940s, and over 300 films in the 1950s. For years, American films dominated the film market, but in the 1960s there was an imbalance between the number of American and the number of foreign films released in the United States. For instance, in 1960, of the 320 movies distributed in the US, 208 were American made and 112 were foreign. But in 1968, of the 380 new pictures, only 176 were American.

By contrast, in the 1960s, the British cinema witnessed a recovery, a real renaissance. Shortly after 1956, which saw the premiere of John Osborne's *Look Back in Anger*, considered to be the turning point in the history of the British theater, a new generation of filmmakers and stage directors, like Tony Richardson and Lindsay Anderson, began to leave their mark on British culture. They were members of an innovative cultural movement, The Free Cinema, the British equivalent of the earlier French New Wave. Among the best works of this group were: Jack Clayton's *Room at the Top* (1959), Karel Reisz's *Saturday Night and Sunday Morning* (1960), Jack Cardiff's *The Loneliness of the Long Distance Runner* (1962), and Lindsay Anderson's *This Sporting Life* (1963).

But the popularity of British films and players in the 1960s also indicated that the previous provincialism and parochialism of American culture had declined. This decade saw the repudiation of the 1950s ideology of conservatism and isolationism, represented by Senator Joseph McCarthy and the hearings of the House Un-American Activities Committee. These ideological changes affected American culture and its movies. Furthermore, the melting-pot ideology that had prevailed in American culture for decades, ignoring ethnic and class differences, began to disintegrate. In the 1960s, youth and ethnic segments of the population became more fervid in their demands for subcultural representation.[9] For the first time, youth not only required films specifically dealing with its problems, but could also determine which movies would become successful at the box office. These younger and more sophisticated audiences greeted with enthusiasm the new European Films, not only British, but also Italian, French, and Swedish.

Indeed, the proportion of foreign-made films, particularly British, among the top money-making films was at its greatest in the 1960s. In the 1940s and 1950s, only five of the 100 most commercial movies in each of these decades were foreign-made. But in the 1960s, their proportion increased dramatically, amounting to sixteen movies.[10] The most successful British films, nominated for Oscars and ranking among the top ten money grossers of the year, were: David Lean's *Lawrence of Arabia*, Tony Richardson's *Tom Jones*, Richard Lester's Beatles movie *A Hard Day's Night* (1964), Lewis Gilbert's *Alfie* (1966), Silvio Narizzano's *Georgy Girl* (1966), Carol Reed's *Oliver!* (1968) and, of course, the James Bond movies starring Sean Connery.

The Oscar race reflected the popularity of British films. In 1963, for example, four of the five supporting actresses were British: Diana Cilento, Dame Edith Evans, and Joyce Redman (all for *Tom*

Jones), and Dame Margaret Rutherford (*The VIPs*), who won. And in 1964, four of the five Best Actor nominees were British: Rex Harrison (*My Fair Lady*) the winner, Peter Sellers (*Doctor Strangelove*), Peter O'Toole and Richard Burton (both for *Becket*). Indeed, 1964 was probably one of the most "international" years in the history of the Academy. In addition to Harrison, the other winners in the acting categories were all foreign: Julie Andrews (*Mary Poppins*), Peter Ustinov (*Topkapi*), both British; and French-Russian Lila Kedrova (*Zorba the Greek*). "This will be an unusual night," emcee Bob Hope predicted at the beginning of the ceremonies, "tonight Hollywood is handing out foreign aid." And Julie Andrews, overwhelmed by her win, said in her acceptance speech: "You Americans are famous for your hospitality, but this is ridiculous." A leading trade magazine described the show: "It was a reminder that Hollywood has never been chauvinistic. Its great days are those when artists from throughout the world flocked here or were imported." "The winners are reminders," he concluded, "that the movies are the true international medium."[11]

In 1983, when British actors again dominated the race, various explanations were offered. Critics simply found it strange that four of the five Best Actors were English: Michael Caine (*Educating Rita*), Albert Finney and Tom Courtenay (both for *The Dresser*), and Tom Conti (*Reuben, Reuben*, an American film). The fifth nominee was American, Robert Duvall (*Tender Mercies*), who turned out to be the winner. One voice of reason, who understood the roots of the problem, was critic Vincent Canby. Canby observed that the "customary respect" for English players by the Academy was no greater in 1983 than in previous years, and that "Hollywood today is no more or less Anglophile than it's ever been."[12] However, he stated that "If you are a good American actor and you want to make it big in contemporary American movies, you've got to be able to upstage special effects and futuristic hardware, with very little or no help from the screenwriters." Canby used as examples Roy Scheider, who was engaged in an unfair competition with a marvelous space-age helicopter in *Blue Thunder*, and Harrison Ford who, despite being a box-office champion, failed to get nominations for either Han Solo in *Star Wars* or Indiana Jones in *Raiders of the Lost Ark*. In addition to competing with high and chic technology, Canby claimed that American actors tend to be stereotyped as macho types or psychopaths (Al Pacino in *Scarface*, Robert De Niro in *The King of Comedy*), roles that usually don't get recognition by the Academy. Significantly, it was no accident in that year that the British dominated the Best Actor, but not Best Actress, categories. As Canby noted, for the first time in many years, the American cinema was offering better and richer parts for women than for men.

Other Foreign Films and Artists

In the entire Academy's history, very few foreign-language movies have been nominated for Best Picture. Jean Renoir's antiwar masterpiece, *Grand Illusion* (1938) competed for the prestigious award, but that was before the creation of a distinct category for foreign pictures. Officially, the first winner in this category was Federico Fellini's *La Strada* (1956), in which Anthony Quinn and Giulietta Masina probably gave their most memorable performances as two traveling performers. But prior to the creation of a separate category, the Academy honored several foreign films with an Honorary Oscar, beginning with Vittorio De Sica's neorealistic movie *Shoeshine* in 1947, and the French film *Monsieur Vincent* in 1948. The citation for De Sica's movie read: "The high quality of this motion picture, brought to eloquent life in a country scarred by war, is proof to the world that the creative spirit can triumph over adversity."

However, since the creation of the Foreign Picture award, only three foreign movies have been nominated: Costa-Gavras's political thriller *Z* (1969), a French-Algerian production starring Yves Montand and Jean-Louis Trintignant; Jan Troell's *The Emigrants* (1972), dealing with the emigration of Swedish peasants to America in the nineteenth century and starring Liv Ullmann and Max Von Sydow; and Ingmar Bergman's *Cries and Whispers* (1973), one of the most haunting films about death and dying, featuring unforgettable performances by Liv Ullmann, Ingrid Thulin, and Harriet Andersson.

Z enjoyed a special position in 1969, for it was nominated and won the Best Foreign Picture award and was also nominated in the competitive category of Best Picture. This could happen because, according to Academy rules, foreign pictures that have opened in the United States are eligible to compete in the legitimate categories. To qualify for Foreign Picture, however, a film must be sent by its country of origin to the Academy, where a committee selects the five foreign nominees. *Z* qualified on both grounds: it was nominated by its country, Algeria, and opened in the US in December.

Most of the foreign (non-British) nominees have come from countries with major film industries, such as France, Italy, and West Germany. There have been twelve German, twelve French, seven Italian, four Russian, three Scandinavian, and three Japanese Oscar-nominated players. But smaller countries, such as Greece, Israel, Egypt, and Hungary, have also had representation in the Oscar race, though only if their players appeared in American-made movies. One of the few exceptions has been the nomination of the distinguished Polish actress Ida Kaminska, for her performance in the Czech film *The Shop on Main Street*, which was voted as the 1965 Best Foreign-Language Picture.

All foreign male winners received awards for work in American movies. For example, Emil Jannings was German, but earned the award for two American films (*The Last Command* and *The Way of All Flesh*). And Maximilian Schell was born in Switzerland and worked in Germany and Austria prior to winning the 1961 Best Actor for *Judgment at Nuremberg*. The same is true of most foreign nominees, such as French actor Charles Boyer (*Conquest*), Austrian Oskar Werner (*Ship of Fools*), and Israeli Topol (*Fiddler on the Roof*). The only actors nominated for performances in foreign-language pictures were two Italians, Marcello Mastroianni (*Divorce Italian Style* and *A Special Day*) and Giancarlo Giannini (*Seven Beauties*).

In the Best Actress category too, most foreign women have won for American movies. Austrian actress Luise Rainer won two Oscars for American films, *The Great Ziegfeld* and *The Good Earth*, and Italian actress Anna Magnani won for Tennessee Williams's *The Rose Tattoo*. The one exception in this category was Sophia Loren, the only foreign actress to have won for a foreign-language film, *Two Women* (1961), directed by Vittorio De Sica.

None of the foreign winners in the supporting categories (male or female) has ever won for a role in a foreign-made film, though several foreign actresses earned the award for an American film: Greek actress Katina Paxinou in *For Whom the Bell Tolls*, Japanese Miyoshi Umeki in *Sayonara*, and Russian-French Lila Kedrova in *Zorba the Greek*. The chances of foreign players to get a nomination for a performance in a non-American film have been very slim, but they have been slightly better for leading players.

Perhaps more significantly, the foreign players nominated for lead acting awards have all appeared in commercially popular movies. To get Academy recognition for high-quality acting, foreign players have had to appear in movies that are successful at the box-office; a good performance has no impact if it is contained in an unsuccessful picture. Similarly, most foreign pictures nominated for writing or technical awards have been box-office hits.

For example, *Never on Sunday* (1960), produced, written, and directed by Jules Dassin, who starred in it with his wife-actress Melina Mercouri, would not have been nominated in major categories (Director, Best Actress) had it not been a commercial success. A kind of contemporary version of *Pygmalion*, focusing on the relationship between a serious American writer and a joyous Greek prostitute, the movie is also credited with stimulating the touristic trade to Greece. *Never on Sunday* won one award, Best Song (written by Manos Hadjidakis), thus becoming the first song in a foreign picture to win an Oscar since the Academy began to recognize achievements in this category in 1934. Federico Fellini's satiric view of high society in Rome, *La Dolce Vita* (1961), would not have been nominated for screenplay, director, and other awards had it not created a world sensation with its view of Italian decadence. Praised by many critics, it became one of the most popular foreign films in America, grossing in domestic rentals about eight million dollars. By the time *La Dolce Vita* was shown in the US, it had already received recognition at the Cannes Film Festival and had achieved immense popularity in Europe. It won, however, only best costume design, with the Academy failing to recognize the great acting of Marcello Mastroianni as the journalist whose experiences are the focus of the movie.

In 1976, Marie Christine Barrault won a Best Actress nomination for her performance in the French comedy *Cousin, Cousine*, written and directed by Jean-Charles Tacchella, whose screenplay was also nominated. Her performance was good, though not distinguished, but she won the nomination because the movie proved to be a commercial hit in New York and Los Angeles. The screenplay, however, deserved recognition for being funny, witty, and original, recounting the story of an open adulterous affair between two cousins. In the same year, Giancarlo Giannini won Academy recognition for his performance in Lina Wertmuller's controversial movie *Seven Beauties*. This film put Wertmuller, nominated as writer and director, at the front rank of international filmmakers. Giannini excelled as the contemptible Neopolitan macho, driven to self-degradation in his attempts to survive, but his performance would not have been singled out if the movie had not been successful at the box office.

The most recent and encouraging example of a foreign movie that got the Academy's recognition was the West German *Das Boot* (1982), directed by Wolfgang Peterson, and chronicling the physical and psychological hardships endured by a Nazi crew of a U-boat. This fascinating movie occupied the fifth place among 1982s most nominated pictures, receiving six, some in major categories (writing, directing). *Das Boot* was not only unanimously acclaimed by the critics, but was also very popular with the public, grossing in domestic rentals $4,500,000, making it the most popular German film ever to be shown in the United States.

By contrast, distinguished performances by foreign players in films that were artistic, but not commercial, successes have been consistently overlooked by the Academy. This list is too long to document, but two recent examples should demonstrate the point. Ettore Scola's *La Nuit de Varenne* (1983), which opened to great acclaim but did poorly at the box office, featured a great performance by Marcello Mastroianni as the aging Casanova in a story set during the French Revolution. And Gérard Dépardieu, one of the best and most popular actors in Europe, has never won a nomination, despite excellent performances in film after film, including the frustrated husband in Bertrand Blier's *Get Our Your Handkerchiefs*, and the title role in Andrzei Wajda's *Danton*.

Of all award categories, the best chances for a foreign artist to get a nomination has been in the two writing categories: best original screenplay and best adaptation from another medium. Indeed, the 1945 Swiss film *Marie-Louise*, about a group of French children during World War II, was the first European movie to win in the best original screenplay category. Some of the best Italian neorealistic movies were nominated for writing awards, Roberto Rossellini's *Open City* (1946) and Vittorio De Sica's *Umberto D* (1952). And in the last decade, the writers of the French *Day for Night* (1974), the Italian *Seven Beauties* (1976), the French *Mon Oncle d'Amerique* (1980), the West-German *Das Boot* (1982), the Swedish *Fanny and Alexander* (1983), and the Argentinian *The Official Story* (1985) have all received writing nominations, if not awards.

In addition to being generally overlooked by the Academy, it takes longer for foreign artists to get recognition in the United States, particularly if they don't make American movies. Despite the fact that the distribution of foreign movies in the US has improved significantly in the last two decades, especially in such big cities as New York, Los Angeles, and Chicago, many good "art" films are not widely shown if they don't feature an internationally known star or are not made by a prestigious director, such as Fellini, Truffaut, or Bergman. The distribution of these movies greatly depend on favorable review by major critics in New York and Los Angeles.

This is one of the reasons why foreign players, particularly men, tend to be older than their American counterparts by the time they earn Academy nominations. Marcello Mastroianni's career is a good example, because he is not only one of the most distinguished film actors in the world but one who has been extremely popular outside his own country. Mastroianni made his screen debut in 1949, at the age of twenty-five, after studying acting and acquiring stage experience with Luchino Viscont's theatrical troupe. In the 1950s, he achieved stature as an actor in Italy, but he attained international stardom in 1960, following his starring role in Fellini's *La Dolce Vita*. A year later, he appeared in another Fellini masterpiece, *8½*, which was even more commercially successful than *La Dolce Vita*. The Academy failed to nominate him for either of these performances, though the movies themselves were nominated for a number of awards. Mastroianni earned his first Best Actor nomination in 1962, for the Italian comedy, *Divorce Italian Style*, in which he excelled as the bored Sicilian baron who plans to get rid of his nagging wife. He was then thirty-eight years old. Mastroianni would probably not have received the nomination were it not for the publicity and awards that *Divorce Italian Style* got at both the Cannes Film Festival and Hollywood's Golden Globes.

But even foreign players who work in the US tend to be older than their American colleagues, because they first have to excel in their own countries before they are brought to Hollywood. This explains why Anna Magnani (Italian) and Maggie Smith (British) have been older than American actresses when they won, both for American pictures.

Significantly, American and foreign players tend to make their debuts at more or less the same age: the women in their early and the men in their late twenties. Women, foreign and American, are also younger than men when they are first nominated and first win the Academy Award. The gap between American and foreign players is bigger in the men's careers. For example, American actors have won their Oscar at the median age of thirty-six, foreign actors at forty-three—a significant difference of seven years.

The greatest difference between American and foreign artists prevails in the filmmaker's careers. The foreign directors have made their debuts at a younger age than their American peers (thirty and thirty-two respectively). American directors, however, are younger (thirty-six) than the foreign (thirty-nine) when they get their first nomination. And this difference increases by the time they win their directorial award: the American at forty and the foreign at forty-four.

Consider British director Carol Reed, whose international reputation reached a peak with *The Fallen Idol* (1949), earning him his first directorial nomination, and *The Third Man* (1950), his second. Nonetheless, Reed won the award many years later and for a lesser work, *Oliver!* (1968). This Oscar, long overdue, was received by an aging director (sixty-nine) whose prestige was in severe decline. Most foreign filmmakers have done their best work by the time they earned their first Academy nomination. Jean Renoir received his one and only directorial nomination for *The Southerner* (1945), a film he made in the US when he was fifty-two, but the Academy had failed to nominate him for his French masterpieces, *Grand Illusion* and *The Rules of the Game* (1939). Federico Fellini, another film master, has never won a directorial Oscar despite four nominations: *La Dolce Vita, 8 ½, Satyricon* (1970), and *Amarcord* (1975). Moreover, Fellini was older (forty-two) than his American peers at his first nomination and, like other foreign filmmakers, had not been nominated for his earlier, more modest, masterpieces, *La Strada* and *The Nights of Cabiria*, though both won the Best Foreign Picture Award in their respective years, 1956 and 1957.

But perhaps the best example of how the Academy has consistently ignored the work of foreign filmmakers is provided by Ingmar Bergman. It is hard to believe, but Bergman received his first nomination as late as 1973 for *Cries and Whispers*, when he was fifty-six years old. None of his earlier landmarks, *The Seventh Seal* (1957), *The Virgin Spring* (1960), or *Persona* (1966) was recognized for their directorial genius, though *The Virgin Spring* and *Through a Glass*

Darkly won Best Foreign Picture of 1960 and 1961. Ironically, Bergman, like Fellini, has not won to this day the Best Director Award, though he earned a second nomination for *Face to Face* (1976) and a third for *Fanny and Alexander*, which also won Best Foreign Picture. In all likelihood, Bergman will win an Honorary Oscar for his entire career, but the opportunity to confer the award on a unique artist while at his peak was missed. Bergman's story is no exception: The foreign directors cited by the Academy have all had established reputations in the international film forums by the time they earned their first nominations.

Nationalism and Film Awards

Despite the fact that over one-fourth of the Oscar nominees have been foreign, attesting to the prize's international visibility and prestige, the Academy has been accused of displaying "chauvinism"—that is, of favoring American artists. Just how distinctly American or "nationalistic" has the Oscar been compared with other prestigious film prizes, such as the New York Film Critics and the Cannes Film Festival Awards?

Not surprisingly, American players have dominated all three awards, though in differing degrees. The Oscar has been the most "American" award (76 percent of all winners), followed by the New York Film Critics Award (58 percent) and the Cannes Film Festival Award (42 percent). British players have occupied the second place in all three prizes, but their representation was greater in the New York Critics (25 percent) than in the Oscar (19 percent) or the Cannes awards (14 percent).

In all three awards, there has been more national diversity among female than male winners. For example, most of the foreign male Oscar winners have been British, whereas their female counterparts have been drawn from a variety of nationalities: Swedish, Italian, and French. No man of these nationalities has ever won the Oscar. And the percentage of American men who won the New York Critics Award (67 percent) has been larger than the women's (50 percent). Among the women cited by the New York Critics were two Italian (Anna Magnani and Sophia Loren), one French (Isabelle Adjani), and most recently an Argentinian actress (Norma Aleandro).

Interestingly, some of the Oscar's "great losers" have been foreign actresses who have won multiple New York Critics Awards. For example, British actress Deborah Kerr, a six-time Oscar nominee, won three New York Critics Awards for *Black Narcissus*, *Heaven Knows Mr. Allison*, and *The Sundowners*. Swedish Greta Garbo, a three-time Oscar nominee, was cited twice by the New York Critics for *Anna Karenina* and *Camille*. And Liv Ullmann, the quintessential Bergman actress, has earned two Oscar nominations but three New York Critics citations, for *Cries and Whispers*, *Scenes from a Marriage*, and *Face to Face*. There have been no such striking cases among the men, though two British winners of the New York Critics Award were not even nominated for their performances. The first was Ralph Richardson, singled out by the New York critics for his performance in *Breaking the Sound Barrier*, and the second, John Gielgud for *Providence*. Both actors were nominated by the Academy for other performances, and Gielgud won a supporting Oscar for *Arthur*.

The Cannes Film Festival, an officially international forum, has been more "international" in its distribution of awards than either the New York Critics Circle or the Academy. Among its award recipients were players of Spanish, Brazilian or Algerian origins, nationalities that have not been represented at all in the Oscar contest. However, there is some evidence to support the charge that the Cannes festival has favored French players. The percentage of French winners at Cannes has been much higher (17 percent) than that at the New York Film Critics (1 percent) or the Oscar Award (also 1 percent). This has been particularly so for women: twice as many French actresses (21 percent) than actors (12 percent) have won the Cannes prize for acting.

But contrary to popular notion, the Cannes festival has not favored French films in its awards. Unlike the Oscar and the New York Critics Circle, this festival does not distinguish between French and foreign-language films in its Best Picture Award; thus it is impossible to compare the three organizations. At the same time, the number of French winning films has been smaller than the number of French winning players. In the forty-year-history of the festival, only seven out of the fifty-five honored pictures were French.

However, these statistical generalizations don't deal with the crucial question of whether or not nationalistic considerations have played a role in bestowing the awards, considering the quality of the competing performances in a *given* year. To use one recent example, in 1980 a furor arose in Cannes, when Peter Sellers's brilliant performance in *Being There* was overlooked by the jury for reasons that apparently had nothing to do with its merits. According to some reports, Kirk Douglas, the jury's president, was furious when he realized that other members had decided to single out Michel Piccoli and Anouk Aimee (both in Marco Bellocchio's *Leap into Void*) because they felt it was time for French performers to win.[13] This incident was not an isolated or exceptional case. In other years, political considerations, though not always favoring the French contestants, have played a crucial role in determining the winners. Many critics felt that the motive for awarding the 1975 Golden Palm to the Algerian film, M. L. Hamina's *Chronicle of the Burning Years*, was based on political considerations: Algeria and other Third World cinemas had been underrepresented and overlooked in the past. This is precisely the reason, as was shown, why the New York Film Festival has refused to bestow "merit" awards. Furthermore, the fact that there have been more ties at the Cannes festival than in other film forums also attests to the operation of irrelevant factors, and subsequently inevitable compromises in making the final choices. There have been seven ties in the Best Movie, six in the Best Actress, and three in the Best Actor categories. For example, in 1979, the Cannes Jury conferred the Golden Palm on both the West German picture *The Tin Drum* and the American *Apocalypse Now*. And in 1980, a tie was declared between the Japanese film, Akira Kurosawa's *Kagemusha*, and the American entry, Bob Fosse's *All That Jazz*. By contrast, there has never been a tie in the Best Picture Oscar, and only one tie in the history of the New York Film Critics, in 1960, when both *The Apartment* and *Sons and Lovers* were cited.

In conclusion, both the size of the three film organizations and, more importantly, the nature of their memberships have affected their film choices. The jury of the Cannes festival has the smallest —about seven—but also the most versatile membership: it is drawn from various countries and represents actors, directors, and critics. The New York Critics Circle consists of a reasonably small membership (twenty-six), but it is quite heterogeneous, composed of critics who write for low, middle, and high-brow newspapers and magazines. And the Academy of Motion Picture is composed of an extremely large membership, 4,523 in 1988, divided along twelve areas of expertise. All three film forums are therefore inevitably biased in their choices; that's the nature of awards determined by a *majority* vote. Yet the disagreements within each organization as well as the differences among them are interesting because they attest to the operation of multiple and complex criteria (artistic, ideological, political, and even moral) in the evaluation of film art.

CHAPTER 5

The Winning Process

Winning an Oscar Award is considered to be the ultimate achievement and the epitome of professional success in the film world. The Oscar is supposed to reward artists for an outstanding achievement, preferably for their best work. Consequently, it is important to know at what age and at what phase of their careers film artists win the award. The relationship between age and professional attainment is crucial to the understanding of the award's operations, because the Oscar has differential effects on artists, depending on the age at which they win. Clearly, its influence is more dramatic if the winners are young and at the beginning of their careers (see chapter 12).

The Winners' Age

In theory, it is possible to win the award at any age. Indeed, there have been winners in practically every age group. However, the best chances of winning have been between the ages of thirty and forty-nine; two-thirds of all Oscar winners have been in these age brackets. But there have also been very young (13 percent under thirty) and elderly winners (21 percent over fifty).

As with age at first nomination, actresses have been much younger than actors when they received their first award. About two-fifths (38 percent) of the women, compared with a scant minority (3 percent) of the men, have won the Oscar prior to the age of thirty. And two-thirds (69 percent) of the women, but only one-third (32 percent) of the men, have won the Oscar by the time they reached forty. The gap in winning age is particularly large in the lead categories: half—48 percent of the Best Actresses, but only 2 percent of the Best Actors—have been younger than thirty when they won their first award. And conversely, most (65 percent) Best Actors, but few (18 percent) Best Actresses, have been older than forty when they won.

Within each lead category, there has been a concentration of winners in one or two age groups. Among the Best Actresses, the largest concentration of winners has been in their late twenties. By contrast, the dominant group of Best Actors has been in their early forties. There has been no dominant winning age among the two supporting categories. The age range of supporting players has been very wide, with winners in every age, from the early teens to the late seventies.

The likelihood of winning the award at a particular age is determined by the range of screen roles allotted to men and women, and to leading and supporting players. Both biological and aesthetic norms have prescribed these roles, and these normative prescriptions have been more rigid and confining for leading players. The great variability of supporting roles, in age and physical appearance, explains why the age distribution of supporting winners has been so wide. Compared with leading roles, there have been no specific requirements that character roles be played by young and/or attractive players (see chapter 8).

The differences in screen roles assigned to male and female, lead and supporting players, are reflected in the median age at winning, which is thirty-one for Best Actresses, thirty-eight for Supporting Actresses, forty-one for Best Actors, and forty-six for Supporting Actors. But the impact of gender on the winning age has been more paramount than the category in which they were nominated. The median age at first winning is thirty-four for actresses (lead and supporting) and forty-four for actors (in both leagues), a significant difference of a decade!

Thus, in response to the question—Is the Oscar a young artists' game?—the answer is no. Only one-fifth (20 percent) of all winners have received the award prior to the age of thirty. Still, the Oscar has been more a young woman's than young man's game: 13 percent of the Best Actresses have been in their twenties, but only one Best Actor has been in this age group. Middle age seems to be the norm for the male winners: 69 percent of the Best Actors, compared with 24 percent of the Best Actresses, have been between thirty-five and fifty when they won their first Oscar.

Some artists have been particularly lucky to win the Oscar at a young age. The youngest winners in their respective categories have been:

Tatum O'Neal	11	Supporting Actress	*Paper Moon*
Timothy Hutton	19	Supporting Actor	*Ordinary People*
Janet Gaynor	22	Best Actress	*Sunrise, Street Angel, Seventh Heaven*
Richard Dreyfuss	29	Best Actor	*The Goodbye Girl*

Other players have had to wait until old age to win their first Oscar, as the oldest winners demonstrate:

Marie Dressler	62	Best Actress	*Min and Bill*
Henry Fonda	77	Best Actor	*On Golden Pond*
Peggy Ashcroft	77	Supporting Actress	*A Passage to India*
George Burns	79	Supporting Actor	*The Sunshine Boys*

Significantly, Marie Dressler has been the exception among the Best Actresses. Very few women have received their first Oscar after the age of forty. But in the last decade, older actresses have won the award more frequently. For example, Ellen Burstyn (*Alice Doesn't Live Here Anymore*) was forty-three, Shirley MacLaine (*Terms of Endearment*) was fifty, and this year, Geraldine Page (*The Trip to Bountiful*) was sixty-one. To what extent these actresses represent a new trend, of middle-aged and elderly actresses playing leading roles, remains to be seen. By contrast, the elderly supporting winners have been representative of their categories in every decade, like Helen Hayes (*Airport*), John Houseman (*The Paper Chase*), and Don Ameche (*Cocoon*), who have all been over seventy years old at their first winning.

Ruth Gordon's older winning age, seventy-two, is a good illustration of the career opportunities available to supporting players. Gordon was a late bloomer in film, though an accomplished stage actress. Following a few appearances in silent movies and one substantial role as Mary Todd Lincoln in *Abe Lincoln in Illinois* (1940), she dedicated herself almost exclusively to the theater. In 1966, however, she made an impressive comeback as Natalie Wood's demented mother in *Inside Daisy Clover*, for which she earned her first supporting nomination. Two years later, she won the supporting award for playing a modern witch in *Rosemary's Baby*. "Well, I can't tell you how encouragin' a thing like that is!" said Gordon whole-heartedly in her acceptance speech. "The first money I ever earned was as an extra in 1915, and here it is 1969. I don't know what took me so long." Husband Garson Kanin, with whom she collaborated on many screenplays, responded in a similar vein, "Suddenly Holly-wood discovered Ruth, it's only taken them fifty years." Among the many cables she received was one from her colleague Mary Pickford: "Dear Ruth, why did you take so long? Congratulations and love."[1] Ruth Gordon saw in her Oscar not only a tribute to past achievements, but also a prelude to a new career, and it was. For the next fifteen years, up to her death at the age of eighty-eight, she worked nonstop, delivering some of her best performances.

The Oscar as an Instant Reward

How long does it take to win the Oscar after one's film debut? Once again, women have received faster recognition of their acting talent than men. About one-fifth (19 percent) of the actresses, but only 5 percent of the actors, have won the Oscar during the first year of their careers. And over half (54 percent) of the actresses have received it within a decade after their debut, compared with one-third (32 percent) of the actors.

As with nomination, the Oscar has functioned as an instant reward for the women but not for the men. The actresses have experienced a shorter period of time between their film debuts and their Oscars. The median number of years between the first film and the award has been seven for the women and fourteen for the men, a difference of seven years. Consistent with the other career patterns, the Best Actresses have received immediate recognition by the Academy. The median number of years between debut and winning has been six for the Best Actresses, eight for the Supporting Actresses, twelve for the Best Actors, and fifteen for the Support-ing Actors.

Five Best Actresses have received the Oscar for their film debuts or during the first year of their careers: Katharine Hepburn (*Morn-ing Glory*), Shirley Booth (*Come Back Little Sheba*), Julie Andrews

(*Mary Poppins*), Barbra Streisand (*Funny Girl*), and Louise Fletcher (*One Flew Over the Cuckoo's Nest*). By contrast, only one Best Actor, Ben Kingsley (*Gandhi*) has received the Oscar for his first major film.

It has been much easier for supporting players to win the award. Twice as many supporting (17 percent) as leading players (8 percent) have won the Oscar during the first year of their careers. But overall supporting players have had to wait longer before winning: 27 percent of them, compared with 13 percent of the lead players, have won the Oscar more than two decades after their first films. The supporting players have displayed one of two extremes: they have either won very early or very late. Their careers have not been as orderly and structured as those of the leading players.

The Academy has been more likely to bestow the award for a film debut or during the first year of one's career on the *female* supporting players. Of the fifteen supporting winners in this group, ten have been women, including: Gale Sondergaard (*Anthony Adverse*), Mercedes McCambridge (*All the King's Men*), Eva Marie Saint (*On the Waterfront*), Jo Van Fleet (*East of Eden*), and Goldie Hawn (*Cactus Flower*).

Instant recognition through an Oscar has often been gained by players who repeated on screen a successful stage role in which they had excelled. At times, several members of the original stage cast were rehired for the film version. For instance, Lillian Hellman's 1941 stage hit, *Watch on the Rhine*, an anti-Fascist play, was made into a movie two years later. Two of its cast members, Paul Lukas, as the freedom fighter, and Lucille Watson, as the benevolent matriarch, were recast; Lukas won for it Best Actor, and Watson a supporting nomination.

Three of the four principals in Tennessee William's prize-winning play, *A Streetcar Named Desire*—Marlon Brando, Karl Malden, and Kim Hunter—were rehired for the 1951 film, directed by Elia Kazan, who had staged the play on Broadway with great success. Jessica Tandy, who had originated the role of Blanche DuBois, was not; Warner Brothers wanted a major star. Instead, they cast Vivien Leigh, an Oscar winner who had played the part in London under Olivier's direction. Brando earned his first Best Actor nomination, and Vivien Leigh, Karl Malden, Kim Hunter, and director Kazan all won Oscars.

Other stage players recruited by producers for the film versions of their work and who received nominations and awards include: Nancy Kelly and Patty McCormack in *The Bad Seed* (1956), Paul Newman and Burl Ives in *Cat on a Hot Tin Roof* (1958), Rosalind Russell and Peggy Cass in *Auntie Mame* (1959), Anne Bancroft and Patty Duke in *The Miracle Worker* (1962), James Earl Jones and Jane Alexander in *The Great White Hope* (1970), and Richard Burton and Peter Firth in *Equus* (1977).

Four Best Actresses have won the Oscar for stage roles with which they were intimately connected: Judy Holliday (*Born Yesterday*), Shirley Booth (*Come Back Little Sheba*), Anne Bancroft (*The Miracle Worker*), and Barbra Streisand (*Funny Girl*), all four won critical acclaim for their stage portrayals. For example, Barbra Streisand established herself as a musical star on Broadway in *Funny Girl*, won for it a Tony nomination, and went on to become a movie star after the film version. Director Herbert Ross believes that Streisand was "extremely lucky to make her film debut in *Funny Girl*. Having had the advantages of playing Fanny Brice for two years on Broadway, Streisand knew her part inside out." It was a perfect part "ideally suited to her range as an actress and as a singer."[2]

The number of women nominated for recreating previous stage roles has been even more considerable than those winning: sixteen out of the 129 Best Actresses. Despite the fact that many of them appeared in numerous pictures, some are still identified with these roles. Among these memorable stage-screen roles have been: Lynn Fontanne in *The Guardsman*, Katharine Hepburn in *The Philadelphia Story*, Julie Harris in *The Member of the Wedding*, Maggie McNamara in *The Moon Is Blue*, and Geraldine Page in *Sweet Bird of Youth*.

Of the Best Actors too, no less than seven have received the award for recreating famous stage roles, beginning with George Arliss, who played the British statesman in *Disraeli* on the stage, then in both the silent and sound film versions. Yul Brynner made the part of the King of Siam in Rodgers and Hammerstein's *The King and I* so much his own, that it was unthinkable for anyone else to appear in the film. Brynner won for it a supporting Tony Award, an Oscar, and a life-time lease on this role, playing it on Broadway and outside New York in numerous revivals. It was Brynner's very last role, which he played in New York just weeks before his death in 1985. And Rex Harrison scored such a huge triumph in Lerner and Lowe's *My Fair Lady* on both sides of the Atlantic that when the movie was made he was the natural and perfect choice for it. Like Brynner, Harrison became intimately identified with the role, arguably his best in a long and distinguished career. The Academy could not deny the award to other actors who excelled in transferring a "big" stage role to the screen, like Jose Ferrer in *Cyrano De Bergerac* and Paul Scofield in *A Man for All Seasons*.

A large number of the Best Actors nominees received recognition for playing popular roles in both theater and film. The distinguished male performances in this group have included: Walter Huston in *Dodsworth*, Raymond Massey in *Abe Lincoln in Illinois*, Anthony Franciosa in *A Hatful of Rain*, Ron Moody in *Oliver!*, Topol in *Fiddler on the Roof*, James Whitmore in his one-man show, "*Give 'Em Hell, Harry*," and most recently Tom Courtenay in *The Dresser*.

Recreating successful stage roles on screen has been one route for getting instant recognition, but not the only one. Another route, quite frequent though less understood, has been luck, or circumstances over which artists have little or no control. Fluke or happenstance are often-used terms in show business because they describe quite accurately the careers of many artists, from the time they become performers, to getting a "break," to being cast in an important film, to being nominated and winning an Oscar. Having been "the right person at the right time at the right place" has been, at times, more crucial a factor in determining the course of screen careers than talent or acting skills.

For example, many players gave their Oscar-winning performances not at their home studios, but when they were loaned out to other studios. Producer Samuel Goldwyn let Warners borrow Gary Cooper for the title role of *Sergeant York* (his first Oscar) in exchange for Warners' contract player, Bette Davis, cast in *The Little Foxes*, which also earned her a nomination.

Clark Gable and costar Claudette Colbert scored a great success in Columbia's *It Happened One Night*, despite the fact that both were at first reluctant to appear in this comedy, directed by Frank Capra. Colbert, in fact, was about to sail for Europe, and Gable was loaned out to Columbia by Louis B. Mayer as a disciplinary measure, after Gable had rejected some scripts the studio had created for him. MGM considered *It Happened One Night* a minor project at a minor studio. Film history proved otherwise: the film won Best Picture, Director, and acting awards and also changed the previously low status of Columbia Pictures in Hollywood. The unanticipated critical and commercial success of *It Happened One Night* demonstrated again that once a movie is made, it has an independent life of its own. Indeed, there is always an element of unpredictability and adventurism in filmmaking because the audiences' response can never be accurately predicted.

Oscar history is replete with such stories. Warner Baxter was assigned the role of the Cisco Kid in the Western *In Old Arizona* by default; the intended actor was Raoul Walsh who, unfortunately, had a car accident in which he lost an eye. And Mercedes McCambridge believes that she "might have never stumbled onto an Oscar," for *All the King's Men*, "if it hadn't been for a pushy friend of mine," who took her to a "cattle call" in New York.[3] This small part launched a vital screen career, after winning a supporting Oscar for it.

Furthermore, many players won their Oscars for parts for which they had neither been the first nor the second choice. Cary Grant, for example, was given the opportunity to choose between the two male leads in *The Philadelphia Story*: Tracy Lord's ex-husband or the canny journalist. He chose the former and Jimmy Stewart, cast as the reporter, went home with an Oscar. Grant committed another error, in retrospect, turning down the part of Judy Garland's down-and-out husband-actor in *A Star Is Born*, later played with great distinction by James Mason, who received a Best Actor nomination for it.

One cannot guarantee, of course, that had the original actors intended for these roles played them, they would have been singled out by the Academy, but the chances are that they would at least have been nominated for them. A case in point is Norma Shearer who, in the absence of her husband-producer Irving Thalberg (who died in 1938), made what turned out to be some errors in judgment. Shearer turned down the title role in *Mrs. Miniver*, which went to Greer Garson, bringing her an Oscar and her best-remembered role. Joan Crawford is best known for *Mildred Pierce*, but few people know that it was first offered to Bette Davis, who turned it down. And Davis herself delivered what is considered to be the finest performance of her career, Margo Channing in *All About Eve*, by accident. Claudette Colbert started to work on this film, but a back injury prevented her from doing it. Producer Darryl Zanuck's first choice as a replacement was Ingrid Bergman, who was then in Italy. Bette Davis was reportedly his "last-minute" choice; in retrospect, however, it is hard to imagine any actress but Davis in that role.

Director Anatole Litvak wanted Ingrid Bergman to play the mentally disturbed woman in *The Snake Pit*. But she rejected it, claiming "it all takes place in an insane asylum and I couldn't bear that."[4] Instead the role went to Olivia de Havilland, who scored a great success, winning a nomination and a citation from the New York Film Critics. After the film's success, Litvak confronted Bergman, "Look what you turned down!" "It was a very good part," she humorously replied, "but if I had played it, I wouldn't have got an Oscar for it." Ingrid Bergman also rejected the part of a young Swedish maid in *The Farmer's Daughter*, because, as she recalled, "For me to play my own part as a Swedish girl was not what I wanted." Loretta Young was cast in this comedy and received an Oscar for her first and only nomination. But Bergman claims she has "never regretted refusing either of those roles."[5]

Marlon Brando's stunning performance in *On the Waterfront*, as the not too-bright ex-prizefighter Terry Malloy, was first offered to Frank Sinatra, on the strength of his 1953 Oscar-winning role in *From Here to Eternity*. However, when director Kazan learned that Brando was available, he broke his promise to Sinatra and cast Brando. And in 1962, Brando himself turned down the title role in David Lean's epic, *Lawrence of Arabia*, which went to an unknown actor, Peter O'Toole, who was physically wrong for it, but who became an international star overnight, honored with his first of seven Oscar nominations. Rod Steiger scored critical acclaim in Paddy Chayefsky's television drama *Marty*, but when it was transferred to the big screen, he refused to do it again. Instead, a relatively obscure player, Ernest Borgnine, until then cast in villainous roles, was chosen. In addition to broadening Borgnine's range, the film went on to win Best Picture and Best Actor.

Sophia Loren's part in *Two Women* was first intended for Anna Magnani, under George Cukor's direction. The idea was to cast Magnani in the mother's role and Loren as her daughter. Magnani, however, rejected this proposition, apparently because Loren was taller than her and she could not perform with a daughter "I have to look up to." Loren was excited about this casting, particularly at the prospect of performing with Anna Magnani, who at the time was "the doyenne of Italian actresses."[6] She tried to persuade her, but to no avail. As it turned out, this part was single-handedly responsible for breaking Loren's image as a sex symbol, and establishing her as the serious dramatic actress she had always wanted to be.

Fluke played a major factor in two of Peter Finch's best screen roles. Ian Bannen was originally cast as the Jewish homosexual doctor in *Sunday, Bloody Sunday*, but after a month of shooting he became sick and had to be replaced. Finch's first reaction when the role was offered to him was, "I'm not a queer," but on second thought, after reading the scenario, he was convinced that "it was a fabulous script and a fabulous part." Director John Schlesinger later said that he "can't think of anyone who could have done it better," and that Finch was "definitive."[7] Finch won for this role international recognition, including his first Best Actor nomination. Nor was Finch a top choice for the role of the demented television commentator in Sidney Lumet's *Network*. The role had been previously offered to—and rejected by—George C. Scott, Glenn Ford, and Henry Fonda. It was screenwriter Chayefsky who suggested Finch for the part. According to his biographer, the arrival of the script in Jamaica, where Finch was at the time, "absolutely galvanized" him, his major concern being that someone else would take it before "he could stake his claim." As soon as he finished reading it, "he was frantic to let them know he was more than interested."[8]

Finch knew that *Network* was not only a plum role, but "Oscar material," and consequently did not want to miss the opportunity to work on this picture. But it is not always easy for actors to assess the quality of a role before, or even after, filming begins. For example, *Coming Home*, the first Hollywood anti-Vietnam War movie, was in various phases of preparation for six years, until Jane Fonda's production company, IPC, brought it to the screen. Moreover, its casting, which earned Jane Fonda and Jon Voight acting laurels, is now considered to be perfect. Actually Voight's role, as the paraplegic war veteran, was first offered to Jack Nicholson and Sylvester Stallone, the latter fresh from the unanticipated victory of *Rocky*. United Artists, which released the picture, wanted a bankable star, though producer Jerome Hellman and director Hal Ashby managed to convince the studio that Voight was the right actor for the part.

Nomination and Winning

How many nominations does it take to win the award? Officially, the Academy claims that the number of nominations does not—and should not—affect the candidates' chances of winning. Indeed, two-thirds (66 percent) of all winners have earned the Oscar at their first nomination. However, those claiming that the number of nominations *do* count point out that 22 percent of the winners have been nominated twice, and 12 percent three or more times prior to winning. It's one of these cases in which the interpretation depends on how you "read" the statistics.

It has been much easier for supporting players to win the award at first nomination: four-fifths (80 percent) of them, compared with half (55 percent) of the leading winners. Conversely, twice as many lead as supporting players have won the Oscar at their second nomination (27 percent to 15 percent respectively). The gap between these categories widens with those nominated three or more times: 18 percent of the lead, but 5 percent of the supporting. The competition for supporting awards has usually been less intense, and the Academy has been more discriminating in its evaluation of leading performances; the lead Oscars are, after all, much more prestigious and influential.

But once again, of the four groups, the Best Actors have been the least likely to get the award at their first nomination. Two-thirds (65 percent) of the Best Actresses, compared with less than half (45 percent) of the Best Actors, have won at their first nomination. And 6 percent of the women, but 11 percent of the men, have been nominated four or more times before winning. The disadvantageous position of the Best Actors derives from the fact that until the late 1970s American films have provided better roles for men, thus making the competition within this category much fiercer (see chapter 8).

In the first decade of the Oscar, all Best Actresses won at their first nomination. Joan Fontaine was the first actress to win the award at her second nomination, for *Rebecca* in 1941. Until the 1970s, at least half of the Best Actresses won for their first nominated roles. In the last decade, however, Faye Dunaway (*Network*) won at her third nomination, Shirley MacLaine (*Terms of Endearment*) at her fifth, and Geraldine Page (*The Trip to Bountiful*) broke all records by winning at her eighth nomination.

By contrast, except for the first decade, in which most men naturally won at their first nomination, throughout the years it has become a rarity for men to win at their first or even second nomination. In the 1970s, only two of the winning actors, Art Carney for *Harry and Tonto* and Richard Dreyfuss for *The Goodbye Girl*, received the award for their first nomination. The other actors were nominated three or four times before winning. However, in the 1980s the trend seems to have reversed itself, with most actors winning at their first nomination, as demonstrated by Ben Kingsley *(Gandhi)*, F. Murray Abraham *(Amadeus)*, William Hurt *(Kiss of the Spider Woman)*, and Michael Douglas *(Wall Street)*.

Twelve of the 199 Oscar players have been nominated four or more times before winning:

4 nominations	6 players	Laurence Olivier, Marlon Brando, Elizabeth Taylor, Dustin Hoffman, Maureen Stapleton, and Robert Duvall
5 nominations	4	Susan Hayward, Gregory Peck, Jack Nicholson, and Shirley MacLaine
6 nominations	1	Paul Newman
8 nominations	1	Geraldine Page

If the chances of winning an Oscar increase with the number of nominations, as was recently demonstrated by Duvall, MacLaine, and Page, the following players are likely candidates for the award: Peter O'Toole (seven nominations), Al Pacino and Glenn Close (each with five), Albert Finney, Jane Alexander, and Marsha Mason (each with four), and Warren Beatty and Jeff Bridges (each with three). The late Richard Burton was also nominated seven times, six in the lead and one in the supporting category.

The careers of the Oscar directors have resembled those of the women: over half (58 percent) have won at their first nomination, one-fourth (25 percent) at their second, and less than one-fifth (17 percent) at their third or more nominations.

3 nominations	4 directors	Michael Curtiz, Fred Zinnemann, Carol Reed, and Sydney Pollack
4 nominations	1	David Lean
5 nominations	2	William Wyler and George Cukor

The greatest losers in this category are: King Vidor, Clarence Brown, and Alfred Hitchcock (each with five nominations), Sidney

Lumet, Federico Fellini, and Stanley Kubrick (with four), and Ernst Lubitsch, William A. Wellman, Sam Wood, Richard Brooks, Stanley Kramer, Ingmar Bergman, and Steven Spielberg (each with three). Of these, judging by their current work and popularity in Hollywood, Lumet, Kubrick, and Spielberg are likely to win an Oscar in the future.

Ties and Multiple Awards

Ties have been a rare occurrence: neither the Academy nor the nominees like the idea of sharing the coveted award. Indeed, there have never been ties in the Best Picture and only two in the acting awards. The first tie was declared in 1932, when Wallace Beery (*The Champ*) and Fredric March (*Dr. Jekyll and Mr. Hyde*) split the Best Actor award. Beery came within one vote of March, and in those years when a nominee came within three votes of another, a tie was announced. The second tie occurred in the 1968 Best Actress award, which was split between Katharine Hepburn (*The Lion in Winter*) and Barbra Streisand (*Funny Girl*). This time, however, the number of votes for each candidate was not disclosed.

In other film awards too, ties have been quite rare. In its half century of existence, the New York Film Critics Circle has declared a tie only twice. In 1960, two films were cited, *The Apartment* and *Sons and Lovers*; both films were nominated, but the Oscar winner was *The Apartment*. And in 1966, Elizabeth Taylor (*Who's Afraid of Virginia Woolf?*) and Lynn Redgrave (*Georgy Girl*) were singled out for their acting; the Academy winner was Taylor. The Los Angeles Film Critics Association has also refrained from splitting its awards, though in 1976, Sidney Lumet's *Network* and John Avildsen's *Rocky* were named Best Pictures; the Academy winner was *Rocky*. And in 1984, this group honored two male performances: Albert Finney in *Under the Volcano* and F. Murray Abraham in *Amadeus*; the Oscar winner was Abraham.

For most players (86 percent), winning an Oscar has been a once-in-a-lifetime achievement. Yet considering the intensity of the competition, the proportion of players winning multiple awards has been quite impressive: 14 percent. As could be expected, lead players have had better chances than supporting of winning multiple Oscars (20 percent and 7 percent respectively). And consistently, the Best Actresses have had the best prospects of winning a second Oscar: 28 percent compared with 13 percent of the Best Actors.

Multiple winners have earned their awards for performances within the same category (lead *or* supporting) or for performances in two categories (lead *and* supporting). The following players have won two Oscars in the same category:

Best Actor	5	Fredric March, Spencer Tracy, Gary Cooper, Marlon Brando, and Dustin Hoffman
Best Actress	9	Bette Davis, Luise Rainer, Vivien Leigh, Ingrid Bergman, Olivia de Havilland, Elizabeth Taylor, Glenda Jackson, and Jane Fonda
Supporting Actor	4	Anthony Quinn, Peter Ustinov, Melvyn Douglas, and Jason Robards
Supporting Actress	1	Shelley Winters

Two players have stood out in their Oscar achievements. Katharine Hepburn, probably the most respected screen actress, holds the record of the largest number of nominations (twelve) and the largest number of awards (four). Furthermore, these Oscars have been won over half a century, from the first in 1932 for *Morning Glory* through *Guess Who's Coming to Dinner?* in 1967, *The Lion in Winter* in 1968, and *On Golden Pond* in 1981. Walter Brennan holds another kind of a record, having won three supporting Oscars within five years: *Come and Get It* in 1936, *Kentucky* in 1938, and *The Westerner* in 1940.

Seven players have won Oscars in both the leading and supporting categories: Three actors (Jack Lemmon, Robert De Niro, and Jack Nicholson) and four actresses (Helen Hayes, Ingrid Bergman, Maggie Smith, and Meryl Streep). Significantly, with the exception of Jack Nicholson, the men first won a supporting, then a lead award. For example, Jack Lemmon was cited for a featured role in *Mister Roberts* in 1955, and twenty-eight years later for a leading role in *Save the Tiger*. The actresses, however, first won Best Actress, then Supporting Actress. Helen Hayes was one of the first female winners, *The Sin of Madelon Claudet* in 1932, but in 1970 she won a second, supporting award for *Airport*. As was mentioned, these different career patterns were related to the rigid specifications for women's roles, demanding that leading ladies be young and attractive. Nonetheless, the career of Meryl Streep, the only actress to have first won a supporting (*Kramer Vs. Kramer*) and then a leading Oscar (*Sophie's Choice*), is seen as an encouraging development in women's careers in Hollywood.

Multiple winning has been even more characteristic of the directorial category, reflecting the different ratio of supply and demand of directorial talent. The concentration of awards and nominations within a small group of talented filmmakers has been a consistent trend in Hollywood. Of the forty Oscar-winning directors, fourteen (35 percent) have been multiple recipients. The all-time record is still held by John Ford, who won four Oscars, followed by Frank Capra and William Wyler, each with three Oscars. Only nine of the forty directors have received one nomination, but ten directors have been nominated five or more times. The effects of winning may have been more pervasive on directorial than on acting careers.

While a large number of players and directors have been multiply nominated, only four players have won two Oscars in a row: Luise Rainer in 1936 and 1937, Spencer Tracy in 1937 and 1938, Katharine Hepburn in 1967 and 1968, and Jason Robards in 1976 and 1977. And only two directors: John Ford for *The Grapes of Wrath* in 1940 and *How Green Was My Valley* in 1941, and Joseph L. Mankiewicz for *A Letter to Three Wives* in 1949 and *All About Eve* in 1950.

By and large, the Academy has been reluctant to bestow the Oscar posthumously. Peter Finch has been the only player to have won the award after his death for *Network*. Some suspect that the Academy has avoided posthumous awards because of its realization that they would have much less impact on the commercial appeal of the winning films, as if saying it would "waste" the award if it would't be of any help. But others claim that the Academy's reluctance stems from its belief that the awards should affect the careers of practicing artists. Indeed, in some categories, such as the Irving G. Thalberg Memorial Award for distinguished producers, and the Honorary Oscars, the rules state explicitly that the awards "shall not be voted posthumously."

A recent case of a posthumous award also demonstrates how rule-abiding the Academy is. In 1972, Raymond Rasch, Larry Russell, and Charlie Chaplin earned the best original score for

Limelight, a film made twenty years earlier. Both Rasch and Russell were dead, but Chaplin accepted the award for a film that had been banned in the United States for many years, though it was shown in Europe. Released in Los Angeles in 1972 for the first time, the picture was eligible for nominations.

Posthumous nominations have been only slightly more frequent than such awards. There must really be a good reason for the Academy to nominate players after their death. James Dean has been one of the few exceptions, earning two Best Actor nominations posthumously, for *East of Eden* in 1955, and for *Giant* in 1956. Dean was killed in a highway car crash while driving his Porsche to Salinas to compete in a race. *East of Eden* was released a few weeks after his death, on September 30, 1955, and *Giant*, which he did not complete, about a year later. The consensus was that Dean's second nomination was based on sentimental reasons, though his performances in both pictures were outstanding. These nominations not only contributed to the box-office success of *East of Eden* and *Giant*, but also to Dean's legend as an actor.

Spencer Tracy was also nominated posthumously for *Guess Who's Coming to Dinner?*, a film that provided a grand acting reunion with Katharine Hepburn; their ninth film together. Were it not for Hepburn, he would not have made it, for he was very ill. Frightened that he might not get through with the picture, he told director Stanley Kramer four days before shooting ended: "You know, I read the script again last night, and if I were to die on the way home tonight, you can still release the picture with what you've got."[9] Had Tracy lived, he would probably have won an award, both for his acting and also for sentimental reasons. Hepburn's award for this picture was probably based on personal reasons too; she nursed him through it. Aware of this, she is reported to have said: "I'm sure mine [the award] is for the two of us."

The most recent case of posthumous nomination was that of Sir Ralph Richardson, for his bravura performance in *Greystoke: The Legend of Tarzan*, (1984), in which he played the eccentric Lord Greystoke. Undeterred by his death, the New York Film Critics Circle cited him as best supporting actor, and the Academy's Acting Branch, acknowledging Richardson's genius and the fact that it was his last film, nominated him for a featured role; the winner, however, was Hang S. Ngor for *The Killing Fields*.

The Nominees as a Social and Artistic Community

The Academy winners and nominees are in many ways members of a closely knit artistic community. To begin with, it is a small group, comprised of the most distinguished players. In the entire Academy history, only 199 players have won and only 446 players have been nominated for an Oscar. The 645 Oscar-nominated players amount to 1 percent of the members of the Screen Actors Guild and a smaller percentage of all practicing screen players. The Oscar directors have also been a select group, 43 winners and 104 nominees, about 17 percent of the membership of the Directors Guild.

Indeed, the screen professions, particularly acting, have been sharply stratified, marked by tremendous inequality between the elite and the rank-and-file members. According to the Screen Actors Guild, on any randomly chosen day, over 80 percent of its members are unemployed, and only a minority (18 percent) makes more than five thousand dollars a year from screen acting.[10] By contrast, Oscar-winning players can make up to five or six million dollars per picture and tend to work nonstop, moving from one project to another.

The Oscar contest reflects this sharp inequality: the nominations and awards have been concentrated within an extremely small group of artists. The average number of nominations has been 3.7 among the Best Actresses, 3.2 among the Best Directors, and 2.9 among the Best Actors.

The winners constitute a social community in another respect. Many players were under contract to the same studio for the entire duration of their careers, thus appearing opposite the same players and working under the same directors in film after film. Bette Davis, Humphrey Bogart, and James Cagney were Warner Brothers stars. Clark Gable, Spencer Tracy, Joan Crawford, and Norma Shearer defined the film quality of MGM as much as this studio shaped their careers. These lengthy affiliations meant, among other things, that performers appeared in similar films and specialized in similar kinds of screen roles, which helped audiences to distinguish a "Bette Davis" from a "Joan Crawford" film, and a "Clark Gable" from a "James Cagney" movie.

Moreover, most studios deliberately created romantic screen teams, to increase audience identification with their stars, on and offscreen. Janet Gaynor appeared so often with Charles Farrell that they became known as "America's lovebirds." Other famous romantic teams have included: Olivia De Havilland and Errol Flynn (*Captain Blood*), Katharine Hepburn and Spencer Tracy (in nine pictures beginning with *Woman of the Year*), Margaret Sullavan and James Stewart (*The Shop Around the Corner*), Greer Garson and Walter Pidgeon (*Mrs. Miniver*), Humphrey Bogart and Lauren Bacall (*To Have and Have Not*), and Doris Day and Rock Hudson (*Pillow Talk*).[11] With the demise of the studio system, this distinctive aspect of the American cinema completely disappeared.

Direct occupational inheritance—that is, children who step into their parents' occupations—has been more prevalent in acting than in other lines of work, making it a smaller, more intimate community. About 10 percent of the Oscar players had one parent, and 5 percent had both parents in the acting profession. And if related professions (writing, producing, directing) are taken into account, the proportion is even higher (15 percent), particularly among the women (20 percent).[12] In some cases, occupational inheritance has prevailed for three or more generations: the acting dynasties of the Barrymores, the Powers, the Fondas, and the Robards in the United States, and the Redgraves in England.

Many performers were literally born into show business. Paul Muni, for instance, was reared in a theater trunk; his parents were strolling players, touring all over Europe and later America with him and his two brothers. Shunning the financial hazards of acting, his parents hoped he would pursue a career as a violinist, but Muni was stagestruck. At thirteen, he became a regular member of his parents' troupe—he never studied acting in school because there was no need for it. Another Academy nominee, Mickey Rooney, spent his infancy and early childhood backstage and on tour with his parents, both entertainers. He made his stage debut at fifteen months, appearing in a vaudeville act as a midget, wearing a tuxedo and smoking a big rubber cigar. The parents of Oscar-winner Jennifer Jones were the owners and stars of the Isley Stock Company, a tent show that toured the Midwest; beginning as a ticket and soda seller, she made her stage debut at the young age of ten.

The high rate of endogamous marriages—that is, marriages within the same social unit, in this case profession—has been another distinctive characteristic of acting, contributing to the integration of its members into a social group with its own life-style and culture. At least two-thirds of the nominated artists have married within the film colony; most, more than once. The only difference between the genders is that actors usually marry actresses, but actresses tend to marry producers and directors—in addition to actors. In this respect, the Academy nominees could almost be accused of "incest," based on the revealing statistics that 20 percent of all nominated players and directors have been married to each other at one time or other in their careers! Further, many have met their prospective spouses at work, while appearing in a play or shooting a movie. Some have fallen in love and subsequently married their leading men or ladies.

Academy nominee Merle Oberon (*The Dark Angel*) serves as a good example. Married four times, three of her husbands were drawn from the world of show business. Oberon's first husband was British film producer Alexander Korda, and her second, cinematographer Lucien Ballard. Her third, and longest, marriage, was the exception, to an Italian industrialist. However, in 1973, Oberon married her costar, Robert Walders, many years her junior, in her comeback film *Interval*. Ironically, Walders was cast as a young man, falling in love with an aging woman. . . . The issue of whether art imitates life or life imitates art is not easy to resolve when it concerns courtship and marriage in Hollywood. Oberon's example is by no means unique. Another Oscar-nominated actor, James Earl Jones, met his prospective wife, Julienne Marie, when she played Desdemona to his Othello in the New York Shakespeare's production in Central Park.

These marital and familial bonds have been expressed in Oscar nominations and awards. Three types of such family ties can be distinguished: intergenerational nominations of parents and children, marital nominations of husbands and wives, and sibling nominations of brothers and sisters.

The only example of three-generational Oscars is provided by the Huston family. In 1948, John Huston won two Oscars, for writing and directing *The Treasure of the Sierra Madre*, a film that provided his father, Walter Huston, with one of his best roles as the shrewd old gold prospector—for which he won a supporting Oscar. This double winning was the emotional highlight of the evening, after which Walter Huston jokingly remarked: "I always told my boy that if he ever became a director, to find a part for the old man." Thirty-seven years later, John Huston's daughter Anjelica accepted

Best Supporting Actress for her stunning performance as the wild and wronged granddaughter of the don, in her father's *Prizzi's Honor*. The polls had predicted that Huston would win a second directorial Oscar for this film, and many people were excited at the prospects of seeing father and daughter sharing the spotlight. However, the surprise winner was Sydney Pollack for *Out of Africa*. In her acceptance speech, Anjelica, who had made her debut in one of her father's pictures, acknowledged her family debt: "This means a lot to me, especially since it comes for a role in which I was directed by my father, and I know it means a lot to him."

The 1975 awards ceremonies were described as "The Francis Ford Coppola Family Hour," because *The Godfather, Part Two* won six Oscars, including Best Director (Coppola) and Best Dramatic Score for the director's father, Carmine Coppola, shared with Nino Rotta. Talia Shire, Coppola's sister, was nominated for a supporting award, as Connie Corleone, the sluttish sister of Al Pacino in the movie, but did not win.

A family reunion, imbued with symbolic meanings on and off-screen, took place at the 1982 Oscar show, when Henry Fonda won for *On Golden Pond*, based on Ernest Thompson's stage play, whose screen rights Jane Fonda allegedly purchased as a star vehicle for her father. Jane Fonda had made her acting debut opposite her father at the Omaha Community House Theater. But *On Golden Pond* was the first and only movie they made together, with Jane cast as Chelsea, a daughter at odds with her father over some childhood misunderstanding. The film's reconciliation scene, under the sturdy guidance of Katharine Hepburn, who plays Fonda's wife, in which Chelsea finally comes to terms with her past and becomes her father's friend, has been interpreted autobiographically; apparently, Jane's radical politics created tension between them. Jane agreed to play a thankless role in the film, for familial as well as publicity considerations. The Academy respectfully honored Henry Fonda and Katharine Hepburn with Oscars, and Jane with her sixth (and first supporting) nomination. Henry Fonda was unable to attend the ceremonies due to poor health; Jane accepted the Oscar for him.

Other famous Hollywood families have been honored with nominations and awards. Vincente Minnelli was named Best Director for the musical *Gigi*. His ex-wife, Judy Garland, was not nominated for any of their mutual films, but was singled out twice by the Academy: as Best Actress for the musical *A Star Is Born*, and as featured actress in the court drama *Judgment at Nuremberg*. Their daughter, Liza Minnelli, who at the age of two made her film debut in a walk-on part in her mother's musical *In the Good Old Summertime*, was also nominated twice: for *The Sterile Cuckoo*, and for *Cabaret*, winning Best Actress for the latter.

The Redgrave family is probably the most renowned acting dynasty in England, consisting of five generations of players. The grandfather and both parents of Sir Michael Redgrave were actors, and he was married to Rachel Kempson, known for her stage and television work. Moreover, all of their three children—Vanessa, Lynn, and Corin—chose acting careers. On the evening of Vanessa's birth, her father was playing opposite Olivier in *Hamlet* at the Old Vic. Olivier was so excited by the news that in his curtain speech he announced: "Tonight a lovely new actress has been born. Laertes [played by Redgrave] has a daughter."[13] Olivier's prophecy was self-fulfilling and Vanessa not only decided to become an actress at an early age, but also made her first screen appearance, playing the daughter of her real-life father in *Behind the Mask*.

As in the Fonda family, acting talent has been in abundance in the Redgrave dynasty, some of it certified by the Academy. Three of the family members have been nominated: Sir Michael, as Best Actor, for the film version of Eugene O'Neill's *Mourning Becomes Electra* in 1947. And Vanessa and Lynn won their first Best Actress nominations in 1966, the former for *Morgan*, the latter for *Georgy Girl*. Lynn recalled that for the part of Georgy, described as a young woman "who just missed being beautiful," the producers "tried to get every girl in London," including her sister Vanessa, who turned it down because of other commitments. But the nomination of Vanessa and Lynn in the same year apparently did not affect their close relationship. Both made sure to dispel in public any feelings of rivalry or animosity, and Lynn is reported to have said: "We like each other's work and each other as people. Vanessa takes the spotlight one week, I get it the next."[14] In the following decade, however, it was Vanessa who distinguished herself as a performer; she is considered to be the best actress in the English-speaking world. Vanessa has been nominated five times, and won a supporting Oscar for *Julia*.

The Redgrave acting torch seems to be passing down from generation to generation, judging by the fact that all three of Vanessa's children have already appeared on stage and/or in film. Most recently, her daughter Joely Richardson appeared in David Hare's *Whetherby*, in which she played Vanessa's character as an adolescent. And her other daughter, Natasha Richardson, played Nina to her mother's Irina in a British production of Chekhov's *The Sea Gull*, which, in the 1968 film directed by Sidney Lumet, had been one of Vanessa's earlier roles.

The friendly sportsmanship of the Redgrave sisters in the 1966 nominations did not prevail when another pair of sisters was nominated in the same year: Joan Fontaine for *Suspicion* and Olivia de Havilland for *Hold Back the Dawn*, in 1941. Rumors of the "feuding sisters," who were of similar age and both ambitious, circulated in the movie colony. De Havilland's beginning was much more auspicious than her sister's, having made a number of popular films opposite Errol Flynn. But Fontaine recalls that when she won the award for *Suspicion*, "Olivia took the situation very graciously. I am sure it was not a pleasant moment for her, as she'd lost the previous year for Melanie in *Gone with the Wind* in the supporting actress category." In later years, however, "Olivia made it up with two Oscars, for *To Each His Own* and for *The Heiress*, so the evening was only a temporary setback."[15] But reports from magazines of the time tell in great detail how Olivia backed off and cut her sister dead when Joan tried to shake her hand at her first winning.

Oscar-related frustrations also prevailed in the Barrymore family. Two of the Barrymore siblings have won Oscars. Lionel Barrymore earned the 1930/31 Best Actor, as Norma Shearer's alcoholic lawyer-father in *A Free Soul*. His sister, Ethel Barrymore, was nominated four times for supporting actress within five years, winning for *None But the Lonely Heart*, as Cary Grant's poor mother. Nonetheless, John Barrymore, the most famous of the three, was never nominated, despite a number of excellent performances. The Barrymores, like the Redgraves, have been a genuine acting clan, extending (so far) over five generations. The most recent member of this family to have graced the screen has been Drew Barrymore, of *E.T.* fame.

The Oscar race has also included marital nominations. Three husband-wife teams have been nominated for the same film. Alfred Lunt and Lynn Fontanne were the first team, nominated for recreating on screen their famous Broadway roles, as the jealous husband-actor and his flirtatious wife-actress, in the Hungarian comedy *The Guardsman*. The second team, Charles Laughton and Elsa Lanchester, made a number of films together, and were both nominated for Billy Wilder's *Witness for the Prosecution*, in which Laughton, in his third nomination, played Sir Wilfred Robards, the eccentric Queen's defense counsel, and Lanchester, in her second supporting nomination, played his maidenly owlish nurse. In one of many memorable scenes, Lanchester tells Laughton, "It's time for our nap," to which he replies, "You go ahead, start it without me." Neither Laughton nor Lanchester won, for 1957 was a year of particularly intense competition, with Alec Guinness winning for *The Bridge on the River Kwai*, and Miyoshiu Umeki as Supporting Actress for *Sayonara*.

Elizabeth Taylor and Richard Burton, one of Hollywood's most glamorous couples, was the third acting team to be nominated for the same film, also playing husband and wife. Taylor, as the earthy Martha, and Burton, as her husband-professor George, probably gave their finest screen performances in Mike Nichol's adaptation of Edward Albee's prize-winning *Who's Afraid of Virginia Woolf?* Taylor won a second Oscar for this picture, but Burton lost to Paul Scofield in *A Man for All Seasons*.

Paul Newman and wife-actress Joanne Woodward met while they were performing on Broadway in *Picnic*, and went on to appear in many films together, *From the Terrace*, *Paris Blues*, *A New Kind of Love* among them. But none of their acting collaborations won critical acclaim or nominations. They were more successful as a director-actress team. *Rachel, Rachel* (1968) earned Woodward her second nomination and, though Newman was not nominated for his direction, the film was nominated for Best Picture.

The careers of several performers can be described quite accurately in terms of their Academy nominations and awards. Burt Lancaster occupies a special position among them, being an accomplished actor himself with many Oscar-winning films to his credit, and also performing opposite other Oscar-winning players. Lancaster was cast in an unsympathetic role in *Sorry, Wrong Number* (1948), which brought Barbara Stanwyck her fourth nomination, and costarred in *Come Back Little Sheba* (1952), which earned Shirley Booth a Best Actress Oscar. In 1953, he appeared in Fred Zinnemann's *From Here to Eternity*, which won two supporting awards to Frank Sinatra and Donna Reed, and three leading nominations, Montgomery Clift, Deborah Kerr, and Lancaster, who was singled out by the New York Film Critics. In 1955, Lancaster costarred in Tennessee Williams's *The Rose Tattoo*, which earned Anna Magnani an Oscar, and a year later in *The Rainmaker*, which brought Katharine Hepburn her seventh nomination.

Lancaster also coproduced and appeared in *Separate Tables* (1958), which was nominated for Best Picture, and won his costars, David Niven and Wendy Hiller, acting awards. In 1960, he won Best Actor and a second New York Film Critics Award for a flashy performance in *Elmer Gantry*. Lancaster was not nominated for *Judgment at Nuremberg*, but the film was, and costar Maximillian Schell won an Oscar. For his performance in the prison drama *The Birdman of Alcatraz* (1962), he earned his third nomination, and Thelma Ritter, as his mother, her sixth supporting nomination. And in 1981, he surprised critics and audiences with a great performance in Louis Malle's offbeat *Atlantic City*, for which he received his fourth nomination and his third New York Film Critics Award.

Of the postwar generation of stars, Lancaster is one of the few practicing actors, celebrating this year the fortieth anniversary of his screen career. Bette Davis and James Stewart belong to an even older generation of performers, but they do not make feature movies any more. The only surviving member of this generation is Katharine Hepburn, who had received her first Oscar in the sixth year of the Academy. Having made her film debut in 1932, her career almost parallels the Academy's entire history.

CHAPTER 6

The Oscar-Winning Films

Every year hundreds of movies are released in the United States and are thus eligible for Academy nominations. But regardless of the number of films made, only five films are selected by the Academy for the top award, the Best Picture of the year. How are these five chosen out of hundreds of motion pictures? What are the criteria for selection in the nomination and in the final winning processes? Have there been any consistent patterns of selection?

The Oscar-nominated films have, of course, differed in theme, style, and artistic merits. Still, an interesting question arises as to whether or not the Academy has displayed consistent bias in favor of or against particular kinds of film. More specifically, how crucial has the films' genre been in the nomination and in the winning? To answer these questions, all 367 films nominated for Best Picture, from 1927 to the present, were classified according to genre. Two kinds of comparisons are made: between the winning and nominated films, and between the nominated and the kinds of films produced.[1]

Biographical and Fictional Films

Considering the fact that the vast majority of films are based on fictional stories and characters, the Academy has displayed a clear bias in favor of what might be called "biopictures," that is, pictures inspired by actual events and personalities.[2] The degree of accuracy or truthfulness of these biopictures to their respective source materials is an interesting issue, though not under examination here. Furthermore, in the final account, every film is fictional, even if it seriously attempts to recreate the life of a particular individual or reconstruct a specific historical era.

Eighteen (29 percent) of the sixty-one Oscar-winning films have been inspired by real-life events or personalities. These movies have been diverse in themes and concerns, ranging from show-business figures *(The Great Ziegfeld)* to scientists *(The Story of Louis Pasteur)* to writers *(The Life of Emil Zola)* to military *(Lawrence of Arabia)* and historical figures *(A Man for All Seasons)*. More significantly, biopictures have featured more prominently in the last two decades: Six of the eight winning films in the 1980s have been inspired by real-life figures. In 1981, *Chariots of Fire*, the inspirational tale of two British runners, Harold Abrahams and Eric Liddell, in the 1924 Paris Olympics, won Best Picture. *Gandhi*, a stricter and even more noble biopicture, was the 1982 Oscar winner. In 1984 *Amadeus* offered an interesting view of the life of genius composer Wolfgang Amadeus Mozart in eighteenth-century Vienna. *Out of Africa*, based on the life of Karen Blixen, the Danish writer who published under the name of Isak Dinesen, won in 1985, and *The Last Emperor*, an expansive epic about Pu Yi, the last Manchu emperor of China, was the 1987 winner.

There has been no difference between the prominence of the biopictures among the winning and the nominated films: eighteen (29 percent) of the former and seventy (24 percent) of the latter, a considerable proportion compared with the number of biopictures made. These pictures have used the narrative conventions of different genres: musicals *(Yankee Doodle Dandy)*, war films *(Patton)*, Westerns *(Butch Cassidy and the Sundance Kid)*, historical epics *(Mutiny on the Bounty, Ben-Hur)*, and even action-adventure *(The French Connection, The Right Stuff)*.

There have been interesting historical trends, qualitative as well as quantitative, in the nomination of biopictures. In the 1930s, the studio most associated with the production of biopictures was Warner Brothers. Their cycle actually began with *Disraeli* (1929), starring George Arliss as the wily British statesman. But it became more prominent later in the decade, with the release of some notable Warners biopictures, two of which were nominated, both starring Paul Muni.[3] In 1936, *The Story of Louis Pasteur* recounted the life of the French chemist who discovered the anthrax vaccine, which saved French cattle from the black plague. The Oscar winner of 1937 was *The Life of Emil Zola*, which dealt with the exposure of anti-Semitism in the French government. These films, as historian Lewis Jacobs suggested, were predominantly social in outlook, realistic in interpretation, and imbued with strong messages about democratic values. Indeed, they all drew a direct parallel between the past and the present, particularly in their condemnation of Fascism and Nazism.[4]

The number of biopictures in the 1940s (23 percent) was much higher than that in the 1950s (only 7 percent). And the movies of the two decades also differed in subject matter. The direct involvement of the United States in World War II in 1941 affected Hollywood's film production. Many war films, inspired by actual military figures, were made in this decade, of which the best known was *Sergeant York* (1941), celebrating the courage of the World War I hero. By contrast, the few 1950 films inspired by real events or personalities dealt with biblical (*The Ten Commandments*) or Christian heroes (*Quo Vadis?*, *The Robe*). The 1950s films were historical epics that, unlike the 1940s biopictures, did not even attempt to be realistic in their treatment.

The biopictures nominated in the 1960s were either about show-business personalities (*Funny Girl*), or royalty intrigues and affairs (*Cleopatra*, *Becket*, *The Lion in Winter*, *Anne of the Thousand Days*, *Nicholas and Alexandra*). However, from the mid-1970s, the range of nominated biopictures has been wider. They included, of course, the perennial topic of show biz, *Lenny* and *All That Jazz*, both directed by Bob Fosse, with the latter drawing on his own life. But there were also movies about working-class protagonists, which in the past were neglected by the American cinema. Sidney Lumet's *Dog Day Afternoon*, based on a Brooklyn bank robbery, depicted the life of marginal people through the figure of Sonny (Al Pacino), the doomed bisexual whose motive for the robbery was to provide money for his lover's sex-change operation. The heroine of *Norma Rae* would have been an unlikely topic for a Hollywood film of the past, but Martin Ritt made an uplifting movie, inspired by the life of a Southern hillbilly (Sally Field) in a small dormant town who gains political consciousness.

This trend of biopictures reached an apogee in the 1980 Oscar contest, in which three of the nominated films were based, to varying degrees of accuracy and interest, on real-life figures. *Coal Miner's Daughter* recreated the life of country and western singer Loretta Lynn (Sissy Spacek), from her backwoods childhood to her success. Martin Scorsese's *Raging Bull* offered an uncompromisingly tough look at the disintegrating life of middleweight champion Jake La Motta (Robert De Niro). And *The Elephant Man* probed the life of John Merrick (John Hurt), the grossly deformed victim of neurofibromatosis, in the context of nineteenth-century Victorian society. It was also the first year in which both lead acting awards, to De Niro and Spacek, honored contemporary personalities; Jake La Motta and Loretta Lynn were guests of honor at the ceremonies.

In addition to favoring biographical over fictional features and real-life over fictional personalities, the Academy has given priority to some specific genres while overlooking or underestimating others. The concept of genre is used here as a classificatory system, grouping together films of similar narrative conventions, plots, situations, and characters. All Oscar nominated films are divided into eight genres: action-adventure, comedy, serious-problem drama, historical epic, musical, suspense-mystery, war, and Western.[5]

The most dominant genres among the Oscar-winning films have been serious drama (41 percent) and historical epic (15 percent). Comedy and musical (each 11 percent), war films (10 percent), action-adventure (5 percent), suspense and Western films (each 2 percent) have been less frequent. The rank order of the nominated films by genre is similar to that of the winning films, with a few exceptions. Musicals, historical epics, and war films have been more prominent among the winners than among the nominees. And conversely, serious films, adventures, comedies, suspense, and Westerns have been slightly underrepresented among the winners. But the differences are not big, showing that the same types of films have been nominated and won awards.

The Serious-Problem Film

The most dominant and most respected genre in the Oscar competition for Best Picture has been the serious-problem film. Twenty-five (41 percent) of the Oscar-winning, and 141 (46 percent) of the nominated pictures have been serious dramas dealing with "important" issues. The greatest representation of this genre in the Oscar contest was in the 1930s and 1940s, over half of the nominated films in each decade, and the weakest in the 1960s, with only one-third.

What marks the serious-problem film is its great reliance on other literary sources, mostly best-sellers. With one major exception, in the 1950s, the primary source for the Hollywood problem picture was the Broadway theater. Three of Tennessee Williams's stage hits, for example, were nominated for Best Picture: *A Streetcar Named Desire* in 1951, *The Rose Tattoo* in 1955, and *Cat on a Hot Tin Roof* in 1958. Indeed, the impact of Broadway on Hollywood was apparent in every film genre. Most film musicals, in the 1950s and in later decades, originated on the New York stage, such as *The King and I* in 1956, and *Gigi* in 1958. Along with stage plays, some television dramas were made into films, like *Marty* in 1955, *Twelve Angry Men* in 1957, and *Judgment at Nuremberg* in 1961.

The serious-problem films are intimately connected with the social and political contexts in which they are made, reflecting timely, relevant issues. As such, they also tend to appear in cycles whose duration is about three to five years. For example, in the late 1940s, Hollywood produced a cycle of films dealing with racial prejudice and discrimination, two of which were nominated, *Crossfire* and *Gentleman's Agreement*. In the late 1960s, there was a cycle of films about the position of blacks in America, such as *In the Heat of the Night* and *Sounder*. And in 1979, *Kramer Vs. Kramer* launched a cycle of serious family dramas, which included *Ordinary People* and *On Golden Pond*.

Because the number of serious-problem films is very large and it is impossible to describe each one of them, this genre is classified in terms of the films' chief domain and specific concerns. There seem to be three basic types of problem films. The first includes films dealing with the *domestic* or private arena whose primary concerns are love, marriage, and the family. The second type concerns the *public* domain, focusing on the workplace, career problems, and portraits of various occupations. And the third type consists of movies about the *political* arena, concerned with societal issues, such as wars, crime and violence, poverty, and racial discrimination. These three are pure types, however, and in actuality many films are hybrids, like *domestic-public* films, dealing with both private and public lives, conflict between work and the family, tension between career and marriage. Or films dealing with both *domestic and political* problems, like the impact of war and politics on individual behavior, marriage, and the family.

Most nominated films, as could be expected, have been about

domestic-public or domestic-political issues; few have been concerned with strictly public or political themes. This is characteristic of the American cinema in general, not just of the nominated pictures. Even a committed political filmmaker on the order of Costa-Gavras understands that to attract large publics to "message" films, they must deal with some personal and emotional problems. The two Costa-Gavras Oscar-nominated films, *Z* in 1969 and *Missing* in 1982, are good examples of political films that deliver their strong ideological messages through personal stories.

The Serious Woman's Film

There are significant differences between problem pictures that contain male and female roles. Most female-nominated roles have been in the domestic type of film known as "the woman's film," because it features a woman as protagonist and is specifically designed for female audiences. These films were very popular in the 1940s, and some were nominated for Best Picture.

Bette Davis distinguished herself in such vehicles. In William Wyler's *Jezebel* (1938), a romantic melodrama of the Old South, advertised by Warners as "Half-angel, half-siren, all-woman," she won an award for playing a Southern belle. Edmund Goulding's *Dark Victory*, with a screenplay by Casey Robinson about a society girl who discovers she is dying of a brain tumor, was one of the most popular films of 1939, earning Best Picture and Best Actress nominations. And *All This and Heaven Too* (1940), based on Rachel Field's book about the love of a nineteenth-century married French nobleman (Charles Boyer) and his governess (Davis), was also nominated but did not win any awards.

In the same year, William Wyler's *The Letter*, a remake of the 1929 film based on Somerset Maugham's tale of an adulteress wife (Davis) who shoots her lover in a jealous rage, was marked by a distinctive visual style, and was nominated for Best Picture and six other awards. The wonderful role of Leslie Crosbie had been played on stage by Katharine Cornell and by Jeanne Eagles in the first film version; both Eagles and Davis were nominated for it, though neither won. Wyler cast Davis again, as the conniving and greedy Regina Giddens, in Lillian Hellman's *The Little Foxes* (1941), which was nominated for nine but did not win any awards.

None of the so-called woman's pictures has ever won the Oscar

Award, and after the 1940s few were nominated. The only two Oscar-winning films that come close to this genre, featuring strong women as their heroines and dealing with women's problems, were *Grand Hotel* and *All About Eve*, though neither was a typical woman's film.

Based on Vicki Baum's novel, adapted to the screen by William A. Drake, *Grand Hotel* was a MGM prestige production, winning the 1931/32 Best Picture. It featured an all-star cast, demonstrating that MGM had indeed "more stars than in heaven." And there were *five* star performances, each exhibiting his or her particular screen persona, though best of all were Greta Garbo, as the fading dancer, and John Barrymore, as the declining nobleman. Their scenes together were the strongest in the film; some of Garbo's lines, like "I want to be alone," became forever identified with her screen image. Also good were Joan Crawford, as a determined secretary, Wallace Beery, as her brutish tycoon-employer, and Lionel Barrymore, as a pathetic dying man. The movie, as a whole, lacks coherence; it's too much of a patchwork, with each star having a "big scene," but audiences apparently did not mind; it was the top money-maker of the year. Viewed from today's perspective, *Grand Hotel* still serves as an example for a type of film that "Hollywood does not make anymore."

Grand Hotel competed against seven other movies, including John Ford's *Arrowsmith*, King Vidor's *The Champ*, *One Hour with You*, codirected by George Cukor and Ernst Lubitsch, and Josef Von Sternberg's *Shanghai Express*. Strangely enough, none of *Grand Hotel*'s star players or director, Edmund Goulding, was nominated. It is one of the three Oscar-winning films to have received only one award.[6] At present, the tendency is for a few films to get a large number of nominations and awards, but in the 1930s and 1940s, the votes were spread among a larger number of pictures.

In contrast to *Grand Hotel*, the 1950 Oscar-winning *All About Eve* received the largest-ever number of nominations, fourteen, winning six awards. Joseph L. Mankiewicz won two Oscars, as writer (original screenplay) and director. George Sanders won the Supporting Actor Oscar, as the acerbic drama critic, Edith Head and Charles LeMaire won black-and-white costume design, and W. D. Flick and Roger Heman won best sound recording. Its two leading ladies, Bette Davis and Anne Baxter, were nominated, but did not win (see chapter eight).

All About Eve's major competitor that year was Billy Wilder's *Sunset Boulevard*, a dark probing of the film industry that contrasted the old and the new Hollywood through the relationship of a fading, demented silent queen, played by Gloria Swanson, and a young gigolo-writer, played by William Holden. Neither film was very successful at the box office when initially released; each made less than three million dollars in domestic rentals.[7] However, both have acquired cult status over the years and for the same reasons —the star performances of Davis in *Eve* and Swanson in *Sunset*. And, of course, their witty, campy dialogue, with such lines as Davis exclaiming, "Fasten your seat belts, it's going to be a bumpy night," or Swanson telling Holden, "They don't make faces like that anymore," or better, "I'm still big. It's the pictures that got small."

Nominated features with strong female protagonists have usually dealt with show business, like *Stage Door* and *A Star Is Born*, both in 1937. Gregory La Cava's *Stage Door*, nominated for four Oscars, describes a group of would-be actresses living in a theatrical boarding house, all anxious to get their "big break." Katharine Hepburn, playing one of her rich girls, and Ginger Rogers have the best parts in an all-female cast that included Eve Arden, Lucille Ball, and Ann Miller. Andrea Leeds was the only one to be nominated, for playing a woman who, after waiting for a whole year for "the one role," commits suicide. Like *All About Eve* and *Sunset Boulevard*, it has become a cult film over the years, with such memorable lines as Hepburn declaring: "If I can act I want the world to know it, but if I can't act, *I* want to know it."

Along with Bette Davis and Katharine Hepburn, Greer Garson was the third female star to appear in prestige films nominated for Oscars. Indeed, only one of the other Oscar-winning films up to 1950 features a woman as its heroine, played by Greer Garson in *Mrs. Miniver*. Garson was MGM's most respected star and Louis B. Mayer's favorite actress, for whom he chose the best vehicles. No other MGM actress has enjoyed as complete a support of the studio as Garson. From 1939 to 1943, five of her movies were nominated, all serious dramas. She was introduced to the American public in Sam Wood's 1939 *Goodbye Mr. Chips*, as the actress who humanizes the public-school teacher, rescuing him from failure. In Mervyn LeRoy's *Blossoms in the Dust* in 1941, based on Anita Loos's script, playing the child welfare crusader Edna Gladney, she exclaimed: "There are no illegitimate children; there are only illegitimate parents!" And in 1943 she recreated the life of the noted French scientist in *Madame Curie*, one of the more distorted biopictures of the era.

Except for the three aforementioned women, few of the leading female stars made films that were nominated for Best Picture. Rosalind Russell and Barbara Stanwyck, for example, received their nominations for films that, for one reason or another, were not considered "Oscar stuff." Stanwyck received her first nomination for playing the self-sacrificing mother in King Vidor's *Stella Dallas* (1937), a prototype of the woman's film, and her second, as the striptease queen in Howard Hawk's *Ball of Fire* (1941); neither film was nominated. And Russell first won the Academy recognition for the comedy *My Sister Eileen* (1942), then for the biopicture *Sister Kenny* (1946), as the woman who devoted her life to get the medical profession's approval of her unorthodox method of treating infantile paralysis.

What is more revealing about the status of the "woman's" film, and the screen roles allotted to women, is the weak correlation between the Best Picture and the Best Actress awards—in sharp contrast to the awards for Best Actor. Only eleven of the sixty male-winning roles were contained in films that were *not* nominated for Best Picture, compared to twenty-two of the sixty-one female-winning roles.[8] This was particularly apparent during the heyday of the studio system. For example, Mary Pickford (*Coquette*), Marie Dressler (*Min and Bill*), Helen Hayes (*The Sin of Madelon Claudet*), Katharine Hepburn (*Morning Glory*), Bette Davis (*Dangerous*), Olivia De Havilland (*To Each His Own*), and Loretta Young (*The Farmer's Daughter*), all won awards for roles that were *not* contained in Oscar-nominated films.

This shows that the movies that featured these strong female roles were not considered good enough to compete for Best Picture. And further, that films nominated for Best Picture featured no, or few, lead roles for women. Films with women as their protagonists were probably not taken as seriously by the Academy as those featuring men. Indeed, up to the late 1970s, there was a strong correlation between the Best Picture and Best Actor—but not Actress—awards.

The Problem-Message Film—Race, Politics, and Crime

More male than female-winning roles were in the genre of the serious-problem film, attesting to the prestigious status of both films and male performances. The overwhelming majority of Best Actor roles were contained in message films that propagated dominant values and dealt with important political issues.

For example, Warners' *The Life of Emile Zola* was nominated for the largest number of awards in 1937, ten, and won three: film, screenplay, and supporting actor to Joseph Schildkraut, in the role of the wrongly accused Captain Alfred Dreyfus. Had Paul Muni not won the previous year for another biopicture, *The Story of Louis Pasteur*, he would have received it for his portrayal of the French writer, who exposed anti-Semitism in the French government. Reviewing *Emil Zola*, one critic suggested that "Along with *Louis Pasteur*, it ought to start a new category—the Warner crusading films, costume division."[9] Nine other movies competed with *Emil Zola* in 1937, including Leo McCarey's marital comedy *The Awful Truth* with six nominations, and Gregory La Cava's *Stage Door*, with four. The other nominees were: William Wyler's social drama set in a New York city slum, *Dead End*, Frank Capra's utopian comedy *Lost Horizon*, and Henry King's adventure *In Old Chicago*.

The political crusading drama reappeared in the late 1940s, when Hollywood devoted its efforts to exploring racial discrimination, first against Jews, then against blacks and Indians. The 1947 winning film was Elia Kazan's *Gentleman's Agreement*, baesd on Laura Z. Hobson's novel, adapted to the screen by Moss Hart. Gregory Peck plays a crusading journalist, who decides to pose as a Jew in order to experience, first hand, racial prejudice. Like most serious films, it also has a romance, here with the daughter (Dorothy McGuire) of Peck's publisher, who turns out to be slightly bigoted herself. The film is preachy, particularly in the lengthy dialogues between Peck and a Jewish military captain (John Garfield), who has just returned from occupied Germany. But it was praised by most critics, with one finding it to be "more savagely arresting and properly resolved as a picture than it was as a book," and describing its script as "electric with honest rapportage."[10] *Gentleman's Agreement* won two other awards, for director Kazan, and for its supporting actress, Celeste Holm, who has the film's most pungent lines.

Its major competitor was Edward Dmytryk's *Crossfire*, which lost in each of its five nominated categories. Its nominated screenplay, by John Paxton, was based on Richard Brooks's novel *The Brick Foxhole*, though in a typically Hollywood manner it changed the book's homosexual hero into a Jew. In retrospect, *Crossfire* is a better film than *Gentleman's Agreement* in every aspect: theme, characterization, acting, and visual style. Dealing with racial bigotry, it was directed by Dmytryk as a tense noir thriller about an obsessive, psychopathic sergeant (Robert Ryan, who specialized in this kind of role), who beats a Jewish ex-sergeant to death. Detective Finlay (Robert Young), helped by Sergeant Keely (Robert Mitchum) sets out to trap the killer. Like *Gentleman's Agreement*, it is a heavy message film, with many speeches against prejudice, but it boasts great acting by Ryan and Gloria Grahame, as a floozy dance-hall girl; both were nominated for supporting awards.

That *Gentleman's Agreement* was voted Best Picture for ideological, not artistic, considerations is clear not only from its win over *Crossfire*, but also from its win over David Lean's materpiece, *Great Expectations*. However, the Academy could not ignore *Great Expectation*'s cinematic innovations and honored its black-and-white cinematography and art direction and set decoration. Yet the Academy proved that when weighing a film's content against its style, the former counts more.

None of the late 1940s films dealing with racial prejudice against blacks or Indians was nominated for Best Picture. Stanley Kramer's 1949 *Home of the Brave* started this cycle, which was followed by two other films released in the same year, *Intruder in the Dust* and *Pinky*. Directed by Kazan, *Pinky*, one of the first films about racial identity, was singled out for its acting, nominating all three of its female performers: Jeanne Crain, as a light-skinned black trying to pass for white; Ethel Waters, as her benign grandmother; and Ethel Barrymore, as an old Southern matriarch. Considered at the time a "courageous" film because of its subject matter, it was not the first nominated film about white-black relations. That place is reserved for the first version of *Imitation of Life*, starring Claudette Colbert and Louise Beaver, though this 1934 film was a lone voice.

Sidney Lumet's first feature film, *Twelve Angry Men*, was nominated for the 1957 Best Picture, but did not win the award. A courtroom drama, it is confined to a jury room, where twelve jurors debate the fate of a black boy accused of murdering his father. In the course of the drama, Henry Fonda, as the liberal Juror No. 8, succeeds in reversing the majority's opinion. In the following year, Stanley Kramer's *The Defiant Ones* was more successful, critically and commercially. Nominated for Best Picture, it tells the story of two escaped convicts in the South, one black (Sidney Poitier), the other white (Tony Curtis), forced to spend their short-lived freedom together because they are chained by the wrist. *The Defiant Ones* was cited as Best Picture by the New York Film Critics Circle and won two Oscars, for story and for black-and-white cinematography.

Otto Preminger's *Anatomy of a Murder* and Robert Mulligan's *To Kill a Mockingbird* were nominated in 1959 and 1962 respectively. Among other things, *Anatomy* contains one of the longest trial scenes in film history, over an hour, in which James Stewart's small-town lawyer defends a white army lieutenant (Ben Gazzara), accused of killing a black tavern owner for allegedly raping his wife (Lee Remick). Universal's *To Kill a Mockingbird* featured more prominently in the Oscar race than *Anatomy*, which did not win any award. Based on Harper Lee's Pulitzer Prize novel, it cast Gregory Peck in his Oscar-winning role as a widowed liberal lawyer, defending a black man against a rape accusation in a Southern town rampant with prejudice. Peck, in a perfectly suitable role, concentrated all his acting energies on the courtroom scene, the most powerful in the film, a nine-minute close-up speech, delivered to the jury (i.e., the audience). In addition to Best Actor, *To Kill a Mockingbird* won a screenplay award for Horton Foote, and black-and-white art direction and set decoration.

For unaccountable reasons—other than its "noble" subject matter—Ralph Nelson's *Lilies of the Field*, was nominated for five awards in 1963. It won, however, only Best Actor for Sidney Poitier, as Homer Smith, an ex-GI light-hearted handyman who helps a group of nuns from behind the Iron Curtain build a chapel in the Arizona desert. Poitier thus became the first black actor to win an Oscar for a leading role and the second black, following Hattie McDaniel as supporting actress in *Gone with the Wind*, ever to win an Oscar.[11] Black players and films about racial prejudice left their most impressive mark in 1967, with the release of three films all starring Sidney Poitier: *To Sir with Love, Guess Who's Coming to Dinner?* and *In the Heat of the Night*. Consequently, Poitier became the first black actor to be selected as the most popular star in America in 1968.[12]

All of a sudden, black was not only beautiful, but also good business at the box office. The Academy showered both *Guess Who's Coming to Dinner?* and *In the Heat of the Night* with multiple nominations and awards. A flawed comedy, *Guess* tells the story of a liberal couple (Spencer Tracy and Katharine Hepburn), he a publisher and she an art gallery owner, whose value system is challenged when their only daughter (Katharine Houghton) announces one day her intention to marry a famous black surgeon (Poitier). Nominated for ten Oscars, it won two: Best Actress to Hepburn, and screenplay and story.

Norman Jewison's *In the Heat of the Night* is the only problem film about racial discrimination against blacks to have won Best Picture, though later pictures with similar issues, like Martin Ritt's *Sounder* in 1972, and *A Soldier's Story* in 1984, also directed by Norman Jewison, were nominated. But in 1967, the timing was "right" to honor a topical film, and *In the Heat of the Night*, about the collaboration of a bigoted police chief (Rod Steiger) and a black homicide detective (Poitier), won five Oscars, including Best Actor for Steiger. Of the nominated films that year, the best was Arthur Penn's *Bonnie and Clyde*, a revolutionary film in more senses than one. But its glamorizing attitude toward the two gangster characters, and the fact that it was made by the New Hollywood—Warren Beatty served as producer and star—all worked against it. To think that the Academy honored *In the Heat* for best editing and sound over the amazing achievements in these areas in *Bonnie and Clyde* is still shocking.

In addition to racial prejudice, serious winning films have dealt with other societal issues, such as social adjustment to a changing society, abuse of political power, corruption, the loneliness of urban life, and crime. Each of the winning films was a representative, not always the best, of a larger cycle.

The Best Years of Our Lives was the most honored film in 1946, receiving the largest number of awards to date, seven regular and two Special Oscars. It captured the mood of postwar America so effectively and so realistically that even the more critical reviewers failed to see its flaws at the time. Independent producer Samuel Goldwyn, who released the film through RKO, was allegedly inspired by an article in *Time* magazine of August 7, 1944, recounting the story of war veterans coming home. He commissioned MacKinlay Kantor to write a screenplay, which was first published as a book, *Glory for Me*, then adapted to the screen by Robert Sherwood. Released on November 21, 1946, it was still a relevant subject, with many Americans struggling with readjustment to civilian life after the war.

James Agee wrote a rave review, describing *The Best Years* as "profoundly pleasing, moving and encouraging." He particularly liked its script, which was "well differentiated, efficient, free of tricks of snap and punch and over-design," and its visual style of "great force, simplicity and beauty" in many scenes.[13] Wyler's direction of *The Best Years* was described by Agee as being "of great purity, directness and warmth, about as cleanly devoid of mannerisms, haste, superfluous motion, aesthetic or emotional overreaching." And it was photographed by Gregg Toland in black and white, stressing long shots, deep-focus, and crisp images. The acting was also superb, particularly by Fredric March, who won a second Oscar for his mentally anguished banking executive and ex-sergeant, who realizes that in his absence his family—and society as well—have tremendously changed.

All the King's Men, a political drama about the corruptive nature of excessive power and the danger of populist dictatorship in America, won the 1949 award. Broderick Crawford won Best Actor as Willie Stark, a self-styled demagogue, who starts as a self-made lawyer from rural Louisiana and ends up establishing a corrupt political empire that results in his assassination. Mercedes McCambridge won supporting actress as his tough, unscrupulous secretary-mistress. The film drew on Robert Penn Warren's 1946 Pulitzer-winning book about the life of Southern Senator Huey "Kingfish" Long. *All the King's Men* competed against four other films, each critical of some aspect of American life: two realistic analyses of men at war, *Battleground* and *Twelve O'Clock High*; a tale of a greedy courtship, *The Heiress*; and an examination of middle-class marriage and suburban life, *A Letter to Three Wives*.

James Jones's *From Here to Eternity*, about the public and private lives in an Army base, was a best-seller before Fred Zinnemann adapted it to the screen. Set in Hawaii prior to the Pearl Harbor attack, it captures the essence of military life in all its complexity and detail, centering on the conflict between individualism, embodied by Montgomery Clift's Private Prewitt, and rigid institutional authority, represented by the Army. Prewitt refuses to fight for the unit's team despite promises for rewards and then pressures from his officer, having once blinded a man in the ring. A stubborn yet decent soldier, he admires the Army, but is unwilling to compromise his notion that "if a man don't go his own way, he's nothin'," which sums up the film's message as well as director Zinnemann's favorite cinematic theme (see chapter 7). Daniel Taradash's fine screenplay contains half a dozen sharply etched characterizations, including Burt Lancaster's Sergeant Warden, an efficient but human officer; Clift's Prewitt, an inner-directed man, guided by his own code of ethics; Frank Sinatra's Maggio, the cocky but honest Italian-American soldier; Deborah Kerr's Karen Holmes, the frustrated adulterous wife married to a weakling (Philip Ober), and Donna Reed's Alma, a dance-hall hostess.

Zinnemann's direction was restrained but excellent, bringing to the surface the film's issues which, as Pauline Kael observed, represented new attitudes on the American screen that touched a social nerve. Indeed, *From Here to Eternity* is genuinely honest in treating career problems, personal frustrations, and most important of all sexuality—the sexually charged beach scene with Lancaster and Kerr was highly daring and innovative at the time and is still interesting to watch. *From Here to Eternity* was nominated in 1953 along with two historical features, *Julius Caesar* and *The Robe*, George Steven's classic Western *Shane*, and William Wyler's elegant comedy *Roman Holiday*, its serious competitor. Nominated in thirteen categories, it won eight, the largest number of awards for a film since *Gone with the Wind*. "The industry which voted the honors now merits an appreciative nod,"[14] wrote Bosley Crowther with enthusiasm, having convinced his colleagues earlier to honor the film, director Zinnemann, and actor Lancaster with the New York Film Critics Awards. The casting and acting by each of the performers was perfect, partly due to the fact that Zinnemann rehearsed the entire film with props, an uncommon practice in Hollywood, which gave the actors a sense of continuity. All five players were nominated, with Burt Lancaster and Montgomery Clift canceling each other out as Best Actors (the winner was William Holden in *Stalag 17*), but the film honored its two supporting players: Frank Sinatra and Donna Reed.

Political corruption, this time in the context of labor unions, was also the topic of Elia Kazan's *On the Waterfront*, the 1954 winner. The film works both as an exposé of union racketeering and as a thriller, involving the murder of an innocent longshoreman. Filmed on location, *On the Waterfront* was photographed in black and white, almost documentary style (Boris Kaufman won an Oscar), which was perfect for its realistic subject matter and commonplace characters. Marlon Brando won Best Actor for one of his most touching performances as Terry Malloy, an ex-prizefighter, who is transformed, with the assistance of his girl (Eva Marie Saint) and the neighborhood's priest (Karl Malden), from a passive dock worker into an active fighter of corruption in trade unionism. The film won eight Oscars, for director Kazan, supporting actress Saint, story and screenplay (Budd Schulberg), art direction, and editing. The only category in which it lost was Supporting Actor, probably because three roles were nominated, each wonderfully acted. Rod Steiger was nominated for playing Brando's brother, an opportunistic lawyer working for the arrogant racketeer-boss, a crooked monarch of the docks, played by Lee J. Cobb, who was also nominated. And Karl Malden was nominated for his militant Father Barry.

Much has been written about Kazan as a friendly witness, testifying twice before the HUAC in 1952, in which he repudiated his leftist past and named names. The movie itself has been interpreted as a "McCarthy film" in favor of informing,[15] though the analogy between informing on Communists and informing on corrupt crooks is quite problematic. But the movie is powerful and enjoyable without this ideological reading, and it would have won Oscars regardless of its politics, considering the poor competition in 1954: a court drama based on Herman Wouk's *The Caine Mutiny*, starring Humphrey Bogart; Clifford Odets's backstage melodrama *The Country Girl*, starring Bing Crosby, Grace Kelly, and William Holden; MGM's musical *Seven Brides for Seven Brothers*, starring Jane Powell and Howard Keel; and the romantic comedy *Three Coins in the Fountain*. *On the Waterfront* was not only superior to its competitors, but also the only film not based on another literary source and, along with *The Caine Mutiny*, the only serious film dealing with a contemporary issue.

In the late 1960s, the urban crime drama, which had been very popular during the depression, reemerged. *Midnight Cowboy*, John Schlesinger's 1969 Oscar winner, is a touching tale of a strange friendship between Joe Buck (Jon Voight), a good-looking, uneducated and naive Texan, who under the influence of radio and television commercials fancies himself to be a stud, and Ratso Rizzo (Dustin Hoffman), a sickly, crippled poor drifter. The film captured the ambience of night life at Times Square and its alienated, lonely creatures, but perpetuated the myth of New York as a big, sleazy, dehumanized, impersonal city. The acting of Voight and

Hoffman was superb, both were nominated, and the screenplay (Waldo Salt won an Oscar), based on James Leo Herlihy's novel, was witty and sharp. *Midnight Cowboy* surprised audiences with its candid view of sex and daring dialogue—though by today's standards, it is conservative and mild.

The phenomenal success of *Bonnie and Clyde* revived interest in the crime-gangster film. More crime films were nominated in the 1970s than in any previous decade, and three won Best Picture: the action-thriller *The French Connection*, and the two Francis Ford Coppola crime sagas, *The Godfather* in 1972, and *The Godfather, Part Two* in 1974. Of the two, *The Godfather* was more critically acclaimed and more popular, grossing over eighty million dollars in rentals. But it was less honored by the Academy, winning a second Best Actor for Marlon Brando, as Mafia don Vito Corleone, and screenplay, written by Coppola in collaboration with Mario Puzo, upon whose best-seller it was based. Its major competitor in 1972 was Bob Fosse's musical *Cabaret*, which captured the largest number of awards, eight, including Best Director. The two *Godfathers* broke new grounds in several ways. They are still the only crime-gangster movies to have ever won Best Picture. And *Part II*, which won the largest number of awards in 1974, six, is the only movie sequel to have ever received an Oscar.

The Problem-Message Film—Individual and Family

Problem films have also dealt with personal issues, such as alcoholism, physical deformities of deafness and blindness, and mental anguish and insanity.

Billy Wilder's *The Lost Weekend*, which won the 1945 Oscar, is important because it was the first major Hollywood film about alcoholism. Prior to that, alcoholics in film were either comic or secondary characters—but never heroes. *The Lost Weekend* depicts the inner degradation and torment of Don Birnbaum (Ray Milland) who, unable to realize his writing ambitions, turns to the bottle. Despite a stark portrayal of alcoholism in all its misery and horror, the changes made in the adaptation of Charles Jackson's novel to the screen are instructive because they shed light on Hollywood's morality standards at the time and on the conventions of portraying screen heroes. In the book, Birnbaum's frustration derives from an indecisive sexuality—he is a troubled bisexual—whereas in the film he suffers from a writer's creative block. And the picture also changed the book's ending by providing a solution to his drinking problem, using the ploy of a patient, loving girl (Jane Wyman) who helps to regenerate him.

The Lost Weekend had earlier won the New York Critics Award, then under the leadership of Bosley Crowther, who found its "most commendable distinction" in being "a straight objective report, unvarnished with editorial comment or temperance morality."[16] *The Lost Weekend* won over Hitchcock's *Spellbound* and Leo McCarey's *The Bells of St. Mary's*, both starring Ingrid Bergman. And surprisingly, it appealed to large audiences, ranking as the ninth most popular film of the year.

Suffering and victimization have been almost exclusively the domain of women in the American cinema, as the Oscar-winning performances of Jane Wyman's deaf-mute girl in *Johnny Belinda*, Joanne Woodward's schizophrenic Eve in *The Three Faces of Eve*, and Patty Duke's blind-deaf Helen Keller in *The Miracle Worker* demonstrate. But it was due to the success of *The Lost Weekend* that pictures about mental illness and insanity could be made. Anatole Litvak's *The Snake Pit*, nominated for the 1948 Oscar, was a rather faithful adaptation of Mary Jane Ward's partly autobiographic novel about the harrowing experiences of a mentally ill woman (Olivia De Havilland) in an asylum. Considered at the time a breakthrough film because of its realistic treatment of insanity, it was honored with six nominations.

Hollywood has usually been very careful in its treatment of mental problems, for fear of alienating movie patrons. However, one such movie, *One Flew Over the Cuckoo's Nest*, the Oscar winner of 1975, was so popular that it even shocked its filmmakers, producers Saul Zaentz and Michael Douglas, and director Milos Forman. Ken Kesey's 1962 novel, which was first adapted for the stage, enjoyed some popularity, but it is Jack Nicholson's flamboyant performance, as Randle Patrick McMurphy, a bright, free-spirited, antiestablishment hero, that made all the difference. Further, the film's conflict between individualistic, nonconformist behavior (Nicholson's) and the repressive established society, represented by Nurse Ratched (Louise Fletcher), the head of the mental ward, was absorbed by younger audiences as timely and relevant. Vincent Canby singled out the film's comic scenes, which he thought were the best, and the fact that Forman did not patronize the patients as freaks, but presented them as variations of "ourselves," ordinary citizens.[17] Whatever the specific cause, *One Flew Over the Cuckoo's Nest* won all five major Oscars and became the most widely seen problem film, grossing in rentals over fifty million dollars, ranking second to Spielberg's *Jaws* among the year's blockbusters.

The family is probably one of the most sacred and most revered institutions in American culture, but family dramas, like other serious pictures, have appeared in cycles. *Cavalcade*, the Oscar winner of 1932/3, was Fox's most prestigious production to date. Based on Noel Coward's play, adapted to the screen by Reginald Berkeley, it is a tale of an upper-class British family, spanning thirty years, beginning on New Year's Eve in 1899, and continuing through the Boer War, the sinking of the *Titanic*, World War I, and the depression. Diana Wynyard gave a wonderful (nominated) performance as the strong mother who loses both of her sons in tragic circumstances. *Cavalcade* won over nine other pictures, including *Forty-Second Street*, *I Am a Fugitive from a Chain Gang*, *Little Women*, and *The Private Life of Henry VIII*.

The next Oscar-winning family drama was John Ford's 1941 *How Green Was My Valley*, which, like *Cavalcade*, had been a smash hit at the box office even before earning a nomination. But unlike *Cavalcade*, it celebrates what Bosley Crowther described as "the majesty of plain people," and "the beauty which shines in the souls of simple, honest folk."[18] Indeed, it reaffirmed Ford's populist ideology, propagated the year before in another Oscar-nominated family saga, *The Grapes of Wrath*. However, *How Green* was not associated with the leftist, angry politics of John Steinbeck's book. The story of a Welsh mining family narrated by its youngest son, it is one of Ford's most beautiful, if sentimental, pictures. Andrew Sarris has described *How Green* as an elegiac poem, and it was; its portrayal of the disintegration of a mining community is of epic, heroic dimensions.

It won five Oscars, honoring Ford's direction, Arthur Miller's cinematography, and art direction. Sara Allgood was nominated for her gentle mother, and Donald Crisp won supporting award for his stern father, killed in the mine. Not to be underestimated is the fact that the film was selected while the US was already involved in the war. Its warm, sympathetic depiction of family unity must have hit deep chords in the country's collective consciousness, which may explain, at least in part, why its two major competitors,

Orson Welles's masterpiece debut *Citizen Kane* and William Wyler's *The Little Foxes*, each with nine nominations, lost. Both were dark, somber visions of the American family, particularly *Foxes*. Once again, content and ideological approach counted, though Ford's *How Green* was as visually distinguished as thematically acceptable (see chapter 12).

If Ford's *How Green* was one of the most pictorially stunning celebrations of ordinary life, the next winning film about ordinary, "little people," *Marty*, was possibly the most pedestrian—intellectually as well as emotionally. The competition in 1955 was one of the weakest in the history of the award. What better sign than the fact that three of the five nominees were mediocre screen adaptations of Broadway's stage hits, *Mister Roberts*, *Picnic*, and *The Rose Tattoo*; *Marty* was based on Paddy Chayefsky's television play. The fifth nominee was the romantic melodrama, *Love Is a Many Splendored Thing*. In this case, movie politics, rather than societal politics, might give a clue as to why *Marty* was favored over the other films. It was the first American picture to win the Golden Palm at the Cannes festival, a fact that apparently could not be ignored by the Academy or the critics; *Marty* also won the New York Film Critics Award.

Marty is the love story of its eponymous hero, a thirty-four-year-old lonely bachelor-butcher from the Bronx (Ernest Borgnine), and Clara, a shy teacher (Betsy Blair), following their meeting in a dance hall. Filmed in the Bronx, its American-Italian locale is described with meticulous attention. But the screenplay patronizes its little, lonely protagonists, an attitude demonstrated in the scene in which Marty assures Clara, "You're not really as much of a dog as you think you are." Nominated for eight awards, *Marty* won four: film, director Delbert Mann, writer Chayefsky, and actor Borgnine. The Oscar was not much help at the box office; *Marty* is still one of the least commercial of all Oscar-winning films.

Two decades later, an unemployed actor named Sylvester Stallone took some of *Marty*'s ideas, mixed them with conventions of the sports-prizefighting genre (*The Champ*, *Golden Boy*, *Champion*, and *Somebody up There Likes Me*), and came up with the formulaic *Rocky*. This movie proved the impossible by becoming the first, but not last, sports film to win the Best Picture of 1976; *Chariots of Fire* was the second. *Rocky* and *Bound for Glory*, the biopicture of singer-labor organizer Woody Guthrie, featured as the weakest nominees of 1976. Each of the others was far more interesting. Alan Pakula's *All the President's Men*, produced by Robert Redford, was a good political thriller about the Watergate scandal, based on the best-seller by two *Washington Post* reporters, Carl Bernstein (Dustin Hoffman) and Bob Woodward (Robert Redford). Sidney Lumet made an outrageous farce, *Network*, about the potential power of television; for some reason many people took it as serious drama. And Martin Scorsese followed up his *Mean Streets* with *Taxi Driver*, a film about political and social alienation, embodied by Robert De Niro in a grand performance. Of the five, *Rocky*'s message, the rise to stardom of an obscure "nobody," which paralleled both the actor's life offscreen and President Jimmy Carter's 1976 election, was the most upbeat and the least controversial. But it was also the most befitting of the nation's mood in its Bicentennial celebrations.

The impact of *Rocky*'s success is still felt by the American public. The film made Stallone the most popular star and the most dominant male image in the 1980s, surpassing the powerful persona of Clint Eastwood's *Dirty Harry* films. And it also led to three sequels of the Rocky Balboa saga, which raises two questions: Will *Rocky IV* be the last part of the series? And, if not, who will Rocky fight next? After defeating the Russian champion and being cheered up by the entire Soviet Union—what else is left?

Rocky was not a family drama, but a romance between Rocky and Adrian, a shy, plain salesclerk (Talia Shire), whom he later marries; it was conducted along the movie lines of Marty and Clara in *Marty*. Moreover, it paved the way to the making and acceptance of other conventional, old-fashioned, movies about ordinary families and ordinary folks. After being saturated for a decade with the action-adventure "disaster" film the American public seemed to turn to such fare. Moviegoers must have noticed that the family had almost disappeared from American films for most of the 1970s. And the last major pictures to have dealt with marriage and the family were mostly negative portrayals, like Mike Nichols's two nominated features, *Who's Afraid of Virginia Woolf?* and *The Graduate*.

The reentrance of family drama into film was gradual, with such romantic melodramas as *The Turning Point* and Paul Mazursky's socially relevant comedy *An Unmarried Woman*. But it was Robert Benton's *Kramer Vs. Kramer*, the 1979 Oscar winner, that gave legitimacy and definition to the new cycle of family pictures. The cycle lasted about four years, the average duration of such, during which two other films won, *Ordinary People* and *Terms of Endearment*, and five others were nominated, *Breaking Away, Coal Miner's Daughter, On Golden Pond, Tender Mercies,* and *Places in the Heart.* Each of these movies was loaded with human messages, the most important of which was the centrality and strength of the American family. And some, like *Tender Mercies* and *Places in the Heart,* were imbued with Christian morality of love, togetherness, and forgiveness.

Like other films that started cycles, no one associated with *Kramer's* production initially expected such an extraordinary success, and the film's carefully designed advertising campaign, using different posters for different target audiences, proves this point. Nonetheless, based on Avery Corman's novel, it was a timely film, describing the confusion of many women who wanted to establish a firm identity, independent of their roles as wives-mothers. Beautifully shot on location in Manhattan, it featured a great cast, headed by Dustin Hoffman and Meryl Streep as the splitting couple, Justin Henry as their son, and Jane Alexander as their sympathetic neighbor. All four were nominated for their performances, with Hoffman and Streep winning.

In 1980, a year after *Kramer's* release, Robert Redford made a stunning directorial debut in *Ordinary People,* adapted to the screen by Alvin Sargent from Judith Guest's novel about the disintegration of an upper-middle-class suburban family that, following an accidental death of one son and a suicide attempt of another, is unable to communicate its feelings and deal with its strains. *Ordinary People* was emotionally effective, but decidedly unsentimental. Redford's direction was restrained and tremendously supported by an excellent cast, with Donald Sutherland as the sympathetic father, Mary Tyler Moore, as the undemonstrative, extremely controlled mother, Timothy Hutton, as the surviving troubled youngster (who won an Oscar), and Judd Hirsch as the understanding Jewish psychiatrist.

At first sight, Dustin Hoffman's award for *Kramer,* and his second Oscar, for *Rain Man,* have nothing in common but high-caliber acting. However, thematically both films celebrate the sanctity of the American family. Indeed, the immense success of the 1988 Oscar-winning *Rain Man* could be attributed to its ideological message. In this case, the rediscovery of love between two brothers: an autistic savant (Hoffman) and a young hustler (Tom Cruise), a fast-talking car salesman. At first, the younger brother wants to rob his older of the inheritance his father has left. However, he gradually gets to know his brother, of whose existence he has been completely ignorant, and both realize that they not only love but also need each other. Blending conventions of the comedy-drama and road film, *Rain Man* propagated mainstream family values of the 1980s. The public embraced the film even before it was nominated for eight awards—and won four.

Comedy Films

The second most prevalent genre among the Oscar films has been comedy: eight (13 percent) of the sixty-one winning and fifty-six (18 percent) of the 306 nominated pictures. Thus, comedies have amounted to 17 percent of all 367 nominated pictures. Compared with the number of comedies produced, this genre has been under-represented among the winning and nominated films. The Academy has displayed its biases not only against comedy films, but also against comedic performances and performers.

It took seven years for the first comedy to win Best Picture: Frank Capra's *It Happened One Night* (1934). And it won by surprise, for it was directed by a relatively unknown director and produced by a lesser studio (Columbia Pictures). *It Happened One Night* held a record for forty-one years as the only film to capture all five major awards: film, director, actor (Clark Gable), actress (Claudette Colbert) and screenplay (Robert Riskin). A "road" comedy, it describes the romance between a runaway heiress (Colbert) and a tough reporter (Gable) who, having been fired by his editor, plans a comeback by getting the exclusive story of her rebellious flight to marry a man her family does not approve of.

The picture was rooted in the context of the depression, embodying the values of upward mobility, ambition, individual success, and romantic love. But *It Happened One Night* was influential in other ways. It is credited with exerting tremendous impact on the fashion industry. When Gable took off his shirt and exposed a bare chest, the sale of undershirts is reported to have substantially declined. The film also affected domestic tourism; the number of women traveling by bus increased tremendously.

The second winning comedy was also directed by Capra for Columbia Pictures, *You Can't Take It with You* (1938), based on George S. Kaufman and Moss Hart's Pulitzer Prize stage hit, and adapted to the screen by Robert Riskin. A zany comedy, about a madcap family believing in free enterprise, each member is dedicated to his awards, winning two: film and director. It boasts a large excellent cast, of which only Spring Byington was nominated for a supporting role, as Penny, the eccentric mother who starts writing endless plays when a typewriter is left at her house by mistake. Strangely enough, Jimmy Stewart and Jean Arthur, as the romantic couple, Lionel Barrymore as the charming grandfather, and Edward Arnold, as the stuffy millionaire, were not singled out for their wonderful acting.

In the 1940s, the only Oscar-winning comedy was *Going My Way* (1944), directed by Leo McCarey and starring Bing Crosby, as a progressive priest who turns a group of young delinquents into a choir, and Barry Fitzgerald, as the old and irascible priest, still attached to his ninety-year-old mother. Both Crosby and Fitzgerald won acting awards, the former in the lead and the latter in the supporting category. *Going My Way* was the only nominated comedy in 1944; the other nominees were two noir pictures, *Double Indemnity* and *Gaslight*, and two patriotic fares, *Since You Went Away* and *Wilson*. Sweeping seven Oscars, *Going My Way* proved to be the sentimental favorite of the public too, ranking as the top grossing film of the year.

No comedy won Best Picture in the 1950s, but two were cited by the Academy in the 1960s: Billy Wilder's comedy-drama, *The Apartment*, and Tony Richardson's adventure-comedy *Tom Jones*. Among other distinctions, *The Apartment* (1960) is the last black-and-white film to win Best Picture. Excessive and disjointed, it is not one of Wilder's best, though it offers some biting comments on the world of big business, the ethos of success and getting ahead, and adultery, one of the most consistent themes in the director's oeuvre. The acting of Jack Lemmon, as the ambitious, upwardly mobile IBM operator, and particularly of Shirley MacLaine, as the elevator woman, was superb; both were nominated, though neither won. But the film lacks a clear point of view, vacillating between sympathy and pity for its protagonists. It opened to mixed reviews, ranging from outright rejection, with critic Dwight MacDonald describing it as "without either style or taste,"[19] to moderate praise. Hollis Alpert regarded the film as a "dirty fairy tale, with a shnook for a hero, and a sad little elevator operator for a fairy princess."[20] But 1960 was not a particularly strong year, which may have accounted for its winning. *The Apartment* is also one of the few winners whose Oscar was not much help at the box office.[21]

By contrast, *Tom Jones* was a commercial success prior to winning the 1963 Oscar and an extraordinary smash hit afterward. It is easily one of the most popular films of the entire decade. As was mentioned, it was the first all-British film to win the Oscar since *Hamlet* in 1948, making its star, Albert Finney, a household name in the United States. Based on Henry Fielding's famous novel, which was adapted to the screen by playwright John Osborne (winning an Oscar), it features Finney as the adventurous, amorous illegitimate son of a servant in eighteenth-century England. All three supporting women were nominated for their superb work: Dame Edith Evans, as the intrepid aunt; Diane Cilento, as the wild gatekeeper's daughter; and best of all Joyce Redman, as a lady of easy virtue, who seduces the hero over a large meal; the seduction is probably the picture's best-remembered scene. The production values were very high in every department: cinematography by Walter Lassally (which won), editing, and musical score. Influenced by the French New Wave, Richardson used his camera in a jazzy and dynamic manner. *Tom Jones* was far superior to all the other nominees: *America, America, Cleopatra, How the West Was Won,* and *Lilies of the Field.*

The choice of the next winning comedy, George Roy Hill's *The Sting* (1973) was controversial and the Academy found itself under severe attack by its more serious critics. Cashing in on his previous success, the comedy Western *Butch Cassidy and the Sundance Kid,* the director reteamed its stars, Paul Newman and Robert Redford, in a depression-era comedy set in Chicago, about the elaborate scam of two con men (Newman and Redford) against a big-time racketeer (Robert Shaw). Released to mostly good reviews, *The Sting* grossed an immense amount of money, ranking twentieth on *Variety's* list of all-time film champions. The film has a lot of charm, and its music —Scott Joplin's piano rags, adapted by Marvin Hamlisch—became immensely popular throughout the country. Still, many felt that such a commercial blockbuster should not have been nominated for an Oscar in the first place, let alone win.

Woody Allen's comedy with autobiographical overtones, *Annie Hall* (1977), is a bitter-sweet, introspective look at the unstable affair between Alvin Singer (Allen), a Jewish, anxiety-ridden comic, and Annie Hall (Diane Keaton), a WASPish insecure singer. It is funny and serious at the same time, free-wheeling and self-reflective, with Allen addressing the audiences directly in witty monologues. The contrast between the Jewish and the Gentile ways of life is also extremely poignant. *Annie Hall* established Allen, with the assistance of the award, as a major director and also became his most popular film to date. Competing against two Herbert Ross's films, *The Goodbye Girl* and *The Turning Point*, Lucas's *Star Wars*, and Zinnemann's *Julia*, the Academy honored *Annie Hall* with four awards out of its five nominations: film, director, original screenplay, co-written by Allen and Marshall Brickman, and actress Diane Keaton; the fifth nomination was for Allen as an actor. It is Allen's only film to be nominated for Best Picture; *Manhattan* was unaccountably ignored in 1979, though it is expected that *Hannah and Her Sisters* would be nominated for the 1986 award.

The last comedy to win an Oscar was James Brooks's *Terms of Endearment* (1983), basically a television situation comedy expanded for the big screen. Brooks's triple win, as producer, writer, and director, was an astonishing achievement considering the fact that the screenplay had been turned down by several studios before Paramount decided to finance it. In its sentimental tone and traditional view of women, *Terms of Endearment* resembled many old-fashioned, well-made movies. However, most audiences enjoyed the honest, loving relationship between a possessive mother (Shirley MacLaine) and her daughter (Debra Winger), and especially the amusing sexual encounters between MacLaine's middle-aged widow and her boozy ex-astronaut neighbor (Jack Nicholson). The film's candid honesty toward sexuality in middle age was highly refreshing, and its release at a time when most Hollywood movies were either action-adventure or teenage movies explains its acclaim by the Academy and its huge popularity with the public.

It's hard to detect specific patterns for the nomination of comedies because in every decade many are made, though few excel. Still, the largest number (sixteen) of comedies was nominated in the 1930s, arguably the golden age of comedies in the sound era. Indeed, every brand of comedy was nominated in this decade, including Mae West's 1933 sex farce *She Done Him Wrong*, which would not have been nominated a year later because of the Production Code. In 1934, the most popular of the nominated films was MGM's comedy-mystery, *The Thin Man*, which made William Powell and Myrna Loy big movie stars and also role models for many married couples across the nation. Charles Laughton gave a wonderful performance in Leo McCarey's 1935 political comedy *Ruggles of Red Gap*, which contrasted values of British aristocracy and American democracy. McCarey was also represented in the contest with the sophisticated marital comedy, *The Awful Truth* (1937), starring Cary Grant and Irene Dunne. MGM's female stars also distinguished themselves in comedies: Jean Harlowe in *Libeled Lady* (1936), and Greta Garbo in Ernst Lubitsch's romantic comedy, *Ninotchka* (1939).

Of the comedies nominated in the 1940s, some stood out. One such was MGM's *The Philadelphia Story* (1940), starring Katharine Hepburn in one of her really great performances, assisted by James Stewart and Cary Grant. In the same year, Charlie Chaplin's *The Great Dictator*, in which he plays a dual role, Adenoid Hynkel, the dictator of Tomania (standing in for Hitler), and the little Jewish ghetto barber, won recognition as both slapstick comedy and political satire.

Columbia's *Here Comes Mr. Jordan* won the two writing awards of 1941, original story and screenplay, recounting a fantasy in which a prizefighter (Robert Montgomery) is sent by mistake to heaven and then back to earth in search of a new body. Extremely popular at the time, this film later served as the inspiration for Warren Beatty's blockbuster *Heaven Can Wait*, winning a 1978 nomination for Best Picture. The original *Heaven Can Wait* (1943), was a Lubitsch account of family life in the nineteenth century, with gorgeous sets and costumes. In the same year, George Stevens's *The More the Merrier*, a war comedy about housing conditions in Washington, starred Jean Arthur as a civil servant renting her small apartment to an old gentleman (Charles Coburn) who in turn rents it to an attractive young man (Joel McCrea); Coburn won a supporting Oscar for his elderly, daffy millionaire, and Arthur was nominated for Best Actress.

Not many comedies were nominated in the 1950s. The most popular, by commercial appeal, was the service comedy *Mister Roberts* (1955), starring Henry Fonda in his best-known screen role, as the first officer on the *Reluctant*, a cargo ship miles away from the battle zone, whose route is described by him as "from Tedium to Apathy, and back again, with an occasional side trip to Monotony." The war is close to an end, and Roberts is anxious to get into combat before it is too late, which he does. Fonda's performance was unaccountably ignored by the Academy in a shameful oversight. By contrast, Jack Lemmon's Ensign Pulver, a flighty fellow assigned to the ship's laundry, won him his first (supporting) Oscar.

Rosalind Russell, like Fonda, recreated her successful stage role in the 1958 film version *Auntie Mame*; with over nine million dollars in domestic rentals, it outgrossed the box-office receipts of the Oscar winner that year, *Gigi*.

The most distinguished of the 1950s nominated comedies was George Cukor's *Born Yesterday* (1950), based on Garson Kanin's stage play, in which Judy Holliday's dumb-shrewd blonde Billie Dawn is victimized by a rough, rude junk dealer (Broderick Crawford) and educated by a sensitive Washington correspondent (William Holden). The first part of the picture is better and funnier than the second; many wished her character did not have to be socialized, for the romantic, "educational" sessions with Holden are not very interesting. The appeal of *Born Yesterday* was also due in part to its political message, the attempt of a scrap metal dealer to bribe a bill through Congress and the successful fight of a not-very-bright individual against political corruption, which was timely after World War II, condemning the dealers who profited from the war economy; Arthur Miller dealt with a similar issue in *All My Sons*, first as a Broadway play, then a Hollywood movie.

The decade also had its share of romantic comedies. William Wyler's *Roman Holiday* (1953), starring Audrey Hepburn as a European princess and Gregory Peck as an American reporter, was stylized and elegant and featured location shooting, albeit in black and white. In the following year, the Academy nominated Twentieth Century-Fox's romantic comedy, *Three Coins in the Fountain*, also set in Rome, which received an award for its sumptuous color cinematography of Rome. It also won Best Song, by Sammy Cohn and Jules Styne, which contributed a lot to the film's popularity, demonstrating, like *High Noon*'s ballad before, how useful a good song can be to the marketing of a movie.

The comedies nominated in the 1960s were of great variability and originality. In 1964, Stanley Kubrick's black comedy, *Doctor Strangelove, Or How I Learned to Stop Worrying and Love the Bomb*, was ahead of its time in its antinuclear message, depicting military generals as irresponsible puppets, enamored with their limitless power. Peter Sellers excelled in three widely contrasting roles: the United States President, a British RAF Captain, and best of all a mad German scientist, whose heavy accent was inspired by physicist Edward Teller. The film was relatively popular with audiences, though not as much as *Mary Poppins*, which was also nominated in

1964. It must have been a good year for comedies, for a third nominee was Michael Cacoyannis's *Zorba the Greek*, based on Nikos Kazantzakis's popular novel. Anthony Quinn was cast in what became his best-known role, the commonsensical, garrulous force of virility and vitality, contrasted in the picture with Alan Bates's civilized Englishman.

Toward the end of the decade, two sociological comedies, reflecting the ideological concerns of their times—youth and ethnicity—were nominated. Mike Nichols's second feature, *The Graduate*, was nominated for seven awards, and won only Best Director. But it legitimized the youth counterculture and the generation gap through the nonconformist Benjamin Braddock, played to perfection by Dustin Hoffman. The other 1967 nominated comedy was Stanley Kramer's *Guess Who's Coming to Dinner?*, one of Hollywood's first films about interracial marriage. Both pictures aimed at younger film audiences, and both were stronger in ideas than in artistic execution, which is the reason why neither, particularly *Guess*, holds up well.

The 1970s were not good years for screen comedies, judging from the few nominated films. George Lucas's nostalgic view of youth, *American Graffiti*, set in California in 1962, was used as a metaphor of "what we once had and lost." Made on a shoe string budget, it soon became the sleeper of 1973, launching a whole cycle of rock 'n' roll high school movies. But as the decade came to an end, more comedies were made and more were nominated. Paul Mazurski's *An Unmarried Woman* (1978), starring Jill Clayburgh, was a timely comedy that reflected the changing position of women. This cycle of comedies about changing gender roles continued into the 1980s. Of these Sydney Pollack's *Tootsie* (1982) was probably the best and also the most (ten) nominated. This witty situation comedy, written by Larry Gelbart and Murray Schisgal, is not only funny but also provides commentary about love, sex, friendship, and even television. It stars Dustin Hoffman as Dorothy Michaels, a middle-aged unemployed actor, who becomes daytime television's most popular star after disguising himself as a woman. Each member of the cast played to the hilt, and four received nominations: Hoffman; Terry Garr, as his unemployed and rejected girlfriend; Jessica Lange, as the submissive, sexy actress; and Charles Durning, as Lange's widowed father who falls in love with Hoffman.

Lack of Respect for Comedy Players

Perhaps more revealing than the underrepresentation of winning comedy films is the Academy's lack of respect for comedic performances that, for some reason, are considered to be "easy." Unlike other genres, there have been no differences between the frequency of male and female performers in comedy. Here the crucial variable is the category, with more supporting than leading performances in comedies. Indeed, leading players have seldom won an Oscar for a comic role. For example, following Audrey Hepburn's award for *Roman Holiday*, it took twenty years until the next woman won for a comedy—Glenda Jackson in *A Touch of Class*. Male winning performances in comedies have not been much more visible: no Best Actor won for a comic role between Jimmy Stewart's gossip columnist in *The Philadelphia Story* back in 1940 and Lee Marvin in *Cat Ballou*, a quarter of a century later.

Supporting performances in comedies have been more frequent and usually more distinguished. For instance, Peter Ustinov won a second supporting Oscar for playing a petty con man, talked into a robbery in Jules Dassin's *Topkapi* (1964). His misadventures, as a tourist guide afraid of his own shadow, were the best scenes in the movie. George Burns also excelled in Neil Simon's *The Sunshine Boys* (1975), as a veteran vaudevillian reunited with his old partner (Walter Matthau) after many decades. Of the female supporting comedians, Josephine Hull gave a great performance in *Harvey* (1950), as Jimmy Stewart's distraught, scatter brained sister, ending up in a mental institution she had intended for him. And Eileen Heckart received a supporting award as the overbearing, overprotective mother of her blind son in *Butterflies Are Free* (1972).

That comedy as a genre has been overlooked by the Academy is also reflected in the unfair representation of comedy writers-directors. Take Charlie Chaplin, whose contribution to the genre is undisputable. Of his major works, only *The Great Dictator* was nominated for Best Picture, though it did not win any award. His masterpieces, *The Circus* (1928), *City Lights* (1931), and *Modern Times* (1936), failed to win nominations. Chaplin was nominated twice as Best Actor, for *The Circus* and for *The Great Dictator*, losing on both occasions.

Preston Sturges, another extraordinary comedy filmmaker, won only one Oscar, best original screenplay, for his first film as director, *The Great McGinty* (1940). But despite originality, urbane sophistication, and a biting sense of humor, none of his comedies were nominated for Best Picture or other major awards, though at least three deserved serious consideration: *Sullivan's Travels* (1941), *The Palm Beach Story* (1942), and *Hail the Conquering Hero* (1944).

None of the "classical" clowns has ever won a legitimate Oscar or even a nomination. True, most of them did their best work in the silent era, prior to the age of Oscars, but even those who contributed to the genre later were overlooked by the Academy. In addition to Chaplin, the two other members of the "clowns' triumvirate," Harold Lloyd and Buster Keaton, were also ignored by the Academy, which later awarded Honorary Oscars as corrective measures. In 1952, Lloyd was awarded a Special Oscar as "a master comedian and good citizen." Unlike Lloyd, Buster Keaton made some excellent comedies in the sound era, when he was under contract at MGM, *Cameraman* (1928), and *Spite Marriage* (1929), but he never won the Academy recognition. Once again, a 1959 Special Oscar cited Keaton, the "king of comedy," for his "unique talents which brought comedies to the screen."

A most popular comedy team, Oliver Hardy and Stan Laurel, were also underrated during their creative careers. Joining forces in 1926, Laurel and Hardy delighted audiences with their inventive acts for two decades. In 1960, three years after Hardy's death from cancer, the Academy honored the surviving member, Laurel, who had refused to perform after his colleague's death, with an Oscar "for his creative pioneering in the field of cinema comedy."

The Academy's bias against comedic performances was also apparent in the case of players who excelled in comedies, but had to deviate from this genre to win the Academy's respect. The best example of these players is Cary Grant, who distinguished himself in romantic as well as screwball comedies. It was comedy, beginning with *The Awful Truth*, that made him a big star. The public preferred to see him in comedies, the best of which were those opposite Katharine Hepburn (*Bringing Up Baby*, *Holiday*) and Rosalind Russell (*His Girl Friday*), neither of which brought him a nomination. Grant had to step outside of his specialty to earn his two nominations. The first for a sentimental melodrama, *Penny Serenade* (1941), as a married man who loses his adopted daughter, and the second for a "serious-dramatic" role in Odets's *None but the Lonely Heart* (1944), as a Cockney drifter. No other actor of Grant's generation contributed more to screen comedy, but he was "victim" of the Academy's wrong notion that his acting looked "easy" and "effortless," while in actuality it was a product of hard work and meticulous preparation. It took many years and many talents to perfect the genius at timing, spontaneity, and naturalness, in which Grant, Carole Lombard, Claudette Colbert, and others excelled. The Academy "corrected" this injustice by honoring Grant with a 1969 compensatory Oscar "for his unique mastery of the art of film acting."

Jack Lemmon's awards also demonstrate the favoring of "serious" over comedy acting. Lemmon began his screen career in high comedies, often cast opposite Judy Holliday (*It Should Happened to You*, *Phfft*). He later became the quintessential Billy Wilder actor, appearing in seven of his films, including *Some Like It Hot* (his first lead nomination) and *The Apartment* (his second). The Neil Simon comedies *The Odd Couple* and *The Prisoner of Second Avenue* further established him as a foremost comedian. Ironically, Lemmon received his great acting accolades for straight, "dramatic" performances; first for his alcoholic in *Days of Wine and Roses* (1962), the breakthrough of his career for which he earned a nomination. And Lemmon won his Best Actor (and second) Oscar for *Save the Tiger* (1973), a film about the moral disintegration of a garment manufacturer who, in financial desperation, resorts to arson. The self-pity of the character and his disenchantment with the American values system for some reason made his acting appear more "serious" and more "substantial."

The underestimation of comedy performers is not exclusive to the Academy. Other film associations have also failed to honor comedy films and performers. Neither Cary Grant nor Jack Lemmon has ever won a New York Film Critics Circle Award, for example. And Steve Martin, honored in 1984 by the New York Film Critics and the National Society of Film Critics for his excellent physical comedy in *All of Me*, has been the exception rather than the rule. Indeed, most performers know when they are cast in comedies that they may be popular with the public but won't get recognition from the Academy. Julie Walters's reaction to her nomination for *Educating Rita*, in which she played a hairdresser anxious to achieve education, was: "I won't win. They don't tend to give Oscars for comedy."[22] The Golden Globes and the Tony Awards distinguish between comedy and drama for this specific reason—to make sure that comedy as a genre will get its fair representation and due respect. Paradoxically, by doing so they also increase the number of awards, thus diminishing their relative meaning and prestige.

Wings, the first film ever to win Best Picture (1927/28), receiving a second Oscar for engineering effects. Its spectacular aerial sequences and running time (136 minutes) set a trend favoring grand-scale, epic films. (Courtesy of The Museum of Modern Art/ Film Stills Archive)

The Broadway Melody, MGM's first musical and the Academy's first winning musical (1928/29). (Courtesy of The Museum of Modern Art/Film Stills Archive)

Cimarron, the only Western ever to win Best Picture (1930/31). (Courtesy of The Museum of Modern Art/Film Stills Archive)

Greta Garbo and John Barrymore in *Grand Hotel*, the 1931/32 Best Picture and the only Oscar winner to be nominated in one category. The two legendary players never won an Oscar Award. (Courtesy of The Museum of Modern Art/Film Stills Archive)

Clark Gable and Claudette Colbert in Frank Capra's *It Happened One Night* (1934), the first comedy to win Best Picture and the first film to sweep all five major awards. (Courtesy of The Museum of Modern Art/Film Stills Archive)

Charles Laughton and Clark Gable in *Mutiny on the Bounty* (1935), the only film to contain three Best Actor nominations; the third was Franchot Tone. (Courtesy of The Museum of Modern Art/Film Stills Archive)

Vivien Leigh and Hattie McDaniel in *Gone with the Wind*, the 1939 Best Picture, sweeping eight competitive and one Special award. McDaniel became the first black actress to be honored with an Oscar. (Courtesy of The Museum of Modern Art/Film Stills Archive)

Rebecca (1940), the only suspense-thriller to win Best Picture. Its famous director, Alfred Hitchcock, was nominated five times, but never won a regular Oscar. (Courtesy of The Museum of Modern Art/Film Stills Archive)

Mrs. Miniver (1942), the first film to be nominated for 12 awards, winning six, including Best Picture. One of William Wyler's less impressive features, it won for ideological rather than artistic considerations. The Best Actress for Greer Garson (left) typecast her for the rest of her career as a gentle, civilized lady. (Courtesy of The Museum of Modern Art/Film Stills Archive)

Casablanca, the 1943 Best Picture, features Humphrey Bogart (right) in his best-known role, as Rick Blain, the most famous cafe owner in film history. Bogart should have won an acting award, but did not. (Courtesy of The Museum of Modern Art/Film Stills Archive)

Ray Milland in *The Lost Weekend* (1945), Billy Wilder's first Oscar-winner and Hollywood's first major film about alcoholism; Milland won Best Actor for playing an alcoholic writer. (Courtesy of The Museum of Modern Art/Film Stills Archive)

Fredric March (right), Harold Russell (left), and Dana Andrews (back) in *The Best Years of Our Lives*, the 1946 Best Picture and one of the greatest social problem films. March won his second Best Actor Oscar, and Russell received two awards, Supporting Actor and a Special Oscar. (Courtesy of The Museum of Modern Art/Film Stills Archive)

Gregory Peck at his best, a liberal crusading journalist in Elia Kazan's 1947 Oscar-winning *A Gentleman's Agreement*. It was Peck's third nominated performance. (Courtesy of The Museum of Modern Art/Film Stills Archive)

Broderick Crawford (left), Mercedes McCambridge, and John Ireland in the 1949 Best Picture, *All the King's Men*, a serious warning against political corruption and demagogery. Its director, Robert Rossen, was blacklisted during the McCarthy era. (Courtesy of The Museum of Modern Art/Film Stills Archive)

A "meaningful" look between Bette Davis (left) and Anne Baxter (right), as the "aging" and "rising" actresses, watched by George Sanders (right) and Gary Merrill in *All About Eve*, the 1950 Best Picture, the most nominated (fourteen) film in the Academy's history, and the first to feature two Best Actress nominations. (Courtesy of The Museum of Modern Art/Film Stills Archive)

Marlon Brando (center) finally won an Oscar at his fourth nomination for *On the Waterfront* (1954), which was also named Best Picture and honored Eva Marie Saint with a supporting award. It was the first film to feature three supporting actor nominations, all of whom lost. (Courtesy of The Museum of Modern Art/Film Stills Archive)

The chariot race in the blockbuster *Ben-Hur* (1959), the only remake to win Best Picture and the only film to win eleven awards. (Courtesy of The Museum of Modern Art/Film Stills Archive)

Rita Moreno, the only Hispanic player to win an Oscar (Supporting Actress), in a production number from the musical *West Side Story* (1961), which won Best Picture and nine other awards. Her award typecast her as a "Latin spitfire" for over a decade. (Courtesy of The Museum of Modern Art/Film Stills Archive)

Peter O'Toole should have won an Oscar for his performance in David Lean's historical epic *Lawrence of Arabia*, the 1962 Best Picture, but did not. With seven nominations, all in the lead category, O'Toole is the greatest loser of the Academy. (Courtesy of The Museum of Modern Art/Film Stills Archive)

My Fair Lady, the 1964 Best Picture: Rex Harrison (right) received the Best Actor award, Wilfrid Hyde-White (left) a supporting nomination. Audrey Hepburn was ignored by the Academy, which resented the fact that Julie Andrews, who created the role on stage, was not cast by Warners. (Courtesy of The Museum of Modern Art/Film Stills Archive)

Paul Scofield (right) was honored as Best Actor for his noble portrayal of Sir Thomas More in *A Man for All Seasons*, the 1966 Oscar winner. Robert Shaw was nominated as supporting actor for his eccentric interpretation of King Henry VIII. (Courtesy of The Museum of Modern Art/Film Stills Archive)

In the Heat of the Night (1967), one of the least distinguished Oscar winners, featured good performances by Rod Steiger (right), who won Best Actor, and Sidney Poitier (left), and set a trend for films celebrating male friendship. (Courtesy of The Museum of Modern Art/Film Stills Archive)

Dustin Hoffman (right) and Jon Voight (left) cancelled each other out as Best Actor nominees in John Schlesinger's *Midnight Cowboy*, the 1969 Best Picture about friendship in sleazy and impersonal New York City. (Courtesy of The Museum of Modern Art/Film Stills Archive)

George C. Scott shocked the film world when he refused his nomination for *Patton* (1970), but his colleagues honored him as Best Actor and the film as Best Picture. One thing was beyond doubt: the brilliance of Scott's acting. (Courtesy of The Museum of Modern Art/Film Stills Archive)

Francis Ford Coppola's crime saga, *The Godfather* and *The Godfather, Part II*, won Best Picture of 1972 and 1974 respectively. Marlon Brando (Best Actor, 1972) and Robert De Niro (Supporting Actor, 1974) won the award for playing the same character, Don Vito Corleone in different ages. (Courtesy of The Museum of Modern Art/Film Stills Archive)

Films about mental illness and asylums were never big box office until Milos Forman's *One Flew Over the Cuckoo's Nest* (1975), winning Best Picture, Best Actor (Jack Nicholson), and Best Actress (Louise Fletcher). (Courtesy of The Museum of Modern Art/Film Stills Archive)

Annie Hall, the 1977 Oscar-winning comedy, established its heroine, Diane Keaton, as a household word and its director, Woody Allen, as one of America's foremost directors. (Courtesy of The Museum of Modern Art/Film Stills Archive)

Robert Benton's *Kramer vs. Kramer*, the 1979 Oscar winner, summed up the changes in gender roles, male and female, of the decade. Dustin Hoffman won Best Actor, and Justin Henry's supporting nomination made him the youngest nominee in the Academy's history. (Courtesy of The Museum of Modern Art/Film Stills Archive)

Terms of Endearment (1983), the last comedy to win Best Picture, was popular with the public because of its honest treatment of sexuality among the middle-aged and relationship between mother and daughter. The acting of Shirley MacLaine (Best Actress) and Jack Nicholson (Supporting Actor) was superb. (Courtesy of The Museum of Modern Art/Film Stills Archive)

CHAPTER 7

The Oscar-Winning Films— Other Genres

Musical Films

Musical films have been overrepresented in the Best Picture category: eight (13 percent) of all winning films. Musicals featured most impressively during the depression: about half of all nominated musicals were made in the 1930s. By contrast, the weakest representation of musicals was in the 1940s, with only two nominees: *Yankee Doodle Dandy* and *Anchors Aweigh*. Ironically, the 1940s are considered to be the heyday of musicals in the American cinema. Indeed, there is no connection between the number or quality of musicals made and their representation in the Oscar Award. For example, more musicals won in the 1960s than in any other decade, despite the fact that not many were made. It seems that as the genre declined in production, it gained in prestige, and the Academy members showed their respect for the effort of making musicals by honoring more of them. Hollywood was not willing to take risks with new ideas and subsequently most of the nominated musicals from the 1950s on were based on Broadway smash hits, with a few exceptions, such as *Seven Brides for Seven Brothers* (1954) and *Mary Poppins* (1964).

The first winning musical, *The Broadway Melody* (1928/9), was MGM's first musical and also the first talking film to be honored by the Academy. Advertised as "All Talking, All Singing, All Dancing," it also featured the technological innovation of color. One number, "The Wedding of the Painted Doll," was presented in two colors. A backstage musical, it is the tale of two sisters (Bessie Love and Anita Page), who seek fame in the New York theater, and in the process fall in love with the same song-and-dance man. By today's standards, the story and characters are cliché-ridden because they have been used so many times, but in 1929, the novelty of sound, color, and form proved winning. And the nominated performance of Bessie Love, as the older, wiser sister who sacrifices herself for her sister's career, was truly excellent. A big-budget film, close to half a million dollars, *The Broadway Melody* opened to rave reviews, soon becoming the second[1] top money-maker of the season, with three million dollars in domestic rentals.

The Broadway Melody was such a big box-office hit that MGM made three more "Broadway Melody" films, of which *The Broadway Melody of 1936*, released in 1935, is considered to be the best, and is one of the few sequels to be nominated for Best Picture. The supporting cast, particularly Jack Benny, as the columnist, and June Knight, as a no-talent who wants to become an actress, was more impressive than the leads, played by Robert Taylor and Eleanor Powell. But the movie won one Oscar: dance direction for David Gould's sequence, "I've Got a Feeling You're Foolin'."

In the 1930s, most studios produced musicals, each developing its own distinctive style. In addition to "the Broadway Melody" films, MGM was represented in the Oscar with *The Great Ziegfeld* (1936), the second Oscar-winning musical, and later with *The Wizard of Oz* (1939). Paramount participated with a number of sophisticated operettas, marked with "the Lubitsch touch," such as *The Love Parade* (1929), *The Smiling Lieutenant* (1931), and *One Hour with You* (1934), all starring Maurice Chevalier. RKO left its imprint on the musical map of the decade with the fabulous dancing of Fred Astaire and Ginger Rogers; two of their musicals were nominated: *The Gay Divorcee* (1934) and *Top Hat* (1935).

Of Warner Brothers' major musicals during the depression, only one was nominated, *Forty-Second Street* (1933), with Warner Baxter, Ruby Keeler, and Dick Powell, though it did not win any award. Harry Cohn, head of Columbia Pictures, was not in favor of making musicals, yet having Grace Moore, the Metropolitan Opera diva, under contract inspired him to make *One Night of Love* (1934), a variation on the Svengali theme. Moore, in the role of the rising star, was also nominated, and the film won sound recording and music score. *Alexander's Ragtime Band* (1938), Twentieth Century-Fox's big-scale musical, with a wonderful score by Irving Berlin and a cast headed by Tyrone Power, Alice Faye, and Don Ameche, also received a nomination for Best Picture and an award for Alfred Newman's musical direction.

In the 1940s and 1950s, MGM dominated the musical genre in the Oscar Award. Of the six nominated musicals, four were produced by MGM, two of which won. *An American in Paris*, George Gershwin's musical about the romance of a young American painter (Gene Kelly) and a poor French girl (Leslie Caron), was the big winner of 1951, with six Oscars, for story and screenplay (Alan Jay Lerner), scoring of a musical (Johnny Green and Saul Chaplin) and several technical awards. The second winning musical was MGM's *Gigi* (1958), based on Colette's story, also set in Paris and also starring Leslie Caron as a shy girl who becomes an elegant lady. Combining French charm with the American tradition of film musicals, *Gigi* won the largest number (nine) of awards to date, including direction (Vincent Minnelli), screenplay (Alan Jay Lerner), and color cinematography (Joseph Ruttenberg).

Paradoxically, more musicals won Best Picture in the 1960s, when the genre was in severe decline, than in any other decade. Four of the ten Best Pictures in the 1960s were musicals: United Artist's *West Side Story* (1961), Warners' *My Fair Lady* (1964), Twentieth Century-Fox's *The Sound of Music* (1965), and Columbia's *Oliver!* (1968), a British-made movie. All four musicals were based on Broadway hits, but in each one of them a major cast change was involved, the most publicized of which was the casting of Audrey Hepburn as Eliza Doolittle, a role played with great success by Julie Andrews on the stage.

Each of these winning musicals is some kind of a landmark in the history of the genre and of the Academy. Transporting Shakespeare's *Romeo and Juliet* to the slums of New York and boasting great music by Leonard Bernstein and lyrics by Stephen Sondheim, *West Side Story* is the only winner in the Academy's history to receive awards in all (ten) but one area in which it was nominated. Further, it is the only winner to be codirected; Robert Wise and Jerome Robbins shared the directorial award. It still ranks second, next to *Ben-Hur*, as the most Oscar-honored film.

The stylized and elegant *My Fair Lady*, nominated for twelve awards and winning eight, was selected in 1964, a year that saw the decline of the great classic musical and the rise of a new type, beginning with Richard Lester's *A Hard Day's Night*, starring the Beatles. George Cukor, who won an Oscar, directed an opulent production in grand manner and with fabulous costumes, designed by Cecil Beaton. With the conspicuous omission of Audrey Hepburn in the lead (chapter 9), its three British players, Rex Harrison, Stanley Holloway (as Alfred P. Doolittle), and Gladys Cooper (as Mrs. Higgins) were nominated, and Harrison deservedly won. *My Fair Lady* won over another musical, *Mary Poppins*, the only Walt Disney production to ever be nominated for the top award, but was much less commercially successful than the latter.

By contrast, the immense success of the 1965 winner, Robert Wise's *The Sound of Music* is still a desirable goal to repeat for every studio in Hollywood. Winning five of its ten nominations, it is, along with *Gone with the Wind*, one of the two most commercial Oscar winners, grossing in rentals close to eighty million dollars. Based on Howard Lindsay and Russel Crouse's long-running Broadway musical, with highly melodic music by Richard Rodgers and Oscar Hammerstein II, it represented Hollywood's approach to filmmaking at its most conservative and most calculating. Set in Austria in 1938, the narrative consists of old-fashioned and stilted devices, each aiming to appeal to a different segment of the movie-going public. Advertised as an entertainment for all the family and a genuine celebration of life, it is high corn, though not camp. At the center of the story is the motherless Von Trapp family of seven children, headed by Christopher Plummer, which becomes a troupe of singers under the benevolence of Maria, the nun-turned-governess (Julie Andrews), in order to elude the Nazis and successfully escape to Switzerland and then to America. The movie includes, most shrewdly, two generational romances: Plummer and his haughty baroness (played by Eleanor Parker in an embarrassing performance), whom he later deserts for the simple but maternal Andrews; and a youthful romance. And it cherishes the moral strength of the family and the benevolence of religion, placed in a political setting imbued with anti-Nazist feelings and, more importantly, filmed in a stunning landscape, the Austrian Alps and Salzburg.

The Sound of Music was not only mechanically made, but most shrewdly packaged and sold to the public. It was deliberately released in March, while Julie Andrews was the talk of the town following *Mary Poppins* and when it became clear that she would be the Best Actress winner for this film in the awards ceremonies scheduled for April. Indeed, her win made *The Sound of Music* even more popular at the box office. The competition for Best Picture in 1965 was rather weak. Stanley Kramer's flawed *Ship of Fools* and the screen adaptation of the Broadway comedy *A Thousand Clowns* had no chance in the final balloting, and the other two contenders were made by British directors, David Lean's *Doctor Zhivago*, a romantic historical spectacle, and John Schlesinger's *Darling*, clearly the most interesting and most innovative of the five nominees, singled out earlier by the New York Film Critics. For most Academy members the choice thus boiled down between *The Sound of Music* and *Doctor Zhivago*, which interestingly each received ten nominations. The awards were also equally divided, with each movie getting five; with the exception of screenplay (Robert Bolt), *Doctor Zhivago* received mostly technical and music awards.

Twentieth-Century-Fox hoped to repeat the success story of *The Sound of Music* with two subsequent musicals that were poorly conceived and executed: *Doctor Dolittle* (1967), starring Rex Harrison, and *Hello Dolly* (1969), starring Barbra Streisand. These movies received multiple nominations, *Dolittle* nine and *Dolly* seven, not because of their merits but because of extensive, shameless publicity campaigns (chapter 12). From the 1970s to the present, only three musicals have been nominated for Best Picture: *Fiddler on the Roof* (1971), *Cabaret* (1972), and *All That Jazz* (1979). Michael Apted's *Coal Miner's Daughter* (1980), was a biopicture of country singer Loretta Lynn rather than a conventional musical. Similarly, *Amadeus*, the 1984 winner, was at once more and less than a genre musical, though one of its greatest achievements was the integration of Mozart's music into the narrative.

Up to the 1950s, the filmmakers of the winning musicals were not honored by the Academy for their direction. For example, Vincente Minnelli was nominated, but did not win, for *An American in Paris*; the winner was George Stevens for *A Place in the Sun*. Minnelli won his first and only directorial Oscar for *Gigi*, at his second nomination. By contrast, all the directors of the winning musicals in the 1960s received an Oscar, some long overdue. George Cukor is the only filmmaker to have won the directorial award (*My Fair Lady*) at his fifth nomination. And British director Carol Reed was singled out for his direction of *Oliver!* at his third nomination. The separation between the Picture and Director awards has been rare, but in 1972, the Academy chose Bob Fosse as Best Director for *Cabaret*, but *The Godfather* was voted Best Picture.

For some reason, musicals have not been very generous to their performers as far as acting Oscars are concerned. Only eleven players have won an Oscar for a musical, but, significantly, there have been more women than men. Luise Rainer was the first actress to win for a musical, as Ziegfeld's first wife, Anna Held, in *The Great Ziegfeld*. The next musical winner was Julie Andrews, almost three decades later, as the magical governess in Walt Disney's *Mary Poppins*. Two winners appeared in musical biographies: Barbra Streisand as Fanny Brice in *Funny Girl*, and Sissy Spacek as Loretta Lynn in *Coal Miner's Daughter*. And one of the most brilliant performances in a musical was delivered by Liza Minnelli in *Cabaret*, as Sally Bowles, the ambitious nightclub singer in pre-Nazi Germany. The two male winners have been Yul Brynner in *The King and I*, and Rex Harrison in *My Fair Lady*.

What is interesting about the acting nominations in musicals is that most were selected after 1950. Very few performers had been nominated for a musical before, Bessie Love and Gene Kelly being the only exceptions. Neither Fred Astaire nor Ginger Rogers was ever nominated for any of their nine musicals, despite brilliant dancing. Indeed, Ginger Rogers won recognition as an actress only when she proved she could handle a dramatic role as the Irish girl from the wrong side of the tracks in *Kitty Foyle* (1940). She herself was anxious to demonstrate that she was much more than Fred Astaire's dancing partner, though it is precisely in this capacity that she is best remembered. The Academy bias against musical performers has unfortunately been similar to those against comedy performers.

Historical-Epic Films

Judging by the locale of the Oscar winners, over one-third—twenty-one pictures—have featured historical stories or characters. These movies have been widely diverse in genres, Westerns (*Cimarron*), historical romances (*Gone with the Wind, Out of Africa*), historical musicals (*Gigi*), historical political dramas (*Gandhi*), and even historical comedies (*Tom Jones*). But not every movie whose narrative occurs in the past is an historical *epic*, a genre that has to do as much with locale as with scope and intent. Epic films tend to be big-budgeted, big-scaled, and super-produced.

The historical epic as a distinct genre has featured prominently in the Oscar competition. No less than nine (15 percent) of all

Oscar-winning films have been historical epics: *Mutiny on the Bounty* (1935), *Gone with the Wind* (1939), *Hamlet* (1948), *Ben-Hur* (1959), *Lawrence of Arabia* (1962), *A Man for All Seasons* (1966), *Gandhi* (1982), and *Out of Africa* (1985). There is some difference between the rank of historical epics among the nominees and the winners, which demonstrates the overrepresentation of this genre in the Oscar. Not many epics are produced, but those made have a good chance to be nominated.

MGM's *Mutiny on the Bounty*, produced and directed by Frank Lloyd, was based on the true story of the famous 1787 mutiny aboard the British ship HMS *Bounty*. It features three great male performances: Charles Laughton, as the ruthless and sadistic Captain Bligh; Clark Gable, as the romantic and dashing Fletcher Christian; and Franchot Tone, as the decent midshipman Roger Byam. It is still the only film honored by the Academy with nominations for all three of its players as Best Actor, though none won. *Mutiny on the Bounty* was reportedly Gable's favorite film because "It was something you could get your teeth into, for it was history, a story of the struggle of real he-men with a refreshing absence of the usual load of love-interest."[2] Acclaimed by the critics, the movie enjoyed immense popularity with audiences, but it won only one award: Best Picture. The directorial and male acting awards went that year to John Ford and Victor McLaglen for *The Informer*.

Mutiny on the Bounty has withstood the test of time well. In fact, it is vastly superior to its two remakes, the first by MGM in 1962, also nominated for Best Picture, starring Trevor Howard in the Laughton role and Marlon Brando in the Gable role. The second remake, produced by Dino De Laurentiis in 1984 and starring Anthony Hopkins as Captain Bligh and Mel Gibson as Fletcher Christian, is reportedly more accurate to the source material than its two predecessors, but lacks the excitement and epic scale of the 1935 version.

Like other genres, historical epics have been more prominent in some decades than others. Their greatest representation was in the 1930s and in the 1950s and 1960s. But there are interesting differences between the epics of the two eras. The decade of the 1930s is dominated by MGM's prestige, studio-made films, such as *Viva Villa!* (1934) starring Wallace Beery as the Mexican rebel; *David Copperfield* (1935), based on Charles Dickens's novel and directed by George Cukor; Irving Thalberg's production of Shakespeare's

Romeo and Juliet (1936), with Norma Shearer and Leslie Howard in the leads; *A Tale of Two Cities* (also 1936), based on Dickens's book with Ronald Colman; and the film version of Pearl Buck's *The Good Earth* (1937), starring Paul Muni and Luise Rainer as the Chinese farmers.

Based on classic novels, these movies were marked by high literary values as well as high production values, though like other films at the time, they were confined to the studio lot. Their budgets were immense by the time's standards. The costs of *The Good Earth*, for example, were reported to be three million dollars (equivalent of thirty million at present), and the film itself was in production for over three years, due to producer Thalberg's death and changes in its directors: George Hill began and Sidney Franklin finished. This picture won an acting award for Luise Rainer and best cinematography, possibly for the locust attack sequence, an impressive special effect.

Not many historical epics were made in Hollywood in the 1940s, which is why David Lean's masterpiece *Great Expectations* and Laurence Olivier's screen adaptations of Shakespeare, *Henry V* in 1946 and *Hamlet* two years later, stood out in the American film scene and were honored by the Academy. *Henry V*, the more experimental of the two, was shot in Technicolor and blended stylized as well as realistic conventions. The movie begins at the Globe Theater, where the actors prepare for the performance, then switches to a more realistic setting, including one spectacularly photographed battle scene. *Henry V* was nominated for four, but did not win any awards; Olivier received a Special Oscar for his effort. *Hamlet*, the 1948 winner, was filmed in a different style, emphasizing the camera as an active participant in the narrative, and shot in black and white, based on Olivier's metaphor that it was like an engraving rather than a painting.[3] The Castle, with its massive and gloomy corridors, framed the human characters in a cool, detached way, and the Oscars for art direction and costume design were well deserved. Despite criticism of the adaptation, which omitted characters and whole scenes, *Hamlet* is an exciting film with fine acting by Olivier and Jean Simmons (as Ophelia).

But in the 1950s, because of the fierce competition with the new medium of television, Hollywood somehow believed that its survival depended on big-scale epic films, with production values that could not be imitated or seen on the small screen. Thus, almost every year saw the nomination of big epics. Once again, the field was dominated by MGM. But this time, the epics were massive historical tales, on the order of *Quo Vadis?* (1951), the most expensive film to date, starring Robert Taylor and Deborah Kerr; or *Ivanhoe* (1952), a medieval romance, based on Sir Walter Scott's novel, also with Robert Taylor, this time with two leading ladies, Elizabeth Taylor and Joan Fontaine. Each of these pictures was nominated in multiple categories, but won few if any awards. *Quo Vadis?* for example, received eight nominations but no awards.

Cecil B. De Mille, one of Hollywood's greatest showmen, was represented in the Oscar with two epics: *Cleopatra* (1934), starring Claudette Colbert, and *The Ten Commandments* (1956), with an all-star cast, headed by Charlton Heston. *Cleopatra*, which won best cinematography, is far more entertaining than the later remake, directed by Joseph L. Mankiewicz and starring Elizabeth Taylor, which was nominated in 1963. Nominated for multiple awards, *The Ten Commandments* also won only one: best special effects, a tribute to the parting of the Red Sea. It was De Mille's last picture, and one of the top-grossing pictures of all time.

Historical epics have also been the specialized genre of David Lean, with two of them winning Best Picture: the war epic *Bridge on the River Kwai* (1957) and *Lawrence of Arabia* (1962). One of the achievements of Lean as a master filmmaker is that he knows how to combine values of epic adventures on a grand scale with interesting human characters. Indeed, *Lawrence of Arabia* is great filmmaking on any level, visually as well as narratively. The complex character of T. E. Lawrence, the British officer who organized Arab tribes in an effort to drive the Turks out of their lands, remains an enigma in the film, but it is stunningly portrayed by Peter O'Toole, then a newcomer. Produced by Sam Spiegel, it won seven Oscars, best director, cinematography, art direction, editing, sound recording, and musical score. Lean was represented in the Oscar contest with two other historical epics: *Doctor Zhivago*, based on Boris Pasternak's novel, which won five Oscars, and *A Passage to India*, adapted to the screen from E. M. Forster's book, which won three.

MGM's *Ben-Hur*, the 1959 winner, boasted achievements in a number of departments. It was then the most expensive film ever made, with a budget of fifteen million dollars, one fifth of which was allocated for advertisement. The film was produced in Rome by Sam Zimablist who reportedly constructed 3,000 sets and employed over 50,000 people. *Ben-Hur* is still the first remake to ever win Best Picture, and it has won the largest number of awards to date: eleven out of its twelve nominations. The only category in which it lost was screenplay, credited to Kral Tunberg, though at least four distinguished writers contributed to its writing: Maxwell Anderson, S.N. Behrman, Christopher Frye, and Gore Vidal, which might have been the reason for its loss; the winner was Neil Paterson for *Room at the Top*. *Ben-Hur* was also the only historical spectacle in the 1959 Best Picture contest, up against small, intimate movies, such as Otto Preminger's *Anatomy of a Murder*, George Stevens's *The Diary of Anne Frank*, Fred Zinnemann's *The Nun's Story*, and Jack Clayton's *Room at the Top*.

Based on Lew Wallace's popular novel about the rise of Christianity, it features spectacular visual effects, the stunning chariot race, choreographed by Hollywood's top second unit directors, headed by Yakima Canutt. Its acting, by contrast, is not spectacular and Charlton Heston, who was cast after Universal refused to loan out Rock Hudson, is reasonably good in the title role of a converted Christian, in conflict with Massalla (Stephen Boyd), the Roman commander and his former childhood friend. But it did not matter, for the film was endowed with a visual sweep and enough pageantry to entertain its audiences for its epic length, 217 minutes. Overcoming MGM's fears, *Ben-Hur* was such an instant commercial success that its grosses were reported weekly to the public to make it seem "a must see" movie, which it became, with the assistance of mostly good reviews and word of mouth, grossing over eighty million dollars in world-wide rentals.

The trend of the 1950s continued into the 1960s. In addition to David Lean's epics, the decade began with John Wayne's historical Western, *The Alamo* (1960), about Texas's 1836 battle for independence, which Wayne considered his magnum opus. In 1962, Lewis Milestone's version of *Mutiny on the Bounty* was nominated for seven, but did not win any awards. And in 1963, *Cleopatra*, the picture that almost destroyed Twentieth Century-Fox, was nominated for nine and won four technical awards. In the following year, the British film *Becket*, based on Jean Anouilh's stage play, about the conflict between church, represented by the Archbishop of Canterbury (Richard Burton), and state, by King Henry VII (Peter O'Toole), was nominated in twelve categories, but won in just one: screenplay for Edward Anhalt.

The most talked about film in 1966 was Fred Zinnemann's *A Man for All Seasons*, based on Robert Bolt's smashing stage play, concerning the battle of will between Sir Thomas More (Paul Scofield), the Roman Catholic Chancellor, and Henry VIII (Robert Shaw), who broke with the Vatican and established the Church of England with himself as its head. Bolt's screenplay simplified his stage play and accentuated the differences between the characters, making More a noble saint, thus lacking the humor and dramatic wit that the play possessed. Zinnemann's direction was decent and serviceable, but Scofield's restrained and dignified acting was so sublime and Shaw's so eccentric that it became enjoyable viewing. Indeed, despite cinematic flaws, *A Man for All Seasons* was favored by the Academy for its noble and human message over its major competitor, Mike Nichols's *Who's Afraid of Virginia Woolf?* winning five awards in addition to Best Picture, for its director, actor, screenwriter, cinematographer, and costume designer.

The critical and commercial success of these historical films encouraged producers to make others of their kind, some good and others far from that. Franco Zeffirelli's handsome production of *Romeo and Juliet* (1968) cast two unknowns in the lead roles and stressed visual excitement at the expense of Shakespeare's text. In the same year, James Goldman's stage play, *The Lion in Winter*, was transferred to the screen without its original players, Robert Preston and Rosemary Harris. A gossipy, modern version of the court intrigues of Henry II, it was marked by such anachronistic dialogue as the Queen's comment, "Hush, dear, mother's fighting," or better, "Well, what family doesn't have its ups and downs?" which reminded many of *The Little Foxes* or *Who's Afraid of Virginia Woolf?* But Douglas Slocombe's exquisite cinematography and the acting by Peter O'Toole and Katharine Hepburn made its viewing tolerable. British royalty, this time the courtship between Henry VIII (Richard Burton) and Anne Boleyn (Genevieve Bujold), was featured again in the 1969 nominated film, *Anne of the Thousand Days*, which received only the costumes award, out of ten nominations!

Of the two historical epics nominated in the 1970s, one, *Nicholas and Alexandra* (1971), did not deserve nomination. The script by James Goldman was based on Robert K. Massie's novel, which meticulously reconstructed the last years of Russian czarist history, but despite their tragic fate, the characters were neither interesting nor moving as film characters. Even the art direction and costumes (which won Oscars) were not very imaginative, and despite publicity campaigns and nominations, it died at the box office. By contrast, Stanley Kubrick's *Barry Lyndon* (1975), based on William Makepeace Thackeray's novel, set in the eighteenth century, was an interesting experiment at adapting a novel to the screen. Endowed with a breathtaking visual vision, albeit lacking a dramatic sense, it won four awards, one for John Alcott's distinguished photography.

Roman Polanski's *Tess* (1980), inspired by Thomas Hardy's novel, and imbued with a contemporary viewpoint, excelled more in its cinematography and production values, winning three Oscars, than in its dramatic effects. *Reds* (1981), with Warren Beatty functioning as producer, cowriter (with Trevor Griffith), director and star, was an overambitious attempt to make at once a historical epic, romantic adventure, and political drama. But it was intelligent and original in its use of informants, contemporaries of John Reed, the adventurous journalist, who was in Russia during the 1917 Revolution and wrote the influential book, *Ten Days That Shook the World*. *Reds* also provided good parts for Diane Keaton, as Louise Bryand, Reed's wife, and particularly for Jack Nicholson, as Eugene O'Neill, and Maureen Stapleton, as the revolutionary Emma Goldman, which won her a supporting Oscar.

Out of Africa, starring Meryl Streep, as Danish writer Isak Dinesen. was a routine rendering of a tedious romance, set in Africa between 1913 and 1931. *Out of Africa* is unclear about its heroine, failing to provide any clues about the meaning of Africa for her and how it made her the kind of writer she later became. Nor does the film work as a love story, because it lacks any chemistry between its stars, with Robert Redford, as the white hunter, giving an embarrassing performance. Episodic rather than dramatic, and with cinematography that is beautiful in the manner of a travelogue but not well integrated into the narrative, *Out of Africa* does have redeeming qualities. It is an adult movie, about adult characters, and for adult audiences, standing out as such from the teenage films at present. Along with *The Color Purple*, the film was nominated for the largest number of awards (eleven), winning seven: film, director Pollack, adapted screenplay (Kurt Luedtke), cinematography (David Watkin), and others.

The latest Oscar-winning epic is Bernardo Bertolucci's *The Last Emperor,* sweeping most (nine) of the 1987 awards. Boasting a stunning cinematography, it is another episodic film with no coherent story and no epic hero. Its protagonist, Pu Yi (who became emperor of China at the age of three), was a passive man who lacked any power over his life. This may have accounted for the fact that none of the performers was nominated and the win was mostly in the technical categories. But what a feat to the eye the film is in terms of visual images, art direction, costumes, and editing. Bertolucci's win at his second nomination (the first was for *Last Tango in Paris*), made him the first Italian filmmaker to receive the Best Director Award.

War Films

War films as a genre have featured poorly, amounting to only 19 (five percent of the 367 nominated movies. However, the ratio of winning war films to those nominated is three to one, showing the Academy's bias for war films. All six Oscar war films have been on a grand epic scale: *Wings* (1927/8), *All Quiet on the Western Front* (1929/30), *The Bridge on the River Kwai* (1957), *Patton* (1970), *The Deer Hunter* (1978), and *Platoon* (1988). And with the exception of William Wellman, who was not nomimated for *Wings*, all the other directors were honored: Lewis Milestone for *All Quiet*, David Lean for *The Bridge*, Franklin J. Schaffner for *Patton*, Michael Cimino for *The Deer Hunter*, and Oliver Stone for *Platoon*.

Wings, the first Oscar film, is the only silent feature to win the award. It was in production for over a year because of its aerial sequences, which are still exciting to watch, and was the most expensive (two million dollars) film at the time. The first collaborative effort between Hollywood and the Army Air Corps, it enjoyed the latter's assistance on the condition that the movie project a positive image of the military. It was just the beginning of a later, more intimate connection between the film industry and the Administration during World War II.

If *Wings* celebrates heroism, action, and male camaraderie, the next winning film, *All Quiet on the Western Front*, has a different, antiwar, message. Based on Eric Maria Remarque's famous novel, adapted to the screen by a team of writers headed by playwright Maxwell Anderson, it describes the initial excitement, then disillusionment of a group of German soldiers in World War I, none of whom survives. Uncompromising, it makes a clearly bleak statement of war fighting in trenches, stressing the insanity of war for both sides, the Allies and Germans. *All Quiet on the Western Front* proved a huge success at the box office; it was Universal's biggest movie, but was poorly received in Germany prior to Nazism and officially banned following Hitler's rise to power. Reissued in the US in 1939 in a substantially truncated version, it enjoyed a second successful run.

The largest number (six) of war films were nominated in the 1940s, during World War II. But interestingly enough, none of them won Best Picture. Furthermore, few of the nominated films were action pictures, depicting men in the battle zone. Rather, most concerned the home front during the War, such as *Mrs. Miniver*, the 1942 Oscar winner, about a "typical" British family during the Blitz. Or *The Human Comedy* (1943), based on William Saroyan's book about the lives of ordinary folks in a small California town, with Mickey Rooney as a Western Union messenger whose role is to deliver death telegrams. And in 1944, David Selznick produced an American version of *Mrs. Miniver*, which he entitled *Since You Went Away*, dealing with a "typical" American family during the war, with Claudette Colbert playing the indomitable mother that Greer Garson played in *Mrs. Miniver*. Most of Hollywood's serious examinations of the war and its effects were made after the war was over, like MGM's *Battleground* and Twentieth Century-Fox's *Twelve O'Clock High*, both nominated in 1949.

One exceptionally good film was Paramount's *Wake Island* (1942), a moving, though fictionalized, report of the defense of the Pacific Island base, with strong emphasis on the heroic gallantry of three marines, played by Robert Preston, Brian Donlevy, and William Bendix, who won a supporting nomination. Despite the fact that it was shot in California, the battle scenes seem convincingly realistic. The film got rave reviews, though it was clear that the reviews themselves were tainted by the politics of the times. For example, one critic wrote that "Although the United States has been at war for nine months, *Wake Island* is Hollywood's first intelligent, honest, and completely successful attempt to dramatize the deeds of an American force on a fighting front."[4] Bosley Crowther, who saw the film at a marine base, praised the filmmakers who "deserve a sincere salute," and predicted that the picture "should surely bring a surge of pride to every patriot's breast."[5]

The British were represented with two war pictures. The first, *The Invaders*, made in 1941 and released in the US a year later, deals with six survivors from a Nazi submarine attempting to cross the Canadian border to the United States. Its real distinction is its wonderful cast: Laurence Olivier, Leslie Howard, Raymond Massey, and best of all Eric Portman as a heartless, relentless Nazi. The other, *In Which We Serve*, was the creative product of Noel Coward. Inspired by the sinking of HMS *Kelly* off Crete, this saga recreates the biography of a ship from its building to her last battle, interspersed with flashbacks of its crew's lives at home (see chapter 4).

The first winning war films usually received few awards. *Wings* won two Oscars, film and engineering effects, a category discontinued the following year. *All Quiet on the Western Front* also won two awards, for film and director. Conferring on one film many awards began with *Gone with the Wind* and became a trend in the 1950s, as David Lean's epic, *The Bridge on the River Kwai* demonstrated with its seven awards.

Like other Lean movies, *The Bridge on the River Kwai* is rich in characterization and ambiguity of point of view, here in the manner in which it presents the conflict between Colonel Nicholson (Alec Guinness), a rigid British officer committed to the military code of integrity at all costs, the Japanese commander of the prisoner of war camp (Sessue Hayakawa), and the American man of action (William Holden). The construction of the bridge has different meanings for these men and, at the end, when the colonel dies by falling on the detonator that destroys the bridge, the irony of the story becomes explicit. *The Bridge* is strong as a psychological study of character, suspense action, and a visual epic and, as Ivan Butler suggests, it is one of those rare pictures that satisfy audiences emotionally, cerebrally, and aesthetically.[6]

In the 1960s, three big war movies were nominated, beginning with *The Guns of Navarone* in 1961, an action movie about a tough sabotage team sent to destroy two giant guns on a Turkish island in 1943. The second, *The Longest Day* in 1962, about the preparations and landings of the Allies on Normandy on D Day, June 6, 1944, was much better and, were it not for the competition with *Lawrence of Arabia*, it would have probably won Best Picture. Of its five nominations, it won two awards: black-and-white cinematography and special effects. However, Twentieth Century-Fox's 1966 attempt to make another blockbuster war movie, *The Sand Pebbles*, failed. An unabashed publicity campaign got the film eight nominations, though it lost in every category. Screenwriter Richard Anderson and director Robert Wise were not exactly sure what kind of message to send in their story about the involvement of an American gunboat patrol, led by Steve McQueen, with Chinese warlords in its 1926 rescue attempts of American citizens and missionaries.

Patton, the 1970 Oscar film was also ambiguous in its message, attempting to please right-wing as well as left-wing audiences, letting each type of audience read the film the way it wanted. But unlike *The Sand Pebbles*, it works. Made on a twelve-million-dollar budget, with an original screenplay by Francis Ford Coppola and E. H. North, it presents a multi-faceted view of World War II General Patton, as a noble hero, demented psychopath, genius strategist, megalomaniac devoid of any human feelings,˙ and poet. George C. Scott, in a brilliant performance, dominated every frame of the film, to the exclusion of the other actors, whose roles were underwritten and underdeveloped. It was a one-character, one-star movie, and the response of the country, in the midst of the Vietnam War controversy, was overwhelming, grossing in rentals over twenty-eight million dollars. *Patton* won seven major awards out of its ten nominations, for director Franklin J. Schaffner, actor Scott, screenplay, art direction, editing, and sound.

In 1978, two major films about the Vietnam War competed for Best Picture, *The Deer Hunter* and *Coming Home*. Both films were set in 1968, though they differed substantially in their orientation and style. Michael Cimino's *The Deer Hunter* is more ambitious and multi-layered, dealing with a group of five Russian-American friends and their harrowing experiences in Vietnam. The film starts with ordinary life in a small Pennsylvania steel town, then sharply switches to Vietnam. It says something about male friendship and camaraderie, survival of ordeals, violence in political and personal contexts, and even family life, though none of it is too deep. There was no doubt that the picture was stronger in its lyrical-expressive imagery than in its story or ideas. Winning all major critics awards, *The Deer Hunter* also won five Oscars.

Francis Ford Coppola's *Apocalypse Now* (1979), was inspired by Joseph Conrad's *Heart of Darkness*, though it is intellectually vapid and dramatically incoherent as a statement of American involvement in Vietnam. The Academy honored it with two Oscars for its major achievements—Vittorio Storaro's stunning cinematography and sound.

In the 1980s, the war genre is well and alive, judging by the crop of action films about Vietnam. Some of these films are made under the guise of the action-adventures, but in actuality are imbued with a strong political subtext, reminiscent of the anti-Communist Cold War movies of the 1950s; for some, they represent an American version of fascist ideology. Prominent in this genre are the three Sylvester Stallone *Rambo* films which, in their comic-strip revision of the Vietnam War, proved to be bonanza at the box office but completely ignored by the Academy. The Oscar-winning *Platoon*, honored in four out of its eight nominated categories, was different in texture and ideology. Based on director Stone's service in Vietnam, it is an exploration of "the everyday realities of what it was like to be a nineteen-year-old boy in the bush for the first time." Depicting realistically the routine activities of a single infantry platoon, the film focuses on the battle between the "evil" sergeant Barnes (Tom Berenger) and the "good" sergeant Elias (Willem Dafoe) over the soul of "innocent" grunt Chris (Charlie Sheen). It took Stone ten years to get his script produced because the country was not ready to deal with the issues of the war. Released in December 1986, at a time when President Reagan's popularity was in decline, the film challenged the national consciousness concerning its ambivalent feelings toward the war and its veterans.

Action-Adventure Films

The action-adventure genre has been popular with the public, but not very respected by the Academy. Only three adventures (5 percent) have won Best Picture and only twenty-three such films (7 percent) have been nominated.

The first Oscar-winning adventure was Cecil B. De Mille's *The Greatest Show on Earth* (1952), which also earned, for no apparent reason, the writing award. Produced by Paramount, it was the only De Mille film to win Best Picture. Its inspiration derived from the Ringling Bros., Barnum and Bailey Circuses, with a melodramatic romantic triangle, between a tough manager (Charlton Heston), his beautiful aerialist (Betty Hutton), and a trapeze artist (Cornell Wilde). The picture contains some interesting circus acts, but the most spectacular sequence is a train crash, with hundreds of animals running around. A mass entertainment, *The Greatest Show on Earth* still ranks as one of the least accountable and least distinguished Oscar winners in the history of the Academy. Furthermore, this film began the tradition of honoring big-budget, special-effects blockbusters with a large number of nominations.

Cecil B. De Mille got his first and only directorial nomination for this picture, but the winner that year was John Ford for *The Quiet Man*. The Academy must have anticipated De Mille's failure to win a competitive award for it decided to honor him with a Special Oscar, in recognition of *The Greatest Show on Earth* as well as his other blockbusters. This tribute was well timed: DeMille made just one more film, *The Ten Commandments*, before dying in 1959 at the age of seventy-eight.

Mike Todd's *Around the World in 80 Days* (1956) was the second winning adventure. It was directed by Michael Anderson and based on Jules Verne's best-seller about a Victorian gentleman (David Niven) and his valet (Cantinflas), and their attempt to go around the world in eighty days on a wager. It was not the first film to use the technique of Todd-AO, which produced sharper images than the previous innovation of Cinerama, but it put it to great effect as an exciting travelogue that took audiences to exotic locales. The film was big-budgeted, seven million dollars, much above the average at the time, and featured over fifty cameo appearances of famous stars, such as Charles Boyer, Marlene Dietrich, Ronald Colman, Buster Keaton, Cesar Romero, and Frank Sinatra. Spotting the stars was a great joy for most audiences, which set another trend, using many stars in small roles, as was later demonstrated in *The Longest Day* and *How the West Was Won.*

Around the World's five Oscars honored the adapted screenplay, color cinematography, editing, and musical score. Victor Young, the noted Hollywood composer, won his first Oscar posthumously, after nineteen nominations. The picture ranked second among the top-grossing films of the year, following *The Ten Commandments*, and was the most commercially popular Oscar film until *Ben-Hur* in 1959.

While it was in production, no one expected William Friedkin's *The French Connection* to become either such a major critical and commercial hit or to win the 1971 Oscar. But it did, capturing additional awards for the director, actor (Gene Hackman), screenplay (Ernest Tidyman), and editing (Jerry Greenberg). The importance of *The French Connection* could not be overestimated, with the Oscar legitimizing its status as the best "cop and caper" film of the decade. The film contributed, as film scholar James Monaco observed, to the brief resurgence of film noirs in the 1970s and also in setting a style for visceral excitement.[7] It also made the cop film the most popular and the most distinctive genre of the decade, preceding the release of Clint Eastwood's *Dirty Harry* by a few months.

Every element in *The French Connection* is good in its own right but even better as part of the whole movie, which is highly coherent. It has a good screenplay, based on the adventures of two real-life policemen, Eddie Egan and Sonny Grosso (who served as technical advisers for the film and also appeared in minor roles), involved in tracking down a large shipment of pure heroin hidden in a car transported from Marseilles to New York City. But in addition to a good thriller, containing the best chase scene in American films, imitated since in many pictures, it revolves around an interesting character. Popeye Doyle (Hackman) is a tough, vulgar, bigoted cop, obsessed with breaking up the international narcotic ring. To think that the filmmakers considered other actors for the role (Jackie Gleason and Steve McQueen, among others) is hard to believe, for it provided Hackman with the best role of his career. *The French Connection* also boasts breathtaking, ultra-realistic cinematography and sound track of the streets of New York, and well-paced editing, all of which contributed to a well-made, entertaining movie. Praised by most critics, *The French Connection* went on to earn in domestic rentals twenty-six million dollars, ranking third among the year's top grossers.

Nominated adventure films seem to have appeared in two cycles: in the 1930s (ten films) and in the 1970s (seven films). No adventure films were nominated in the 1940s and 1960s, and few in the 1950s. A recurrent feature of adventure films is their high production values and special effects, but there are important differences between the adventure films of the 1930s and of the 1970s.

In the earlier decade, adventure films tended to be more coherent, with melodramatic stories and well-built, if contrived, plots. For example, MGM's *Trader Horn* (1931), a jungle melodrama distinguished by its location shooting in Africa, which was a novelty at the time, cast Harry Carey as a white hunter in a series of encounters with hostile tribes. An even better example is another MGM production, the popular hit *San Francisco* (1936), featuring the most spectacular earthquake ever recorded on screen, which occupies close to ten minutes of screen time. But in addition to these special effects, it is a well made film with an emotionally engaging love story, between a tough saloon owner (Clark Gable) and a singer (Jeanette MacDonald), with a third character, a no-nonsense priest (Spencer Tracy, who stole the show). Indeed, an attempt was made to engage the audiences in the plot and its characters.

Warner's two major swashbuckling adventures of the decade, both featuring Errol Flynn, *Captain Blood* (1935) and *The Adventures of Robin Hood* (1938), were also nominated. The former did not win any award, but the latter, the first Technicolor version of the Robin Hood legend, won three: art direction, editing, and original score. Paramount's adventure, *Lives of a Bengal Lancer* (1935), for which Henry Hathaway received his only directorial nomination, was based on Francis Yeats Brown's novel and starred Gary Cooper, Franchot Tone, and Richard Cromwell as courageous British officers in India's northwest frontier, involved in treacherous border intrigues. One of the most nominated (six) pictures of the year, it was honored with one Oscar, for best assistant direction.

The World War II years were not particularly conducive to the production of adventures. And they continued to be missing in the 1950s, with this decade's emphasis on historical epics. Yet MGM's *King Solomon's Mines* (1950) stands out as the most entertaining adventure of the decade, similar to the earlier *Trader Horn*, and marked with distinguished color cinematography of Africa's jungles, by Robert Surtees, who won an Oscar, nicely edited by Ralph E. Winters and Conrad A. Nervig, who also won.

After a decade of no adventures competing for Best Picture, the 1970s brought a new cycle of action-adventures, labeled as "disaster movies," because they depicted all kinds of catastrophes, man- and nature-made, set on earth (*Earthquake*, 1974), in the air (*Airport*, 1970 and its many sequels), on the sea (*Jaws*, 1975 and its sequels) as well as under the sea (*The Poseidon Adventure*, 1972). This genre exploited its narrative possibilities in a few years, saturating the market so fast that it resulted in a hilarious send-up of the various "airport" movies, *Airplane* (1980).

The disaster adventures were packaged, calculated entertainment, each with an all-star cast, rather than *made* movies. Most of them proved to be extremely popular with the general public, at once cashing in on and promoting collective fears of the most ordinary behaviors, such as flying (*Airport*), swimming on Long Island's beaches (*Jaws*), and working in a high-rise building *(The Towering Inferno)*. The pattern of these blockbusters, as far as the Academy was concerned, was to bestow a large number of nominations, in recognition of their technical aspects and their commercial appeal, but few awards. The disaster adventures provided employment for many actors, some in forced retirement, but they were not very generous to them, with each actor getting at best one good scene. This may explain the large number of technical and the paucity of acting nominations, though the latter were usually given to elderly performers for sentimental reasons. For example, Helen Hayes won a second (supporting) Oscar, for portraying a cute, eccentric and compulsive stowaway in *Airport*, who upon being caught, says: "I don't think it would be very good public relations to prosecute a little lady for visiting her daughter." In his review of the film, Canby wrote that Helen Hayes plays "with such outrageous abandon you believe she must have honestly thought it would be her last performance,"[8] which it was not—but maybe the Academy thought so. The Academy also honored Maureen Stapleton as the slow-witted, distraught wife of a mad bomber, played by Van Heflin, with a nomination.

The Poseidon Adventure honored Shelley Winters with her fourth nomination, for playing a fat Jewish grandmother, a passenger in a sinking ship. Sentimentality, onscreen and off, explains the first and only nomination of Fred Astaire in *The Towering Inferno*, as a widower who loses his new friend (Jennifer Jones) in the disaster. And the multi-nominated *Star Wars* received only one acting nomination, Alec Guinness as a whiskery wizard.

Star Wars began a new cycle of action-adventures in 1977, the science-fiction film, which, unlike its 1950s counterpart, was now highly sophisticated and elaborate in its technological and production values. The impact of *Star Wars* and its sequels and imitators on popular culture was immense, influencing fashion and interior design, television programming, the toy industry, and even the way children are brought up. The Academy acknowledged its status with six regular and one Special Award, but *Star Wars* was the exception. The Academy proved its respect for these blockbusters in the nomination process, but when it came to the "real thing," the Oscar itself, a more cautionary vote was displayed:

In 1970, *Patton* was selected over *Airport*.
In 1974, *The Godfather, Part II* over *The Towering Inferno*.
In 1975, *One Flew over the Cuckoo's Nest* over *Jaws*.
In 1977, *Annie Hall* over *Star Wars*.
In 1981, *Chariots of Fire* over *Raiders of the Lost Ark*.
In 1983, *Terms of Endearment* over *The Right Stuff*.

Suspense Films

Mystery and suspense films, like action-adventures, have been more appreciated by filmgoers than the Academy, judging by the scarcity of nominated films in this genre. Considered to be purely commercial escapism, some critics regard the well-made thriller as a product of craftsmanship rather than art.

In the Academy's history, only one suspense film, Alfred Hitchcock's *Rebecca* (1940), has won Best Picture. Based on Daphne du Maurier's popular novel, it was Hitchcock's first American movie, in which he cast Laurence Olivier and Joan Fontaine in the starring roles. The film is distinguished by exquisite cinematography—

George Barnes won an Oscar for it—and great ensemble acting, particularly in the supporting cast, headed by Judith Anderson as the malevolent housekeeper in one of her most memorable portrayals.

In the same year, *Rebecca* competed against another Hitchcock film, *Foreign Correspondent*, which, imbued with political overtones, deals with espionage in 1938 Europe. The film was interpreted by some as an endorsement of the American involvement in the war, because its producer, Walter Wanger, was known for his anti-Fascist views. Both *Rebecca* and *Foreign Correspondent* were extremely popular at the box office; *Rebecca* was one of the hits of the season, grossing in rentals a phenomenal $1,500,000.

No filmmaker has ever won a directorial Oscar for a suspense picture or a thriller, including Hitchcock, the acknowledged master of this genre. Hitchcock was nominated five times for five masterpieces: *Rebecca*, *Lifeboat* (1944), *Spellbound* (1945), *Rear Window* (1954), and *Psycho* (1960), his last undisputed success. Furthermore, four Hitchcock films were nominated for Best Picture, the aforementioned *Rebecca* and *Foreign Correspondent*, and *Suspicion* (1941) and *Spellbound*. However, Hitchcock never won a legitimate directorial Oscar, though the Academy later compensated him with an Honorary Award.

Other filmmakers specializing in thrillers have shared similar fate at the hands of the Academy. Carol Reed established an international reputation with two extraordinary suspense pictures, both based on Graham Greene's books: *The Fallen Idol* (1949), starring Ralph Richardson, and *The Third Man* (1950), with Orson Welles. Both pictures had high production values, particularly cinematography; Robert Krasker won an Oscar for his black-and-white photography of Vienna in *The Third Man*. Reed received directorial nominations for these films, but won the Oscar at his third nomination for a less distinguished and less characteristic movie, *Oliver!*

Suspense films have also featured marginally among the nominees. Strictly speaking, only 12 suspense pictures (3.2 percent) have been nominated, most in the 1940s. In addition to Hitchcock's four films, they included John Huston's first, and still one of his best, features, *The Maltese Falcon* (1941), George Cukor's Gothic tale *Gaslight*, and Billy Wilder's *Double Indemnity*, both in 1944. No suspense films were nominated in the 1950s and 1960s, and only two in the 1970s: Roman Polanski's *Chinatown* and Francis Ford Coppola's *The Conversation*, both in 1974.[9] Note that most of the nominated thrillers have employed the thematics and stylistics of film noir.

Some, like *The Maltese Falcon* and *Double Indemnity* are proto-typical of this interesting genre.

The Academy's lack of respect for thrillers and mysteries is also reflected in the underrepresentation of acting awards in this genre. Only 2 percent of all winning performances have been for roles in suspense pictures, and most of them by women. Women in this genre have typically played victims, threatened to be murdered and/ or victimized by their husband/lovers (see chapter 8).

Western Films

The Western, the most uniquely American film form, was until the late 1960s also one of the most popular genres. For decades, it was regarded as the "bread and butter" of the film industry, consisting of numerous B Westerns that functioned as the bottom of the double-feature bill. In the 1950s, for example, the production of Westerns amounted to one-third of Hollywood's entire film output; it is arguably the best decade for A Westerns in the genre's history.

Yet, only one out of the fifty-eight Oscar-winning films has been a Western; it was *Cimarron* (1930/31), based on Edna Ferber's best-selling book about the opening of the Oklahoma frontier and the land rush of the late 1890s. Directed by Wesley Ruggles, the film is episodic, covering three decades in the Cravat family. It provided good roles for Richard Dix as a dashing, adventurous romantic, and Irene Dunne as his strong, indomitable wife Sabra, who starts as a fragile, dependent wife but later becomes the editor of the local newspaper and a congresswoman. In addition to Best Picture, *Cimarron* won writing adaptation and art direction, and proved to be a blockbuster with the public.

Of all genres, the Western has been the most peripheral in the Oscar contest: only seven Westerns (2 percent) have been nominated: *In Old Arizona* (1928/9), *Stagecoach* (1939), *The Ox-Bow Incident* (1943), *High Noon* (1952), *Shane* (1953), *How the West Was Won* (1963), and *Butch Cassidy and the Sundance Kid* (1969). With the exception of John Ford's *Stagecoach*, all the other Westerns were directed by filmmakers who did not specialize in the genre, which may have had something to do with the nomination of their pictures. These were "prestige" filmmakers, like Fred Zinnemann *(High Noon)* and George Stevens *(Shane)*, who made only one Western in their entire careers, for which they were nominated.

The lack of respect for Westerns is also reflected by the fact that no filmmaker has ever won a directorial award for this genre. John Ford, undoubtedly the master of Westerns, was nominated five times, but only once for a Western *(Stagecoach)*. Significantly, Ford's four Oscars were for other genres: *The Informer, The Grapes of Wrath, How Green Was My Valley,* and *The Quiet Man.* Indeed, many critics hold Ford in high regard for his achievements outside the domain of Westerns. Astonished by the Academy's biases, Ford is reported to have said: "I don't think a lot about honors, but I think it is demeaning to the Westerns that I have received honors for other films and none for my Westerns."[10] Ford also failed to win a nomination for what is considered to be his chef d'oeuvre, *The Searchers* (1956).

Ford is not an exception; other directors excelling in Westerns have similarly skirted Academy recognition. The list is too long to chronicle, but one example is indicative of the trend. Howard Hawks failed to get nominations for his Westerns, particularly *Red River* (1948) and to a lesser extent *Rio Bravo* (1959), but was nominated for his patriotic flag-waver *Sergeant York,* though did not win.

Being a typically "masculine" genre, the Western has contained more and better male than female performances. This has been acknowledged by the Academy: seven men, but no women, have won acting Oscars in a Western. The first winner was Warner Baxter, as the legendary Mexican bandit the Cisco Kid in *In Old Arizona.* Gary Cooper, the second Best Actor for a Western, gave one of his finest performances as Marshal Will Kane in *High Noon.* In the 1960s, two actors won the lead award for comic performances in a Western. Lee Marvin played a dual part in *Cat Ballou* (1965): as Kid Shellen, a whiskey-soaked gunfighter, and as Shellen's antagonist, Tim Straun, a villain with a silver nose. And *True Grit* (1969) provided John Wayne with one of the richest roles of his career, as the fat, aging, eye-patched, Marshal Rooster Cogburn, who helps a teenager avenge his father's death.

Three supporting awards honored roles in a Western. The first was Thomas Mitchell, as the drunken Doc Boone in *Stagecoach.* Walter Brennan won his third supporting Oscar for the portrayal of Judge Roy Bean in William Wyler's *The Westerner.* Finally, Burl Ives won for his patriarch landowner in *The Big Country,* another Wyler Western.

Few players have been nominated for a Western, not for lack of distinguished performances, but for the low prestige of the genre itself. Indeed, actors identified with some of the best Westerns failed to get recognition, including Henry Fonda, James Stewart, William Holden, Kirk Douglas, and Burt Lancaster. Moreover, the few nominated received recognition because of their status as players, not necessarily because of good work in Westerns. For example,

Geraldine Page was nominated for her supporting role in a John Wayne Western, *Hondo* (1953), for no apparent reason other than the fact that it was her first Hollywood movie, arriving in California with the acclaim of being Broadway's brightest star after her stunning work in *Summer and Smoke*. Jennifer Jones and Lillian Gish were nominated for their roles in King Vidor's *Duel in the Sun*, an erotic though rather silly Western, because it was a blockbuster. And Julie Christie won her second nomination, as the frizzy-haired, opium-smoking whore in Robert Altman's symbolic Western *Mc-Cabe and Mrs. Miller* (1971), because she was then in vogue.

Ironically, only when the Western became self-conscious and started to take itself less seriously did it begin to win some respect. Lee Marvin won the Oscar for a Western spoof, *Cat Ballou*, which caricatured the traditional Western and its cowboy hero, and was sold to the public as a "put-on" of previous Westerns. John Wayne won acclaim only when he poked fun at his own screen image. And comedienne Madeline Kahn received a supporting nomination in Mel Brooks's spoof, *Blazing Saddles* (1974), which made jokes about every convention of the genre. Kahn was cast as Lily von Shtupp, an explicit impersonation of Marlene Dietrich's numerous cabaret-singer roles.

Conclusion

What then are the crucial attributes of an Oscar-winning film? One way to answer this question is to examine the filmmakers whose movies have dominated the competition. William Wyler, Fred Zinnemann, and David Lean have occupied special positions in the annals of the Academy in two ways: many of their films have been nominated for Best Picture, and many of the performers in their films have won nominations and awards. All three filmmakers probably qualify as auteurs, though in different ways and for different reasons.

Of the three, Wyler's film oeuvre is probably the most diverse, at least in genre, ranging from serious dramas to Westerns to romantic comedies and even musicals. Three of Wyler's films won Best Picture: *Mrs. Miniver*, *The Best Years of Our Lives*, and *Ben-Hur*. Moreover, he brought out the best of many performers, with thirteen (out of 188) winning the award for roles in his films: Walter Brennan (*Come and Get It*, co-directed with Howard Hawks; and *The Westerner*), Bette Davis and Faye Bainter (*Jezebel*), Greer Garson and Teresa Wright (*Mrs. Miniver*), Fredric March and Harold Russell (*The Best Years of Our Lives*), Olivia De Havilland (*The Heiress*),

Audrey Hepburn *(Roman Holiday)*, Burl Ives *(The Big Country)*, Charlton Heston and Hugh Griffith *(Ben-Hur)*, and Barbra Streisand *(Funny Girl)*. Wyler was the Academy's most respected and most honored director; over half of his thirty-five sound movies brought their players nominations.[11] It could be that Wyler's films contained the largest number of Oscar-winning and Oscar-nominated performances due to his revolutionary use, with cinematographer Gregg Toland, of long takes and deep-focus shots, in which characters appear in the same frame for the duration of entire scenes, thus enabling them some continuity in their acting. Indeed, this technique required a great deal of discipline on the part of screen players, most of whom were used to acting in bits and pieces, the predominant norm of filming. A meticulous craftsman, he was nicknamed "90-take Wyler," for the many takes he demanded.[12] Accused of being a tyrant, he often clashed with his players, yet most of them have done their best work in his movies.

Note that the Wyler films which won Best Picture and honored him with Best Director did not represent his most distinguished or, for that matter, characteristic work, among which one would have to include *Dodsworth, The Letter,* and *Little Foxes*. As will be shown, *Mrs. Miniver* won for political rather than artistic reasons, and the historical epic *Ben-Hur* did not bear Wyler's signature as an artist, since he was at his best when adapting literary works to the screen. Still, the Academy recognized Wyler as a distinguished auteur before the auteurist critics themselves. Wyler's reputation, in fact, suffered in the 1960s and 1970s, along with that of Billy Wilder and Fred Zinnemann, because critics failed to identify the idiosyncratic elements in his work, when they compared it with the more obvious auteurs, Eric Von Stroheim, Fritz Lang, John Ford, and Howard Hawks. Yet, as Vincent Canby recently observed, Wyler was best at "submerging his own personality to obtain the most effective realization of the work of others," and it is precisely this "extraordinary consistency of purpose and achievement" that is his distinctive trademark.[13]

If consistent quality was Wyler's signature as a filmmaker, Fred Zinnemann's contribution has been in his humanist concept of filmmaking, which was mainstream in Hollywood of the 1950s and 1960s. Zinnemann directed two Oscar winners, *From Here to Eternity* and *A Man for All Seasons,* and four Oscar-nominated pictures, *High Noon, The Nun's Story, The Sundowners,* and *Julia*. Considering the duration of his career, over half a century, his film oeuvre has been rather small: twenty-two features and a number of documentaries. Nonetheless, the number of Oscar-winning performances in Zinnemann's films has been disproportionately large. Eighteen players have been nominated in his movies, some more than once, like Montgomery Clift in *The Search*, as a sensitive American soldier befriending an orphan in Europe right after the War, and in *From Here to Eternity*, as yet another sensitive soldier. And six of these players have won Oscars: Gary Cooper *(High Noon)*, Frank Sinatra and Donna Reed *(From Here to Eternity)*, Paul Scofield *(A Man for All Seasons)*, and Vanessa Redgrave and Jason Robards *(Julia)*. Some players have done their best work in his films, like Marlon Brando in his debut, *The Men*, Audrey Hepburn in *The Nun's Story*, and Julie Harris and Ethel Waters in *The Member of the Wedding*.

Being cast in a Zinnemann movie increases the chances of getting a nomination. He is considered to be a "dream director" because of his great respect for acting and actors. His movies have been perfect "Oscar material," with their sensitive subject matter and humanistic orientation, containing complex or interesting character roles. Zinnemann is an auteur thematically: his films have displayed a good deal of consistency in their narrative concerns. Asked to describe the kinds of stories that attract him, he said: "I just like to do films that are positive in the sense that they deal with the dignity of human beings and have something to say about oppression."[14] "It is this moral courage," Zinnemann elaborated, "which has interested me most. I look for the universal theme that will allow the audience to identify with the characters."[15] What fascinated him about *Julia*, his last nominated film, was "the story of the friendship of the two women," and "the fact of conscience." "I always find questions of conscience very photogenic," he explains, "that kind of interior drama is to me very, very exciting."[16]

Zinnemann's earlier films were produced by a young filmmaker, Stanley Kramer, who was highly committed to problem-message films propagating liberal causes, such as racial equality *(Home of the Brave, The Defiant Ones)*, political justice *(Judgment at Nuremberg)*, interracial marriage *(Guess Who's Coming to Dinner?)*. Kramer's contribution to American film is in being the first to make mainstream movies about pressing, often unpopular issues.[17] Many of his films were nominated for Best Picture, despite often unimaginative approach and flat and static direction. *Ship of Fools* was nominated for eight Oscars in 1965, including Best Picture—probably because it was considered to be important—dealing with a group of passengers (a sort of "*Grand Hotel* on water") aboard a ship bound for Germany in 1933. The movie was intellectually pretentious and technically crude and shapeless, yet a number of powerful performances and its symbolic message overshadowed its weakness, and the Academy proved again the primacy of subject matter over style and artistic form in its winners. Like Zinnemann, Kramer was a "sociological" director, but he lacked the veteran director's technical skills and polished style.

Zinnemann's humanist approach to filmmaking is almost nonexistent in Hollywood of the present. However, David Puttnam, the British producer (*Chariots of Fire, The Killing Fields*), who was appointed chairman of Columbia Pictures, which incidently produced Zinnemann's Oscar-winning *From Here to Eternity*, hoped to reinstate Zinnemann's kind of films, as he recently said: "If I had to characterize them [films] in terms of another filmmaker, they're not unlike Fred Zinnemann's films. I think they're about people finding within themselves resources they didn't know were there, and coming from the best of them."[18]

One of the few filmmakers to combine interesting issues, complex characters, and grand epic style is David Lean, whose work is a *perfect* example for the kinds of films that win awards. Six of Lean's movies have been nominated, from *In Which We Serve*, co-directed with Noel Coward, through *Great Expectations, Doctor Zhivago*, and *A Passage to India*. Unlike other directors, Lean was good at small, intimate films (*Brief Encounter*), literary adaptations (*Oliver Twist*), and documentary-style narratives (*Breaking through the Sound Barrier*), but he achieved international recognition when he switched to grand, epic-style movies, beginning with *The Bridge on the River Kwai*.

This brings us to the second crucial feature of the Oscar films: high production values, expressed in visual style, epic vision, and also in big-budget and long-running time. Indeed, *Ordinary People* and *Terms of Endearment* were the last modest films to have won Oscars, in 1980 and 1983 respectively. The other winning films of the 1980s have all been, independent of their genre, big-scaled and super-produced: *Chariots of Fire* won in 1981, *Gandhi* in 1982, *Amadeus* in 1984, *Out of Africa* in 1985, and *The Last Emperor* in 1987. Most of the Oscar-winning films have been big-budgeted, from the very first one, *Wings*, through *Gone with the Wind* in the 1930s; *Ben-Hur* in the 1950s; *Lawrence of Arabia* and *Tom Jones* in the 1960s; *The Godfather* movies in the 1970s. The decade of the 1940s is conspicuously underrepresented here because of the austere economy of the war and the dominance of war pictures.

Excessive running time has impressed not only moviegoers, but also Academy members. The running time of over half (thirty-five of sixty-one) of the winners has been in excess of the average ninety to 110 minutes. *Wings's* running time was 136 minutes, *The Great Ziegfeld* 179, *Gone with the Wind* 220, *The Best Years of Our Lives* 182, *Around the World in 80 Days* 178, and *The Last Emperor* 166 minutes. Woody Allen's *Annie Hall* is the exception: with a running time of ninety-three minutes, it has been the shortest film among all Oscar winners.

CHAPTER 8

The Oscar-Winning Roles

W hich roles have tended to get Academy nominations and awards? Assuming that most nominated performances have been of relatively high quality, it is interesting to examine whether the Oscar roles have also shared similar thematic attributes. Is it possible to generalize about the kinds of roles that have received the Academy's attention? Have there been consistent or "typical" Oscar roles, for men and for women?[1]

The advantage of analyzing the Oscar roles is that they have usually been contained in popular and/or important movies, widely seen by the public, thus functioning as potential agencies of socialization, particularly for adolescents who in the last decade have been the most frequent moviegoers. Seen from this angle, the Oscar roles can serve as indicators of what the American cinema has been telling its audiences about the appropriate and inappropriate behaviors of men and women in society.[2] The typical Hollywood movie has been designed to appeal to the largest potential audiences, which means that filmmakers (producers, directors, and writers) have tried to make movies that they thought would be acceptable to the American public.[3] Thus, the particular attributes of the male and female Oscar-winning roles can shed light on basic cultural guidelines, proscriptions and prescriptions, that the American cinema has provided for men and women over the last half century, from the beginning of the Oscar to the present.

The Oscar Roles and Film Genre

As was shown, the Academy has favored biopictures over fictional films. But it has also favored biographical roles: about one-fifth (21 percent) of all Oscar roles have been inspired by real-life personalities. The recreation of real-life figures brings some measure of prestige to their performers, particularly if these screen characters were important in their time. Nonetheless, a clear gender-related bias has been in operation: the number of biographical Oscar roles has been twice as large among the men (27 percent) as among the women (14 percent), particularly in the lead categories: 35 percent of the Best Actors, compared with only 15 percent of the Best Actress roles.

But in addition to quantitative there have been qualitative differences. The men's biographical roles have been more diverse than the women's, historically as well as occupationally. For example, the men have portrayed military figures: Gary Cooper as Alvin York, the Tennessee farmer who became a hero in World War I, in *Sergeant York;* and George C. Scott, as General Patton, the controversial but brilliant strategist of World War II, in *Patton.* Or historical figures, such as Charles Laughton as the English monarch in *The Private Life of Henry VIII*, and Paul Scofield as Sir Thomas More in *A Man for All Seasons.* The men have also recreated the lives of political personalities, like George Arliss, as the British prime minister in *Disraeli,* and Ben Kingsley as the venerated Indian leader in *Gandhi.* Women, by contrast, have mostly portrayed show-business personalities, like Luise Rainer, as the first wife of showman Florenz Ziegfeld in *The Great Ziegfeld*; Barbra Streisand as musical comedy star Fanny Brice in *Funny Girl*; and Sissy Spacek as country singer Loretta Lynn in *Coal Miner's Daughter.*

The overrepresentation of men, or underrepresentation of women, in biographical pictures celebrating real-life achievements suggests that perhaps there have not been as many prominent women in science, politics, and literature for the movies to draw upon. Thus, films have not had a large pool of "important" women as sources for their narratives. But one could also argue that movies have been reluctant to use the real-life heroines who were appropriate for screen biographies, thus functioning as agencies of social control, keeping women in their place, by confining them to the domestic arena or to show business, both traditional female domains.

Moreover, the Oscar roles have been contained in *specific* film genres. The most frequent film genre, for both male and female roles, has been the serious-dramatic picture with three-fifths (59 percent) of all Oscar roles, followed by comedy (15 percent). Interestingly, there have been no differences between the genders in straight-dramatic films and in comedies, but the particular kinds of roles that men and women have assumed in these two genres have been radically different, as will be shown.

Few of the Oscar roles have been in romantic melodramas (7 percent), musicals (5 percent), suspense films (2 percent), and Westerns (also 2 percent). But there has been unequal distribution of male and female roles in these genres, attesting to the prevalence of "masculine" and "feminine" genres—that is, types of films regarded as appropriate for men and for women. The second most frequent genre among the men has been the action-adventure (including war films and Westerns), amounting to one-fifth (19 percent) of all male roles, whereas only few (6 percent) of the female roles have been in this genre, usually in the supporting league. The most "feminine" genre, the female equivalent of the action-adventure, has been the romantic melodrama, with 14 percent of the female roles, and even a higher percentage (19 percent) in the Best Actress category; no man has ever won an Oscar for such a film. Furthermore, in the suspense genre, there has been only one male, but four female roles, and significantly, the women have been typically cast as victims, like Joan Fontaine in *Suspicion*, and Ingrid Bergman in *Gaslight*.

Gender and the Oscar Role: The American Hero and Heroine

Mention has been made of the fact that actors have tended to win the Oscar at an older age than actresses. But their screen characters have also been older than the women's.[4] According to the Oscar roles, the American screen heroine has typically been young: four out of five Oscar roles in which the character is young in age have been female. Further, three-fifths (62 percent) of all female Oscar roles have been young, compared with only one-sixth (16 percent) of the males. And conversely, over half (57 percent) of the male characters have been middle-aged, but only one-fifth (22 percent) of the female. One-fourth (27 percent) of the male roles have been elderly characters but only one-eighth (13 percent) of the females.

By and large, characters in supporting roles have been older than those in leads: about half (47 percent) of the lead roles have been young compared with one-third (29 percent) of the supporting.

And twice as many supporting as leading roles have been old (29 percent and 13 percent respectively). The most dramatic difference between the lead and supporting roles prevails among the women: the vast majority (81 percent) of Best Actress roles have been young compared with only one-third (38 percent) of the Supporting Actresses. By contrast, the Supporting Actor roles have been either younger or older than the Best Actors.[5]

Supporting roles, both male and female, have been more varied in their ages than the lead roles. Within each of the lead categories, there has been one dominant age group: young for women and middle-aged for men. American popular culture, as expressed in the medium of film, has prescribed quite consistent biological distinctions: the screen heroine is normatively young, whereas the screen hero is middle-aged. Moreover, attached to these biological limits is an aesthetic normative prescription: the leading lady has been young and attractive, whereas the leading man has been middle-aged and preferably, but not necessarily, handsome.

These normative prescriptions have had confining results for the range of screen roles allotted to women: leading roles have almost exclusively been cast with young and beautiful actresses. Indeed, up to the 1970s, leading actresses over the age of forty were forced to make a career choice: to retire from the screen or to switch to character roles, which are usually smaller and secondary. Early retirement was therefore not a matter of choice, but rather forced upon many actresses by restrictive normative prescriptions while they were at the peak of their acting careers. For example, Deborah Kerr, a leading lady and a six-time Oscar nominee, decided to retire in 1969 after appearing in Kazan's *The Arrangement* at the age of forty-eight.

The Oscar roles also reveal important information about the norms of marriage for men and women in the US. There have been no differences in the proportion of single men (43 percent) to single women (41 percent), or divorced men (4 percent) to divorced women (5 percent). But two-fifths (40 percent) of the female Oscar roles have been married, compared with one-fourth (26 percent) of the men. And close to one-fifth (18 percent) of the male Oscar roles have made no reference to their marital status. This is in sharp contrast to a paucity (3 percent) of female roles with no information about their marital position. Clearly, screen men's marital status has been less crucial to their functioning than has been the case for women. There has been no role among the Best Actresses in which her marital position was irrelevant to the screen narrative. If our knowledge of gender roles were based entirely on information provided by movies, it would have been impossible to understand women's roles in society without knowing whether they are single, married, divorced, or widowed. By contrast, statuses other than the marital are important in understanding men's place in society.

The difference between men and women pertains to their supporting roles as well. The proportion of Supporting Actor roles with no reference to their marital status has been five times greater than that of the Supporting Actresses' (31 percent and 6 percent respectively). These differences are particularly salient due to the fact that films usually don't provide much information about supporting roles whose screen time is often limited to a few scenes. However, the chances are that if it's a female supporting role, even limited to one scene in the picture, there will be some revelation about her marital status.

Furthermore, in the course of the films' plots, the women's marital status tends to change more frequently than the men's. These transformations (from singlehood to marriage, from marriage to widowhood, from widowhood to second marriage) have constituted the heart of the narrative—not just in the genres of romance or melodrama. And they have followed one consistent pattern: regardless of the heroine's initial status (single, married, widowed, or divorced), by the film's end she is either married, going to be married, or attached to one man. Most of these films have made a point, at times using the most incredible and illogical plot devices, to resolve their heroine's marital position, if it were undetermined. This is the reason why the percentage of married or attached women is higher by the film's conclusion than at its start.

The occupational portrayal of men and women in American film, as reflected in the Oscar-winning roles, has distinguished between them even more sharply than their depiction in terms of age and marriage. The vast majority (97 percent) of the male Oscar roles had identifiable occupations and were gainfully employed. By contrast, over one-third (36 percent) of the female characters have had no gainful work. In sharp contrast to the women, there have been no men who did not work. It has been inconceivable for the screen male *not* to engage in a gainful employment—unless he is a criminal or convict. And whereas there is always a "good" reason for screen males not to work, there is nothing "wrong" with women who sit idle and don't work. A second difference between men and women concerns their range of occupations, which has been much wider for men. Males have been portrayed in three times as many occupations as women, ranging from the top of the occupational hierarchy (kings, judges, governors, generals) to the least prestigious occupations (manual workers, butchers, and miners).

Prevalent Male Oscar Roles

There has been a tremendous concentration of men in occupations related, directly or indirectly, to the maintenance of law and order in society. The two most frequent occupations among male roles have been soldiers (14 percent) and sheriffs and policemen (9 percent).

Fourteen actors have won the Oscar for portraying a military figure: Emil Jannings in *The Last Command*, Gary Cooper in *Sergeant York*, Fredric March and Harold Russell in *The Best Years of Our Lives*, Dean Jagger in *Twelve O'Clock High*, William Holden in *Stalag 17*, Frank Sinatra in *From Here to Eternity*, Jack Lemmon in *Mister Roberts*, Alec Guinness in *The Bridge on the River Kwai*, Red Buttons in *Sayonara*, George C. Scott in *Patton*, John Voight in *Coming Home*, Christopher Walken in *The Deer Hunter*, and Louis Gossett Jr. in *An Officer and a Gentleman*. And the number of screen soldiers among the nominees has been even more substantial.

Law enforcers (sheriffs, marshals, detectives) have also been dominant among the male roles: Gary Cooper in *High Noon*, Lee Marvin in *Cat Ballou*, Rod Steiger in *In the Heat of the Night*, John Wayne in *True Grit*, and Gene Hackman in *The French Connection*.

Furthermore, if all male roles concerned with the control of violence and crime are combined, their proportion is extremely high: 41 percent of the Oscar roles. In addition to military figures and sheriffs, this group will include kings (Yul Brynner in *The King and I*), politicians (Broderick Crawford in *All the King's Men*, Ed Begley in *Sweet Bird of Youth*), freedom fighters (Paul Lukas in *Watch on the Rhine*), and judges and lawyers (Lionel Barrymore in *A Free Soul*, Walter Brennan in *The Westerner*, Maximilian Schell in *Judgment at Nuremberg*, and Walter Matthau in *The Fortune Cookie*). Screen priests have also fulfilled important functions in maintaining social order. In *Boys' Town*, Spencer Tracy's Father Flanagan creates a school for tough and poor street children, and Bing Crosby in *Going My Way* rehabilitates a group of juvenile delinquents by turning them into a choir.

Most of the male roles have depicted men preoccupied with their professional careers, single-mindedly and at times at the expense of fulfillment in their personal lives. In some cases, there are no women in their lives. For example, Rod Steiger's Billie Gillespie in *In the Heat of the Night* is a thick-witted, bigoted sheriff, investigating a murder in his small Southern town. The film deals with his relationship with Virgil Tibbs (Sidney Poitier), a black homicide detective from the North, brought in to help him resolve the mystery. In the course of the movie, their relationship is transformed from initial suspicion and contempt to mutual respect and understanding. But *In the Heat of the Night* illuminates their personalities in terms of two statuses, occupation and ethnicity, which are exclusively explored in the contexts of their public roles; nothing of their private lives enters into the film. Similarly, *Patton* focuses on the wartime career of the arrogant and authoritarian general, who is in love with war, and incapable of coping with peacetime. This movie differs radically from the cinematic conventions of biopictures by *not* presenting any material about his personal life.

In case of a conflict between the requirements of the job and those of family life, a clear priority is given to the former. Gary Cooper's second Oscar was for the role of Will Kane in *High Noon*, a marshal who faces a serious dilemma on his wedding day: to leave town, as his Quaker wife (Grace Kelly) and most of his friends urge him to do, or to face the four outlaws by himself—nobody in this cowardly town is willing to help him. Despite burdens of fear and isolation, the danger of losing his wife, and the fact that he has retired from the job, he decides to meet the challenge alone, head-on. "A man's got to do what a man's got to do," has been a consistent motto of the screen male hero in all genres, not just in Westerns and war movies.[6]

It is also illuminating that two out of the four male Oscar roles that primarily dealt with privacy and leisure have been those of elderly men who had retired from their professions. In *Harry and Tonto*, Art Carney's Oscar-winning role, Harry is an aging widower who, having been dispossessed from his New York apartment, goes on a transcontinental tour with his cat Tonto. And

Henry Fonda's Norman Thayer, the protagonist of *On Golden Pond*, is an eighty-year-old retired university professor, spending what is perhaps his last summer with his spunky wife of fifty years.

Screen men have also enjoyed a relatively greater freedom from the legitimate social order than women. Several men have won the award for playing deviants or criminals. Marlon Brando and Robert De Niro won Oscars for the same screen role. The former portrayed mafia don Vito Corleone in *The Godfather*, and the latter played the same character as a younger man in *The Godfather, Part II*. De Niro studied Brando's performance meticulously, though, as he explained, "I didn't want to do an imitation, but I wanted to make it believable that I could be him as a young man." For him, the challenge was similar to "a mathematical problem—having a result and figuring out how to make the beginning fit."[7]

By contrast, there have been few Oscar roles of female deviants. Tatum O'Neal's 1973 supporting award in *Paper Moon*, as a tough-talking nine-year-old girl who becomes an accomplice to a con man, a Bible salesman (played by her real-life father Ryan O'Neal), has been a rare exception.

However, there have been more nominations than actual awards for screen portrayals of criminals, demonstrating a greater normative range in the nomination than in the winning. Indeed, several players have had to deviate from their previous screen image, if it were that of a gangster, before winning the award. Actors who started their careers by playing heavies and villains have had to switch to playing heroes, or good-bad guys, to get the award. Wallace Beery played a wide array of villains in his Paramount silent pictures, but with the advent of sound he shook off his image and started to play the "lovable slob," the "good-bad" guy, as exemplified by his Oscar-winning role, *The Champ*, in which he played an errant father, a drunk, a gambling ex-champion, who makes a comeback for the sake of his idolizing son (Jackie Cooper).

Ernest Borgnine's looks made him a natural screen villain; a wide face, beady eyes, and gap between his teeth. His appearance was used in his early years as an actor, when he was cast as a sadistic sergeant (*From Here to Eternity*) and other menacing villains (*Bad Day at Black Rock*).[8] Nonetheless, Borgnine won the award for a role that represented a change of pace, an utterly sympathetic hero: the lonely and kind butcher in *Marty*.

More significantly, great performances in crime-gangster movies

have been either ignored by the Academy or, at best, nominated—
but seldom have won. It is a curious fact, but none of the Warner
Brothers' actors who specialized in gangster movies won the award
for such a role. James Cagney's image is most closely associated
with the gangster film, but neither his performance in *The Public
Enemy*, the film that made him a star, nor his distinguished work
in the Freudian gangster movie *White Heat*, were even nominated.
Still, unlike other gangster heroes, Cagney received two nominations for such movies: *Angels with Dirty Faces*, which won him the
New York Critics Award, and *Love Me or Leave Me*, as the tough
racketeer Martin Snyder married to singer Ruth Etting (Doris
Day).

Still, Cagney had to step outside of this realm and portray the patriotic showman George M. Cohan in *Yankee Doodle Dandy* to win an
Oscar. This role, however, did not change his screen persona, as
Frank S. Nugent wrote: "Mr. Cagney has the faculty of being taken
for granted. Although he is not in the least public enemyish off the
screen, he has done so well in the role that producers entered a
happy conspiracy to keep him there. His few breaks for freedom—
Boy Meets Girl among them—have not been successful, whether
through Cagney's fault or our inability to adjust ourselves to seeing
him without an armpit holster."[9]

Paul Muni, another noted Warners player, started his career in
gangster films, delivering an indelible performance in Howard
Hawks's *Scarface*, but failing to get nominated for it. Like Cagney,
he won the respect of the Academy when he portrayed a series of
"important" historical figures, like the French scientist in *The Story
of Louis Pasteur*, his Oscar role, or the writer in *The Life of Emile Zola*,
for which he won a nomination.

But most revealing of all in this regard is the career of Humphrey
Bogart, who for a decade specialized in playing villains usually shot
down in the last reel of the film. No other actor has died so many
times on the screen. But after *High Sierra*, and particularly *The Maltese Falcon*, his screen image underwent a radical transformation,
and he was rewarded by the Academy for his new tough-but-
romantic heroic persona in *Casablanca*, his first nomination and
best-remembered film and in *The African Queen*, for which he won
an Oscar. Bogart was cast as Charlie Allnut, a tough, unshaven,
gin-soaked riverboat captain who becomes a hero, helping a missionary (Katharine Hepburn) in Africa to torpedo a German battle-

ship. As Andrew Sarris has observed, because the Academy members have been conservative they are not likely to vote for anarchic, virile roles.[10] The socialization and taming of Bogart's Charlie by Hepburn in *The African Queen*, in one scene pouring all his gin into the river, proves Sarris's argument.

Until recent years, mainstream roles, deeply rooted in dominant culture, have had much better chances to get nominations and awards than rebellious, antiestablishment roles. Dustin Hoffman's career, five nominations, and Oscar demonstrate this point well. Hoffman received his first nomination for *The Graduate*, as the college graduate who first violates sexual mores by having a simultaneous affair with a mother and her daughter, but then rejects the predatory old woman and the bourgeois life-style of his parents. His second nomination was for *Midnight Cowboy*, in which he played Ratso, a drifter and an outcast at the margins of society. For his portrayal of Lenny Bruce, Hoffman received a third, though playing the foul-mouthed comedian was almost an assurance that he would *not* get the award. Hoffman continued to play other countercultural roles, such as in *Papillon*, as a prisoner on Devil's Island, and in *Straw Dogs*, for which he was not nominated. But it was only when he was cast in a mainstream role in *Kramer Vs. Kramer*, as a self-absorbed executive who becomes the most affectionate and responsible father, that he won the Oscar, for which he was long overdue.

For years, Hoffman was highly critical of the Oscar award, which made him, along with other reasons, one of Hollywood's enfants terribles. However, when the preaward polls predicted his likelihood to win, he mellowed his public utterances and also decided to attend the show. Hoffman was incorporated into mainstream Hollywood, along with other famous Hollywood rebels, such as Jane Fonda and Barbra Streisand. Indeed, anti-Hollywood and antiestablishment players are now abiding by the rules of the Academy and the industry. Their dissenting voices seem weaker, fewer, and mellower—they have realized that being rebellious might have damaging effects on their careers and on their box-office popularity. And the new generation of stars, Meryl Streep, Sissy Spacek, Sally Field, William Hurt, have been "obedient" from the very start, refraining from attacking Hollywood or the Academy. They either believe in the system or understand that in order to exercise power in Hollywood and win awards, one has to play the rules of the game!

Enduring Female Screen Stereotypes

In comparison with the men, gainfully employed screen women have been confined to highly stereotypical professions, those considered to be "appropriate" for women. There have been two major lines of work for screen women, both reflected in the Oscar roles, in service (as teachers, nurses, secretaries) and in entertainment (as actresses, singers, and dancers). The two most prominent professions among the women have been actresses (15 percent) and prostitutes (12 percent). At least one out of every three gainfully employed women has been an actress or a prostitute and, at times, both actress and prostitute. In both professions, a woman is paid, as critic Molly Haskell has observed, "for doing what already she did: prostitution, in which she was remunerated for giving sexual pleasure, and acting, a variant on natural role-playing."[11] What is common to both lines of work is "playing roles and adapting to others, aiming to please."[12] Moreover, neither acting nor prostitution has enjoyed a particularly high prestige in the occupational hierarchy, probably because it is possible to practice both works without any formal education or professional training.[13]

Actresses playing actresses have had the best chances to win nominations and awards for two major reasons. The Acting Branch of the Academy consists of the largest number of members, who usually are sympathetic, even biased in favor of screen portrayals of show-business personalities. And screen roles of peformers, as much as they can be stereotypical, also provide "meaty" parts, lending themselves to a display of histrionic antics and an intense gamut of emotions.

There have been two prevalent roles of screen actresses, both quite stereotypical. One is that of the fading star, slipping from the top to skid row because of aging, the loss of looks, drinking problem, frustrated love, or unhappy marriage. The other is almost the reversal, the young ambitious ingenue, who gets her big break at the very last moment, usually on opening night, when the veteran is unable to perform, as epitomized in *Forty-Second Street*. Some movies, like the 1950 Oscar-winning *All About Eve*, juxtaposes the two stereotypes. Bette Davis, in the greatest performance of her career, is Margo Channing, the aging star who cannot come to terms with her progressing age, forty, which by today's standards is still young, but in the 1950s was considered to be old. And Anne Baxter is the young, driven Eve Harrington, scheming to take over everything Davis possesses, her roles, friends, and even her man.

Bette Davis, in fact, specialized in portraying suffering actresses, and four of her ten nominations were for such roles. In her first Oscar role, *Dangerous*, she plays Joyce Heath, a bottle-swigging, once-famous stage actress, bent on her own destruction until she meets an admiring young architect (Franchot Tone) who befriends her and sponsors her comeback. When her husband (John Eldredge) refuses her a divorce so she can marry the architect, she attempts to kill both of them by driving into a tree. They survive, but her husband is crippled for life. Returning triumphantly to the stage, she now understands the values of sacrifice, giving up her real love for duty to her husband. In *The Star*, her ninth nomination, Davis's Margaret Elliot is a has-been, a former Oscar winner who is now pathetic, bitter, and violent. As in *Dangerous*, an admirer (Sterling Hayden) saves her by convincing her, as in *All About Eve*, that she must give up her career and live a more normal—i.e., domestic— life. Davis's last nomination was in the cult film, Robert Aldridge's *Whatever Happened to Baby Jane?* She is cast as Jane Hudson, the genius child star whose talent faded when she grew up, turning her into a demented alcoholic, sadistic and vindictive toward her crippled sister (Joan Crawford). It was a flashy, quite grotesque performance, but it opened a new phase in her career— playing horror queens.

Gloria Swanson created an indelible shading as Norma Desmond, the aging silent movie queen, terrified of the camera but dreaming of a comeback, in *Sunset Boulevard*. And Geraldine Page did some of her best work, on the stage and in film, as Alexandra DeLargo in Tennessee Williams's *Sweet Bird of Youth*, as another aging, drug-addict star, entertained by an opportunistic stud (Paul Newman), only to find out that her last film was not as disastrous as she had thought.

But the portrayal of actresses on screen need not be tragic; this stereotype has been exploited in comedy too. For example, Maggie Smith won her second Oscar in Neil Simon's *California Suite*, as

British actress Diana Barrie, a hard-drinking, hard-talking performer, arriving in California for the Oscar ceremonies. Disenchanted after losing, she complains, "Acting doesn't win Oscars—what I need is a dying father." And Valentina Cortesa was nominated in Truffaut's comedy *Day for Night,* as yet another fading movie star who hides a bottle on the set and cannot remember her lines.

The best example of the reverse stereotype, the young, stage-struck ingenue, is Katharine Hepburn's first Oscar-winning performance in *Morning Glory,* as Eve Lovelace, a naive girl from Vermont who creates a sensation by stepping in for a recalcitrant leading lady on opening night. Some lines from this picture have entered movie lore, as when she is warned by a veteran actor not to succumb to her fame, "How many keep their heads? You've come to the fore. Now you have the chance to be a morning glory, a flower that fades before the sun is very high." Or Hepburn's vow, "I'm not afraid of being like a morning glory. I'm not afraid. I'm not afraid." And, of course, Adolphe Menjou as the producer telling her: "You don't belong to any man now, you belong to Broadway!"

The prostitute, with or without "the golden heart," has been one of the most enduring female images and the *second* prevalent Oscar role among the women. Elizabeth Taylor won her first Oscar in *Butterfield 8,* based on John O'Hara's novel, as Gloria Wandrous, a New York call girl. She describes herself as "the slut of all times," but basically she is a good-natured woman, whose main ambition in life is to gain respectability by marrying a decent man and living a suburban, middle-class life. However, trapped and unable to forget her past, there is no hope for her and, after a disastrous affair with a wealthy, married Yale graduate (Laurence Harvey), she meets death in a fatal car crash.

Jane Fonda's first Oscar-winning performance in *Klute* was of great distinction. For no apparent reason, the film was titled after its detective's name (played by Donald Sutherland), but it should have been named after its real heroine, Bree Daniel, a New York call girl who is at once a victim of her circumstances but also powerful—she enjoys the control she possesses over her clients. This film, like many others, makes an explicit association between the two traditional female professions, actresses and prostitutes. When Bree complains to her analyst that she has had no luck as an actress in auditions, the latter responds, "What is the difference? You're successful as a call girl, you're not successful as an actress." Other films also make these links, like Claire Trevor's Oscar role in *Key Largo*, as a gangster's alcoholic mistress, who is a faded torch singer.

There have been more supporting than leading Oscars for playing prostitutes. Jo Van Fleet won a supporting award in *East of Eden*, for playing James Dean's presumably dead mother who actually broke free of her family and becomes a notorious madame of a brothel. And Dorothy Malone gave an intense performance in Douglas Sirk's *Written on the Wind*, as a frustrated rich nymphomaniac who enjoys seducing gas-station attendants in motel rooms.

What is interesting about these Oscars is that they have often rewarded actresses for deviating from their previous screen image as wholesome and sweet girls. For example, Anne Baxter began her career as "the girl next door," in patriotic war films (*The Pied Piper, Crash Dive, The Fighting Sullivans*), but she won an Oscar for a major departure from that image, as the tragic woman in *The Razor's Edge*, who becomes a dipsomaniacal prostitute after the death of her husband and child in a car crash. Donna Reed built a name for herself as a sincere, wholesome girl—in *It's a Wonderful Life* she was Jimmy Stewart's loyal wife—but she won for a role that was the exception in her career, Alma, the hostess in *From Here to Eternity*; the film was less explicit about her occupation than the book, in which she was a prostitute.

Shirley Jones was recruited to Hollywood from the Broadway stage, having established herself as a singer. At first, she played romantic and shy girls in a series of musicals (*Oklahoma!, Carousel, April Love*). But only when she changed her appearance and her image in *Elmer Gantry*, as Lulu Bains, the prostitute, did she get recognition from the Academy. Thus, the two 1960 female awards were given to actresses who played prostitutes: Elizabeth Taylor in *Butterfield 8* and Shirley Jones. "I am sick of portraying ingenues with sunny dispositions, high necklines and puff sleeves, who are girlishly aggressive about happiness being just around the corner,"[14] Jones is reported to have said after her Oscar.

In addition to actresses and prostitutes, the other women's roles have also conformed to cultural stereotypes of traditional family roles, such as wives, mothers, and daughters. The two most distinctive attributes of the female Oscar roles have been sex and suffering. The combination of family roles with sex and victimization has created some of the most enduring screen stereotypes, such as the adulteress-mistress, the sacrificing mother, the suffering wife, the oppressed spinster-daughter. These stereotypical roles, reflected and reinforced by the Oscar Award, have persisted in the American cinema for half a century—with few or minor alterations. Most female roles up to the 1970s have been variations or reworkings of these formulaic conventions, as the following examples demonstrate.

The Southern belle has been a uniquely American literary and cinematic type. Bette Davis won a second Oscar for *Jezebel*, as the rich, spoiled, and willful Julie Marsden, whose entire behavior is motivated by her failure to win the love of Pres Dillard (Henry Fonda). He breaks their engagement when she disregards the norms and wears a red gown to New Orleans's Olympus Ball; all the other girls are wearing the traditional white dress. Punished, she secludes herself, waiting for him to return, only to find out that he has married another girl. However, when he falls victim to a yellow-fever epidemic, she convinces his wife that *she* should accompany him to a quarantine island, but promises to send him back if he survives.

Vivien Leigh's memorable Oscar performance as Scarlett O'Hara, a tempestuous self-centered belle, in the popular film of Margaret Mitchell's *Gone with the Wind*, is another good example. So is her second Oscar, for Blanche DuBois in Tennessee Williams's *A Streetcar Named Desire*, the sordid tale of the mental deterioration of a repressed Southern belle. Blanche DuBois, a challenge for every living actress, is a perfect prototype of the kinds of screen roles that win Oscars, because it includes all the "necessary" elements of a good role, thus allowing for a display of great range of emotions and acting skills.

Tennessee Williams has written some of the best female roles on stage and on screen. The eccentricity of his characters, their rich inner selves, often dominated by repressed sexuality, have called for great acting. It is therefore not surprising that most of his films, based on his plays, have earned nominations and awards for their women, and sometimes for their men too. In *Baby Doll*, Carroll Baker was nominated for playing "a white trash," a retarded, thumb-sucking child-wife, seduced by her husband's revenge-seeking rival; Mildred Dunnock was nominated for playing a pathetic, demented aunt. *Cat on a Hot Tin Roof* was one of 1958's most nominated pictures, in which Elizabeth Taylor excelled as Maggie, the sexy wife who is punished by her alcoholic husband (Paul Newman, also nominated) who won't sleep with her. *Suddenly Last Summer*, a study of incest, cannibalism, and insanity, confronted Katharine Hepburn, as a demented aristocratic mother in love with her homosexual poet-son, with Elizabeth Taylor, as her niece, who almost goes mad after witnessing the rape and murder of her cousin; both Hepburn and Taylor won nominations; neither won.

Vivien Leigh was not nominated for playing the widowed American actress who drifts into lassitude and moral decline in *The Roman Spring of Mrs. Stone*, but Lotte Lenya, as a vicious female pimp, was. In *Summer and Smoke*, a drama of earthly and spiritual love, Geraldine Page was nominated for the role of Alma, the sexually repressed spinsterish minister's daughter. In addition to Geraldine Page, *Sweet Bird of Youth* provided a nomination for Shirley Knight, as the victimized daughter-girlfriend who had contracted syphilis from her boyfriend (Paul Newman). And in *Night of the Iguana*, Grayson Hall received a supporting nomination as the leader of the vacationing schoolteachers whose animosity toward the defrocked priest (Richard Burton) reflected a repressed lesbianism and interest in the nymphomanical teenager (Sue Lyon).

The spinster, or the old maid, has been another distinctive and enduring female stereotype. Olivia De Havilland won her second Oscar in *The Heiress*, as the timid ugly duckling daughter of a strong, domineering father (Ralph Richardson), who is deceived and bitterly disappointed when she finds out that her admirer (Montgomery Clift) is a scoundrel interested only in her wealth. Other distinguished performances of frustrated spinsters who received nominations have included Agnes Moorehead's neurotic, spinsterish aunt in *The Magnificent Ambersons*, and Joanne Woodward in *Rachel, Rachel*, as a spinster teacher in a small town who experiences her first sexual encounter at thirty-five, and is then deserted by the man. Most of these spinsters have domineering mothers, against whom they finally rebel, usually for the love of a man. One of Bette Davis's most popular roles was in *Now Voyager*, as a desperate, humiliated, mother-driven spinster who finds a fulfilling love at a later age. In *Separate Tables* too, Deborah Kerr starts as a timid, sexually repressed virgin, dominated by her cruel mother (Gladys Cooper), but in the end she rebels against her.

Katharine Hepburn has gone through several distinct phases in her lengthy screen career. In the earlier phase, up to the late 1940s, she played strong, independent but attractive women (*The Philadelphia Story, Woman of the Year*). When she started to age, she continued to play strong-willed women, but they became unglamorous and spinsterish. If the role of Tracy Lord in *The Philadelphia Story* summed up the earlier part of her career, *The African Queen* (her fifth nomination), in which she was cast as a missionary, fulfilled the same function for a later phase. She was cast in a similar role in *Summertime* (her sixth nomination), a spinsterish teacher vacationing in Venice and falling in love with Rossano Brazzi, and in *The Rainmaker* (her seventh nomination), as an unattractive tomboyish girl whose womanhood is eventually brought to the surface by Burt Lancaster's con man.

Suffering and Victimization

One chief attribute of the female Oscar roles, running through all genres, has been suffering or victimization. According to the Oscar roles, women have suffered a disproportionately large number of disasters and catastrophes, natural and man-made. The vast majority (71 percent) of the female Oscar roles have included suffering of one form or another. Men have suffered much less, and the source of their victimization has been substantially different. Women have tended to be victims of their spouses or lovers: 42 percent of the Best Actress roles, compared with only 2 percent of the Best Actors. The male heroes have been in charge of their emotional lives, whereas women have exercised little or no control over their romantic, marital, and even familial bonds—all of which have caused them a great deal of torment and anguish.

Sexual assault has been the most obvious form of victimization, with 5 percent of the Oscar roles describing actual rapes. In *Johnny Belinda*, Jane Wyman is cast as a deaf-mute girl, a victim of a brutal rape by a drunken fisherman, who later attempts to steal her illegitimate baby; this forces her to kill him and stand trial. And Blanche DuBois, the genteel belle in *A Streetcar Named Desire*, is tortured, then raped by her brutish brother-in-law, an act which drives her into insanity.

An even larger number of Oscar roles has depicted women betrayed by their husbands. Adultery has been one of the most consistent male privileges on the screen and, correspondingly, a continuous source of suffering for women. Janet Gaynor won an Oscar for *Sunrise*, as a farmer's loyal wife, betrayed by her husband, for a glamorous, sexy city woman, who almost succeeds in persuading him to kill her. And Luise Rainer's second Oscar was for playing a selfless, slavelike Chinese farmer's wife in *The Good Earth*, first neglected by her husband, then further humiliated when he marries a younger wife. Serafina Della Rose, Anna Magnani's Oscar role in *The Rose Tattoo*, is a tempestuous widow who idolizes her dead husband, only to be the last to discover that he has been unfaithful to her. A deeply religious woman, she is obsessed with sexual memories of him to the point of becoming a recluse and a domineering mother.

The notion that women's status in American society can be instructively, though unfortunately, examined through such concepts as deviance, stigma, and victimization, is clearly demonstrated in the Oscar-winning roles.[15] Any attempt by screen women —until the 1970s—to deviate from their prescribed, stereotypical roles has been consistently and continuously punished. Strong-willed, determined heroines have not only been depicted as deviants, but have also been oppressed if their conducts were considered a threat to the status quo of male dominance. These forms of punishment have ranged from the most extreme sanction, death, to lesser sanctions, such as humiliation, ostracization, and relegation to domestic life.

Bette Davis's Julie in *Jezebel* is punished for violating social conventions of clothes, wearing a red gown; the film implies that she has destroyed her chances at real happiness, through marriage, by defying the social norms. Sexual promiscuity by women has also been regarded as a severe violation of mores, which is the reason why most screen prostitutes (Elizabeth Taylor's in *Butterfield 8*) have paid with their lives for engaging in such a direputable occupation.

Death, by "accident," has also been the fate of screen adulteresses. Gloria Grahame specialized in playing floozies and loose girls (*Crossfire*, *The Big Heat*). She received a supporting Oscar for *The Bad and the Beautiful*, as an attractive, social-climbing wife, urging her screenwriter-husband to move to Hollywood for its glamorous life-style. But his ruthless producer (Kirk Douglas) considers her to be an interruptive force in his creative career and, subsequently, arranges for her an affair with a Latin lover. Needless to say, she ends up tragically in an airplane crash. Simone Signoret's Alice Abigal in *Room at the Top* also finds death in a fatal automobile accident. An aging actress who is unhappily married, she is desperate for some genuine affection. But she falls in love with an ambitious, calculating working-class man (Laurence Harvey), who mistreats her. In the end, she is sacrificed by him for a younger woman, the daughter of the town's rich tycoon, and dies on his wedding day.

Screen death seems to have "solved" the problem of having to deal with women as equal partners, particularly women who participate actively in the economic and political structures. Vanessa Redgrave's role in *Julia* is a good example, for Julia is a young intelligent woman, who rebels against her aristocratic family by becoming a fighter in the European anti-Fascist movement. But she too is killed off in the course of the narrative, thus becoming a symbol of political heroism and courage rather than a real living woman. Screen death has often functioned as a safety valve, permitting audiences to admire courageous independent women as martyrs, but relieving men of the burden of dealing with them as equals on a realistic level.[16] If the hero of *Julia* were a man, he would probably have survived. Male fighters in American film have usually succeeded in accomplishing their missions, as Paul Lukas's Oscar role in another Hellman work, *Watch on the Rhine*, demonstrates. Lukas, in fact, plays a similar role to Vanessa Redgrave's—an anti-Fascist fighter.

Ambitious career women have also been consistently punished for stepping out of their place, entering into men's domain, and thus competing with them for desirable jobs and rewards. The best example of this type is Joan Crawford's Oscar role as the suffering mother in *Mildred Pierce*. An ambitious woman, she builds up a chain of restaurants in order to provide her ungrateful daughter (Ann Blyth) all the rewards she was deprived of. Throughout the movie she is punished. Her younger daughter dies of pneumonia while she is spending her *first* weekend off from work with her lover. She then throws herself into a second, loveless marriage with a playboy, whom she ends up supporting. But her eldest daughter despises her for her lower-class origins and job as a waitress, and flirts with her stepfather, whom she later kills out of jealousy. At the film's end, having lost everything, including her business, Mildred Pierce goes back to her first husband—and to a second life as a housewife, where, apparently, she belongs.

Mildred Pierce is by no means an exception. The portrayal of career women was quite consistent up to the late 1970s. Screen career women have been typically single, suggesting that it is impossible for them to combine successful careers with satisfactory personal lives—which screen men, on the other hand, have managed to achieve with relative ease. Even women choosing the perennial female occupation, acting, have been single, as in *All About Eve*: Margo Channing, while she was professionally successful, and Eve throughout the film. Career women have been ridiculed and condemned as grotesque, "unfeeling monsters." This dehumanization is illustrated in Louise Fletcher's Oscar role in *One Flew Over the Cuckoo's Nest*, as Big Nurse Ratched, a tyrannical nurse in charge of a state mental ward. She is a severe, humorless woman, representing an oppressive establishment whose major goal is to tame her patients, all men, using all kinds of controls, including electroshock treatment and lobotomy. Endowed with a bureaucratic personality, she is rigid, indoctrinary, and adheres to the rules by the book. Nurse Ratched is sympathetic to her patients only when it promotes her own interests and authority. In the course of the film, she drives one of her young patients (Oscar-nominated Brad Douriff), a mother-fixated kid, into suicide by consciously playing on his guilt complex. Her character is not written or played on the same level of realism as her patients; she is more of an abstract symbol of sexual inhibition and repressive authority.

Faye Dunaway's Oscar role as Diana Christensen, a ruthless, power-hungry television executive in *Network*, is also more of an abstract, or "type," than a realistic character. In fact, some believe that Dunaway was rewarded for being a good sport, poking fun at her own screen image as an ambitious career woman. In this film, her chief goal is to upgrade the network's ratings, as she unashamedly boasts: "All I want out of life is a 30 share and 20 rating," for which she is willing to use illegitimate, disreputable means, like a program featuring a terrorists' organization. Obsessed with her work, which permeates every aspect of her life, she talks about it nonstop, even during a sexual encounter. In this scene she even sets the tone and the speed of the act with a sensitive married executive (William Holden) by sitting on top of him and reaching orgasm prematurely, thus imitating what is considered a typical masculine sexual practice. Efficient and rational, she is cold and incapable of any human feelings. Neither Diana nor Nurse Ratched have any meaningful personal lives outside the contexts of their work.

The most prevalent female screen stereotypes have combined show business with suffering, as demonstrated in the various versions of *A Star Is Born*. Janet Gaynor and Judy Garland were both nominated for the same role in the 1937 and 1954 versions respectively: the story of a young actress, ascending to stardom while her husband's career goes on the skids. Show-business biopictures about women have been based on simple formulaic conventions: the achievement of fame costs a high price, and stardom does not last long because it is often accompanied by afflictions and problems that have damaging effects on both career and personal life.

The following list is just a sample of this type of Oscar-nominated role: Eleanor Parker as crippled singer Marjorie Lawrence in *Interrupted Melody*; Susan Hayward as alcoholic singer Lillian Roth in *I'll Cry Tomorrow*; Diana Ross as heroin-addict, discriminated-against black singer Billie Holliday in *Lady Sings the Blues*; Bette Midler as a drug-addict rock star, loosely based on Janis Joplin's life, in *The Rose*; and Jessica Lange as the doomed, antiestablishment actress Frances Farmer in *Frances* who, tormented by her overbearing mother, turns to the bottle and ends up in a mental asylum.

The Oscar Roles, Hollywood, and Male Dominance

Cinema, like other social institutions, does not operate in a social or political void. Rather, it is interrelated with the economic and political structure of society and with its dominant ideology. Hollywood can be instructively analyzed as a commercial industry of products as well as an ideological system that produces and transmits cultural symbols. These two intertwining facets of movies—as ideological constructs of meanings and as commercial products—have never been more explicit than in the Hollywood formulaic genre movies. The cultural world articulated in the Hollywood movie has expressed the ideological dominance of one powerful group in society: white, middle-class men. This group has defined and controlled the normative order and has imposed it on other, less powerful groups, such as women and ethnic minorities. The notion of cultural dominance is therefore crucial to the understanding of the specific images that men and women have embodied, best reflected in the Oscar-winning roles.

The typical screen hero and heroine have differed substantially in such attributes as age, physical appearance, marital status, and occupation. Moreover, the male roles have been in serious, dramatic pictures dealing with important issues, such as crime, racism, and injustice. Assigned to screen roles that control and maintain the social order, men have perpetuated the status quo symbolically, onscreen, and pragmatically, offscreen. Female roles, by contrast, have been based on fictional figures mostly contained in the genres of romance and melodrama, known as the "woman's" film. According to the Oscar roles, the contribution of women to society has been in marital and familial roles, as wives-mothers, or in service professions, as entertainers and prostitutes.

The men's Oscar roles can be described as social *types*, whereas the women's are *stereotypes*. There is a crucial difference between the two concepts: social types are shared, recognized, easily grasped norms of how people are expected to behave while playing certain roles, but stereotypes are based on much more stringent and confining guidelines.[17] Stereotypes involve strong value judgments, both approval and disapproval of particular ways of behavior, and imply that "persons not conforming to the specified ways of appearing, feeling, and behaving are inadequate as males or females."[18] Stereotypes may not only be distorted, but also harmful, confining people to narrowly defined ranges of norms and behaviors.

The function of the male types and female stereotypes, from the point of view of dominant ideology, is to keep women in their place, to reward them for accepting their traditional roles and for *not* challenging the status quo. These screen roles have provided an ideological rationalization much needed to reconcile women to marriage and family life.[19] Comprehensive and all-embracing, these images go beyond the socioeconomic area, providing a mental state of mind, a whole way of life for women. The persistence of these roles, for over half a century, indicates that a large segment of moviegoers accepted at least passively the ideological message of the Hollywood movies.

However, the limited, stereotypical portrayal of women also shows that Hollywood has basically been out of touch with reality, ignoring the progress that women were beginning to make in the social structure. Indeed, the media's images and symbols are not necessarily up-to-date: a culture lag[20] often prevails between society's material conditions and its cultural representations. Such a gap has existed between the economic and occupational roles of women in society and their ideological treatment in film.[21] Moreover, the most negative screen portrayal, trivializing women's domestic roles and condemning career women, occurred in the late 1960s and early 1970s—just when women were beginning to make their mark offscreen. It would not be an exaggeration to claim that there was an ideological backlash in Hollywood, manifested in three important ways.

First, there was a paucity of screen roles for women, particularly leading roles. For a while it seemed as if women had completely disappeared from the American screen.[22] The worst year in the history of the Best Actress category, marked by extremely weak competition, was in 1975, when members of the Acting Branch had difficulties in nominating five actresses for lead performances. No wonder Louise Fletcher won—there was not much competition. The other four nominees were: Isabelle Adjani in *The Story of Adele H.*, Ann-Margret in the musical *Tommy*, Glenda Jackson in the film version of Ibsen's *Hedda*, and Carol Kane in *Hester Street*. Ellen Burstyn, the previous year's winner, asked her colleagues in the Acting Branch not to nominate actresses in the lead category as a protest against the marginal position of women in Hollywood. Under other circumstances, Fletcher's role in *Cuckoo's Nest* would have been nominated for a supporting Oscar.

Men dominated Hollywood not only quantitatively, but also qualitatively. The typical, big-budget movies of that era were the action-adventures, focusing on male heroism, male friendships, and male courage. The major movies, artistically as well as commercially, usually featured two male stars in the leading roles, with few or no women in their narratives. The list of these movies is too long to reproduce here in its entirety, but it is sufficient to name a few of the Best Picture nominees that were also blockbusters: *In the Heat of the Night* starring Rod Steiger and Sidney Poitier; *Midnight Cowboy* with Jon Voight and Dustin Hoffman; *Butch Cassidy and the Sundance Kid* with Paul Newman and Robert Redford; *M.A.S.H* boasting a mostly male cast headed by Donald Sutherland and Elliott Gould; *Patton* with George C. Scott and Karl Malden; *The French Connection* with Gene Hackman and Roy Scheider; *Deliverance* with Jon Voight and Burt Reynolds, *The Godfather*, Parts I and II, with an all-male cast, Marlon Brando, Robert De Niro, Robert Duvall, and Al Pacino; *The Sting* with Paul Newman and Robert

Redford; *The Towering Inferno* with Paul Newman and Steve McQueen; *Dog Day Afternoon* with Al Pacino and Chris Sarandon; *Jaws* with Richard Dreyfuss, Roy Scheider, and Robert Shaw; and *All the President's Men* with Robert Redford and Dustin Hoffman.

Finally, most of the box-office stars in the late 1960s and 1970s were men, with the exception of Barbra Streisand, the only woman among the ten Box-Office Champions. Moreover, the biggest names in the industry were all male stars with a strong, tough "macho" image, such as Steve McQueen in *The Thomas Crown Affair* and *Bullitt*, Clint Eastwood in his *Dirty Harry* movies, Lee Marvin in *The Professionals* and *The Dirty Dozen*, and Charles Bronson in *Death Wish* and its many variants.

Recent Changes in Oscar-Winning Roles

In the last decade there have been some significant changes in the Oscar roles, mostly in the female and to a lesser extent in the male. In fact, the cinematic depiction of women has undergone such basic transformation that some critics are talking about the new screen heroine. The first changes in the cinematic treatment of women occurred in the mid-1970s and became more visible toward the end of the decade—almost ten years after the appearance of the women's movement.

Alice Doesn't Live Here Anymore (1974) is considered to be a turning point, because it was the first major film with a strong, central role for a woman, and because it also attempted to challenge the male cultural dominance on screen and offscreen. Ellen Burstyn, who won Best Actress for it, was instrumental in bringing the project to the screen. She allegedly discovered Robert Gotchell's screenplay, persuaded a major studio, Warners, to distribute it, chose a rising director, Martin Scorsese, and even had a say on its casting, selecting women for its production crew. Thematically, however, *Alice* was compromising and far from the feminist film it was intended to be. Its eponymous heroine is a recent young widow, struggling to launch a new career for herself as a singer, and a new life for her and her adolescent son. But at the end, she becomes dependent again, settling into what seems to be a second, complacent relationship, albeit with a more sensitive man (Kris Kristofferson) than her first husband. Nonetheless, *Alice* showed that there is interest in women's stories and that such films are also commercially viable.

The real turning point occurred in 1977, when for the first time, four of the five Best Picture nominees were about women and contained at least one strong female character. The Oscar winner was Woody Allen's *Annie Hall*, starring Diane Keaton, competing against Neil Simon's romantic comedy *The Goodbye Girl*, with Marsha Mason, and Fred Zinnemann's *Julia*, a sensitive picture about friendship between two women. The other nominee, *The Turning Point*, was about the costs and rewards of life choices, contrasting two women: an ex-dancer, now a wife-mother (Shirley MacLaine) and an aging and lonely ballerina (Anne Bancroft).

In these as well as other movies of the late 1970s, a new screen woman was depicted, professional and career-oriented, but without the dehumanization and condemnation of Fletcher's nurse in *Cuckoo's Nest* or Dunaway's television executive in *Network*. The range of occupational roles widened considerably, going beyond the traditional female professions of actresses, secretaries, or prostitutes. In recent years, Glenda Jackson won a second Oscar for playing a fashion designer in *A Touch of Class*, Liv Ullmann was nominated for her psychiatrist in Ingmar Bergman's *Face to Face*, and Ingrid Bergman was nominated for playing a concert pianist in another Bergman movie, *Autumn Sonata*. Geraldine Page excelled as an interior decorator in *Interiors*, and Jane Fonda received a nomination as a television investigative reporter in *The China Syndrome*.

The new screen woman is concerned not only with her career, but also with asserting herself as a worthy human being whose status neither derives from nor entirely depends on her marital and familial roles. Meryl Streep won a supporting Oscar in the role of Joanna Kramer in *Kramer Vs. Kramer*, a young woman who walks out on her self-absorbed husband, leaving him the responsibility of raising their six-year-old son alone. She is depicted as a confused woman, deeply dissatisfied with her mother-wife chores, but not as a career woman. She has a profession, but her dilemmas are not confined to career frustrations. *Kramer* was the first major Hollywood movie to deal with a married woman who deserts her family in order "to find herself" and to regain her self-worth. Further, in sharp departure from previous cinematic conventions, she willingly gives up her son, after winning a cruel custody battle, telling her ex-husband: "I came here to take my son home, and I realized he already is home." The movie also changed the traditional image of the husband-father, played by Dustin Hoffman, who won Best Actor. Ted Kramer starts as a tense, egotistic advertising executive, so engrossed in his career that he neglects his family and forbids his wife to work. But he is capable of changing and, by the film's end, he is transformed into a loving, caring father who has learned the lessons of parenthood.

Another recent trend has been to portray women as much more concerned with the public and political domains. In the past, screen heroines were not only confined to their domestic lives, but also exhibited little interest in what was happening in the big outside world. However, several movies in the last decade have dealt with the process by which women are gaining social and political consciousness. At the center of Martin Ritt's *Norma Rae*, Sally Field's first Oscar, is the politicization of a Southern working-class woman in a small dormant town, after meeting a Jewish labor-organizer (Ron Liebman) from New York. The movie describes her fiesty struggle to unionize a mill, which involves the organization of a general strike. What is innovative, from the point of view of gender, is that her relationship with the Jewish intellectual is neither romantic nor sexual, but based on mutual respect. At the end, they part with a friendly handshake, not with the cliché kiss. This friendship, between such unlikely partners (a simple, uneducated woman and an urban Jewish intellectual) would have been impossible in the past, but in the context of this film it is mutually engrossing, with each party learning and benefiting from the friendship.

The new screen woman has also gained in the areas of sexual mores and conduct. In the past, it was the exclusive privilege of men to engage in illicit, adulterous affairs. But recently women have become more sexually liberated—without having to pay for it with their lives. *Coming Home*, Jane Fonda's second Oscar, describes the change of Sally Hyde, a bored, middle-class wife, married to a hawkish, chauvinistic marine captain (Bruce Dern, who was also nominated) into a politically aware citizen, while volunteering in a war veterans hospital, where she meets and falls in love with a sensitive war paraplegic (Jon Voight). For a change—and it is a *big* change—the film does not condemn her adultery; in fact, it is not only justified but favorably described.

Finally, there have been dramatic changes in that perennial screen role: the mother. The new, liberated mother is no longer suffering and self-sacrificing as Mildred Pierce or Stella Dallas were for the future of their children or husbands. She is no longer weak or submissive, but determined and in full control of her life and in full charge of her emotions. Sally Field won a second Oscar as Edna Spaulding in *Places in the Heart*, a young Texan housewife, whose husband-sheriff is killed in an accident. After fifteen years of marriage, she suddenly finds herself with no talent or skills for anything except cooking and taking care of her children. But with tremendous willpower, steadfastness, and hard work she faces successfully a series of hardships, a foreclosing bank, a greedy cotton dealer, and even a tornado. A very similar type of mother was portrayed by Jessica Lange in *Country*, inspired by the farmers' plight in Iowa, and Sissy Spacek in *The River*, both of whom were nominated. These three movies, labeled as "Hollywood's farm trilogy," also challenged the traditional screen images of men, depicting them as less committed to the cause of keeping the land, weaker, and more emotional than their female counterparts.

What better indication of the changing gender roles in American society—and film—than the roles played by the five women nominated for the 1988 Best Actress Award? The winner, Jodie Foster in *The Accused*, plays Sarah Tobias, a fast-food waitress (traditional female profession), who is gang-raped in a roadside bar (also conventional stereotype). However, in the course of the film she transforms from a good-time, hard-drinking girl to a woman fighting for the decency and self-esteem she never had. Like Foster, in *A Cry in the Dark* Meryl Streep was cast as a defiant working-class woman, accused of being responsible for the death of her baby girl. Based on the 1980 story of Lindy Chamberlain, this complex role shows her to be proudly stubborn, a victim of the sensationalistic and merciless Australian media. In *Dangerous Liaisons*, Glenn Close's Marquise de Merteuil is another proud woman who refuses to live by the sexual mores of France's ancient regime. "I was born to dominate your sex and avenge my own," she tells the Vicomte de Valmont (John Malkovich) with whom she engages in games of sex and power. Sigourney Weaver, in her self-assured portrayal of the late anthropologist Dian Fossey, dominated every frame of *Gorillas in the Mist*, a film about her heroic struggle to save Africa's gorillas from poaching. And finally, Melanie Griffith's Tess McGill, in the modern fairy tale *Working Girl*, is a victimized secretary from Staten Island who decides to take charge of her life and in the process also gets her boss's lover. Indeed, the Oscar-winning roles have been accurate reflections of the current trends in the screen portrayal of men and women.

Mary Pickford, "America's Sweetheart," in her Best Actress role in *Coquette* (1928/29), the only departure from her screen image, cast as an impetuous belle. Her win was not unrelated to her husband Douglas Fairbanks, Sr. being the Academy's president. (Courtesy of The Museum of Modern Art/Film Stills Archive)

Katharine Hepburn and Adolph Menjou in *Morning Glory* (1932/33). Hepburn's first Oscar was for playing a rising actress, one of the most enduring female roles. (Courtesy of The Museum of Modern Art/Film Stills Archive)

Joan Crawford in her
Oscar-winning role
in *Mildred Pierce* (1945),
her most famous film;
Bette Davis and Barbara
Stanwyck had turned down
the role.
(Courtesy of The Museum
of Modern Art/Film
Stills Archive)

Jane Wyman deviated from her previous glamorous roles and won the 1948 Best Actress in
Johnny Belinda, as a deaf-mute girl and rape victim, a stereotypical female role in the 1940s.
(Courtesy of The Museum of Modern Art/Film Stills Archive)

Broderick Crawford and Judy Holliday, the 1950 Best Actress, as the "dumb-intelligent blonde," in George Cukor's political comedy *Born Yesterday*. (Courtesy of The Museum of Modern Art/Film Stills Archive)

Playing Southern belles became a specialty for British player Vivien Leigh, here with Marlon Brando in her second Oscar-winning performance in *A Streetcar Named Desire* (1951), based on Tennessee Williams's prize-winning play. (Courtesy of The Museum of Modern Art/Film Stills Archive)

Anna Magnani (left) in her 1955 Oscar performance in *The Rose Tattoo*, the first Italian actress to win an Oscar, though in an American movie. (Courtesy of The Museum of Modern Art/Film Stills Archive)

Susan Hayward was one of the few women to win Best Actress for playing a criminal, as Barbara Graham in *I Want to Live!* (1958). (Courtesy of The Museum of Modern Art/Film Stills Archive)

Jane Fonda's first Best Actress was for playing a New York call girl in *Klute* (1971), one of the most complex female characterizations and one of the best performances of the whole decade. (Courtesy of The Museum of Modern Art/Film Stills Archive)

Sophia Loren won Best Actress in *Two Women* (1961), a film which made a career difference, changing her image from a sex symbol to a serious dramatic actress. (Courtesy of The Museum of Modern Art/Film Stills Archive)

Katharine Hepburn received a ninth Best Actress nomination for portraying Mary Tyrone in Sidney Lumet's version of Eugene O'Neill's *A Long Day's Journey into Night* (1962). Her superlative acting in this movie surpasses each of her four acting Oscars. (Courtesy of The Museum of Modern Art/Film Stills Archive)

The two female awards in 1962 honored Anne Bancroft (as Anne Sullivan) and Patty Duke (as Helen Keller) in Arthur Penn's *The Miracle Worker*. Bancroft had earlier won a Tony award for playing the role on stage. (Courtesy of The Museum of Modern Art/Film Stills Archive)

Ellen Burstyn (right) received Best Actress and Diane Ladd a supporting nomination in Martin Scorsese's *Alice Doesn't Live Here Anymore* (1974), which resurrected the woman's film in the 1970s. (Courtesy of The Museum of Modern Art/Film Stills Archive)

Faye Dunaway parodied her own screen image, as a ruthlessly ambitious television executive, in Sidney Lumet's political farce *Network* (1976), winning Best Actress at her third nomination. (Courtesy of The Museum of Modern Art/Film Stills Archive)

Sally Field gave a stunning performance, as a working-class woman who gains political consciousness, in Martin Ritt's *Norma Rae* (1979), for which she was rewarded with her first Best Actress Award. (Courtesy of The Museum of Modern Art/Film Stills Archive)

The 1988 Oscar-winning and blockbuster, *Rain Man,* also serves as a testament to the kind of film made in the New Hollywood. Packaged by a powerful agency and dominated by stars (Dustin Hoffman, left, and Tom Cruise, right), its message was in tune with the neo-conservative times: the importance of brotherly love and the nuclear family. (Courtesy of The Museum of Modern Art/Film Stills Archive)

CHAPTER 9

The Oscar as a Reward System

Strictly speaking, the selection of Oscar winners should be determined by two factors—the quality of the nominated achievement and the intensity of competition in the relevant category. But both factors, quality and degree of competition, have fluctuated greatly from year to year. Logical reasoning assumes a strong correlation between the intensity of competition and the quality of the winning achievements, which means that in years of stiff competition the chosen nominee will be the best. However, many cases attest to a reverse relationship—that is, in years of fierce contest, the winning performance is not necessarily the strongest and, at times, may even be the weakest.

In 1940, for example, the competition in the two lead acting categories was particularly intense. The nominees for Best Actress were: Bette Davis in *The Letter*, Joan Fontaine in *Rebecca*, Katharine Hepburn in *The Philadelphia Story*, Ginger Rogers in *Kitty Foyle*, and Martha Scott in *Our Town*. The consensus was that Hepburn gave the year's best performance, arguably the best performance of her career, for which she was cited by the New York Film Critics. The Academy winner, however, was Ginger Rogers, earning the Oscar for her first and only nomination. In the same year, James Stewart's winning performance in *The Philadelphia Story* was not the most distinguished, compared with Charlie Chaplin in *The Great Dictator* and Henry Fonda in *The Grapes of Wrath*; the two other nominees were Laurence Olivier in *Rebecca* and Raymond Massey in *Abe Lincoln in Illinois*.

In 1947, the best performance by an actor was probably delivered by William Powell in *Life with Father*, for which he won the New York Film Critics Award. Yet the Academy winner was Ronald Colman in *A Double Life*, winning over stiff competition from Gregory Peck in *Gentleman's Agreement*, and particularly John Garfield in *Body and Soul*. The fifth nominee was Michael Redgrave in *Mourning Becomes Electra*. The female category that year was not particularly marked by strong performances. The winner was Loretta Young in *The Farmer's Daughter*, who was up against Joan Crawford in *Possessed*, Susan Hayward in *Smash-Up: The Story of a Woman*, Dorothy McGuire in *Gentleman's Agreement*, and Rosalind Russell in *Mourning Becomes Electra*.

Bette Davis was denied an Oscar for the greatest performance of her career, Margo Channing in *All About Eve*, but she competed against her costar, Anne Baxter, in the same category, which might have split the votes. And it was a year of extraordinary performances, including Gloria Swanson's in *Sunset Boulevard*. Interestingly, the surprise winner was Judy Holliday in *Born Yesterday*, the only comedic role in a year of heavy dramatic roles; the fifth nominee was Eleanor Parker, as the victimized wife-convict in the prison drama *Caged*.

Ben-Hur was the biggest winner in 1959, sweeping eleven of its twelve nominations, including Best Actor for Charlton Heston in the title role. An actor of limited range, Heston possibly won his Oscar as a result of the patterned habit to vote for one film in most categories, deservedly or undeservedly. The competition in this category was extraordinary: Laurence Harvey in *Room at the Top*, Jack Lemmon in *Some Like It Hot*, Paul Muni in *The Last Angry Man*, and James Stewart in *Anatomy of a Murder*, who was the New York Critics' winner.

The Error of Omission

The nomination process has been repeatedly criticized as slighting and bypassing many film achievements. The Academy's apologetic response has been consistent: there can be only five nominees and only one winner in each category. This inevitably means that not every worthy achievement will be nominated. Yet, errors of omission have been particularly visible in years in which the nominated achievements have been mediocre—compared with the excellence of those omitted.

In this respect, all the winners of the New York Film Critics Award have probably deserved nomination. The most conspicuous omissions in this group have been: Greta Garbo in *Anna Karenina*, Ida Lupino in *The Hard Way*, Tallullah Bankhead in *Lifeboat*, Ralph Richardson in *Breaking the Sound Barrier*, Liv Ullmann in *Cries and Whispers* and *Scenes from a Marriage*, John Gielgud in *Providence*, Glenda Jackson in *Stevie*, and most recently Norma Aleandro in *The Official Story*.

Furthermore, some players have been consistently passed over by the Academy. Edward G. Robinson was never nominated, despite a large number of excellent performances, such as in *Little Caesar* and *Flesh and Fantasy*, and despite considerable range, excelling in playing men on *both* sides of the law, like his detective in *Double Indemnity*.

Jean Arthur occupies a special position among the Academy's underestimated actresses. At least three of her performances should have been nominated: *Mr. Deeds Goes to Town*, opposite Gary Cooper; *Mr. Smith Goes to Washington*, as Jimmy Stewart's secretary; and in George Stevens's Western *Shane*, with Alan Ladd and Van Heflin. Note that all three movies were nominated for Best Picture and that most of her costars earned acting nominations: Cooper in *Deeds*, Stewart and others in *Smith*, and Brandon De Wilde and Jack Palance in *Shane*. Jean Arthur was nominated only once, in George Stevens's *The More the Merrier*.

Many films earned nominations for most of their players, excluding one or two performers who deserved to be nominated but for some reason were not. Eleanor Parker and Lee Grant were nominated for *Detective Story*, but not Kirk Douglas, in one of his best roles as the obsessively righteous detective. Burt Lancaster and Shirley Jones earned awards for *Elmer Gantry*, but Jean Simmons, as the devout evangelist, was conspicuously omitted. Similarly, Spencer Tracy received a nomination for the courtroom drama, *Inherit the Wind*, but his costar, Fredric March, did not. And Greer Garson was nominated for playing Eleanor Roosevelt in *Sunrise at Campobello*, but Ralph Bellamy, who recreated his Tony-award role as President Roosevelt, was not. *The Sundowners* was nominated in 1960 in many categories, including acting nominations for Deborah Kerr and Glynis Johns, but not for Robert Mitchum. Incidentally, Mitchum earned only one supporting nomination in his entire career, in the war film *The Story of G.I. Joe*.

Almost every year, film critics compile lists of achievements bypassed by the Academy. Vincent Canby noted that in 1980 "there have been more glaring omissions than in any year in the recent past."[1] On his list were six male performances, each of which he thought was more worthy of a nomination than Peter O'Toole's in *The Stunt Man* or Jack Lemmon's in *Tribute.* Canby singled out Alan King's tycoon in *Just Tell Me What You Want*; James Caan's blue-collar worker in *Hide in Plain Sight*, Michael Caine's psychiatrist in *Dressed to Kill*, Brad Douriff's antiprophet in *Wise Blood*, David Bennet in *The Tin Drum*, and Anthony Hopkins's doctor in *The Elephant Man.* Note that three of these, *Just Tell, Hide in Plain*, and *Wise Blood*, were all box-office failures; *The Tin Drum*, a foreign film; and *Dressed to Kill*, a suspense-thriller—which might have had something to do with their omissions. The Academy's bias against foreign films and thrillers has already been documented.

Of the supporting performances overlooked by the Academy in 1980 Canby singled out: Levon Helm in *Coal Miner's Daughter*, Keith Gordon in *Dressed to Kill*, Debra Winger in *Urban Cowboy*, Charlotte Rampling in *Stardust Memories*, Pamela Reed in *Melvin and Howard*, Elizabeth McGovern in *Ordinary People.* It is interesting to mention that two of these, Winger and McGovern, who made their debuts in these films, later received nominations: McGovern in *Ragtime*, and Winger in *An Officer and a Gentleman.*

Many of the aforementioned omissions were in films that were not commercially successful, which leads to another charge against the Academy: popular films and popular performers have at times been undeservedly nominated *because* of their popularity. In general, performers have better chances to get nominated for a lukewarm work in a blockbuster than for a distinguished performance in a fiasco.

The Oscar as a Popularity Contest

Popularity with audiences rather than acting skills or quality of performance have at times been yardsticks for nomination. Bing Crosby was a dominant box-office draw in the 1940s, following his "Road" movies with Bob Hope and Dorothy Lamour and his recordings. His 1944 Oscar, *Going My Way*, and second nomination, *The Bells of St. Mary's*, were as much a reward to his long-enduring popularity as a tribute to his natural, effortless style of acting; it also helped, of course, that both movies were commercially successful.

Doris Day was the most popular female star in America for close to a decade. Her first and only nomination, for the sex comedy *Pillow Talk*, coincided with her appearance on the "Ten Most Popular Stars" poll in 1959. As she herself recorded: "I was surprised at being nominated for an Academy Award for my performance in *Pillow Talk*, and even more surprised to find that by the end of that year, I had shot up to number one at the box-office."[2] Day's performance in this film did not match her work in Hitchcock's *The Man Who Knew Too Much*, or the biopicture of singer Ruth Etting, *Love Me or Leave Me*, arguably the best role of her career.

Robert Redford was catapulted to the pantheon of movie stars in 1969, following the immense success of *Butch Cassidy and the Sundance Kid*, costarring Paul Newman. The two stars were reteamed in a bigger hit, *The Sting*, proving that there was no need for love interest to make a movie a smash hit. Redford received his one and only nomination for *The Sting*, (Newman did not), possibly because of its immense box-office appeal and the fact that Redford was in another blockbuster that year, *The Way We Were*. His embarrassment over it, however, is somehow understandable—his work in Michael Ritchie's political satire *The Candidate*, and in Sydney Pollack's *Jeremiah Johnson*, was more interesting. But, by the time of the 1974 nominations, Redford ranked as the most popular star in America and the Academy could not ignore it. Richard Dreyfuss's Oscar for *The Goodbye Girl* was probably also related to the fact that he had appeared in three all-time blockbusters, *American Graffiti*, *Jaws*, and *Close Encounters of the Third Kind*.

Some players would not have received a nomination had they not appeared in a commercial hit. Take Ali McGraw, a beautiful if undistinguished actress. She began her film career after a successful turn as a model and established herself as star material in *Goodbye Columbus*, as the Jewish princess. Her third movie, *Love Story*, based on Eric Segal's best-seller, opened to mixed reviews but was such a smash hit that it was nominated in every major category: Picture, Actress, Actor (Ryan O'Neal), Director (Arthur Hiller).

Similarly, John Avildsen's *Rocky* would not have been nominated for ten awards, winning three, including Best Picture, had it not been the top money-maker of the year, with over fifty million dollars in domestic rentals. Popular films tend to make those associated with them appear more gifted than they really are. Moreover, had Talia Shire's performance, as Rocky's shy girlfriend, been contained in another film, she would not have received a supporting nomination for it.

The choice of winners, more than the choice of nominees, has been based on a *popularity* rather than a *talent* contest, because the final voting is by the Academy's entire membership—not by the relevant branch. Consequently, many artists stress the nomination because it is based on peer evaluation, which is allegedly less biased. Furthermore, because the final selections are made by a large and varied body, many irrelevant factors—advertising campaigns, studio politics, the nominees' personality, and popularity within the film industry—play a considerable role. Even when there is agreement over the deservability of the five nominated achievements, it is hard to choose the *one*, among supposedly equal-caliber achievements. It is therefore inevitable that emotional and political factors interfere in the final selections.

The charge that the choices are based on the validity of the nominees' personalities offscreen rather than on their work onscreen is double-edged. On the one hand, brilliant actors have been denied the Oscar (and nomination) because of their real or alleged politics or life-styles. But mediocre artists have won the award for sentimental and other personal reasons, such as an impressive comeback, durability of career, and old age. In these cases, the Oscar has been used as a symbol of forgiveness and social acceptance, granted to previously wayward or neglected members of the film colony.

For example, Joan Crawford had been in Hollywood for two decades, and a major MGM star for a decade. One of the highest paid women in the US, and an extremely ambitious actress, she lacked, however, one important thing—peer recognition as epitomized by the Oscar. In the 1940s, her career was in a rut and she was proclaimed a washout. In fact, Louis B. Mayer "released" her from her long-term contract, after eighteen years of loyal service. For two years, she did not make a picture until Warners came to her rescue with *Mildred Pierce*. Crawford demonstrated in this movie as much willpower as acting talent, which was limited, in a perfect role that captured the essence of her life offscreen. She was as good as she could ever be, and the Academy rewarded her with an Oscar. Ironically, this Oscar rejuvenated her career and she survived as an actress decades longer than her previous rivals at MGM; Greta Garbo and Norma Shearer both retired in 1942.

Olivia De Havilland, like Bette Davis, fought Warners for better roles and better contracts, for which she was occasionally put on suspension. At the end of her seven-year contract, Warners refused to release her, demanding that the contract be extended to include the duration of her suspensions. She sued them, winning a landmark victory, with a court's decision setting the outside limit of a contract player at seven years, including suspensions. Absent from the screen for three years, she celebrated her comeback with an Oscar for *To Each His Own*. Similarly, Gary Cooper's second Oscar for *High Noon* was also a comeback victory, after a faltering career in the late 1940s.

The impact of offscreen factors on the Oscar has never been more clearly demonstrated than in the case of Ingrid Bergman. Her career was severely damaged after she left her husband and daughter and went to Italy to work with director Roberto Rossellini. This open adulterous affair, bearing him a child out of wedlock, shocked the film community. After all, Bergman had been advertised as a "normal" and "wholesome" star, living a quiet idyllic family life. Her screen roles, particularly Sister Mary Benedict in *The Bells of St. Mary's*, perpetuated this image. Consequently, her affair with Rossellini, while officially married, made her the subject of a most vicious campaign. Fan magazines, church, and even school organizations condemned her, and there was serious talk of boycotting her films in the US. Moreover, Senator Edwin C. Johnson denounced her on the Senate floor as "a free love cultist," "a common mistress," "a powerful influence for evil," and "Hollywood's apostle of degradation,"[3] demanding that she be barred forever from the country on grounds of "moral turpitude."

For almost a decade, Bergman was persona non grata in the US. Unfortunately, none of the pictures she made with Rossellini was successful, artistically or commercially, and neither artist benefited from their professional collaboration; her star charisma was somehow foreign to his simple, neorealistic style that, among other things, boasted the use of nonprofessional actors and nonglamorous looks. Soon the marriage itself was in troubled waters.

However, in 1955, producer Darryl Zanuck came to the rescue, offering her the lead in *Anastasia*, as the amnesiac refugee, passing herself off as the surviving daughter of czars Nicholas and Alexandra. This was done against the advice of Twentieth Century-Fox's executives, who believed that the American public had not forgiven her yet. But with Zanuck's insistence and a new publicity campaign, now advertising Bergman as a courageous woman who sacrificed her career and her family for the sake of love, her public image began to change. The story of her comeback reads like a Hollywood fairy tale. Ed Sullivan, the noted television host, flew to London, where *Anastasia* was filmed, to interview her—not before soliciting his viewers' opinion concerning her return to America.[4] Many believed that it was Sullivan and his popular program that turned the tide of public opinion in her favor. Bergman's reputation was restored with a second Oscar for this film, though she did not accept it in person. She returned to the US in 1959, when the Academy asked her to be a presenter on the show.

However, in the 1950s the very mention of Ingrid Bergman's name evoked an extremely negative response. Shelley Winters recalls that during her affair with Italian actor Vittorio Gassman, her agents at Universal told her: "We have invested a great deal of money in you. And now you are destroying our investment." "You may not have noticed," they warned, "but Ingrid Bergman's career is finished in the United States and perhaps throughout the world. Are you ready to have that happen to you?"[5] Winters was also asked to keep a low profile during the 1951 nominations, to assure her placement on the ballots. Thus, her dispute with costar Frank Sinatra on the set of *Meet Danny Wilson* infuriated Leo Spitz of Universal. "From all the rumors we hear," Spitz told her, "you're going to be nominated for Best Actress for *A Place in the Sun*. If you keep your publicity as dignified as possible—given your explosive personality—there's a good chance the Academy members will vote for your performance, and you will get the Oscar." She was surprised to hear from him that "most of the newspapers owe us favors and we can keep all this nonsense out of the press."[6]

Many of Elizabeth Taylor's nominations and one award were related to events in her life *offscreen*. Her chances to win the award for her second nomination, *Cat on a Hot Tin Roof*, were good because MGM's publicity department had started an early campaign for her, and it was an estimable performance. Furthermore, the 1958 death of husband Mike Todd in an airplane crash had earned her the sympathy of the industry and the press. However, a few months prior to the 1959 ceremonies, she broke up Eddie Fisher's marriage to Debbie Reynolds, one of Hollywood's most celebrated unions; this immediately changed public opinion, which resented her rush to marry him. Still, she was nominated the following year in *Suddenly Last Summer*, but lost out to Simone Signoret in *Room at the Top*.

But once again, personal factors that had denied her the 1958 Oscar operated in her favor in 1960 when she was nominated for *Butterfield 8*. This time, it was her almost fatal illness that brought sympathy—and the Oscar. Indeed, the Academy, the press, and the public had forgiven her "sins," and her bout with death restored her to public favor. Taylor herself believed that "the reason I got the Oscar was that I had come within a breath of dying of pneumonia." And although "it meant being considered an actress and not a movie star," she still felt "it was for the wrong picture," for "any of my three previous nominations was more deserving."[7] In retrospect, however, her winning performance was not all that bad—contrary to popular opinion, it is not the worst performance honored by the Academy! Still, Taylor was delighted when she won her second Oscar for *Who's Afraid of Virginia Woolf?* because, as one critic put it, "it was for what happened on the screen rather than off."[8] In this picture she demonstrated, once and for all, to those who still doubted, that she could act.

The Oscar as a Reward for Mediocrity

"The curious thing about awards," composer Jules Styne observed, "is that one receives them for work one does not expect to receive them for, and does not receive them for work one does. For instance, I received the Tony for *Hallelujah, Baby!* and not for *Gypsy*."[9] Similarly, many performers have been nominated for mediocre, not best, work. There is usually agreement over the candidate's talents and abilities, but not over the *particular* film for which one has received a nomination.

Such cases exist in every category. Lew Ayres was not nominated for his portrayal of the pacifist soldier in *All's Quiet on the Western Front*, but he was nominated for his doctor in *Johnny Belinda*, because the latter was nominated in every category. Cary Grant failed to earn recognition for any of his great comedies—*The Awful Truth*, *Bringing up Baby*, and *His Girl Friday*—or for his wonderful performance in Hitchcock's *North by Northwest*, but he *was* nominated for two pedestrian performances in *Penny Serenade* and *None But the Lonely Heart*. And John Wayne was not nominated for his excellent Westerns, *Red River* and *The Searchers*, but for the patriotic war film, *Sands of Iwo Jima*.

Lee Marvin undoubtedly gave a better performance in a more demanding role in *Ship of Fools*, as a vulgar Texas tycoon, than in *Cat Ballou*. And Steve McQueen's one and only nomination was for his inscrutable, alienated sailor in the big-budget *The Sand Pebbles*, but not for his more interesting work in the "small" but sensitive *Baby, the Rain Must Fall*, Horton Foote's story of a violent parolee in a small Southern town.

A group of British players were nominated, not for their distinguished work in British films, but for mediocre American movies. Sir Michael Redgrave was nominated just once, as Orin in *Mourning Becomes Electra*, but not for his teacher in *The Browning Version*, or for Oscar Wilde's *The Importance of Being Earnest*. And Sir Ralph Richardson received his first supporting nomination for *The Heiress*, but not for his servant in *The Fallen Idol*, or *Breaking the Sound Barrier*.

Similar patterns have characterized the winners, with many receiving the Oscar for average work in popular films. The quality of these Oscar performances was inferior to their previous nominations. Even the Oscar's supporters concur that while the winners might not be those who gave the best performance of the year, they are, nonetheless, Oscar-caliber artists, worthy of the award. Thus, there is no doubt about the winners' deserving the award, but about the *particular* achievement for which they won. Once again, the Academy claims that in the final account, the Oscars "even out the odds," by honoring (sooner or later) artists who have consistently made Oscar-caliber films. Some members vote for the *overall* quality of the nominee under consideration, including past achievements, not just the present nomination.

Bette Davis once said that her two Oscars, for *Dangerous* and *Jezebel*, did not mean much, because they were for the "wrong" films; she would have been more gratified had she won for *The Letter* and particularly *All About Eve*. And James Stewart gave a finer performance in *Mr. Smith Goes to Washington* than in his Oscar role, *The Philadelphia Story*. The best example of an actress nominated for *distinguished*, but winning just for good roles, has been twelve-time nominated and four-time winner Katharine Hepburn. Three of her nominated performances represent not only the best of *her* career, but the best of the American cinema. These are: *Alice Adams, The*

Philadelphia Story, and Mary Tyronne in Sidney Lumet's brilliant version of O'Neill's *Long Day's Journey into Night*. But Hepburn won for *Morning Glory*, *Guess Who's Coming to Dinner? The Lion in Winter*, and *On Golden Pond*.

The Academy voters have been naturally influenced by the selection of the New York Film Critics. There are players who received the critics' award for a role that also brought them a nomination—but not the award. Almost invariably, they later went on to win the Oscar for a lesser performance. Jon Voight was singled out by the New York critics for his Jo Buck in *Midnight Cowboy*, for which he was also nominated, but he received the Oscar for *Coming Home*. Jack Nicholson won the New York Critics Award and an Oscar nomination for his private eye in *Chinatown*, but the award was given to him a year later, for *One Flew Over the Cuckoo's Nest*.

In the last decade, some players actually won the Oscar for the weakest of their nominated performances. Jack Lemmon did not win for *Some Like It Hot*, *The Apartment*, or *Days of Wine and Roses*, but for *Save the Tiger*. Faye Dunaway lost twice, for her portrayal of Bonnie Parker in *Bonnie and Clyde*, and for her mysterious femme fatale in *Chinatown*, but she won for *Network*. And Dustin Hoffman's Oscar performance in *Kramer Vs. Kramer* was not on a par with or as original as his other nominated roles.

The Oscar as a Reward for Eccentricity

One of the common attributes of both male and female performances has been eccentricity, often manifest in major transformations in their physical appearances and looks while playing particular screen roles. "The best way to win awards in Hollywood," Andrew Sarris observed, "is to plaster a young face with old-age makeup," for "artificial aging" is interpreted as "an infallible sign of 'character' for those who confuse the art of acting with the art of disguise." But there have been tricks other than heavy makeup that players have used to impress audiences—and their colleagues at the Academy. These tricks do not win awards in themselves but they have contributed to the overall effectiveness and power of many performances. And they have made reasonable or passable performances look more impressive than they really are.

Heavy accents or just different accents have been used to great effect. For example, Spencer Tracy developed a heavy accent for playing the primitive Portuguese fisherman in *Captains Courageous*, and Mischa Auer used a droll accent for his eccentric role in *My Man Godfrey*; in one scene, he is asked to play a gorilla. Loretta Young attempted a Swedish accent in *The Farmer's Daughter*, and Ingrid Bergman used her native Swedish for the role of the neurotic missionary in *Murder on the Orient Express*; in the same film, Albert Finney was unrecognizable, donning a wig and speaking in a Belgian accent as Hercule Poirot. Alan Arkin used a Russian accent in *The Russians Are Coming*, and Michael Caine spoke directly to the audience with a Cockney accent in *Alfie*. At present, Meryl Streep is nicknamed "the queen of accents," using a different accent in every film, from Polish in *Sophie's Choice* to British in *Plenty* to Danish in *Out of Africa*.

The art of disguise has a long theatrical tradition, encouraging stage players to exploit mimicry and makeup as a form of sensationalism.[10] In film too, heavy makeup and on screen aging have been embraced by screen players, who somehow believe that it demonstrates a greater range. Fredric March's makeup transformation in *Dr. Jekyll and Mr. Hyde* was, of course, necessary, but it also contributed to the effectiveness of his performance and the film itself. Irene Dunne and Richard Dix aged extensively during the thirty-year story span of *Cimarron*. Greer Garson progressed from boarding-house slave to wealthy matriarch in *Mrs. Parkington*, a story that covered half a century in the life of a family.

Similarly, attractive leading ladies have been rewarded for consenting to deglamorize their screen appearances and appear drab or frumpy. Bette Davis wore paddings on her legs, donned glasses, and pulled her hair back tight in *Now Voyager*. Olivia de Havilland played an ugly duckling in *The Heiress*, and Grace Kelly won an Oscar for *The Country Girl*, as an embittered, humiliated wife, wearing the most unglamorized and unflattering wardrobe of her career. Similarly, Elizabeth Taylor portrayed a woman much older and fatter than herself, also harsher and quite deglamorized in *Who's Afraid of Virginia Woolf?* Lynn Redgrave still finds it difficult to shake her image from *Georgy Girl*, as a pathetic ugly duckling weighing 180 pounds!

Men have also used tricks: Yul Brynner shaved his head for *The King and I*, and continued to use it as a professional trademark for the rest of his career. Lee Marvin played a dual role in *Cat Ballou*, a drunken gunslinger and a killer with a silver nose. John Wayne put on an eye patch for *True Grit*, and Marlon Brando puffed out his cheeks in *The Godfather*. Robert De Niro gained sixty pounds to play the gluttonous Jake LaMotta in *Raging Bull*, and Jack Nicholson a substantial amount of weight for *Terms of Endearment* and *Prizzi's Honor*. There have been fabulous performances of men in drag, from Jack Lemmon in *Some Like It Hot* to Dustin Hoffman in *Tootsie*. Furthermore, playing homosexuals or transexuals has helped to get recognition through the eccentric, campy behavior of their characters, as shown in the same year (1982) by Robert Preston, as Julie Andrews's mentor in *Victor/Victoria*, who has a flamenco-drag number; and John Lithgow in *The World According to Garp*, as Roberta, the former football player who has undergone a sex-change operation.

These have all been great screen performances by wonderful players. Still they have been based on great roles, which raises the unanswerable question: which is more important—the written role in the scenario or the delivered performance on the screen? As Sally Field said of her second Oscar-winning role: "The script of *Places in the Heart* is so well done that it brings more attention to the role. Edna is such a complex character that she gives the actor a lot to do." Vanessa Redgrave felt the same way about her nominated role in *The Bostonians*: "I feel that all I've done is play the lady Henry James wrote about." One wonders if this modesty is a kind of noblesse oblige norm on the part of performers or, perhaps, in the final account it is the written role that is crucial, and less so the specific interpretation of the actors.

The Oscar as a Compensation

Artists who unaccountably lost the award are not forgotten—the Academy compensates the losers, usually in the near future, with belated Oscars. These consolatory awards have served the function of corrective mechanisms to the imperfections of the Academy as a reward system.

Bette Davis's award for *Dangerous* is believed to be a compensation for missing out on the previous year's nominations. As was shown, the attempt to introduce new selection procedures in 1934, the write-ins, failed to get Davis a much deserved nomination for *Of*

Human Bondage. In 1935, upon being nominated for *Dangerous*, Davis herself cited Katharine Hepburn's performance in *Alice Adams* as the year's best, but the Academy selected her. Davis's Oscar is considered to be the first consolation or hold-over award.

Robert Donat's first nomination was for *The Citadel*, as the struggling doctor, but he lost out to Spencer Tracy in *Captains Courageous*. In the following year, this was "corrected" and Donat received the award for a nobler, if not better, performance in *Goodbye Mr. Chips*. But by correcting this error, the Academy created a new "error" and a new "victim," Jimmy Stewart, who gave the best performance of 1939 in *Mr. Smith Goes to Washington*. Once again, this was corrected in 1940, when Stewart got the award for a weaker performance in *The Philadelphia Story*. The fact that he had already enlisted into military service, thus becoming Hollywood's first major star to join the war effort, was probably not unrelated to his win—Stewart accepted the Award in uniform.

One of the more interesting compensatory awards was Julie Andrews's for *Mary Poppins*. The film musical *My Fair Lady* was nominated that year in every major category, except Best Actress, despite an elegant performance by Audrey Hepburn as Eliza Doolittle. The production of this film was marked by initial resentment over Jack Warner's refusal to cast Julie Andrews in a role that she had played to great acclaim on the stage. Under other circumstances, Hepburn would have been nominated, but the Academy's Acting Branch expressed its moral indignation by denying her a nomination and by conferring on Julie Andrews a nomination and later the award for *Mary Poppins*. It felt as if Andrews got the award for the "wrong" film—had she played in *My Fair Lady*, she would have won an Oscar for it. *Mary Poppins* served as an excuse to compensate Andrews for the "injustice" done to her by Warners.

Another "corrective" mechanism has been to award artists who have been nominated multiple times. In theory, the number of nominations should not be a factor in the chances to win. In practice, however, the chances of winning increase with the number of nominations. This corrective mechanism has prevailed in other prestigious awards, such as the Nobel Prize, where scientists passed over in a given year are not considered "lost cases." As shown, about one-tenth of the Oscar winners have received the award at their third or more nominations. Ellen Burstyn (*Alice Doesn't Live Here Anymore*) and Faye Dunaway (*Network*) won at their third nominations; their previous nominations must have played some role. Susan Hayward won for a very good performance in *I Want to Live!* at her fifth nomination, but the fact that she has been nominated four times in the past decade must have counted. Robert De Niro officially won for *Raging Bull,* but how could the Academy forget his memorable performances in *Taxi Driver* and *The Deer Hunter* a few years before? Gregory Peck was honored with Best Actor for *To Kill a Mockingbird,* but the vote also acknowledged his status as a perennial nominee with four nominations to his credit.

The Academy has devised other organizational mechanisms to counter the inevitable imperfections of its evaluation process. The Honorary Awards, set apart from the competitive merit awards, are given "for exceptionally distinguished service in the making of motion pictures or for outstanding service to the Academy." The regulations also stipulate that they "are not limited to the awards year," and "shall not be voted posthumously."

Charlie Chaplin never won a legitimate award, but he was honored with three Special Oscars, the first of which was in 1927/28 for his "versatility and genius," in writing, producing, directing, and acting in *The Circus*; Chaplin was nominated for this film in the competitive categories, but did not win. Whenever the Academy sensed that a major contribution has no chance of winning a legitimate award, they voted a Special Oscar. Laurence Olivier received the 1946 Special Award for his first Shakepearean film, *Henry V.* "One of the greatest foreign films," the citation stated. "No play of classic theatre was ever translated to celluloid with such faithful flawless art." Olivier received nominations for this film, but did not win. Similarly, when rumors circulated that Fred Astaire was going to retire, the Academy hurried and honored him with a Special Oscar in 1949, for "his unique artistry and contributions to the techniques of musical pictures"; Astaire had never been nominated for his musical films.

Greta Garbo, one of the screen's great actresses, was nominated three times but never won. In 1954, she received a Special Oscar. In 1958, the Academy voted a Special Oscar for French actor Maurice Chevalier "for his contribution to the world of entertainment for more than half a century." The Academy Board denied rumors that there was a connection between the award and the fact that Chevalier failed to receive a nomination for *Gigi,* which won most of the year's awards. But it was probably a compensation for this oversight as well as for his having lost the Best Actor in 1929/30, when he was up for two films. Lillian Gish, another screen legend, received an Honorary Oscar in 1970 for her cumulative work, which still goes on. Gish had been nominated only once, for a supporting role in *Duel in the Sun*.

A look at the Honorary Oscars of the last decade shows that there is always some meaningful connection with the legitimate Oscars. For example, Edward G. Robinson, who was never nominated, received an Honorary Award in 1973 for a half-century career; unfortunately, the ceremonies took place just months after his death of cancer. A four-time nominee, Rosalind Russell, was honored with the Jean Hersholt Humanitarian Award in 1972 for her charity work. Barbara Stanwyck, a four-time nominee, received an Honorary Oscar in 1982. It was presented by William Holden, who made his film debut with her in *The Golden Boy*. These have been sentimental, but touching, moments in the history of the award.

Most recipients of the Honorary Awards are aware of their compensatory functions and extremely sensitive about it. Thus, when Mickey Rooney, a four-time nominee, was given the 1983 Honorary Oscar, in recognition of his sixty-year career, which began when he was two years old, he recited all the awards he had recently received so that the Academy would not think it was doing him a favor. "I'd been the world's biggest box-office star at nineteen and, at forty, unable to get work," Rooney said in his acceptance speech, reminding his colleagues and the public of the inherent insecurities of this glamorous profession.

Paul Newman, the recipient of the 1985 Honorary Oscar, was absent from the ceremonies; he was filming in Chicago. One of the great Academy losers, he has been nominated six times for Best Actor. The award was bestowed "in recognition of his many memorable and compelling screen performances and for his personal integrity and dedication to his craft." In his (screened) acceptance remarks, Newman made sure to state that unlike previous recipients, he was neither ill nor close to retirement. "I'm especially grateful that this did not come wrapped as a gift certificate to Forest Lawn," he said. "My best work is down the pike in front of me." Indeed, in the following year the injustice was "corrected" by the Academy with a legitimate Oscar for *The Color of Money*. Though Newman gave a good performance as an aging pool player, the inevitable doubt remains—was it a sentimental compensatory vote for his multiple nominations?

Aside from Honorary Oscars, the Academy established in 1937 the "Irving G. Thalberg Memorial Award" to honor "the most consistent high level of production achievement by an individual producer." Producer-director Stanley Kramer received this award in 1961, coinciding with the release of *Judgment at Nuremberg* for which he received a nomination; Kramer had also been nominated for *The Defiant Ones*, but did not win. Alfred Hitchcock, a five-time directorial nominee, received the Thalberg Award in 1967, and Mervyn LeRoy, nominated once for *Random Harvest*, in 1976. In 1975, Howard Hawks, nominated in 1941 for *Sergeant York*, and French director Jean Renoir, also nominated once for his American-made *The Southerner* in 1945, both won Special Oscars for their cumulative work. King Vidor, who had been nominated five times as a director, *The Crowd* in 1927/28; *Hallelujah* in 1929/30; *The Champ* in 1931/32; *The Citadel* in 1938; and *War and Peace* in 1956, received a Special Award in 1978 to make up for all of these losses.

The Career Oscars

When the Oscar honors veteran artists who have been nominated many times, it is hard to tell if the award is given for the current nomination or for an entire career of achievements. This is yet another corrective device, known as "the career Oscar." In such cases, the official performance, for which artists win, serves as an "excuse" to reward them for careers of many contributions. For obvious reasons, the "career" Oscar has not been well respected, since the recipients can never be sure whether their winning was based on sentimental or meritorious considerations.

The first player to receive a Career Oscar was Mary Pickford, who officially won for *Coquette*, her first talking movie (and the first acting award for a sound film). In actuality, however, the honor paid Pickford a tribute for having been the first international movie star. Her biographer believes that the Oscar was "doubtless as much for past performances and for her service to, and eminence in, the industry, as for *Coquette*,"[11] particularly inasmuch as it was neither a good performance nor a good picture. Marie Dressler's award for *Min and Bill* can also be considered a Career Oscar, for she had been a famous screen (and stage) actress for decades. At sixty-two, she is still the oldest female winner. Both Pickford and Dressler retired from the screen shortly after winning; Pickford made only three more films before quitting in 1933, and Dressler's career was cut short by her death that same year.

Ronald Colman had been an exemplary British actor in Hollywood for three decades, with fifty pictures to his credit, before winning for *A Double Life* in 1947. Further, Colman had been one of the few players who became even more popular with the advent of sound, due to his marvelous voice and impeccable diction, both of which added immensely to his appeal. Colman was possibly rewarded for his enduring popularity in a medium marked by ephemeral success. And he may have also been compensated for previous nominated roles, in *Bulldog Drummond, Condemned,* and *Random Harvest.* His belated Oscar, at the age of fifty-six, was for a career in the silent and sound eras and for box-office popularity. After the Oscar, however, Colman made only a few films before his death in 1958 at the age of sixty-seven.

The 1969 vote for John Wayne's performance in *True Grit* might have been based on sentimental as well as on career-long achievements, though his work in this film was acclaimed by most critics. By 1969, Wayne had been making films for over forty years, and had been a top star for twenty. Some saw in his Oscar an admission by his colleagues that they had been wrong in underestimating his acting skills. Wayne had been nominated once before, for his heroic role in *Sands of Iwo Jima,* which he lost to Broderick Crawford. Winning the Oscar at the age of sixty-two had no pragmatic affect on his career, but it was of great symbolic value to him.

Of Wayne's generation, Henry Fonda was the only major star without an Oscar. Fonda's first and only nomination was for his portrayal of Tom Joad in *The Grapes of Wrath* in 1940. In the late 1970s, the Academy and the American Film Institute realized that his achievements had never received their due recognition—and that he was not very healthy. Consequently, Fonda was showered with special and life achievement awards, from the American Film Institute in 1978, the Golden Globe in 1980, and an Honorary Oscar "for his life-long contributions to the art of filmmaking," in 1981. "It's been a very rewarding forty-six years for me and this has got to be the climax," Fonda said. "I'm very grateful to the Governors of the Academy." But it was not the climax, though neither Fonda nor the Academy could have anticipated that a year later he would be named Best Actor for *On Golden Pond*. Indeed, the Academy restored justice with the most prestigious legitimate Oscar almost at the very last minute. Daughter Jane Fonda received the Oscar for him in a lengthy emotional speech, and the cameras later followed her to his house as she presented the award to him in person. Fonda died a few months later.

Geraldine Page had been nominated eight times, five for Best Actress and three for Supporting Actress. Her winning performance in *The Trip to Bountiful* was good, though not her best; some of her nominated performances, particularly in *Sweet Bird of Youth* and in Woody Allen's *Interiors*, were far more impressive. Like Katharine Hepburn, Page did not win for her best work.

Related to the Career Oscars is the charge that the Academy has favored older over younger and veteran over inexperienced players, at times ignoring the performance's quality. The Academy has been accused of favoring the risk of conservatism over the risk of daring, and of using the award as a validation of survival in the industry rather than as an award of *merit*.

This charge has some validity in the acting categories, especially the male. Of the fifty-seven Best Actors, only seven have been the youngest nominees in their respective years, like Marlon Brando (thirty) in 1954, or William Hurt (thirty-six). But even Brando and Hurt were experienced performers, with notable accomplishments in the theater. In most years, however, the award was bestowed on older, at times the oldest, nominees. In the 1970s, the tendency was to confer the Oscar on relatively older players, such as John Wayne at sixty-two; Art Carney at fifty-four; Peter Finch at sixty; and Henry Fonda at seventy-six. Of the Best Actors, only Ernest Borgnine and Maximilian Schell were both young and unestablished. The priority of age over youth in this category is consistent with the other findings: the Best Actors have been older than the Best Actresses at their film debuts, first nomination, and first winning.

A totally different picture prevails among the Best Actresses, half of whom have been the youngest nominees in their respective years. For instance, Janet Gaynor was twenty-two, Katharine Hepburn was twenty-seven, Claudette Colbert was twenty-nine, and Bette Davis was twenty-seven. Only a few of the Best Actresses have been the oldest nominees, like Marie Dressler, and Katharine Hepburn at her second winning, but they, particularly

Hepburn, have been the exception. Indeed, a large number of Best Actresses—Grace Kelly, Audrey Hepburn, and Joanne Woodward—have been young and had only brief film experience before winning.

Supporting winners, unlike lead winners, have been either young and inexperienced or very old and established. In both the male and female groups, for each young winner, there has been a counterexample of an old and established player. George Chakiris was twenty-nine in 1961, but Ed Begley was sixty-one in 1962, and Melvyn Douglas sixty-two in 1963. And as in the Best Actor category, in the late 1960s and 1970s the pattern was to select the old and established players:

In 1968, Jack Albertson (fifty-eight) won over Gene Wilder.
In 1969, Gig Young (fifty-six) over Elliott Gould.
In 1970, John Mills (sixty-two) over Richard Castellano.
In 1973, John Houseman (seventy) over Randy Quaid.
In 1975, George Burns (eighty) over Brad Douriff.
In 1976, Jason Robards (fifty-seven) over Ned Beatty.
In 1981, John Gielgud (seventy-seven) over Howard S. Rollins.

Timothy Hutton, the youngest nominee (nineteen) has been the exception.

Almost the same pattern describes the Supporting Actresses, who have been either very old or very young. However, there have been more inexperienced and younger winners among the supporting women than in any other category. Teresa Wright was twenty-three, Anne Baxter twenty-three, and Patty Duke, sixteen. But for each of these young recipients, there has been an old one, like Jane Darwell at sixty, Ethel Barrymore sixty-five, Josephine Hull sixty-six, and Margaret Rutherford seventy-two. And recently there has been a conservative trend to honor age over youth:

In 1968, Ruth Gordon (seventy-two) won over Lynn Carlin.
In 1970, Helen Hayes (seventy) over Karen Black and Sally Kellerman.
In 1972, Eileen Heckart (fifty-three) over Jeannie Berlin and Susan Tyrrell.
In 1975, Lee Grant (forty-six) over Ronee Blakely and Lily Tomlin.
In 1976, Beatrice Straight (sixty) over Jodie Foster.

Winners on the order of Goldie Hawn who was twenty-four, and Mary Steenburgen, twenty-seven, two inexperienced performers, have become a rarity.

In conclusion, the Academy has honored age over youth in most categories. The best chance to win the award at an early age and with brief film experience is still for Best Actress. The Academy's tendency to favor established over young artists means that the Oscar has had mostly *symbolic* effects, though it has rejuvenated the careers of veteran artists, at least in the short run. But the Oscar has been most influential when it honored young or beginning artists.

◆CHAPTER 10
_____

The Meanings of the Oscar Award

"There are two types of people," producer Dore Schary once commented on awards winners. "One type asserts that awards mean nothing to them. The second type breaks into tears upon receiving an award, and thanks their mother, father, children, the producer, the director, and—if they can crowd it in—the American Baseball League."[1] Indeed, as Howard Koch, former president of the AMPAS, has observed, the Oscar has been "sought and spurned, revered and reviled, called an incentive for excellence and a commercial tool."[2]

What has the Oscar meant for the winners and nominees? What have been the reactions to both winning and losing the award? The objective effects of winning on the artists' careers are examined in the following chapter. Here the concern is with *subjective* feelings and attitudes toward the Oscar. Is it valid to describe the winning of an Oscar as the ultimate goal of every film artist? Clearly, the attitudes of film artists toward awards have been anything but unanimous, ranging from total embracement to ambivalence and cynicism to outright rejection.

Total Embracement: The Oscar and Peer Recognition

Peer recognition and esteem seem to be primary rewards in the acting profession. Most players regard the winning of an Oscar as great accolade, the supreme praise from one's colleagues. This function of the Oscar was stressed from the very beginning, as William C. De Mille, the second Academy president explained: "The most valuable award a worker can get is to have the acknowledged praise of his fellow workers. It means a great deal more to us than just the acclaim of the public."[3] The Oscar was considered to be the first occasion in film history that "individual creative work has been recognized," and that "meritorious achievements have been passed upon by experts."[4]

Moreover, the very nomination for an award has been considered to be an important achievement in its own right. Indeed, in 1930, the Academy Board announced: "Regardless of which ones of the selected nominees are finally chosen by the Academy to win the statuette trophies, there will be undeniable distinction in winning the preliminary nominations at the hands of their fellow workers."[5] In the first year, all the nominees received an honorable mention, a practice that was later dropped. But the Academy still emphasizes the prestige of being nominated and confers on every nominee a Certificate of Nomination.

The first nomination is highly important because it serves as official acknowledgment of an achievement by peers. Penelope Milford, one of the recent and youngest nominees (*Coming Home*) recalls: "The minute the nominations were announced, the telephone started ringing. A lot of people now are telling me they always knew I had talent and how wonderful it is that I've been nominated. They're the same guys who wouldn't take a phone call from me last week. I'd like to blast them . . . but let's face it, that's not the way to play the game. You've got to keep cool."[6] Milford also said that after the nomination she realized she has become "a known and valued commodity."

Cicely Tyson took great pride in her first nomination (for *Sounder*). "I'm proud and I want every person in the world to see the film." It was a special honor for a black actress to be nominated, and "in a year in which Diana Ross is also a nominee, it is a double honor."[7] Paul Winfield, Tyson's costar in *Sounder*, delighted in his nomination because he was up against "heady competition" (Marlon Brando, Michael Caine, Laurence Olivier, and Peter O'Toole). He felt that, "even though I lost, I think I've already won," because "the nomination came too soon,"[8] and completely suprised him.

One of the most vivid descriptions of the nomination's importance is provided by Ray Milland. Apparently it was the sound mixer of *The Lost Weekend* who first bet that Milland would be nominated—and win—the award; at his urgings, they even had a bet. Milland drove home that night "in a very bemused state, trying not to think about it, but it kept filtering back. 'Could this wonderful thing possibly happen to me? . . . To be acclaimed by one's colleagues in all the cinema crafts, for having given the best performance of the entire year? No! No, stop it! Don't even think about it. Think of the disappointment if nothing happens.'"[9] Even before the nominations were announced, Milland sensed a change of attitude toward him: "I had been getting smiles from people I didn't know, a little more deference from the people in the mailroom, and an unaccountable query from the studio operations wanting to know if I'd prefer a parking lot right outside my dressing room instead of the one I now had."[10]

The day of the nominations' announcement was considered "judgment day," on which "five actors would be in purgatory until the 'Night' four weeks later." Early in the morning, Milland saw his wife, son, cook, butler, and nurse all sitting in the dining room "with their eyes glued to the window." He asked them "what was going on, why they were up so early. As one they replied: 'Same as you. Waiting for the paper.'" Later on, "with the long-suffering look of a man forced to live with mental defectives, I went in to my breakfast. I was just lifting the cup to my lips when I heard the scramble of the front door, and I froze. There was a moment of silence and then one big yelp of exuberance as they all came barreling through the door yelling 'You made it. You're nominated!'"[11]

The nomination not only gives artists some measure of assurance, but also some comparative standard of their quality of performance. As Milland recalled, before the opening of *The Lost Weekend*, "I didn't know whether what I'd done was good or bad; a subject of this kind (alcoholism) hadn't been done before. I had no standards, and it had depressed me terribly."[12] Moreover, for him, the most important effect of the nomination was that "although I had been termed a movie star in the usual magazine concept for five or six years, I was now being accepted as an actor with dramatic merit. It was a wonderful feeling."[13]

That peer esteem is one of the most important functions of the Oscar, even for veteran players, is easy to document. James Cagney believed that "praise from your peers generates a special kind of warmth."[14] "I've always maintained," Cagney said in his acceptance speech, "that in this business you are only as good as the fellow thinks you are." Peer recognition was also the most valued reward to Mercedes McCambridge, who was young and inexperi-

enced when she won. Her Oscar really changed her life: it sky-
rocketed her salary overnight, got her more publicity, many invita-
tions to parties, and an active social life. All of these changes were
"highly enjoyable fringe benefits," conceded McCambridge, but
"best of all was the knowing that you earned it from your peers.
Actors voted for *your* acting."[15]

The Oscar is not the only award to perform this vital role.
"There is something very special about having your work acknowledged by your peers," Joel Grey explained after winning a Tony
for *Cabaret*. "It is a milestone to work for, and the first time something like this happens to you, it is deeply satisfying."[16]

Other film forums may perform the same function, even though
they don't confer prizes. When Martin Scorsese's third feature,
Mean Streets, was selected for the 1973 New York Film Festival, he
is quoted as having said, "For me, it was the most important time of
my life. The festival was a launching pad for my work."[17] This
kind of recognition is crucial for artists who are at the beginning of
their careers: "The Festival can make the difference between recognition and disappearance."[18]

The distinction between being a movie *star* and an esteemed
player is valid, both subjectively and objectively, because the judgment is made by players, film critics, and audiences. One of the
Oscar's functions has been to legitimize the talent of popular stars
who have not enjoyed the respect of their colleagues. "Before I
made *Two Women*" (her Oscar-winning film), Sophia Loren said
succinctly, "I had been a performer. Afterward, I was an actress."[19] This was a pretty accurate description, for Loren had
been a box-office star in Italy and America. Her 1961 Oscar therefore had special meaning for her: "I know some actors have recently
deprecated the value and purpose of the Academy Award, but I'm
certainly not one of them. As far as I'm concerned, if you are a professional actor who has pride in his work, then the judgment of
your peers should be important to you." Loren treasures "each and
every award I have ever received, and my Oscar is in a place of
honor."[20]

The Oscar also fortifies the self-determination of players to pursue their careers in a profession that is far from stable and far from
secure. Asked how *Gandhi* changed his life, in addition to the resulting barrage of scripts and a constantly ringing telephone, Ben
Kingsley said, "I profoundly believe I'm an actor now. I'm not say-

ing I believe I'm a good actor. I just believe there is nothing else in the world I should be than an actor." The Oscar for his first major film made Kingsley "see the tip of the iceberg. I know it's there and it's real."[21]

Contrary to the notion that an artist's main goal is to achieve commercial success, given the choice, many artists would prefer to get their peers' recognition. When Peter Finch's publicist first met her client, she asked him what his main ambition was. He replied unequivocally that the only thing he really wanted was that when he died they would write on his tombstone: "He was a good actor."[22] Finch's wish came true; his Oscar for *Network* was awarded to him posthumously. And another star, Ingrid Bergman, indicated long before she died that she wanted her tombstone to read, "She acted on the last day of her life," which she did: her last acting role was in the television miniseries *Golda*, shown after her death. Bergman's self-chosen epitaph was: "Here lies a great actress."[23]

The Academy Award is not an achievement that just happens. Rather, it is on players' minds early in their careers, considered by them to be the ultimate symbol of achievement. Loretta Young, who started her film career as a child, but won an Oscar after nineteen years of acting, sang out "At long last," when her name was announced winner. And Shelley Winters shouted, when she won her first supporting Oscar, "I've waited fifteen years for this." Susan Hayward was determined to get an Oscar ever since she made her debut. When she was defeated (*Smash-Up: The Story of a Woman*), she tried to take it with a sense of humor. Moreover, the defeat made her even more committed: "I'll be nominated for an Oscar again. Maybe the next year. Maybe I'll have to wait until the fifties. But I intend to win some day. That's my goal."[24] After winning (*I Want to Live!*) at her fifth nomination and following years of hard work, producer Walter Wanger commented: "Thank heaven, now we can all relax. Suzie got what she's been chasing for twenty years." And Hayward herself was convinced that "she now had everything she had ever wanted in life." "I used to make pictures for Academy Awards," she confessed, but "I'm not concerned about winning Oscars anymore. I'm not retiring, but now I'll act for the joy of it and for the money."[25]

Hayward's story is by no means unique. Rather, it attests to the displacement of goals of the Oscar, which was originally designed as a local gesture by Hollywood's artists to honor film achievements. As was mentioned, the Oscar was sort of an afterthought to the Academy's agenda, barely mentioned in the 1927 statement of goals. Nobody intended or anticipated it to become such an important goal and a "sacred" end in its own right. However, film artists now set out consciously to make an "Oscar-winning" film or to give an "Oscar-winning" performance because they regard it as the ultimate symbol of eminence. For better or for worse, winning an Oscar has become a major motive for choosing film projects, based on some knowledge of which films are more likely to get performers a nomination and, preferably, the award.

Take Shirley MacLaine, for example, who turned down the title role in *Mistinguette*, the film version of the legendary French performer, to accept the part of the eccentric, possessive mother in *Terms of Endearment*. It was a conscious and rational decision. Two years before the film was made, MacLaine reportedly told her friends that it was a role that might bring her an Academy Award. "That's one reason I waited," MacLaine told an interviewer, "and didn't work anywhere else for two years." She admitted that she would like to win an Oscar and if she did, "I would think I deserved it"; she would also liked to have won for her previous nomination, *The Turning Point*, in which she played another mother role.[26] She could not have been more perceptive: *Terms of Endearment* provided the best part of her career (so far) and the coveted Oscar.

Artists prefer to win the Oscar for a role they consider important, one with which they have special affinity, professional or emotional. Bette Davis said that she won her first Oscar (*Dangerous*) and, to a certain extent, her second (*Jezebel*) for the "wrong" films; she would have preferred to win for *All About Eve*. By contrast, Gig Young was "crazy" about his part as the marathon dance emcee in *They Shoot Horses, Don't They?* and considered himself "lucky enough to win for the right picture." Young did not hesitate to sum up his career as "Thirty years and fifty-five pictures," of which "there were not more than five that were any good, or any good for me."[27]

The Oscar assumes special meaning for players who worked hard, investing time and other resources, on their winning film, like Charlton Heston who allegedly never worked so hard on a picture as he did in *Ben-Hur*. The Oscar never loses its value, even for those who have won one. When Billy Wilder received his second directorial Oscar (*The Apartment*), Charlton Heston remarked, "I guess, this is old hat to you." To which Wilder replied, "it never gets old hat!"[28]

Indeed, receiving an Oscar not only puts pressure on the winners to prove they have been worthy of it, but it also motivates them to win another one, to prove to themselves and to others that the first win was not by accident or luck. This was demonstrated when Sally Field won her second Oscar (*Places in the Heart*). Genuinely surprised, she shouted: "I've wanted more than anything to have your respect. And I can't deny the fact that you like me now. You really like me!" Field later told reporters that her response was very emotional because she hadn't had "an orthodox career," having started on television in *Gidget*. "The first ten years of my career were in television and it wasn't the finest television, in fact. It's taking me a while to get over that feeling."[29]

In addition to functioning as a symbol of professional attainment, the Oscar also serves as a metaphor of success. Shelley Winters recalls that upon being introduced to Mrs. Roosevelt and Mrs. Stevenson, who congratulated her and Vittorio Gassman for their films, Vittorio behaved "as if we both had just won Oscars."[30] Winters also believes that there are "very definite rules" for public appearances in Hollywood's parties and opening nights: "You must always look beautiful and gloriously happy, and you must be photographed with someone more important than yourself, like people who had won Oscars."[31]

The great subjective meaning of the Oscar for most players is also reflected in the royalty treatment that the statuette receives. Joan Fontaine recalls "cradling it like a doll in my arms."[32] And Ray Milland drove after the Oscar ceremonies to Hillcrest where, "with the golden Oscar in my hand, I walked to the edge of Sunset and looked down at the lights. They seemed very bright that night. After a few moments, I quietly said, 'Mr. Navarro. Tonight they belong to me!'"[33]

Asked if she had a mantel to put the Oscar on, Mercedes McCambridge said, "Got one? I'll build one." And when a photographer asked her to pose while washing the Oscar in a basin, she refused because she "couldn't make fun of it." Regarding the statuette as "a remarkably beautiful piece of furnishing," she used to keep it in front of a mirror so that "it looked like two,"[34] a gimmick used by Louise Fletcher and other winners. Significantly, McCambridge gave that up only when she began to feel "more secure." For years, she also used to wear a miniature Oscar on a golden chain around her neck.

Shelley Winters promised to donate her first Oscar (*The Diary of Anne Frank*) to the Anne Frank Museum in Amsterdam after Otto Frank, Anne's father and the only survivor of the family, visited the film's set and predicted she would win an Oscar for her performance. But after winning, she kept it on a mantel for fifteen years, because "I couldn't bear to part with it; I thought the other one (for *A Patch of Blue*) would get lonely!" Then years later, she brought the Oscar in person to Amsterdam. Initially, the Oscar was put on display openly, but it became such an attraction, with people touching the statuette, that after three days it was put inside a glass case.

Peter Ustinov, a two-time Oscar and a two-time Emmy winner, had on his desk "two emasculated gentlemen and two emasculated ladies," with the four of them making "a fine mixed-double match." Upon winning his third Emmy, he felt he had built "an entire empire."[35] Sophia Loren's Oscar was stolen by thieves, believing it was solid gold. For a sixty-dollar check, she got a replacement from the Academy. Strange, thought Loren, how hard and competitive it was to win the Oscar, but how easy to replace it!

Ambivalence and Rejection of the Oscar

While most film artists have embraced the Oscar completely, with no or very little criticism, some have had a more cynical attitude toward its merits and fairness. Ambivalence and cynicism toward the Oscar have tended to characterize players who have been nominated multiple times but never won. Others have been critical of the award—until they won, at which time their criticism mellowed. Total rejection or contempt toward the Oscar has been the attitude of only a small minority of artists.

Humphrey Bogart provides a good example of initial cynicism that mellowed the moment he won the award. Bogart was the kind of actor who detested Hollywood's phoniness and artificiality, but was extremely conscientious about his work and one of the few men to be really proud of his profession. However, the idea of awards was "diametrically opposed to his concept of noncompetitive acting," claiming that "awards are meaningless for actors, unless they all play the same part."[36] "The only true test of ability," Bogart believed, "would be to have all actors don black tights and recite Hamlet."[37]

Bogart was first nominated for *Casablanca*, then for *The African Queen*. He lost the first time to Paul Lukas, and the 1951 pre-Oscar predictions were that the four actors of *A Streetcar Named Desire* would win. Bogart's friends were certain he would beat Brando, and he was just as certain he would lose. When his friends asked him what he would say in his speech, if he won, he replied, "I'm not going to thank anyone; I'm just going to say I damn well deserve it."[38] Bogart believed he "owed nobody nothing," and that his achievement was due to his own hard work. This attitude, as one critic suggested, was in part "making a shrewd bid for publicity and in part he was giving irascible voice to his honest hatred of the crass and phony side of motion pictures." Indeed, before winning Bogart described the Oscar as "silly" and "all bunk," and once wrote an article calling it "a fake."[39]

However, when Greer Garson announced his name, Bogart, stunned, "jogged up onto the stage, took the Oscar as gently as though it were a newborn baby,"[40] and said, "It's a long way from the Belgian Congo to the stage of the Pantages, but it's a lot nicer here." He then proceeded to thank his director and costar: "No one does it alone. As in tennis, you need a good opponent or partner to bring out the best in you. John [Huston] and Katie [Hepburn] helped me to be where I am now."

Wife-actress Lauren Bacall claims that in spite of Bogart's cynicism, "he was very emotional and very humble. He had really wanted to win, for all his bravado when push came to shove, he did care and was stunned that it was such a popular victory. He had never felt people in the town liked him much and hadn't expected such universal joy when his name was called."[41] Furthermore, Richard Burton recalls that once, when he "dared to challenge Bogart over acting, he stormed out of the room and came back with his Oscar, which he thumped down on the table. 'You were saying?' he growled.'"[42] Thus, consciously or subconsciously, Bogart too used the Oscar as a metaphor of achievement.

John Wayne was another cynic who deprecated the value of the Oscar—before he won. For many years, when asked how he felt about the possibility of winning, he replied, "You can't eat awards. Nor, more to the point, drink them."[43] "My pictures don't call for the great dramatic range that wins Oscars," he used to say, which was based on the unfortunate reality that his specialty, Westerns, have always been overlooked by the Academy. In 1969, however, when his prospects of winning for *True Grit* seemed to be good, he became more cautious in his public utterances about the award. Furthermore, after winning, he praised the award as a great accolade: "The Oscar is a beautiful thing to have. It's important to me. It symbolizes appreciation of yourself by your peers." "The Oscar means a lot to me," he further reasoned, "even if it took the industry forty years to get around to it."[44]

Before Jane Fonda won her first Oscar (*Klute*), she used to say: "I don't care about the Oscars. I make movies to support the causes I believe in, not for any honors."[45] But people close to her believed she was extremely disappointed to have lost the award in her first nomination, *They Shoot Horses, Don't They?* Indeed, despite radical politics at the time, she accepted the New York Film Critics Award for *They Shoot Horses* modestly and appreciatively: "It's the biggest accolade I've ever been given. One tries to be blasé about things, but now that it's happened, it's very nice."[46]

Two actors, George C. Scott and Marlon Brando, have refused the Oscar, but they were not the first to have done so. Dudley Nichols, winner of best screenplay (*The Informer*) refused his in 1935. Nichols, a militant member of the Screen Writers Guild, had resigned from the Academy, along with other actors and writers, during the 1933 labor crisis. The relations between the Academy and the Screen Guilds reached a low point at the eighth annual banquet (March 5, 1936), when the Guilds asked their members to boycott the ceremonies. Bette Davis and Victor McLaglen, the winners of the acting awards, attended, but Nichols and director John Ford, also a winner, boycotted the show. Nichols was reported to have said, "To accept it [the Oscar] would be to turn my back on nearly a thousand members of the Writers Guild."[47]

Nichols's refusal was a minor incident compared with the controversy over George C. Scott's rejection of the award. In 1971, upon notification of his nomination for *Patton*, Scott sent the Academy a telegram requesting that his name be withdrawn from the list of nominees. "I mean no offense to the Academy," wrote Scott, "I simply do not wish to be involved."[48] He had not denied his first nomination for *Anatomy of a Murder*; many believed he gave the year's best performance, but the winner was Hugh Griffith for *Ben-*

Hur, which unfairly swept most of the 1959 awards. Scott's friends said it was extremely important for him to win, but after witnessing the fierce competition and campaigns for votes by his peers, he determined never again to have anything to do with the Oscar, describing it as a "meat parade."

In 1962, Scott was nominated again for a supporting award (*The Hustler*). This time, however, he asked the Academy to withdraw his name from the nominees, but his request was denied by Wendell Corey, the Academy president. "You were nominated by a vote of your fellow actors," Corey stated firmly, "and the Academy cannot remove your name from the list of nominated performances. The Academy nominates and votes awards for performances and achievements as they appear on the screen. Therefore, any one person responsible for achievement cannot decline the nomination after it is voted."[49] But Scott was told he could refuse the award, if he won. He lost, again undeservedly; the winner was George Chakiris in *West Side Story*, which, like *Ben-Hur*, received most of the 1961 Oscars.

Scott regards the politics of the Oscar Award as "offensive, barbarous, and innately corrupt,"[50] encouraging the public to think that awards are more important than acting itself. Thus, when he received his third nomination for *Patton* he declined it again. "Life isn't a race," was his reaction, "and because it is not a race, I don't consider myself in competition with my fellow actors for awards or recognition."[51] "I don't give a damn about the Oscar," Scott said on another occasion, "I'm making too much money anyway."[52] Daniel Taradash, then Academy president, ignored Scott's protests and made it clear that it was not Scott, but his *performance* that was nominated. Taradash felt that to agree to Scott's request would demean his fellow artists. Indeed, many actors believe that this was one of the Academy's finest hours, demonstrating that the vote was not personal, but disinterested and dispassionate—the kind of vote that could not have happened during the studio system (see chapter 12).

Interestingly enough, Scott's attack on the film colony, by thumbing his nose at the awards, had no apparent damaging effects. He won for *Patton* and a year later was nominated for *The Hospital*, which has been interpreted as a positive sign of the Academy's freedom from favoritism and personal considerations. Scott claimed he did not really mean to create a furor by his conduct. Indeed, when the "scandal" grew to unprecedented proportions, he decided that if he were ever nominated in the future, he would accept it. It was too much trouble *not* to accept the award.

The second actor to refuse an Oscar was Marlon Brando, when he was cited for *The Godfather*. Brando's rejection, however, differed from Scott's: he protested against the mistreatment of the American Indian, on screen and off (see chapter 12). Brando did not refuse his first Oscar for *On the Waterfront*, even though his critical views of Hollywood were already established. And, as in Scott's case, Brando's refusal had no impact on his standing in the Academy, for a year later he was nominated for *Last Tango in Paris*.

Other players, like Katharine Hepburn, have been ambivalent toward the Oscar and its publicity. Nonetheless, she did not reject any of her four Oscars. Her form of "protest" (some say eccentricity) was not to attend any Oscar ceremonies until 1968, when she broke her long-standing vow and appeared in a prerecorded tape prepared for the fortieth anniversary show. Hepburn made her first appearance at the 1974 ceremonies, when she presented a Special Oscar to her friend, producer Laurence Weingarten. "I'm living proof," she said afterward, "that someone can wait forty-one years to be unselfish."[53]

Dustin Hoffman has also been critical of the Academy Awards. He attended the ceremonies once, at his nomination for *The Graduate*, but claimed to have been uncomfortable about being nominated. "I hope to God I don't win an Oscar," he is reported to have said. "It would depress me if I did. I really don't deserve it."[54] In 1975, an interview taped earlier was aired on CBS a few hours before the show, in which Hoffman voiced his contempt for the Oscar, calling it "ugly and grotesque." Frank Sinatra, one of the show's emcees, scolded him publicly for these remarks. Hoffman made a point of not showing up at the awards presentations for his next two nominations.

Hoffman also created an uproar when he questioned the validity of film awards at the 1980 Golden Globe ceremonies. "I think that awards are very silly," he said, accepting an award for *Kramer vs. Kramer*. "They put very talented and good people against each other and they hurt the hell out of the ones that lose. And I think they relieve us that win." Addressing his fellow-nominees, Hoffman asserted that "awards make more sense when they're given for a life achievement to a man like Mr. Fonda" (the recipient of the

Cecil B. De Mille Golden Globe Award for career achievements) "and particularly to a man like Mr. Lemmon, who recently gave one of the great performances of his life [*The China Syndrome*]."

Hoffman's criticism was quite similar to that of George C. Scott, deploring the demeaning effects of the Oscar race, particularly the campaigning by actors in the trade magazines. Both protested, as Scott said, the fact that actors are under pressure to enter into competition with their peers that has nothing to do with acting itself. They also resented the idea that actors have increasingly become award conscious. Hoffman repeated his criticism in his Oscar speech, expressing resentment over the Academy's spotlit competition among fellow-artists. "I refuse to believe that I am better than Jack Lemmon, Al Pacino, and Peter Sellers," he said, "and I refuse to believe that Robert Duvall lost. We are part of an artistic family and I am proud to share this award." But unlike Scott, Hoffman did not refuse his award.

There is no doubt that Hoffman was genuinely honest in what he said and there is no doubt that he expressed the opinions of many other artists. Yet it is doubtful that this kind of criticism will change the Oscar's operations and effects. Among other things, the Oscar depends and thrives on individual competitiveness with all of its cruel manifestations.

Reaction to Winning

Many artists consider the winning of an Oscar not just the climax of their professional careers, but also the greatest achievement of their lives. Their immediate reaction to winning usually follows a period of tremendous anxiety, the six weeks between the announcement of nominees and the awards ceremonies. Furthermore, this reaction tends to be more spontaneous or less fabricated than the ordinary behavior in Hollywood: with all the preparations for the event of winning, there are always elements of unpredictability. Ever since the telecast of the awards, the reactions to winning (and to losing) have assumed greater significance because they are shown live to hundreds of millions of television viewers all over the world, which is exciting for the winners but terribly embarrassing for the losers.

In the first years, neither the ceremonies nor the award were highly publicized. Charles Laughton could not attend the 1933

banquet because he was working in London. The Academy telegram, congratulating him for winning for *The Private Life of Henry
VIII*, was put on the board but Laughton made no big fuss over
it,[55] partly because he did not comprehend its meaning and partly
because the award itself did not have much effect.

Joseph Schildkraut (*The Life of Emile Zola*) did not attend the banquet, as the ceremony was called in the 1930s. "My agents discouraged me from going to the affair," he recalled, because they thought
the recipient would be Ralph Bellamy or Thomas Mitchell. He was
already in bed when the telephone rang and "the excited voice of a
man who did not even bother to introduce himself bellowed at me:
'Where in the hell are you? Why aren't you here? The awards are
about to be handed out and you are not here.'"[56] Schildkraut
"could hardly think straight," and thought "was this some practical
joke?" When he blurted out, "If you don't tell me, I won't come,"
the man replied, "Yes, you son of a gun. . . . You won it. Get down
here!" He dressed in style, ordered out the car, and went to the
Biltmore Hotel. "I arrived just in time to be seated at the Warner
Brothers table and to accept the Oscar for my portrayal of Dreyfus
from Frank Capra."[57]

Joan Crawford decided not to attend the 1946 ceremonies out of
fear of rejection. "I know I'm going to lose," she told her publicist
Henry Rogers. Even if she won, she dreaded the idea of having "to
get up in front of all those people and make a speech," fearing she
would be "tongue-tied and make an ass of myself."[58] Neither her
publicist nor producer Jerry Wald could persuade her to go. However, Rogers, who had started her Oscar campaign earlier, arranged
that the photographers of all fan magazines would be at her house.
When Charles Boyer announced on the radio that she won, cheers
erupted over the radio from Grauman's Chinese Theater, and she
exclaimed, "This is the greatest moment of my life."[59] Director
Michael Curtiz, who had accepted the award for her, came to her
house to present it personally. The next morning, newspapers all
over the world printed front page stories of how "Hollywood's Cinderella won the prize without going to the ball."[60] Her house was
filled with flowers and telegrams, and each sender of flowers and
messages received a personal signed letter from her.

Ingrid Bergman did not attend the 1957 show when she was up
for *Anastasia*. Performing in Paris, she asked Cary Grant to stand
by "just in case I got lucky." After the evening's performance, she

went to her hotel, and was awakened at seven o'clock in the morning by a Twentieth Century-Fox publicity man shouting into the phone, "You've won! You've won!" She listened to a repeat of the ceremony over the French radio, and was taking a bath when Cary Grant began his speech, "Dear Ingrid, wherever you are in the world" (and she was saying, "I'm in the bathtub!") "we, your friends, want to congratulate you, and I have your Oscar here for your marvelous performance, and may you be as happy as we are for you."[61]

When Sophia Loren heard she had been nominated for *Two Women*, "I ecstatically announced that I would attend the Academy Awards ceremony in Hollywood. I felt that just being nominated was an honor in itself and a rare one at that for an Italian-speaking actress in an Italian film. But then, upon reflection, I changed my mind. My competition was formidable (Audrey Hepburn, Piper Laurie, Geraldine Page, and Natalie Wood). Besides the formidable opposition, the plain fact was that in its long history, an Academy Award had never been given to an actor or actress in a foreign-language film." Thus, Loren decided, "I could not bear the ordeal of sitting in plain view of millions of viewers while my fate was being judged. If I lost, I might faint from disappointment; if I won, I would also very likely faint with joy. Instead of spreading my fainting all over the world, I decided it was better that I faint at home."[62]

Loren "honestly had no real expectations of winning," but "hope being the eternal rogue that it is, on the night of the Awards, I was too nervous to sleep." Photographer Pier Luigi came to her Rome apartment, "to keep the vigil with me." At three o'clock in the morning, "I tried to go to bed, but my eyes would not close and my heart would not stop pounding, so I went back to the living room to talk to Pier." There was no coverage of the Awards on Italian television or radio. By six o'clock, she knew the ceremony was over and was sure she had not won. Loren was awakened at six forty-five by Cary Grant's pleasant voice, telling her the good news. "I didn't faint," she recalled, "but I went rather giddy. It was incontestably the greatest thrill of my life."[63]

The anxiety and tension during the Oscar show are immense and their effects are equally felt by both male and female nominees. It's one of the few aspects of the "Oscar phenomenon" that does not distinguish between the genders, unlike the kinds of roles they are nominated for or the age at which they win. There seems to be uniformity of response among men and women when it comes to winning (and losing) the Oscar.

Most nominees report that the show seemed endless—that is, until the announcement of winners in their categories. "And we sat, and we sat," Milland recalled, "through the interminable minor awards, applauding dutifully each recipient and the endless speeches of acceptance."[64] He also recalled that after Ingrid Bergman tore the envelope open and "a great big grin appeared on her face," he knew he hadn't won because "she was smiling and I'd never even met her." But then "dimly, I heard the words, 'Are you nervous, Mr. Milland? It's all yours!'" In the applause that followed, he just sat there: "I never thought to move until I felt Mal's elbow in my ribs, a blow which I still feel to this day when it's raining." His wife said, "Get up there, sweetheart! Get up there! It's you! It's you!" He does not remember much of what happened after that. "Everything was a jumble of handshakes, microphones, people with notebooks and pencils, and flashing camera bulbs."[65]

Gig Young, the 1969 supporting winner, also "kept looking away from the program," because he "didn't want to know exactly when my category would be called." But he kept thinking, "I mustn't jump up if they call somebody else's name. I mustn't jump up."[66] And Joan Fontaine recorded her experience of Oscar night:

> I froze. . . . I stared across the table, where Olivia was sitting directly opposite me. "Get up there, get up here," she whispered commandingly. Now what had I done? All the animus we'd felt toward each other as children, the hair-pullings, the savage wrestling matches, the time Olivia fractured my collarbone, all came rushing back in kaleidoscopic imagery. My paralysis was total.[67]

Fontaine also remembers that "cries of 'Speak, Speak!' echoed through the room as I tried to find my voice." She does not have "the faintest idea of what I said in my acceptance speech. God knows I hadn't rehearsed anything."[68]

Indeed, it is never easy to predict the winner. When Broderick Crawford (*All the King's Men*) was asked if he had not been sure of winning, as the polls had predicted, he snapped: "Polls! The polls predicted Dewey would win too!" referring to the failure of the Presidential candidate. "I have no blood," Crawford said after the ceremonies. "I feel like I've been under an anesthetic all day." He also said his wife was in the car and the motor running, "she's taking no chances on a recount."[69]

Year after year, film critics, public opinion polls and filmgoers have attempted to predict the winners. In some years, all pre-presentation favorites have come through as expected. In others, though, there have been major surprises. In 1956, Anthony Quinn's second win (*Lust for Life*) upset the pre-Oscar favorite, Robert Stack (*Written on the Wind*). In 1963, Sidney Poitier (*Lilies of the Field*) won to everyone's surprise; Paul Newman (*Hud*) and Albert Finney (*Tom Jones*) were considered more likely winners. In 1965, Rod Steiger (*The Pawnbroker*) was the critical favorite, and Richard Burton (*The Spy Who Came in from the Cold*) a runner-up, but the winner was Lee Marvin (*Cat Ballou*). In 1968, Peter O'Toole (*The Lion in Winter*) was considered the sure winner; the winner, however was Cliff Robertson (*Charly*). In 1974, most predictions chose Fred Astaire (*The Towering Inferno*), a sentimental favorite, but the winner was Robert De Niro (*The Godfather, Part II*). In the same year, most polls predicted Jack Nicholson (*Chinatown*) would win, but Art Carney (*Harry and Tonto*) was the surprise winner. In 1976, Liv Ullmann (*Face to Face*) was expected to win; the winner, instead, was Faye Dunaway (*Network*). "I didn't expect this to happen quite yet," said the overwhelmed Dunaway. And last year, William Hurt (*Kiss of the Spider Woman*) was the surprise winner; Jack Nicholson (*Prizzi's Honor*) was expected to win.

Artists themselves have been surprised by their nominations and even more surprised by winning. Simone Signoret "had no notion" when she accepted the offer to appear in *Room at the Top*, "that this train I was boarding would lead me to my saying 'thank you' in April 1960 in front of millions of TV viewers, to three thousand people seated in red-velvet seats in a Hollywood cinema."[70] The film's critical acclaim shocked her: "We had made this movie hoping that a few friends would like it."[71] Its success in America came as a great surprise to her.

The lack of assurance prior to the ceremonies have added a great deal of excitement. "When the presenter finally gets the envelope open and the winner is you," Mercedes McCambridge recalled, "the giddiness of delirium sets in, and the long walk to the stage is anesthesia. The dosage diminishes slowly, its effects taking weeks to wear off."[72] Charlton Heston recorded in his diary on April 4,

1960: "I made it. Looking across the orchestra, just before Susan [Hayward] read it off, something popped in my head, 'I'm going to get it.' And I did. I kissed Lydia and walked to the stage dripping wet, except for a pepper-dry mouth: classic stage fright. I'll never forget the moment, or the night, for that matter."[73]

Rita Moreno (*West Side Story*) was sure Judy Garland (*Judgment at Nuremberg*) would win. She was therefore extremely emotional and practically in orbit when she won, shouting, "I can't believe it! Good Heavens." "I never thought I'd win," she said after the awards, "yet, at the same time I was wishing I would win. It's a strange emotional feeling to go around with for days. I'm glad it's over." Gregory Peck was trying "not to work up either undue excitement or nerves" when he earned his fifth nomination for *To Kill a Mockingbird*. "He had lost before and fully expected to lose again."[74]

Sidney Poitier neither expected to be nominated for *The Defiant Ones* nor to win for *Lilies of the Field*. "My anxiety mounted until it was unbearable," he told of the 1964 Oscar night. "I was sitting there being ripped up internally . . . absolutely beside myself with nervousness."[75] Poitier understood "this is an important moment and I have to be here and in fact I want to be here for what it means to us as a people," but he also decided, "never again, under no circumstances am I going to come here again and put myself through this." Although winning seemed a "long-shot dark horse. . . . I was switching from no chance at all to writing my acceptance speech."[76]

When John Mills was watching the daily rushes of his scene with the lobsters in *Ryan's Daughter*, director David Lean asked him, "Johnny, have you ever won an Oscar?" to which he said, "No, I haven't. Why?" "Nothing," said Lean, "I just wondered."[77] A year later, Mills received a cable from the Academy, congratulating him for his supporting nomination. Ever since the nomination, "I had done my best, because I wanted the damn thing so desperately, to persuade myself that I really didn't care, and that I had very little chance." He knew that his part, the village idiot, was small and "without a single line of dialogue." One day, Mills's daughter, Juliet, called from Hollywood to tell him that he had been awarded the Golden Globe. After that, his anxiety was even more acute, because he realized "that the recipient of the Golden Globe Award becomes a top tip for the Oscar." On Oscar day, "the phone rang continually, reporters, gossip writers. . . . Several of them told me that the rumors circulating around town made me favorite. The more of the stuff I listened to, the more convinced I was that I really didn't stand a chance." On Oscar night Mills tried "to look cool and totally relaxed," but he failed. He desperately wanted the Oscar, "knowing that at my age [sixty-three], it was in all probability my last chance of winning one." After "what seemed like an eternity, the moment arrived." Maggie Smith, the award's presenter, opened the envelope and smiled broadly, "I knew before she made the announcement, I'd made it."[78]

I Would Like to Thank. . . . The Acceptance Speech

Prior to the public broadcasts of the show, the acceptance speeches tended to be modest. Janet Gaynor, the first winner, said, "I am deeply honored," but she could not continue as her voice cracked and tears filled her eyes, thus setting a standard of behavior for future speeches by female winners.[79] Embarrassed, she later sent a letter to the Academy: "This is an honor that I deeply appreciate. I regard the opinion of the Academy as so expert and unbiased that to be recipient of the award makes me very happy indeed."[80]

But the speeches have varied in length, content, and originality. Some were simple, as Vivien Leigh's 1940 speech in which she thanked "Mr. Selznick, all my coworkers, and most of all Miss Margaret Mitchell." Others, such as Greer Garson's, were extremely long, thanking everyone, including "the doctor who brought me into the world." "I walked into the wings," she later recalled, "and a man said, 'you spoke for five and a quarter minutes.' " She realized she had broken "a sacred rule," for "leading ladies aren't supposed to get further than, thank you, thank you, and burst into tears."[81] Garson's speech soon became a joke in Hollywood, imitated at parties. Rumor has it that in the next decade she refused to speak in public at all. This kind of speech is impossible at present, the age of television, when every minute of advertising costs a fortune. Still, in recent years, Beatrice Straight's speech was almost as long as her winning part in *Network*, practically one scene.

The "thank you" note has been customary in every speech, but different people have been thanked for different reasons. Wearing a military uniform, Jimmy Stewart (*The Philadelphia Story*) thanked the entire film industry:"I assure you this is a very important moment in my life. As I look around this room, a warm feeling comes over me, a feeling of satisfaction, pride, and most of all, gratefulness for the encouragement, instruction, and advantage of your experience that have been offered to me since I came to Hollywood, and with all my heart I thank you." Joanne Woodward tearfully expressed her thanks to Nunnally Johnson, who wrote, produced, and directed *The Three Faces of Eve*, "for having more faith in me than I ever knew anyone could have." Charlton Heston (*Ben-Hur*) thanked "the first secretary in a Broadway casting office who let me in to get my first job." In the same year, Shelley Winters thanked her agent for getting her the part in *The Diary of Anne Frank*. And Maureen Stapleton (*Reds*) outdid them all, thanking every person she has ever met.

Audrey Hepburn's choice as the presenter of the 1965 Best Actor Award was ironic. She had not been nominated for *My Fair Lady*, but her costar, Rex Harrison, was and his chances to win were excellent. "It was a strange evening," Harrison reported, "I knew that if I won the award I would be on the stage with two Fair Ladies. Julie Andrews had been nominated (*Mary Poppins*); Audrey Hepburn had not, but she was in Hollywood to present the awards to the winners." It all happened, "I won it and Julie won it and things were fairly hectic backstage, trying to keep the factions in the right place for the photographs and interviews. The public relations people had a difficult time, but they are well equipped to for this."[82] "I have to thank two fair ladies," Harrison said in his speech. Hugged by Audrey Hepburn, the television camera caught a close-up of Julie Andrews extremely upset.

In the following year, when Harrison presented the Best Actress Award, another interesting incident happened. The two major contestants were both named Julie and both were English: Julie Christie (*Darling*) and Julie Andrews (*The Sound of Music*). Harrison ripped open the envelope and said with lips pursed, "Julie," then paused for another second and completed, "Christie." Christie, who had been trying to sit calmly, ran to the stage crying, and clutched the Oscar and Harrison at the same time.

Burt Lancaster's speech evoked laughter and applause when he thanked those who worked with him in *Elmer Gantry*, those who voted for him, but also those who did not vote for him. Rod Steiger was truly gracious when he thanked his costar in *In the Heat of the Night*, Sidney Poitier, "whose friendship gave me the knowledge to enhance my performance—and we shall overcome." Gene Hackman (*The French Connection*) thanked his director, William Friedkin, who "brought me through this when I wanted to quit." Jack Nicholson thanked "Mary Pickford who, incidentally, was the first actor to get a percentage of her pictures." "Speaking of percentages," he continued, "last but not least, I thank my agent, who about ten years ago said I had no business being an actor." Jason Robards took the award "in honor of my producer, Robert Redford, who showed such integrity and perseverence in this project (*All the President's Men*)."

One of the more charming speeches was Mary Steenburgen's: She thanked "My patron, Jack Nicholson," who cast her in her first film, *Goin' South*, and concluded by thanking her husband-actor Malcolm McDowell "for making life so nice." "I feel like tap dancing," she said, quoting from her winning role in *Melvin and Howard*.

Some of the speeches have stood out in their humor. Fredric March, who split the 1931/2 award with Wallace Beery, said: "It just happened that this year Mrs. March and I adopted a child and Mr. and Mrs. Beery adopted a child. And here we are, both getting awards for the best male performance of the year." Claudette Colbert was boarding the Santa Fe train to New York when she was announced winner. The Santa Fe officials held up the train and she was taken by taxi to the ceremonies at the Biltmore Hotel. "I'm happy enough to cry," she said, "but I can't take the time to do so. A taxi is waiting outside with the engine running."

Bing Crosby thought he had only slim chances to win and subsequently decided not to attend the presentations. Around six o'clock in the evening of the awards, however, when Paramount learned that he might win, the executives had to persuade him to go: it was not an easy task. "All I can say," Crosby commented, "is that it sure is a wonderful world when a tired crooner like me can walk away with this hunk of crockery." Edmund Gwenn, who won for his Santa Claus in *The Miracle on 34th Street*, said: "Now I know there is a Santa Claus." Jane Wyman, winning for playing a deaf-mute in *Johnny Belinda*, said: "I accept this very gratefully for keeping my mouth shut; I think I'll do it again." Eva Marie Saint (*On the Waterfront*) was in advance pregnancy and feared "I may have the baby right here out of excitement." "I hope this is not a mistake," Yul Brynner (*The King and I*) said, "because I won't give it back for nothing." And the same concern was expressed by Alec Guinness, recipient of the 1980 Special Oscar for career achievement, "I'm grabbing this while the going is good."

David Niven (*Separate Tables*) was so excited, he admitted "I'm so loaded down with good-luck charms I could hardly make the steps." The following day, he published a big "thank you" in the trade magazines:

> In the full glare and under the stress of 'Oscar Night' (if one is lucky enough to be the winner), it is almost impossible not to be corny in the wording of one's thanks. May I now, in the cold light of the morning after, thank from the bottom of my heart, not only those who voted for me, but those who did not vote for me, those who could not vote for me, and those who would not have voted for me in a million years even if they could have voted for me. In other words, I want to thank all show business where, in the midst of the most wonderful and crazy people, I have spent the happiest years of my life.[83]
>
> Love to All
> David Niven

Lee Marvin broke with the tradition of acceptance speeches when he simply said, "Half of this (Oscar) belongs to a horse someplace out in the Valley" [which helped him win in *Cat Ballou*]. Gene Hackman suggested in the same vein, "Maybe the award should really go to my car," referring, of course, to the breathtaking chase scene in *The French Connection*.

Estelle Parsons caused a wave of laughter when she gasped, "Oh, boy, it's heavy!" as she took the statuette from Walter Matthau. Her Broadway show, *The Seven Descents of Myrtle*, closed down for the night so she could attend the event. Barbra Streisand simply looked at the statuette and said, "Hello, gorgeous," her line from *Funny Girl*. In the following year, she saw tears in John Wayne's eyes when she presented him the award for *True Grit*. Yes, the symbol of "macho" cried and was extremely emotional. "I thought some day I might win an award for lasting so long! But I never thought I would get this particular award," Wayne said. "I feel very grateful, very humble." And he concluded on a humorous note: "If I'd known what I know now, I'd have put a patch on my eye thirty-five years ago."

The winners for *One Flew Over the Cuckoo's Nest* referred in their speeches to the movie. "I guess this proves there are as many nuts in the Academy as anywhere else," Jack Nicholson said. And Louise Fletcher said, "It looks like you all hated me so much that you are giving me the award for it, and I'm loving every minute of it. All I can say is I've loved being hated by you." Some speeches have made references to the winners' professional doubts. Olivia de Havilland spoke of the confidence placed on her ability to maintain a high standard of acting when she first won (*To Each His Own*). "Thank you for your very generous assurance that I haven't failed to do so," she said. Jose Ferrer (*Cyrano de Bergerac*) also spoke of the Oscar as a vote of confidence: "It is more to me than an honor accorded to an actor. It's a vote of confidence in me. Believe me, I'll not let you down." Anthony Quinn was deeply moved when he won his second supporting award in *Lust for Life*. "I want to say humbly to my colleagues that acting has never been a matter of competition," he said, "but a fight with myself. And I thank you for letting me win that fight."

A word of consolation to the yet undiscovered and unestablished artists has also appeared in the speeches. Mercedes McCambridge, who won for her first film encouraged other young actors: "Mostly I want to say to every waiting actor, hang on! Look what can happen!" "I meant it with my heart," she later explained, "as a message to all those other actors in the cattle call that day back in New York. I got it that time. Maybe their turn is next. The hanging on is the hard part."[84] Dustin Hoffman also spoke of actors as an intimate artistic community. "How many other Oscar-caliber actors are out there, undiscovered," he said.

An exceptionally honest speech was made by Ingrid Bergman, who was shocked upon learning of her fifth nomination for *Murder on the Orient Express*: "To be nominated for something so small; I really had only one scene." On winning, she rushed up to the stage and said: "This is unfair. I want this award to go to Valentina Cortesa," nominated for *Day for Night*. The spotlights and cameras swept across to Valentina, who stood up and blew kisses at Ingrid Bergman. "It was really sad that she hadn't gotten it," Bergman thought, "because she deserved it." "Please forgive me, Valentina," she apologized, "I didn't mean to." Later, she realized it was not "quite the right thing to say as the movie industry is supposed to be impartial."[85] And there were three other supporting actresses, besides Cortesa, who lost.

Losing the Award: Defeat in the Public Eye

It is not easy to accept failure. Thus, some performers have clung to the importance and prestige of the nomination. "My own disappointment," Gene Tierney observed, "was lessened by the conviction, new to me, that I had developed a difficult character (*Leave Her to Heaven*), not just a pretty face on the screen." "I had been challenged by the role," she explains, "and to have been nominated for an Oscar was excitement enough."[86] Joan Fontaine lost at her first nomination (*Rebecca*), but she "wasn't surprised or sorry," because, "to have won it with my first good role would have been precipitous. The voters might well have thought Hitch was my Svengali, that after so many undistinguished performances in the past, surely it was Hitchcock who had mesmerized me into the performance I was nominated for."[87]

Rosalind Russell, a four-time nominee, is perhaps one of Hollywood's greatest losers. "Glad as I was about it," Russell wrote of her first nomination for *My Sister Eileen*, "the honor put me under heavy pressure. It means too much to the studios to have their people win; I still can't think of the tension surrounding these races without breaking into a sweat."[88] Of her other nominations, she observed, "Half a loaf can feed you (*Sister Kenny* and *Mourning Becomes Electra* had both been critical successes, bringing me two more Oscar nominations), but when you get the whole loaf, you know the difference."[89] Her loss in 1947 was so unexpected that she was in a complete state of shock; some suggested, as a cynical joke, that RKO changed *Mourning Becomes Electra* to "Mourning Becomes Rosalind Russsell." And if three losses were not enough, she lost a fourth race in 1959 (*Auntie Mame*).

That players are expected to care about the award is clear from Gloria Swanson's testimony of her *Sunset Boulevard* experience: "I surprised everyone, except Bette Davis, probably, and Judy Holliday, who sat next to me, by losing." Swanson could not attend the ceremonies in Hollywood because she was performing in New York, but she listened to the broadcast with other stars. "I honestly didn't care, but I could see in the faces of everyone at La Zambra, and everywhere else I went in the weeks after that, that people *wanted* me to care. In fact, they seemed to want more than that. They expected scenes from me, wild sarcastic tantrums. They wanted Norma Desmond, as if I had hooked up sympathetically, disastrously, with the role by playing it." It soon became a problem. "If I said I didn't care, people would pity me and say I had a bad case of sour grapes. If I told them I was an Aries, that it was not in my nature to be dejected, they would think I was mad, and the Gloria-Norma identification would be made forever in the eyes of the press. It was easier to say nothing."[90]

It is especially hard to accept the failure if the nominees attend the ceremonies and expect to win. Shelley Winters was sure she would win at her first nomination (*A Place in the Sun*). On Oscar night, as she described, "I was a wreck," and "the show seemed interminable." When Ronald Colman opened the envelope, she was sure he announced her name and was almost on the steps leading to the stage, when Vittorio Gassman tackled her. She remembered that "as we lay on the floor of the aisle, I thought he'd gone insane." Gassman whispered, "Shelley, it's Vivien Leigh," and they managed to crawl back to their seats "as inconspicuously as possible." But Shelley could not believe it. "The rest of the evening I felt as if Ronald Colman had betrayed me. He could at least have said my name and swallowed the card, if he were any kind of English gentleman." Later, they went to the Governor's Ball, but "I don't remember anything about it. I just knew that the gold statuette was not on *my* table." She believes to this day that Vivien Leigh "had taken my Oscar."[91]

Shelley Winters was not the only nominee to have experienced such embarrassment. Frank Capra, whose *Lady for a Night* got four nominations, was extremely excited. "I became impossible to live with," and "kept telling myself I would win four awards." Preparing for the event, "I wrote and threw away dozens of acceptance speeches. I ordered my first tuxedo, rented a plush home in Beverly Hills to be seen, [and to] sway votes in bistros."[92] When Will Rogers, the presenter of the directorial award, said, "Well, well, well, what do you know? I've watched this young man come up from the bottom, and I mean the bottom," Capra was sure he was the winner. "It couldn't happen to a nicer guy," Rogers continued, "Come up and get it, Frank." Capra rose and headed toward the spotlight, only to realize the winner was Frank Lloyd (*Cavalcade*). "I stood petrified in the dark, in utter disbelief," he recalled, and began "the longest, saddest, most shattering walk of my life. I wanted to crawl under the rug. All my friends at the table were crying." After this awkward experience, Capra vowed that "if they ever did vote me one, I would never, never, *never* show up to accept it."[93] But he did not live up to his vow, as could be expected, and two years later, his dream materialized when *It Happened One Night* set a record, getting all five major awards.

Judy Garland experienced several "Oscar defeats." Of her first nomination (*A Star is Born*), biographer Gerold Frank writes: "It was inevitable that Judy be nominated with almost everyone agreeing she was sure to get it. Though she had received a juvenile award for her work in *The Wizard of Oz*, this was the real thing, and if it were to come true, what a triumph after everything."[94] Prior to her nomination, husband Sid Luft went to an analyst, to help him cope with Judy "as the time drew nearer not only to the birth of her third child but to the resolution of the mounting uncertainty as to whether she would win the Oscar."[95] Judy was determined to attend the ceremonies, but unexpectedly gave birth on March 29, 1955, the night before the Oscar show. Extensive preparations were made at the hospital, with television cameras in her room. The idea was that if she won, she would talk to Bob Hope from her bed. After she learned of her loss (to Grace Kelly's *The Country Girl*) she said: "I knew I wouldn't get it. . . . They wouldn't give it to me, although I deserved it." Her consolation was her newborn son, to whom she referred as "My Academy Award." Her disappointment was indeed profound; she "accepted what was much more of a disaster to her than everyone knew." Comedian Groucho Marx sent her a consolatory telegram: "Dear Judy. This is the biggest robbery since Brink's."[96]

Even players who eventually won the Oscar admitted it had been hard to accept the defeat. Susan Hayward took her first failures with good humor. When she was nominated for the fourth time (*I'll Cry Tomorrow*) and lost, however, she confided: "I managed not to shed any tears until everything was over. Then I sat down and had a good cry and decided that losing was just part of the game."[97] Rod Steiger, who most people believed would win for *The Pawnbroker*, was particularly offended and bitter to have lost to Lee Marvin in *Cat Ballou*. Sylvia Miles, nominated for *Midnight Cowboy*, reacted similarly: "People think I was mad when I didn't win, but they're wrong. It's not that I mind losing, but losing to Goldie Hawn (*The Cactus Flower*)? That was an insult."[98]

Peter Sellers saw his role in *Being There*, as Chance Gardiner, a simple-witted fool who becomes politically powerful in Washington, as his "all-out bid" for an Oscar. He was on an "obssessive quest" to make the film for seven years, hoping that this part would "purge him of the coarse and exploitative roles he had taken in other films. He would finally achieve the perfection that had eluded him.[99] It was a simple, understated performance, devoid of tricks, accents, and multiple impersonations that he had used in earlier films, such as the *Pink Panther* movies, which made him rich and famous. Sellers treated the loss of the Oscar, to Dustin Hoffman in *Kramer vs. Kramer*, with "very little show of emotion but deep down inside he was tremendously disappointed."[100]

Elizabeth Taylor, who won her second Oscar for *Who's Afraid of Virginia Woolf?* was upset that her then husband, Richard Burton, lost, believing he gave the best performance of the year. Burton knew he had no chance of winning after Paul Scofield was cited by the New York Film Critics. And, to his credit, he did not try to conceal that he was hurt, having lost on six previous occasions. "I want the Oscar," he was quoted to have said, "I've won all kinds of little Oscars but not the big one."[101] He therefore convinced Liz Taylor that she should not attend the ceremonies, despite promises made to Jack Warner. The excuse given was filming *The Comedians* in France. On a later occasion, Taylor rationalized their decision: "I've gone to those award dinners four times, and won it once, for not dying. The only time I didn't go was when I was nominated for *Raintree County* and the dinner was just two weeks after Mike [Todd] was killed. They didn't expect me to go. But most of the time you're supposed to, if you possibly can, whether you've got a chance of winning or not. It's for the industry."[102] Anne Bancroft accepted the award for her, which prompted emcee Bob Hope to quip: "It must be nice to have enough talent just to send for one."

There was a lot of criticism of Taylor's absence, particularly because she had excellent chances of winning; all preaward polls predicted her win. "Everybody was talking about it backstage," Walter Matthau, the supporting winner that year (*The Fortune Cookie*) recalled. "When the winners aren't present, it denigrates the whole thing, it cheapens it, it lessens the values, the drama, the excitement."[103] In the same year, the other supporting winner, Sandy Dennis (*Who's Afraid of Virginia Woolf?*) did not attend the show, because she was performing in New York and, besides, hates flying. She later admitted that, given the criticism, it would have been easier to attend.

The contestants in all categories are expected to attend the ceremonies and, indeed, in the last decade most have done so regardless of their chances of winning. Still, the Oscar, like all other awards, is fun for the winners, but not for the losers, particularly when every gesture is mercilessly recorded by the television cameras.

CHAPTER 11

The Multiple Effects of the Oscar Award

How important it is to win the Oscar Award? Most critics agree that winning an Oscar has pervasive effects, but there has been contradictory evidence concerning their precise nature because this issue has not been studied systematically. Some have stressed the "overnight success" syndrome—that is, the winner who becomes an international star overnight. But others have documented the Oscar's negative effects, or the Oscar as "a jinx"—that is, the winner who becomes a "victim" after winning.

The Oscar Award plays a crucial role in both creating and perpetuating the stratification of the film industry in terms of its major rewards: money, prestige, and power. This stratification is based on the principle of cumulative advantage, summed up in the expression, "the rich get richer and the poor poorer."[1] How has the Oscar Award created this cumulative advantage? What have been its effects on the winning films and winning artists in the short and in the long run?

The Oscar's Effects on Films

The highest goal of every studio in Hollywood is to get nominations and win the Best Picture award. Generally speaking, this award increases substantially the box-office success of the winning films, but the extent of its effects on the winners has been all but universal. The first film to have benefited directly from winning, though not Best Picture, was John Ford's *The Informer*, which opened to good reviews but was not popular at the box office. It was only after winning four Oscars, the largest number of awards for a film in 1935, including Director and Best Actor, that it became a hit.

The most dramatic impact of winning occurred in 1947, when *The Best Years of Our Lives* became the most commercial Oscar-winner to date, grossing in domestic rentals over eleven million dollars.[2] Its win of Best Picture and other awards resulted in at least two more million dollars in box-office receipts. But even when the Oscar does not make the winning film a blockbuster, it has *some* effect. For example, *Hamlet* was initially intended for select audiences in the art film circuits. A succès d'estime, its surprise win of Best Picture made it a bigger draw, particularly for audiences who would not have gone to see it had it not won an Oscar.

The commercial value of the Oscar in the first two decades was visible, but not dramatic. In the 1930s, the average domestic rentals of an Oscar-winning film was about two million dollars (see Appendix, Table 4). *Cimarron*, the 1930/1 winner, was the top money-maker of the year with two million dollars in rentals; *Grand Hotel*, the 1931/2 winner, was also that year's top grosser with $2,250,000; and *Cavalcade*, in 1932/3, ranked second among the blockbusters of the season with $3,500,000, becoming the most popular Oscar winner of the decade, with the exception of *Gone with the Wind*.

The strong correlation between the Oscar winners and the blockbusters in the 1930s—that is, between artistic and commercial success—began to decline in the 1940s. Still, in the 1940s, the average box-office performance of Oscar winners was $4,600,000, or twice that of the 1930s.

The three most commercial Oscar films of the 1950s were: *Around the World in 80 Days* with twenty-three million dollars in domestic rentals; *The Bridge on the River Kwai* with seventeen; and *Ben-Hur* with thirty-six. Each of these movies was a blockbuster prior to its nomination, but became even more popular after winning. The average rentals of Oscar-winning films in the 1950s tripled the figures of the 1940s, which was twelve million dollars. But the Academy still honored "small" pictures, whose Oscar had a modest influence on their box-office standings. Contrary to popular opinion, *All About Eve* was not a huge hit, ranking eighth in 1951 with $2,900,000 in domestic rentals. On the other hand, it is doubtful that *Marty* would have grossed two million dollars in 1955 without the Oscar, though the award did not make it one of the year's hits.

MGM's musical *Gigi* was commercially successful before winning the 1958 Best Picture, but the award added about two million dollars to its rentals, and thus made it the fifth money-grosser of the year with over seven million dollars in domestic rentals.

The Oscar's financial effects became much more apparent in the 1960s. Billy Wilder's *The Apartment* was the only Oscar winner in the entire decade to have grossed in rentals less than ten million dollars; the average was twenty-one million. True, more blockbusters were nominated for Best Picture than ever before, which means that most winners were hits prior to the nominations. But the Oscar continued to exert differential impact, depending on the type of the winning film. *The Sound of Music* did not need the 1965 Oscar to become the blockbuster of the decade, but the 1966 Oscar for *A Man for All Seasons* doubled its domestic rentals to about thirteen million dollars, a phenomenal amount for a serious historical film that lacked high production values.

In the last fifteen years, the cash value of the Oscar has been estimated as ranging from five to thirty million dollars in the US and Canada. There is no comparative data on the award's effects in foreign movie markets, though the overseas rentals can match or even surpass the domestic rentals. For example, the 1971 Oscar for *The French Connection* added at least fifteen million dollars to its rentals. And *Annie Hall* had finished its major run by the time of the nominations with twelve million dollars, but the film was re-released after winning the 1977 Oscar, which contributed at least five million dollars more to its rentals. The two films which benefited most from their Oscars in the 1970s were: *One Flew Over the Cuckoo's Nest* and *The Deer Hunter*: about half of the former's fifty-nine million dollars and about half of the latter's thirty million dollars are attributed to the award.

In 1973, two blockbusters were nominated for Best Picture: William Friedkin's horror tale *The Exorcist* and George Roy Hill's adventure comedy *The Sting*, which won. Both films were released in prime time movie-going, at Christmas. In their first fourteen weeks, *The Exorcist* had a clear lead, grossing close to 53 million dollars; *The Sting* followed with 30 million. However, in the first eight weeks after the awards ceremonies, *The Sting* doubled its pre-Oscar weekly pace at the box-office and made 30 million more, whereas *The Exorcist* made 12 million dollars more.[3] The big difference between the box-office behavior of the two films is directly attributable to *The Sting*'s multiple win, making it one of the twenty all-time rental champions in American film history.

The value of the Best Picture award goes beyond box-office appeal. It bestows prestige as well as makes the winning films accessible to a larger public, which might sound contradictory but is not. This effect is particularly important for films that are labeled "art," "specialized," or "highbrow." For example, *Reds* was apparently perceived as highbrow, because of its political contents, and it was hoped that the award would place it within reach of the mass public, but failing to win Best Picture, it didn't even recoup its immense budget.[4] But in the case of the *The Turning Point*, just receiving a Best Picture nomination made the difference. This film made much more money in its second round, after it was nominated in eleven categories, than in its initial run. The nominations were helpful in getting booking dates across the country, for despite its melodramatic content, its locale—the ballet world—was considered an obstacle in attracting large audiences. The nomination performed the same function for *The Elephant Man*, which initially Paramount released mostly in "sophisticated neighborhoods," based on the belief that its appeal was confined to educated audiences. But after the nominations, it got much wider distribution.[5]

Yet, for some films, often good ones, the Best Picture nomination has not helped much at the box office. Louis Malle's *Atlantic City*, nominated in 1981 for five awards and cited as best film by the National Society of Film Critics, gained very little from its reissue after the nominations. Released on April 3, *Atlantic City* finished its run before the end of 1981 with $3,300,000 in domestic rentals. After its nomination, it was rereleased and made another $1,700,000. Thus, its nomination for Best Picture did not create miracles at the box office but, relatively speaking, about one third of *Atlantic City*'s five million in rentals was made as a result of its nomination. And in 1983, *The Dresser* and *Tender Mercies* were among the year's least commercial films, before and after their nominations, with each grossing less than three million dollars.

No one expected *Kiss of the Spider Woman* to be nominated for Best Picture, but it was, and William Hurt's Oscar for that film is estimated at potentially contributing two million dollars to its box-office receipts. Furthermore, the very fact that it was nominated, with clips of the movie shown at the Oscar show, brought it to the awareness of millions, many of whom will make a point to rent it on video cassette, if not see it in a movie house.

Up to the 1980s, the age of video cassette recorders (VCR), winning the top award has almost automatically led to reissuing of the honored films for a second run. For example, *It Happened One Night*, the 1934 winner, was successful in its initial release in late February, but a week after the 1935 ceremonies, it was rereleased by Columbia, on the strength of its mutiple Oscars, and enjoyed a second successful run. However, at present, it takes about six months for a new film to be available in video cassettes, so Oscar-winning films do not get reissued. *Prizzi's Honor*, for instance, one of the five 1985 Best Picture nominees was available on video shortly after the awards show, which means that even if it had won Best Picture, it would have been pointless to rerelease it.

Winning the Best Foreign Film award has not been as commercially influential as winning Best Picture, though it has a considerable impact. For example, *Black Orpheus*, the 1959 French-winning film, has benefited in several ways: at least a fifty-percent increase in bookings, particularly in cities that seldom showed foreign fare, and a double gross in box-office receipts. But in addition to increase in potential profits and wider release, winning of, or even a nomination for, Best Foreign Picture has made their directors instantly and internationally marketable. Polish director Agnieszka Holland, whose *Angry Harvest* was nominated for the 1985 awards, has reported that the nomination of her film has made it easier to get funds for her future work.[6]

Of more limited impact, the acting awards have been particularly important for films with unusual topics or those lacking an immediate box-office appeal. Meryl Streep's 1982 Best Actress award for *Sophie's Choice*, a film about a doomed Polish survivor of the Holocaust, is estimated at increasing its box-office receipts by at least four million dollars. And Geraldine Page's 1985 Best Actress is expected to do the same for *The Trip to Bountiful*.

The producers of Oscar-winning films also get better deals for them when they are sold to television and transferred to video cassettes. In 1984, CBS reportedly paid $4,500,000 to show the 1981 winner, *Chariots of Fire*, and NBC paid more than twelve million dollars for the Oscar nominee *On Golden Pond*.[7] These enormous amounts of money were paid despite the fact that both had enjoyed long runs in movie houses and both were previously shown on cable television.

Effects on the Winners' Careers

Next to Best Picture, the only awards that have impact on the popularity of the winning films are the two lead acting categories, Best Actor and Best Actress. The winning of writing or technical awards has not had much influence on the films involved. But these winning awards, particularly the acting, have had symbolic (prestige) as well as pragmatic (pay, power) effects on the winners' careers, most of which have immediate manifestations.

Skyrocketing Salaries

One of the award's immediate and universal effects is financial: every winner gets a higher salary after winning. "Was my life changed by winning?" observes Mercedes McCambridge. "Oh, yes, yes indeed, if 'change' means money. Salary rocketed overnight, literally overnight."[8]

The Oscar has always had some cash value, but in the first two decades it was not as immense as it later became. And it was not a public issue; the artists' salaries were neither discussed nor revealed. However, the increasing publicity of the awards made its financial effects much more visible. It is difficult to gauge the Oscar's financial worth because the figures have differed radically from one winner to another, as the following examples show. Claudette Colbert's pay jumped from $35,000 to $150,000 per picture after winning the Oscar for *It Happened One Night*. In 1936, Colbert was declared the highest-paid individual in the United States, receiving $302,000 for the year.

Marlon Brando was paid forty thousand dollars for his first film, *The Men*, and seventy five thousand for his second, *A Streetcar Named Desire*. His work in this film, recognized by the Academy with a nomination, brought his salary up to one hundred thousand dollars for his third film, *Viva Zapata!* In 1960, six years after his first Oscar for *On the Waterfront*, Brando earned one million dollars per picture. And after his second Oscar for *The Godfather*, his pay rose again. For *The Missouri Breaks* he was paid about $1,500,000 and a percentage of the profits.

It is hard to believe that Dustin Hoffman was paid only seventeen thousand dollars for his first film, *The Graduate*, which made him an instant star and also brought him his first nomination. Two years later, he got four hundred thousand dollars for *Midnight Cowboy*, earning another nomination. In the 1970s, Hoffman commanded over one million dollars per picture, and for *Tootsie*, his first movie after winning an Oscar for *Kramer vs. Kramer*, he was paid five million dollars.

The Oscar's financial gains have at times been dramatic. Within a decade after Julie Christie's debut, *Billy the Liar*, for which she was paid only three thousand dollars, her salary multiplied over one hundred times! For her Oscar-winning role in *Darling*, Christie was paid the meager sum of $7,500; she was an unknown actress. But for her next film, *Doctor Zhivago*, she received $120,000, and in the late 1960s she could command $400,000 or a percentage of the film's grosses, whichever was higher.

Perhaps more significantly, the award's cash value has been enjoyed by all winners, lead as well as supporting. "All they wanted to know," said Martin Balsam, the 1965 supporting winner, "was how much more money I wanted for my next project." The scripts he received were the same, but "everything was reduced to money. I was an exploitable item."[9] Tatum O'Neal also saw a dramatic increase in her fee after winning a supporting Oscar for *Paper Moon*, commanding three hundred thousand dollars and 9 percent of the net profits of *The Bad News Bears*, thus becoming the highest-paid child actress in Hollywood.

Even the nomination itself has sudden impact on the players' box-office worth. Faye Dunaway's third film, *Bonnie and Clyde*, for which she received her first nomination, changed her career and her status: her pay rose from thirty thousand to three hundred thousand. And the enormous success and nominations for *Love Story*, for which Ryan O'Neal earned only twenty-five thousand dollars, resulted in a fee jump to half a million dollars against 10 percent of the gross profits. O'Neal, then mostly known as a television actor (*Peyton Place*), also became a bankable star whose name alone was a sufficient guarantee to obtain financing for a film.

However, not every winner has reaped the benefits of winning, especially under the old Hollywood studio system. Joan Fontaine, for example, was under personal contract to producer David O. Selznick, who made tremendous profits by loaning her out to other studios. Fontaine's loan-out fee jumped from twenty-five thousand to a hundred thousand dollars after her first nominated film, *Rebecca*, but she was still paid her usual twelve hundred dollars per week. After her Oscar for *Suspicion,* her fee went up, but she received only $100,000 out of the $385,000 that Selznick made from her work. Fontaine's commercial value, like that of other winners, went up but she did not enjoy it because of her contract terms. Furthermore, she did not work for long periods of time, because Selznick was holding out for higher fees, cashing in on her Oscar status.

International Stardom

The award also catapults the winners into the headlines of all the mass media—press and television—with immense coverage of their lives on and offscreen. For some, this effect is more important than the financial benefits. Director Capra observes: "Those who grabbed off the little statuettes didn't give a hang how they got them. They just knew an Oscar tripled their salaries and zoomed them to world fame." "Salary increase didn't whet my appetite," he records, "but world fame—wow!"[10]

This media effect has been quite sudden, even shocking to most players. Joan Fontaine might not exaggerate by describing the winners as "minor members of royalty suddenly elevated to the throne." The press "clamored for some sittings, still photos, and a scrap or tidbit to fill the endless gossip columns, fan magazines, Sunday supplements." But the winners' elevated recognition also has "pragmatic" benefits, such as "the best table in restaurants, preferential treatment whenever one traveled." For Fontaine this "was a fishbowl experience until the next year's awards, when a new winner would occupy the throne."[11]

Mercedes McCambridge also realized that she was "really in the big leagues" after winning. Going to New York on a publicity tour, she was amazed to find out that "for the first time in my life a baggage porter recognized me!"[12] This also meant, as she observes, that "I had moved into a new dimension: from now on my gratuities to such people would have to be stepped up to keep pace with my exalted station!" Indeed, "In the disgracefully broken-down taxi, the driver knew who I was," and "his flattery cost me another five bucks!"[13]

Veteran star and box-office champion John Wayne never realized the worldwide importance of the Oscar—until *True Grit*. "What opened my eyes to how much it means to people," he said, "was the flood of wires, phone calls, and letters I've been getting from all over the world."[14] Wayne regarded them as "a tribute to the industry and to the Academy," fortifying his belief, "never underestimate the power of the movies." Moreover, after claiming for years "I really didn't need an Oscar," because "I'm a box-office champion with a record they're going to have to run to catch," he admitted to have been shocked by the massive media attention he received.[15] For Charlton Heston too, the day after winning an Oscar for *Ben-Hur* was "a fabulous round of phone calls and wires pouring in." "It gets kind of frantic," Heston recalls, but "I wouldn't miss a minute of it."[16]

The impact of the Oscar has been even more dramatic for lesser-known or obscure players. For example, very few moviegoers knew Audrey Hepburn or Joanne Woodward *before* they won the award. Audrey Hepburn made her screen debut with a walk-on part in a British film *Laughter in Paradise*, then appeared in a few more movies, but after her Oscar for *Roman Holiday*, she became an international star. Hepburn would have become a star without the Oscar, but the award made her new status official and legitimatized her talent. Joanne Woodward was virtually unknown before making *The Three Faces of Eve*, a film which put her in the front rank of leading actresses. Lee Marvin had also been relatively obscure until *Cat Ballou*, which made him an instant star. Moreover, Marvin started his career as a supporting actor, specializing in Westerns and crime pictures usually as the villain, but the Oscar led to a new screen image as a leading man and box-office popularity with such films as *The Dirty Dozen* and *The Professionals*.

Respected actors became box-office attractions only *after* the Oscar. Fredric March, for instance, had a reputation as a stage actor, but the Oscar for *Dr. Jekyll and Mr. Hyde* made him a full-fledged movie star. Marie Dressler was unlikely star material, but after her Oscar for *Min and Bill* she became the top female star in the US for four years. Some of these players would have become stars without the assistance of the Oscar, but the win expedited the process and made the winners *internationally* popular, as demonstrated in the case of Sidney Poitier. The first nomination of Poitier for *The Defiant Ones* was a turning point in his career, winning him recognition as a dramatic actor. His popularity rose gradually after winning the 1963 Oscar for *Lilies of the Field*, until he was named the 1968 box-office champion in the US with the tremendous success of *To Sir with Love* and *Guess Who's Coming to Dinner?*

The Oscar also has the power to revitalize dwindling and faltering careers. Take Frank Sinatra, who in the late 1940s enjoyed enormous success on stage, radio, and musical films. In 1952, however, he was dropped by RCA when his vocal cords abruptly hemmorrhaged and his career seemed finished. But Sinatra fought back: he literally begged Columbia Pictures to cast him as Angelo Maggio in *From Here to Eternity*, for which he was paid as little as eight thousand dollars. The supporting Oscar for this performance salvaged his film career and also established him as a dramatic actor with a wider range. But perhaps the Oscar's most surprising effect was experienced by veteran comedian George Burns. In his autobiography, succinctly titled *The Third Time Around*, Burns writes in a chapter called, "A 79-Year-Old Star Is Born": "I hope the title of this chapter doesn't make you think I'm egotistical, calling myself a star, but I can't help it. That's what it says on my stationery." "But it's true," he continues, "I was seventy-nine years old when they asked me to play the part of Al Lewis in *The Sunshine Boys*. And it did start a whole new career for me."[17] Burns has not stopped working since, playing a variety of roles, including God in the comedy *Oh, God!*

Bargaining power for better films has also accompanied the winning. For some players, this power, which translates into a greater say over the choice of projects, directors, and costars, is far more important than better pay or international popularity. In Hollywood, power is the most crucial reward, even though it may not last for long. For example, Meryl Streep's supporting Oscar for *Kramer vs. Kramer* and increasing prestige as an actress helped to finance *The French Lieutenant's Woman*, based on John Fowles's novel and directed by Karel Reisz. Other noted directors, like Mike Nichols and Fred Zinnemann, had tried to bring this project to the screen but to no avail; no studio would finance it. Streep's fame and star power were undoubtedly crucial factors in persuading a major studio, United Artists, to invest ten million dollars in this movie.

Streep also had a say over the choice of her leading man, opting for English actor Jeremy Irons. After winning a third nomination for this film and a second Oscar for *Sophie's Choice*, Streep is one of the few actresses in Hollywood with the power to command any screen role. Her power has also allowed her to demand—and to get— changes in screenplays of her films. Robert Benton, who directed her for the second time in *Still of the Night*, observed that "giving her a script is like giving it to a second author."[18]

The Oscar and Cumulative Advantage in Film

The multiple effects of the Oscar Award point to a broader and more significant phenomenon: the cumulative advantage of the Oscar. This process, which both creates and maintains the stratification system within a profession, basically means that those who have done good work and earned their peers' esteem get more prestige and more recognition for their new work, and they get it faster than they would without it. The result is that the rich and famous become richer and more famous, and the poor get poorer. Indeed, the Academy winners and, to a lesser extent, the nominees, tend to get better roles, better pay, and more publicity at a rate that makes them even more famous and successful, while it makes other players progressively less famous and less successful.

Such cumulative advantage begins to operate once an actor "has made it," which can happen with a single movie, even the first one. Almost every player can point quite accurately to his or her "breakthrough role" or "turning point." However, a successful film debut is neither sufficient nor a guarantee for a successful career. Many prominent players failed or did not make a strong impression in the early phase of their careers.

Jane Wyman, for instance, made two abortive attempts to break into Hollywood: the first at the age of eight, the second at twenty-two. After the first attempt, she became a radio singer, using the name of June Durrell. But she did not give up. In 1934, she tried Hollywood again and her small part in *My Man Godfrey* led to a contract with Warner Brothers. Her apprenticeship at Warners was long, playing at first chorus girls and other bit parts. The turning point in Wyman's career occurred in 1945, when she was cast as

Ray Milland's patient girlfriend in *The Lost Weekend*. Three years later, she was given the chance of her life in *Johnny Belinda*, her Oscar-winning role that made her a top actress.

Anne Bancroft started her career in television in 1950, when she was nineteen, under the name of Anne Marno. Two years later, she made her film debut in *Don't Bother to Knock*, followed by a succession of B films for another six years. In 1958, disillusioned with Hollywood, she went back to New York and scored a huge success on Broadway in *Two for the Seesaw*, opposite Henry Fonda. She received a Tony Award for this part and a second Tony the next year for her performance as the devoted teacher, Annie Sullivan, in *The Miracle Worker*, which she repeated on screen, earning an Oscar for it.

Ellen Burstyn left her home in Detroit when she was eighteen, determined to seek fame and fortune in New York city. At first she worked as a chorus dancer in nightclubs, but in 1957, she landed a part on Broadway in *Fair Game*. Her study at the Lee Strasberg Actors Studio made her more committed to acting. Burstyn's first important role was playing a bitter mother in *The Last Picture Show*, earning for it a supporting nomination and the New York Film Critics Award. By the time she had "made it," she was thirty-nine, and had changed her screen name at least three times.

Cumulative advantage operates for both winners and nominees. Players nominated for an Oscar tend to get more attention and to be taken more seriously by producers and directors. Nonetheless, the effects are much more dramatic for the winners. Their increased popularity and prestige usually lead to additional nominations quite quickly: about half (46 percent) of all winners have earned another Oscar and/or another nomination.

The Oscar exerts a much greater impact on leading players: 59 percent of the lead winners, but only 30 percent of the supporting, have won another Oscar and/or another nomination. And many more lead players have won multiple nominations than supporting, 19 percent and 2 percent respectively. Among the supporting actors, only Walter Brennan received two more awards (*Kentucky, The Westerner*) and a nomination (*Sergeant York*) after his first Oscar. Four supporting actors got a second Oscar: Anthony Quinn, Melvyn Douglas, Peter Ustinov, and Jason Robards. And of the supporting actresses, only Shelley Winters received a second Oscar (*A*

Patch of Blue) and another nomination (*The Poseidon Adventure*), though eight actresses received nominations after their first win.

Women have benefited more from winning: over half (57 percent) of all female, compared with one-third (35 percent) of the male winners, have received another Oscar and/or another nomination. Of the four categories, the Oscar has been most influential for the Best Actresses: four-fifths (78 percent) of them, but only two-fifths (43 percent) of the Best Actors, have won or been nominated again. And twice as many Best Actresses (28 percent) as Best Actors (13 percent) have received a second Oscar. These differences stem from the fact that most Best Actresses have won the award at their first nomination, whereas the Best Actors have been nominated two or three times before winning. Indeed, there is no difference between men and women in their *number* of nominations, but there are in the *timing* of these nominations. The Best Actresses have earned multiple nominations and awards *after* their first win, whereas the Best Actors have received them *before* that.

Katharine Hepburn received three Oscars and eight nominations after her first win, and Bette Davis another Oscar and eight nominations. Ingrid Bergman got two more Oscars and two nominations, and Jane Fonda a second Oscar and four nominations. These multiple awards and nominations show that the same players have been repeatedly nominated. Indeed, 1961 stood out because it was the first time that all four winners of the acting awards (Maximilian Schell, Sophia Loren, George Chakiris, and Rita Moreno) won at their first nomination. At times, previous winners have amounted to half of one year's nominees. In 1964, five of the twenty acting nominees were former winners and six were previous nominees. And in 1982 too, five of the nominees were former winners and four were nominated before, some several times. The five Best Actress nominees in 1985—Anne Bancroft, Whoopi Goldberg, Jessica Lange, Geraldine Page, and Meryl Streep—have been collectively nominated twenty-four times!

This cumulative advantage is also manifest in the distribution of other honorific awards. The Academy winners have been the recipients of awards bestowed by film critics, international film festivals, and other film associations. Most of these awards are announced in late December or early January, about six weeks prior to the announcement of the Academy nominations, in the second week of February. This means that their choices inevitably affect both the Academy nominations and final selections.

There has been quite a consensus between the Academy and the New York critics: 35 percent of all Oscar winners have also won the New York Critics Award. And if the supporting winners are excluded, the correlation between the two awards is even stronger: 52 percent of all lead players have won both prizes. The New York Critics began to honor lead performances in 1935, but supporting performances were first cited in 1969. And some of the Oscar winners have been recipients of multiple critics awards. Ingrid Bergman, Laurence Olivier, and Burt Lancaster, hold the record for having won three New York Film Critics Awards.

The Golden Globes are announced in late January, coinciding with the Academy nominations, which are sent in mid-January. Indeed, 54 percent of all Oscar winners have also been recipients of Golden Globes, with a higher percentage (sixty-four) in the lead than in the supporting (forty-three) categories. Unlike the New York Critics, Golden Globes had been given for supporting performances as early as 1945. More men (60 percent) than women (49 percent) have received the Oscar and the Golden Globes. The stronger connection between the Academy choices and the Golden Globes, compared with that of the New York Critics, is probably based on the fact that the Globes are awarded by journalists, whose yardsticks of evaluation are not as harsh and discriminating as those of the critics. And the Academy's large size and its heterogeneous membership have resulted in choices that are not entirely based on matter-of-fact considerations.

These multiple awards have often been given for the same performance. About one-third of the New York Film Critics winners have been cited for the same role that won them the Oscar. As Ray Milland observed: "I found myself the recipient of more awards than I ever knew existed."[19] For his portrayal of the alcoholic writer in *The Lost Weekend*, Milland received the Oscar, the New York Critics Award, the Golden Globe, the *Look* magazine award, and even a citation from the Alcoholics Anonymous Unwed Mothers of America. Mercedes McCambridge was also surprised that "for the same short performance, I had already won two Golden Globes of the Foreign Press Association, one for Best Supporting Actress and one for Best Newcomer. I'd won the *Look* award, and there were lesser ones."[20]

The increasing number of film awards has meant that players can get six or seven honorific prizes for the same role. Susan Hayward won for her portrayal of the petty criminal Barbara Graham in *I Want to Live!* the Oscar, the New York Critics, the Golden Globe, the Cannes festival, and the Italian Oscar (the Donatello). And George C. Scott was singled out for his work in *Patton* by the Academy, the New York Critics, the Golden Globe, the National Society of Film Critics, the National Board of Review, and the British Film Academy.

The Triple Crown: Oscar-Tony-Emmy

The cumulative advantage also operates outside the film industry. A large number of Oscar winners (and nominees) have been distinguished stage players and recipients of the Tony, the top award in the Broadway theater. Close to one-third (32 percent) of all Oscar winners have won or have been nominated for a Tony.[21] And once again, the Best Actresses have an advantage over the Best Actors: the largest number of Tony winners and nominees (43 percent) has been among the Best Actresses. More women (24 percent) than men (15 percent) have won the Tony, and more women (20 percent) than men (7 percent) have been nominated. As in the case of film awards, a smaller number of women dominate the theatrical scene, with the most interesting stage roles circulating among them.

Interestingly, eight of these players have won the Oscar and the Tony Awards for the same role. The Tony preceded the Oscar for the very reason that motion picture rights are usually purchased after a play has proven to be a commercial success on the Broadway stage. This lucky group of players includes: Jose Ferrer (*Cyrano de Bergerac*), Shirley Booth (*Come Back Little Sheba*), Yul Brynner (*The King and I*), Anne Bancroft (*The Miracle Worker*), Rex Harrison (*My Fair Lady*), Paul Scofield (*A Man for All Seasons*), Jack Albertson (*The Subject Was Roses*), and Joel Grey (*Cabaret*).

The "success syndrome" in both media has often been rapid, occurring within a relatively short period of time. Shirley Booth won her first Tony for a featured role in *Goodbye, My Fancy* in 1949, then won a second Tony as Best Dramatic Actress in *Come Back Little Sheba* in 1950, an Oscar for the same role in the 1952 film version, and a third Tony for *Time of the Cuckoo* in 1953. Furthermore, three players have won the Oscar and the Tony Awards in the same year. Fredric March was the first to claim both prizes in 1947, winning a second Oscar for *The Best Years of Our Lives*, and a second Tony for *Years Ago*. Audrey Hepburn's 1954 Tony for *Ondine* followed the Oscar for *Roman Holiday* by a few weeks only. And Ellen Burstyn's career peaked in 1975, when she won Best Actress for *Alice Doesn't Live Here Anymore* and the Tony for the comedy *Same Time Next Year*, which she later recreated on the screen. But the record holder is undoubtedly Bob Fosse, who in 1973 became the only person in show business to win the Tony for the musical *Pippin*, the Oscar for the film *Cabaret* (which he didn't direct on stage), and the Grammy for the record album *Liza with a Z*.

Successful players have not only "commuted" between the stage and the screen, but also between the big screen and the small screen. This is yet another manifestation of cumulative advantage in the entertainment world. There has been no short supply of talented *or* popular players, but players who are both talented *and* popular have been in great demand, which assures them work in all three media: theater, film, and television. The theater public wants to see the current "hot" players, and players often become "hot" after winning an Oscar or a nomination, like Glenn Close, Linda Hunt, and Elizabeth McGovern. This is also the reason why popular screen players, like Vanessa Redgrave, Meryl Streep, and Jessica Lange, have also played interesting roles on television, often winning the Emmy, the most prestigious prize for television work.

It is therefore not surprising that two-fifths (40 percent) of all Oscar winners have either won (20 percent) or have been nominated (20 percent) for an Emmy. As could be expected, lead players have earned the Emmy more frequently than supporting (24 and 14 percent respectively). And more women (24 percent) than men (15 percent) have won the award, particularly in the lead categories: 33 percent of the Best Actresses, but 17 percent of the Best Actors.

Awards in the performing arts have been concentrated among a small group of players whose success in one medium has often led or "translated" into success in other media. Most players have started their performing careers in the theater, then moved on to film and/or television. As far as awards are concerned, it is difficult to discern one dominant route, beginning, say, with winning a Tony, then an Oscar and an Emmy. But one thing is clear: of all entertainment awards, the Oscar has been the most important and the most pervasive in its effects.

The strong correlation among the various awards also points to the phenomenon of the media star, the player who has been equally successful in all three media. The small minority of media stars is headed by the winners of the "triple crown"—the Oscar, the Tony, and the Emmy Awards. Helen Hayes, Thomas Mitchell, Ingrid Bergman, Shirley Booth, Melvyn Douglas, Jack Albertson, Paul Scofield, Anne Bancroft, and Liza Minnelli have all been genuine media stars. But the group of players who has won or has been nominated for two of the three awards has been substantially larger, particularly in the last decade, in which the same players have dominated Hollywood and the Broadway theater.

Barbra Streisand has been described as "the queen of the entertainment industry," because, as her biographer notes, "at the staggeringly unprecedented age of twenty-seven," she accomplished "an unheard of, indeed, undreamt of feat. She was the only person, male or female, to have won every major entertainment award."[22] Early on in her career, she vowed to scoop all the major awards, which she accomplished in five years. She was nominated for a Tony for her portrayal of Fanny Brice in *Funny Girl*, which provided her screen debut and earned her an Oscar in 1968. Streisand won a Special Tony Award in 1970 as "the actress of the decade," and a multiyear, multimillion-dollar contract, a string of recordings and successful television specials, which earned her Grammy and Emmy awards.

Henry Fonda, one of the most beloved American actors, was a media star in the full sense of the term, though he considered himself primarily a stage actor. Fonda was one of the first screen stars to make a successful transition to stage and television, alternating regularly among them. In 1959, for example, he appeared in the television series *The Deputy*, two theatrical films, *Warlock* and *The Man Who Understood Women*, and a Broadway play. His spate of prestigious awards has included: a Tony for *Mister Roberts* in 1948, the Oscar for *On Golden Pond* in 1982, an Emmy nomination, and multiple life achievement awards.

But no career has better demonstrated the cumulative advantage in the entertainment world than Meryl Streep's, the "hottest" actress in Hollywood today. Streep has achieved stardom on stage, television, and film in an astonishingly brief time. Upon graduation from the Yale School of Drama, she appeared in repertory at the Public Theater. For her Broadway debut, in the Phoenix Theater's production of Tennessee Williams's *27 Wagons full of Cotton* and Arthur Miller's *A Memory of Two Mondays*, she received Tony and Drama Desk nominations, and the Outer Critics Circle and the *Theatre World* awards. This auspicious beginning led to a feature part in the film *Julia* and to a major role in the television series *Holocaust*, for which she received an Emmy. In 1978, she appeared in *The Deer Hunter*, earning her first supporting actress nomination and the National Society of Film Critics Award.

The turning point in Streep's career occurred in 1979, with the release of Woody Allen's *Manhattan*, in which she had a small part, and Robert Benton's *Kramer vs. Kramer*, the film that won her her first Oscar and established her as a household name. In 1981, she made a successful transition from supporting to leading roles in *The French Lieutenant's Woman*, earning her first Best Actress nomination. In the following year, there was a consensus among critics that her doomed Polish heroine in *Sophie's Choice* was the best performance of the year; she won the Oscar as well as every possible film award. In 1983, she won her fifth Academy nomination for playing the title role in *Silkwood*, and two years later was singled out by the Los Angeles Film Critics for her work in *Out of Africa*, winning her sixth nomination.

Negative Effects of the Oscar

Winning an Oscar has dysfunctional as well as functional effects. The Academy Awards have been charged with having negative impact on the winners' careers and on the film world. How valid are these allegations?

Quality of Film Work

There is some justification in the charge that some Oscar winners become victims of their success because they are rushed by their agents or producers into a succession of films designed to cash in on their recently acquired popularity. For example, after her stunning performance in *I Want to Live!* Susan Hayward made a series of B movies that were meant to exploit her status as an Oscar winner.

Paramount and Twentieth Century-Fox held up the release of *Thunder in the Sun* and *A Woman Possessed*, hoping that audiences would flock to see them regardless of their merits. They were wrong; both pictures did poorly at the box office. Moreover, Hayward never had another critical success before retiring.

There have also been attempts to reunite Oscar winners in order to cash in on their popularity. A rare, successful example was *The Bells of St. Mary's*, which reteamed three of the 1944 Oscar winners: Bing Crosby, Ingrid Bergman, and director Leo McCarey. And because Crosby portrayed a priest who was similar to his Oscar role in *Going My Way*, audiences believed this film was a sequel. *The Bells of St. Mary's* was one of the few pictures whose commercial success surpassed that of the movie on which it was modeled. In most cases, however, such attempts have failed. The two 1961 winners, for example, Maximilian Schell and Sophia Loren, were cast together in *The Condemned of Altona*, based on Jean Paul Sartre's play, but the film failed both artistically and commercially.

However, to blame the awards for the winners' dwindling careers is usually unjustified. For every example of an Oscar "casualty" or "victim," there have been counterexamples of Oscar winners whose careers have been rescued and revitalized. Faltering careers have very seldom been the direct result of winning an Oscar. Instead, a combination of factors has accounted for the declining quality of some artists following their awards.

Some winners were not distinguished performers in the first place. Jennifer Jones, for example, was not a formidable actress, but cast in the right role and under a strong director she could give a credible performance, like her Oscar-winning role in *The Song of Bernadette*. It is possible to distinguish between Oscar-caliber performers and a one-time, Oscar-caliber performance. Some players excelled in one screen role, for which they received an Oscar, but they were not really Oscar-caliber actors. Although it may be premature to conclude, so far Louise Fletcher has excelled in one film, *One Flew Over the Cuckoo's Nest*, for which she was singled out by the Academy. By contrast, Jane Fonda, Sissy Spacek, Meryl Streep, and Vanessa Redgrave have been Oscar-caliber actresses, giving consistently high-quality performances.

Furthermore, many players reached the apogee of their careers with their Oscar-winning roles and subsequently have been unable to surpass or to match such quality of work. Sophia Loren (*Two*

Women), Julie Christie (*Darling*), and Elizabeth Taylor (*Who's Afraid of Virginia Woolf?*) have earned the Oscar for the finest performance of their careers, a performance that has been hard to match, let alone surpass. Their film appearances after the Oscar have therefore been inevitably unworthy of their talents. Sophia Loren seldom reached the heights of her Oscar-winning role and, with the exception of her films opposite Marcello Mastroianni, *Marriage Italian Style* and *A Special Day*, her work was mediocre. Julie Christie is another winner who never reached the artistic heights expected of her after *Darling*, though she appeared in many commercial hits, such as *Dr. Zhivago* and *Shampoo*. Critics still wonder whether *Darling* was the only vehicle that could bring out her distinctive talent and intelligence as an actress, or whether she was simply overestimated.

Many players feel that because the Oscar-winning performance is the high point of their careers, it is unfair of critics and audiences to compare it to subsequent roles. Yet it is almost inevitable that such comparisons will continue to be made. Furthermore, given the ratio of acting talent to the number of films produced, it is not surprising that many distinguished players end up making mediocre or bad pictures. For example, Broderick Crawford started and, unfortunately, ended his career with B movies and performances. His Oscar-winning role in *All the King's Men* is not only his best performance but also the exception in his career.

The most devastating example of an Oscar victim in Hollywood's mythology has been Luise Rainer, whose career prompted gossip columnist Louella Parsons to coin the often-used term, "the Oscar as a jinx"—that is, the Oscar as a curse. Rainer was brought to Hollywood by Irving Thalberg to join MGM's great roster of female stars, headed by Greta Garbo, Norma Shearer, and Joan Crawford. Her career took off immediately: she has been the first actress to win two successive Oscars, for *The Great Ziegfeld* and *The Good Earth*. "Those two Academy Awards I got were bad for me," recalled Rainer, for the expectations of her work were so unrealistically heightened that when her next film failed, "I was treated as if I had never done anything good in my life."[23] Rainer made only a few films after her second Oscar and her career terminated abruptly after her last MGM film, *Dramatic School* in 1938. "After Academy Awards you cannot make mistakes," she complained, "in my day making films was like working in a factory. You were a piece of machinery with no rights."[24]

According to some reports, Louis B. Mayer lost interest in her after her sponsor, Thalberg, died. Others put the blame for her premature retirement on poor choice of roles and bad advice from her then husband, playwright Clifford Odets. But judging from the quality of her two Oscar performances, Rainer was not a major talent and the fact that she won twice in a row had to do more with studio politics than with acting skills (see chapter 12).

The decline in the work quality of Oscar winners has been the cumulative result of the tendency to rush players into film projects and an indiscriminating choice of roles by the players themselves and/or their agents. But the permanent imbalance between the supply and demand of acting talent has also accounted for lowered quality. The abundant supply of gifted players, in relation to the number of films made and the number of good films, results in many of them being miscast, misdirected, or giving good performances in bad films.

The Curse of Typecasting

The tendency to typecast players in roles similar to their Oscar roles has had a more prevalent negative effect. Many players complain that they receive scores of film roles, identical or similar to their winning roles, and that it is impossible for them to break away from this typecasting, often created or fortified by the Oscar itself.

Most actors are reasonably aware of their range limits and of their audiences' expectations of them. "When I appear on the screen," Cary Grant said, "I'm playing myself," but he believed that "it's harder to play yourself." Grant attributed a good deal of his success to his conformity to audiences' expectations: "Adopt the true image of yourself, acquire technique to project it, and the public will give you its allegiance."[25] It is possible to describe the Cary Grant or the John Wayne screen persona because of their durable consistency. Most artists distinguish and understand the different responsibilities and rewards involved in being actors and in being movie stars. Critic John Russell Taylor described "the penalty of being a star" in the following way: "An actor is paid to do; a star is paid to be."[26]

Indeed, many have come to resent the screen image imposed on them by the public, because it has limited their range. Mary Pickford was best loved for her typical role, the naive, innocent girl, for which she was dubbed "America's sweetheart." From time to time, however, she would try to deviate from her standardized roles, but under public pressure would be forced to play them again. As late as 1920, when she was twenty-seven, Pickford continued to play teenagers, as in *Pollyanna*. Interestingly, she was cast against type in her winning role, *Coquette*, cutting her curls and acquiring a new hairstyle and a new personality. Nonetheless, neither the film nor her persona convinced her fans. Her ambivalence and resentment toward her image is expressed in her memoirs: "Every now and then, as the years went by and I continued to play children's roles, it would worry me that I was becoming a personality instead of an actress. I would suddenly resent the fact that I had allowed myself to be hypnotized by the public into remaining a little girl. A wild impulse would seize me to reach for the nearest shears and remove that blonde chain around my neck."[27]

Greer Garson also got tired of the image that MGM created for her, the gracious, noble English-like lady (*Mrs. Miniver*), feeling qualified as a professional actress to play a wider range of roles. She was therefore particularly interested in getting the part of the bitter, adulteress wife in *From Here to Eternity*, a role played with great success by Deborah Kerr. Significantly, Kerr wanted this part for the same reason; she too was typically cast as the cool, elegant, somehow reserved lady. Director Zinnemann's decision to cast against type turned out to be a turning point in Kerr's career: after her success in this part, she was able to command any role and, receiving a nomination for the part, it also established her self-confidence as an actress.

Typecasting has characterized the careers of both leading and supporting players. Jane Darwell specialized in playing plump, middle-aged women. She played over sixty standardized roles, modeled on her Oscar-winning role as Ma Joad in *Grapes of Wrath*. "Those mealy-mouthed women, how I hated them," she once observed. "I played so many of them, those genial small-town wives" that "I was getting awfully tired of them."[28] Rita Moreno, the only Hispanic actress to have won an Oscar, became completely identified with the feisty Puerto Rican she played in *West Side Story*, and afterward received many offers all in tune with her stereotypical image as a "Latin spitfire." But she decided not to "get stuck" with this kind of role for the rest of her career and subsequently went back to the theater. After a decade of stage work, she was ready to begin the second chapter of her screen career with a more "neutral" screen image.

Furthermore, because acting involves actual role playing and because of the "realistic" nature of motion pictures, audiences sometimes fail to separate between players' roles onscreen and their real lives offscreen. The difference between life on and offscreen seems to blur. Ray Milland recalled that after the release of *The Lost Weekend*, he found himself being looked upon as an authority on alcoholism. Jack Lemmon, who also played a hard-drinking man in *Days of Wine and Roses*, shared a similar reaction: "You don't know how many people think of me as a drunk and send me letters telling me of the glories of Alcoholics Anonymous."[29]

The trap involved in possessing an established screen image is still exemplified by Julie Andrews, who won an Oscar (*Mary Poppins*) and another nomination (*The Sound of Music*) for a similar role: the virtuous, wholesome heroine. This image stuck so deeply in audiences' collective memory that she could not rid herself of it. Andrews replaced Doris Day as the top female star by playing good-natured, reliable, and maternal women who represented traditional values. However, as critic Linda Gross observed, Andrews remained popular only as long as the status quo was maintained in America. In four years her image became outdated and out of step. Unfortunately, Andrews has never been able "to shake this sugary image in a time when sugary is out of favor, its place taken by conflict and conscience," as represented by the next generation of female stars, Jane Fonda, Diane Keaton, and Ellen Burstyn.[30] Her clean-cut image was so solid that she could not change it even when she played completely different roles, such as *S.O.B.*, in which she appeared in the nude.

"I hope I am not as square as some people might think," Andrews observed, expressing mild resentment at her public image. "I hope I have many facets." She is aware that her career suffered because her image crystallized quite early: "If you have a large success at something, you are inclined to get typed." Andrews further believes that "the lack of good roles for women and the bracketing" have made her a victim of typecasting. She would like to do "more dramatic roles, comedies, and musicals," but "without being typed." Children's films still interest her, though "I don't want to do anything that will seem a pale copy of *Mary Poppins*." Her hope is that at least film critics, if not audiences, would recognize her as a better actress than she was given credit for.[31] In recent years, Andrews went out of her way to break her mold, playing in the musical *Victor/Victoria* a passionate woman, disguised as a man who impersonates women. It remains to be seen whether this and other pictures will succeed in changing her public image.

The effects of typecasting are particularly felt by actresses who played a powerful role that later became their trademark. Gloria Swanson recalls that after her 1950 stunning performance, "more and more scripts arrived at my door that were awful imitations of *Sunset Boulevard*, all featuring a deranged super-star crashing toward tragedy." But being a strong woman, she made a firm vow: "I didn't want to spend the rest of my life, until I couldn't remember lines any longer or read cue cards, playing Norma Desmond over and over again." At the same time, she resented the fact that "serious producers and directors were foolish enough to think that was the only role I could play and get box-office returns."[32]

Hollywood has always believed in repeating a successful formula, which means, among other things, using stars in similar roles. Sylvia Miles "specialized" in portraying tough but vulnerable floozies, earning a first nomination for *Midnight Cowboy* and a second for *Farewell My Lovely*. She claims to have a drawer in her apartment with many similar parts, which she marked as "whores with hearts of gold, waitresses, tough broads." And after playing with great success a prostitute in *Cinderella Liberty*, receiving for it her first nomination, Marsha Mason complained, "if you play down-and-out loser parts, they send you down-and-out loser parts."[33]

Although women have been more trapped by typecasting, men too have been victims of earlier successful roles. Bruce Dern started his career by playing villains, first in NBC's "Alfred Hitchcock Presents," then in *The Cowboys*, in which he "dared" to kill John Wayne onscreen. Dern believes that his recognition as an actor came rather late because "I was sold wrong." "I would have been much further along," he explained, "if I had gotten a better agent earlier. Everyone in this business is sold, and I was sold as a cuckoo, a bad guy, a psychotic."[34] The Academy legitimized his typecasting by conferring on him his only nomination for playing the demented, male chauvinist captain who commits suicide in *Coming Home*.

The second kind of typecasting has been most acutely felt by supporting players, doomed to play for the rest of their careers small and/or secondary parts. The label "supporting" player thus becomes a stigma that is hard to overcome. In some respects, the Academy itself has been responsible for such typecasting, making the distinction between leading and character players *official* in the Academy Players Directory, the chief casting tool of the industry. Players who won or were nominated for supporting awards have almost always remained in this category.

The best example of a strong screen image, created in a first film and certified by a nomination, is that of Sidney Greenstreet, who made an auspicious debut as Kasper Guttman, the ruthless villain in *The Maltese Falcon*. This image suited his size, being a bulky man of three hundred pounds. Greenstreet went on to play many master villains, to the point where he became Hollywood's classic screen heavy. But he resented the fact that Warners relegated him to such limited range and was particularly sensitive to the critics' view that he was only capable of playing villains. Warners never trusted him enough to sell a movie on his own and thus never gave him a starring role.[35] Peter Ustinov suffered from similar typecasting after making his stage debut in London at seventeen, playing older men. He never became a leading man and was always associated with older screen characters. "It was a mistake," Ustinov later conceded. "For years I played nothing but old men."[36]

The same fate was shared by Lee J. Cobb, a leading man in the theater, but a character actor in film. Cobb always played secondary roles, winning nominations for *On the Waterfront* and *The Brothers Karamazov*. His screen range was quite limited, often playing tough racketeers and stern politicians. Gig Young's life-long dream was to be a leading man and the star of a film, but his Oscar (*They Shoot Horses, Don't They?*) and his two other nominations were all in the supporting league. Similarly, Shelley Winters, Celeste Holme, Donna Reed, Shirley Jones, and Teresa Wright, began and ended their screen careers as supporting actresses, especially after winning an award in this category.

Despite the fact that typecasting is still a prevalent norm in Hollywood, it is not as rigid and limiting as it used to be, particularly for men. In the last decade, several actors began their careers and won nominations and awards as supporting players, but later made a smooth transition to leading roles. This group has included: George C. Scott, Roy Scheider, Al Pacino, Robert Duvall, and Robert De Niro. Gene Hackman also started as a character actor, distinguishing himself in secondary parts, such as *Bonnie and Clyde* (first nomination). His important part in *I Never Sang for My Father* brought, to his disappointment, a second supporting nomination. "I guess the Academy is trying to tell me something"[37] was his reaction. At the same time, he was proud to state: "I never approach a film as if I'm playing a supporting character. If I do, then I am just a supporting character." Instead, "I approach it as if it's the most important thing in my life."[38] In 1971, Hackman won Best Actor for *The French Connection*, after which he has played both leading and supporting roles—by choice. Hackman belongs to the new breed of star character actors, who get starring roles without conforming to Hollywood's previous specifications and traditional typecasting, demanding that leading men be attractive and project a romantic image, as was the case with Robert Taylor and Tyrone Power.

Indeed, in recent years leading actors have had to be neither attractive nor romantic to be cast in starring roles. This is probably the reason why Walter Matthau was able to become a leading man. Beginning his career in the 1950s, typically in villainous roles, he seemed to be destined to stay in the supporting league, until he rose to sudden stardom in the Broadway production of Neil Simon's *The Odd Couple*, in a role specifically written for him. Matthau went on to star in a succession of movie comedies, earning a supporting Oscar for *The Fortune Cookie*, and two Best Actor nominations for *Kotch* and *The Sunshine Boys*. Interestingly enough, the same slouching posture, awkward walk, and unhandsome face, which had kept him from becoming a leading man in the 1950s and 1960s were *used* in the 1970s[39] to cast him for the first time in romantic comedy roles, beginning with *House Calls* opposite Glenda Jackson.

Oscar Anxiety

Because of the fierce competition, the desirability of the Oscar, and its immense effects, many artists have been obsessed with winning the award. And those who have won have been under tremendous pressure to prove that they are worthy of it. Professional anxiety, at times to the point of paranoia, has been one of the most devastating consequences of the award.

Some producers, players, and directors have gone out of their way to obtain the coveted award. For example, William Randolph Hearst, the publishing tycoon, was so interested in getting an Oscar for Marion Davies, with whom he was romantically involved, that his activities in the film industry were single-mindedly motivated by this wish, joining forces with MGM and, later, with Warners. He succeeded in getting Davies some good roles, but failed to get her the award; she was never even nominated. David O. Selznick also worked hard to get a second Oscar for his wife, Jennifer Jones, and though failing to achieve that his power and publicity campaigns definitely had some influence over her nominations for unworthy performances, such as in *Duel in the Sun*.

One of the award's dysfunctions is its potential damage to the winner's relation with coworkers, friends, and even family. "A picture taken after the banquet of Brian [Aherne] sitting alone in an empty room," Joan Fontaine observes, "feet up on a chair, my fur coat over his arm, waiting patiently for the photographers to finish with the winners, graphically illustrated the plight of marriage when the wife is more successful than the husband." Furthermore, after winning, "there was many a doubter, many a detractor, many an ill-wisher. It's an uneasy head that wears the crown."[40] Mercedes McCambridge also believes that "there is a price tag" and "mischief in the lovely statue with my name on it." "I mustn't think that taking bows was all that would be expected of me," writes McCambridge. "Oscar was calling the tune now, and it gave me a funny feeling: did the Oscar belong to me, or did I belong to it? Which one of us would always be in debt to the other?"[41]

The permanent pressure to live up to the critics' and audiences' expectations tends to make the award a burden for the winners. "The way to survive an Oscar," Humphrey Bogart said after winning his, "is to never try to win another one. You've seen what happens to some Oscar winners. They spend the rest of their lives turning down scripts while searching for the great role to win another one. Hell, I hope I'm never nominated again. It's meat-and-potatoes roles for me from now on."[42] A generation later, Meryl Streep reiterated Bogart's fears even more succinctly. "I'm freaked out," she said. "It's like a mantle visited on me that has no relation to what I do or who I am." Many of her friends did not speak to her after she was hailed as "America's Best Actress" on the cover of *Time* magazine. It was definitely a traumatic experience. "Hype like that is very destructive," says Streep. "It takes a piece out of every other actress." Baffled by her meteoric rise to stardom, she has no explanation as to exactly how it happened. "It's very difficult. . . . You get a big buildup and it's almost like nothing can live up to it."[43]

The pressure and anxiety involved in getting the award and then living up to it reflect the inherent characteristics of show business in general. Acting is probably one of the most precarious of professions: the rise to stardom may be sudden, but the decline is just as dramatic. One of Hollywood's sad realities is its dictum, "You are as good as your last picture." It is therefore enough for one or two pictures to fail at the box office to destroy a career of multiple achievements. Under these circumstances, the position of film artists is inherently insecure and uncertain, depending on the financial, not artistic, reception of each of their movies. Furthermore, unlike other professions, in which practitioners achieve at one time or another some security, film artists have to struggle constantly in order to maintain their status, over which they have much less control than other professionals.

"Looking back on Hollywood," Joan Fontaine observes, "looking at it even today, I realize that the one outstanding quality it possesses is not lavishness, the perpetual sunshine, the golden opportunities, but *fear*. Fear stalks the sound stage, the publicity departments, the executive offices. Since careers often begin by chance, by the hunch of a producer or casting director, a casual meeting with an agent or publicist, they can evaporate just as quixotically."[44]

Hollywood has always been characterized by its *contemporary* orientation. What counts, in the final summation, is the standing of films at the box office and the *current* popularity of directors and players. Oscar winners of previous years are quickly forgotten, not just by the public, but also by the Academy and the industry. There has been a good deal of resentment among former winners for never being invited to the ceremonies as guests of honor. Many winners tend to become members of a "forgotten legion," unless they win another award and remain active in the industry. There is no hall of fame for past winners, as many feel there should be.

Frank Capra, a three-time Oscar winner and one of the most popular American directors, has made a revealing observation after spending decades in Hollywood: "Show business is brutal to has-beens. Those pushed off the top are rolled into the valley of oblivion; often they are mired in degradation. I saw it all around me: D. W. Griffith—a forgotten man; Mack Sennett—walking unnoticed in the city he had once ruled as a King of Comedy; old stars pleading for jobs as extras."[45]

Most film artists are aware of the inherent insecurities of their work and of the fact that success in show business, which the Oscar symbolizes, does not last long. Yet the Oscar Award exerts such a pervasive influence, on and offscreen, that they continue to regard it as the ultimate achievement of their lives. And as long as they do so, the Oscar and its mythology will continue to thrive.

CHAPTER 12

Politics and the Oscar Award

Cinema, like other social institutions, operates in specific social, historical, and political surroundings. The interplay between films and their political contexts is complex and multifaceted because films are made for the immediate consumption of current audiences. But political considerations have also influenced the types of movies nominated for and winning Oscars. The Oscar Award has not been immune to political pressures and forces operating within and outside the film industry. The relationship between the Oscar, film politics in Hollywood, and societal politics constitutes the focus of this chapter. An attempt is made to understand the roles of politics, of the film industry and society at large, in the nomination and in the winning.

Studio Politics

From the very beginning, the Academy members were asked "to display rare discrimination and honest judgment" in their choices. Members were advised "to evince equal discrimination so that the final awards may be fairly representative of the industry's opinion of its best achievements."[1] After the second Oscar ceremonies, the Academy Board was proud to report that "so far, there has been no evidence of studio politics," and that producers have "freely nominated pictures from studios other than their own."[2] However, as David O. Selznick once observed, the Academy has been "influenced unduly by transient tastes, by commercial success, by studio log-rolling and by personal popularity in the community of Hollywood."[3]

Indeed, the nominations and final selections have been heavily influenced by advertising and publicity campaigns conducted by the production companies, particularly during the heyday of the studio system. There has always been ambivalence toward outright politicking for the studio's movies and contract artists. Some consider advertisement to be a clear violation of *fair* selection procedures, expected to be objective, universalistic, and dispassionate. But those in favor of advertising like to remind that politicking has not been unique or confined to the Oscar and that even in the more esoteric Nobel Prize, there has been extensive campaigning, formal and informal. Still there seems to be a difference: the campaign for Nobel Prizes is usually conducted by peers—other scientists—whereas the campaigns for Oscars have been conducted by the production companies or the individual artists themselves.

The fact remains though, that film artists resort to campaigns because of the tremendous importance they attribute to winning the award, or even to receiving a nomination. The Oscar has become a legitimate measure of evaluating the quality of screen careers. The studios, directors, performers, and other artists have tended to evaluate their, as well as their colleagues', careers in terms of the number of nominations and awards they have received. Apparently, independent producer David O. Selznick took tremendous pride in the fact that his films have won collectively thirty-six nominations and that two, *Gone with the Wind* and *Rebecca*, won Best Picture in 1939 and 1940 respectively.

It has always been easier for the big studios to conduct publicity campaigns for their movies and workers because they had the budgets and the facilities to do it. The publicity departments of these studios have been extremely effective in making stars out of their contract players, in selling their movies to the public, and in persuading the Academy members to vote for their films. Andrew Sarris has claimed that the Academy began its existence as a guild-busting company union, manipulated by the biggest studio, MGM. Louis B. Mayer, who headed MGM until 1951, was one of the Academy's charter founders and as such instrumental in drafting its goals and in financing its first organizational banquets. Mayer was probably more ambitious than other studio heads in Hollywood, and he exerted great power on the Academy and its Oscars.

It is easy to document that MGM had more than its fair share of nominations and awards. In the first decade, MGM received a total of 153 nominations and 33 awards, a record that surpassed all the other studios. Paramount ranked a distant second, with 102 nominations and eighteen awards, followed by Warner Brothers with seventy-one nominations and fifteen awards. By contrast, Twentieth Century-Fox and Columbia Pictures featured poorly, the former with fifty-four nominations and thirteen awards, and the latter with forty-three nominations and ten awards.[4]

Furthermore, in the first twelve years of the award (1927/8-39), of the 102 films nominated for Best Picture, twenty-eight were produced by MGM, seventeen by Paramount, ten by Fox (later Twentieth Century-Fox), fifteen by Warner Brothers, eight by Columbia, seven by RKO, and four each by United Artists and Universal. Only three of the nominated films were foreign-made, the British *The Private Life of Henry VIII* and *Pygmalion*, and the French *Grand Illusion*. Independent producers justifiably complained that their films did not stand equal chance in the nomination process. Indeed, Samuel Goldwyn was represented with only four films (*Arrowsmith*, *Dodsworth*, *Dead End*, and *Wuthering Heights*) and Selznick with two (*A Star Is Born* and *Gone with the Wind*).

MGM's defenders claim that in the 1930s this studio produced *more* films than any other studio, though the differences in output were not substantial. They further claim that MGM made *better* films, though what they probably mean is that MGM made films that were more suitable for Academy Awards. MGM had a particularly impressive record when it came to winning the most important award. Of the first twelve Best Pictures, MGM produced four: *The Broadway Melody* (1928/9), *Grand Hotel* (1931/2), *Mutiny on the Bounty* (1935), and *The Great Ziegfeld* (1936). *Gone with the Wind* (1939), was distributed by MGM, but produced by Selznick. In the early 1930s, MGM had at least two films nominated for Best Picture every year, later in the decade many more. In 1936, five MGM films competed for Best Picture: *The Great Ziegfeld*, which won, *Libeled Lady*, *Romeo and Juliet*, *San Francisco*, and *A Tale of Two Cities*.

In the first decade, MGM also dominated the acting awards. Ten of the twenty Best Actor and Best Actress performances were given by players under contract to MGM. They included Norma Shearer, Marie Dressler, Helen Hayes, and Luise Rainer (in 1936 and 1937) among the women, and Lionel Barrymore, Wallace Beery, Spencer Tracy (in 1937 and 1938), and Robert Donat, among the men.

Smaller studios had limited opportunities when it came to having their movies nominated. Rising director Frank Capra assured his boss at Columbia, Harry Cohn, that he would get nominations for his 1930 comedy, *Ladies of Leisure,* starring Barbara Stanwyck, but was extremely disappointed when it was completely ignored by the Academy. He immediately realized the "disadvantage of working at Columbia." "The major studios had the votes. I had my freedom, but all the honors went to those who worked for the Establishment."[5] The first Columbia movie to be nominated was Capra's 1933 comedy, *Lady for a Day,* and the first Columbia winner was *It Happened One Night* a year later.

In the 1930s, more than in other decades, the Academy was controlled by the big studios and the nominations were dominated by a few powerful cliques within the big studios. "The trick," as Capra observed, "was to get nominated by the clique of major studio directors who had achieved membership—and those Brahmins were not about to doff their caps to the 'untouchables' of Poverty Row," as the small studios were then labeled. "Making good pictures was not enough," Capra learned. "I would have to gain status with big name directors to get them to nominate me."[6]

In the studio era, film workers were loyal to their home studios, on which their very livelihood depended. This meant that they named films and performers of their own studios in the nomination ballots, especially in the final ballots. At times, to assure the nomination of colleagues, they were placed as first choice, followed by unlikely candidates from other studios, which guaranteed that there would not be serious competition in the selection of winners.

Paramount Pictures, under the leadership of Adolph Zukor, was also strongly represented in the Best Picture category during the depression years. In the first year, four of the five nominated films were produced by Paramount, including the winner, *Wings.* A large number of these movies were produced or directed by the prestigious filmmaker Ernst Lubitsch. Columbia's participation in the Oscar in the 1930s can also be described in terms of the output of one man, Frank Capra: six of its eight nominated films were directed by Capra, who won three directorial awards in four years, 1934, 1936, and 1938. By contrast, the few RKO movies were based on the strength of their performers: three of Katharine Hepburn's vehicles were nominated, *Little Women, Alice Adams,* and *Stage Door,* and two by the team of Fred Astaire and Ginger Rogers, *The Gay Divorcee* and *Top Hat.* Similarly, two of Universal's four nominated films featured their star, Deanna Durbin, who single-handedly saved the studio from bankruptcy.

In the 1940s, MGM's domination of the Best Picture category declined, and only ten of the seventy nominated films (14 percent) were produced by it, mostly the Greer Garson vehicles. RKO and Paramount followed, each with seven nominated films. RKO gained prestige from the Orson Welles films, two of which were nominated, *Citizen Kane* in 1941, and *The Magnificent Ambersons* in 1942. Paramount also benefited from the work of one writer-director, Billy Wilder. Three of his movies received nominations: *Hold Back the Dawn* in 1941, which he did not direct but whose screenplay he wrote in collaboration with Charles Brackett; *Double Indemnity*, which he wrote and directed, and *The Lost Weekend*, which won Best Picture.

Up to the late 1940s, the nominations and awards were dominated by the big studios, as was clearly demonstrated with the announcement of the 1948 nominations. Seventy two out of the 102 nominees contending for awards in 25 categories were contained in movies released by the five major studios: MGM, Warners, Twentieth Century-Fox, Paramount, and RKO. The rest were in movies distributed by smaller companies, such as Universal, Columbia, and Republic. (Most of Universal's nominations were for *Hamlet*, which it distributed in America.) The one studio to gain unexpected power in the 1940s was Twentieth Century-Fox, producing thirteen of the seventy nominated films, two of which won: *How Green Was My Valley* in 1941, and *Gentleman's Agreement* in 1947. By comparison, the best decade for Columbia Pictures was in the 1950s, during which three of its movies won Best Picture: *From Here to Eternity* in 1953, *On the Waterfront* in 1954, and *The Bridge on the River Kwai* in 1957. But the power of the big studios as the producers of Oscar-winning films began to decline in the 1950s, when they failed for three years in a row to produce the Best Picture: *On the Waterfront* was produced by Sam Spiegel, *Marty* by Harold Hecht, and *Around the World in Eighty Days* by Michael Todd.

United Artists was fairly represented in the first two decades, though it distributed only one winner, Selznick's *Rebecca*. However, from 1960 to the present, no less than nine of the winners were distributed by it, including: *The Apartment* in 1960, *West Side Story* in 1961, and *Tom Jones* in 1963. United Artists also holds the record for being the only studio to win three Oscars in a row: *One*

Flew Over the Cuckoo's Nest in 1975, *Rocky* in 1976, and *Annie Hall* in 1977.

Overall, there seems to be some balance among the major studios, at least in the Best Picture category. Of the fifty-eight winning films, United Artists received eleven Oscars, Columbia ten, MGM and Paramount eight each, Twentieth Century-Fox seven, and Universal four. The only underrepresented major studio was Warner Brothers, with only three winning films. Independent producers, David O. Selznick received two Oscars and Samuel Goldwyn one. Two of the winning films were British-produced, and one by the new studio, Orion.[7] In the last five years, new, smaller, and independent companies have become such an important force in the American cinema that their chances to be represented in the important categories are now better than ever. The 1984 winner, *Amadeus*, was produced by Orion, and another nominee, *Places in the Heart*, by Tri-Star. And in 1985, *Kiss of the Spider Woman*, a small-budget film financed by the new company Island Alive, was surprisingly nominated for Best Picture.

Advertisement Campaigns

Advertisement campaigns have been used by both studios and individual artists to call the Academy's attention to what they consider "worthy" achievements. These campaigns have become extremely elaborate over the years, reaching their zenith in the late 1960s. But it would be a mistake to believe that advertisement has been a recent phenomenon. There have always been efforts to persuade members to vote for or against a particular film, though they were less explicit and behind closed doors—not out in the open in the trade magazines.

The studio for which the artists worked and their position within the studio's power structure also played some role. There was a clear connection, for example, between Mary Pickford's win for *Coquette* and the fact that her husband, Douglas Fairbanks, Sr. was then the Academy president. And it is doubtful that Norma Shearer, an otherwise mediocre actress, would have received five nominations, were she not married to Irving G. Thalberg, head of production at MGM.

Indeed, with all her popularity and recognized talent, Greta

Garbo was a victim of inner politics at MGM. On her first nomination, for *Anna Christie*, her first talkie, advertised as "Garbo Talks!" she lost to Norma Shearer, who won for *The Divorcee*, another MGM movie. At her second nomination, for *Camille*, Garbo lost out to another lesser actress, Luise Rainer in *The Good Earth*. Rainer was then supported by Louis B. Mayer, though three years later she was dropped by him and her career terminated. And in 1939, when Garbo received her third nomination for *Ninotchka*, she lost because *Gone with the Wind* swept all major awards, including Best Actress to Vivien Leigh. Unlike Garbo's previous competitors, Leigh at least gave a good performance.

Studio politics also deprived Bette Davis of a nomination, and possibly an award, for her great performance in *Of Human Bondage*. She was then under contract to Warners, which loaned her out to RKO for that film. It is conceivable that neither Warner's nor RKO's employees voted for Davis, who was added to the list of nominees as a write-in. RKO knew that if she won the rewards would be reaped by Warners, and Davis was not very popular at Warners.

Clark Gable also believed that he was outvoted for what he considered the best work of his career, Rhett Butler in *Gone with the Wind*, because of strain with producer David O. Selznick and because the publicity department of MGM, which released the film, was not behind him; the winner was Robert Donat for *Goodbye Mr. Chips*, made by MGM.

In 1953, Columbia Pictures made no secret of the fact that it supported Burt Lancaster, and not Montgomery Clift, in *From Here to Eternity*. Both were nominated for Best Actor, though neither won; the winner was William Holden for *Stalag 17*. Clift was not backed because he was an outsider in Hollywood, "suffering" from his reputation as a New York stage actor. Performers who came from the New York stage and continued to appear in both films and plays, like Geraldine Page and Julie Harris, were regarded at that time as suspect in the movie colony. In the same year, Van Heflin and Jean Arthur failed to get nominations for *Shane*, despite good performances, because neither was under contract to Paramount. Instead, the studio campaigned for William Holden, who had been with the studio for many years, and for Audrey Hepburn (*Roman Holiday*); both won.

In 1954, the odds were against Judy Garland, despite an impressive performance in *A Star Is Born*. For one thing, Warners, which produced it, was then in conflict with the Academy, and for another, Garland was not supported by the studio. By contrast, Grace Kelly, who won that year for *The Country Girl*, was probably supported by MGM, her studio, and by Paramount, which produced the film.

The Academy history of some performers is instructive because it brings to the surface the factors responsible for their winning or losing. Consider Shirley MacLaine, a multiple nominee, for example. In 1958, when she was first nominated for *Some Came Running*, MGM supported its veteran performer, Elizabeth Taylor, in the prestige blockbuster *Cat on a Hot Tin Roof*; both lost to Susan Hayward in *I Want to Live!* In 1960, MacLaine gave the best performance of her career to date in *The Apartment*, but once again MGM launched a massive campaign in the trade papers to support the ailing Taylor in *Butterfield 8*. The sympathy of the Academy was with Taylor, whose bout with death was more responsible for her win than her acting.

It is unclear, however, how effective these ad campaigns have been. To document one case in detail, Joan Crawford and her press agent Henry Rogers reportedly conducted one of the biggest campaigns in Hollywood's history in 1945. According to biographer Bob Thomas, during the filming of *Mildred Pierce*, producer Jerry Wald sensed that something extraordinary was happening, upon which he called Rogers and suggested:

> "Why don't you start a campaign for Joan to win the Oscar?"
> "But Jerry, the picture is just starting," replied Rogers.
> "So?"
> "So how would I go about it?"
> "It's simple. Call up Hedda Hopper and tell her, 'Joan Crawford is giving such a strong performance in *Mildred Pierce* that her fellow-workers are already predicting she'll win the Oscar for it.'"
> "Jerry, you're full of shit."
> "Possibly. But it might work. What have you got to lose?"[8]

Indeed, during his daily reports with the famous gossip columnist, Rogers delivered to her this "confidential" report. A few days later, Hopper wrote: "Insiders say that Joan Crawford is delivering such a terrific performance in *Mildred Pierce* that she's a cinch for the Academy Awards." Other columnists followed Hopper, all predicting an Oscar for Crawford. One night, Wald telephoned Rogers, triumphantly announcing, "I think we've got it made." He proceeded to tell him that he just heard from producer Hal Wallis, that "It looks like Joan Crawford has a good chance to win the Oscar. I don't know where I heard it," Wallis said. "I may have read it somewhere."[9] That's exactly what Rogers and the studio wanted, to create a favorable public opinion for Crawford. It helped, of course, that the film opened to quite good reviews and that it was nominated for Best Picture.

However, the interesting question is how crucial was the campaign as a determining factor in Crawford's win? Wouldn't she have won without it? The campaign was, to be sure, a contributing factor, but how much did it contribute? In 1945, Crawford competed against three movie stars, Ingrid Bergman in *The Bells of St. Mary's*, Greer Garson in *The Valley of Decision*, and Jennifer Jones in *Love Letters*. All three had recently won an Oscar: Garson in 1942, Jones in 1943, and Bergman in 1944. The fifth nominee was an unlikely winner, novice Gene Tierney for *Leave Her to Heaven*. Crawford had been an actress for twenty years and enjoyed the sympathy of Hollywood and the press, which resented the way she was mistreated—and fired—by Louis B. Mayer. Furthermore, Mayer himself said in public that he would vote for Crawford, and not for his favorite star Greer Garson, because she deserved it. Crawford would probably have won without this massive campaign.

Campaigning by players reportedly started in 1943, when Teresa Wright called the Academy's attention, through discreet advertisements, to her performances in *Mrs. Miniver* and *The Pride of the Yankees*. She received a supporting nomination in the former and a lead nomination in the latter, winning the award for *Mrs. Miniver*. Wright would probably have won for this movie even without publicity, since *Mrs. Miniver* swept the 1942 awards. One of the biggest and most expensive efforts by an actress for herself, was apparently by Rosalind Russell who reportedly spent over ten thousand dollars in 1948 to get a Best Actress nomination for *Mourning Becomes Electra*. In addition to her personal campaign, RKO spent a large amount of money for her as well as for the movie. Russell received a nomination, but not the award, which some attribute to oversaturating the voters with publicity.[10]

In 1961, Shirley Jones was advised to invest the five thousand dollars she had intended to put into building a new wing on her home into publicity for her performance in *Elmer Gantry*;[11] she won the supporting award, though it is unclear how determining a factor that campaign was. But even if extensive advertisement by players does not result in winning, it still pays off in other important ways. Peter Falk campaigned extensively for his performance in *Murder Inc.* which cost him five thousand dollars. It was his third film, but the first made in Hollywood. Falk considered the campaign worthwhile "because I'm a newcomer out here," thought of "as a New York actor with some reputation," who had difficulty being placed. Moreover, *Murder Inc.* was a small crime film, "the kind that usually gets passed by in the midst of all the big pictures." His motive for the campaign was "to stir up talk," so that "the talk itself will help the career." "Whether I get the nomination or not," he said, "I consider it the best investment I've ever made, and I don't have much money."[12] And it was a fertile investment: Falk received his first supporting nomination, established his reputation in Hollywood, and received other important roles, including one in Frank Capra's 1961 *Pocketful of Miracles*, which honored him with a second supporting nomination.

It is hard to reach definitive conclusions concerning the effects of campaigns on nominations and awards, for two of Hollywood's most respected and most nominated players, Spencer Tracy and Katharine Hepburn, never campaigned for themselves and never pressured their studios to do it for them.

Moreover, politicking and excessive campaigning can sometimes create a boomerang effect, as John Wayne's patriotic campaign for *The Alamo* demonstrated. One ad compared the Alamo's fighters with contemporary politicians, stating: "There were no ghostwriters at the Alamo, only men." The publicity cashed in on the fact that it was an election year: the film was released in July 1960, three months prior to the Presidential elections. "Remember the Alamo," said Wayne, on screen as Davy Crockett, and offscreen as a politically involved actor. Another full-page ad read: "What will Oscar say this year to the world?" with a picture of the battered fortress of the Alamo. Wayne was reported to have spent an extraordinary amount of money on advertising. According to *Newsweek*, publicist Russell Bidwell received the highest amount of money ever paid to advertise a film: a one-year fee of $125,000, plus all costs and salaries of his New York and Hollywood offices for a year, plus a huge operating budget.[13] With this high emotional and financial drive, Bidwell managed to get *The Alamo* seven nominations, including Best Picture, but no acting or directorial nominations for Wayne.

Much more criticized than Wayne was actor Chill Wills, who played Beekeeper, Crockett's whiskey-drinking, humorous sidekick. Wills was charged with using deplorable means in order to get himself a supporting nomination. At fifty-eight and after close to half a century in films, Wills realized that it was his only chance to win an award. Thus, he did not hesitate to print ads on the order of: "We of *The Alamo* cast are praying harder than the real Texans prayed for their lives at the Alamo, for Chill Wills to win the Oscar." "Cousin Chill's acting was great," he wrote, signing it, "Your Alamo cousin." Another ad read: "Win, lose, or draw, you're still my cousins and I love you all." Comedian Groucho Marx, appalled by his methods, wrote back: "Dear Mr. Wills. I am delighted to be your cousin, but I'm voting for Sal Mineo,"[14] nominated for *Exodus.* Wayne himself did not approve of Wills's campaign and reproached him in the press, which prompted Groucho Marx's comment, "for John Wayne to impugn Chill Wills's taste is tantamount to Jane Mansfield criticizing Sabrina for too much exposure."[15] But neither Wills nor Mineo won; the winner was Peter Ustinov for *Spartacus.*

The Alamo's campaigns resulted in a heated controversy over the professional and moral ethics involved in advertising films. Raising the question, "Does advertising for Oscar nominations pay off?" critic Dick Williams saw "nothing reprehensible in artists or productions blowing their own horns," because "it is done in almost every other phase of American life." Nonetheless, Williams objected to the fact that "Oscar voters are being appealed to on a patriotic basis," and resented the implication that "one's proud sense of Americanism may be suspected if one does not vote for *The Alamo.*"[16] At Wayne's request, Bidwell responded to this charge: "Along with Philip K. Scheuer of the L. A. *Times*, you suggest very emphatically that we have conducted a campaign that to vote against *The Alamo* is un-American. This is gratuitous and erroneous conclusion on your part."[17]

The campaign for this movie might have helped in getting it multiple nominations, but there were no awards. *The Alamo* lost in every category but one: best sound. *The Alamo* was not a bad film, but it was up against competition from Billy Wilder's *The Apart-*

ment, which won; Richard Brooks's *Elmer Gantry*, the British *Sons and Lovers*; and Fred Zinnemann's *The Sundowners*. It is noteworthy, that the advertisement campaigns for *Sons and Lovers* and *The Apartment* were estimated to have each cost $20,000, and for *Elmer Gantry* only $6,000.

In 1961, George C. Scott, as we have seen, declined his supporting nomination in *The Hustler*, deploring the demeaning effects of the Oscar race, particularly the explicit campaigning by press agents for "award-conscious" players. But there has been no unanimous agreement in Hollywood over the use of ad campaigns to promote work. Burt Lancaster, for instance, felt that "Ads in the trade papers serve a purposeful function as part of the public relations of our business," which he summed up as "See my pictures before you vote." In response to Scott's accusations, Lancaster also said, "No one's putting a gun to his head to buy any ads. His attitude really doesn't make any sense, he's under no pressure to take any ads."[18]

Following the controversy over *The Alamo* and Scott's protests, the Academy's Board published a statement of policy, "to call the attention of all potential nominees for the importance of maintaining a standard of dignity in any and all media of advertising." Always sensitive to public opinion outside the industry, it stated that "regrettably, in past years a few resorted to outright, excessive and vulgar solicitation of votes," which became "a serious embarrassment to the Academy and our industry." It therefore asked Academy members "to eliminate those advertising practices which are irrelevant to the honest evaluation of artistic and technical accomplishments, and violate the principles under which the Academy was established." But it left the issue "to the good conscience of the nominees, confident that they are well aware of the difference between that which enhances and that which lessens the status of the Academy." "The Academy can command respect," the statement concluded, "only as long as its members and the nominees take onto themselves the responsibility of dignified conduct."[19] However, this request was, as one critic noted, "like asking Pavlov's dogs to ignore their conditional reflexes."[20]

Needless to say, this warning statement did not change the situation. On the contrary, in the 1960s, advertising campaigns for unworthy films reached their peak, resulting in a severe decline in the Academy's public credibility. Twentieth Century-Fox outdid the other studios, after its success with the blockbuster *The Sound of Music*, dubbed in the industry as "The Sound of Money." In the next four years, its executives were determined to win nominations and awards at all costs, for such clinkers as *The Sand Pebbles* in 1966, *Doctor Dolittle* in 1967, and *Hello, Dolly!* in 1969. Through special screening, fancy banquets with wonderful menus, letters and pictures to each member, this studio managed to get multiple nominations for each of the aforementioned movies, which was enough to repudiate the Oscar's prestige in the public eye. Further, it showed that the most dismal films *can* get nominations, granted they are big-budget, star-studded, and, most important of all, "sold" and "marketed" by the "right" campaigns. Thus, many began to suspect that the official function of the awards had changed from honoring "the best" films to rescuing faltering films at the box office. This "rescue" mission by the Oscar soon became a public joke.

To be sure, the Oscar has always had some effects on the box-office receipts of the winning films, and the commercial function of the ceremonies—to promote films and the film industry—has always been a known public fact. Nonetheless, it is one thing to honor good films such as *Chariots of Fire*, which was critically acclaimed but initially commercially unsuccessful. It is another, however, to nominate an undistinguished film, such as *Cleopatra*, as a compensation for its immense budget and years of work. To honor a downright artistic failure, such as *Doctor Dolittle*, in order to recoup its mammoth expenses, is ridiculous and embarrassing.

At the same time, advertisement campaigns have helped in the nominations of small, specialized films that would not have withstood a chance to get nominated without them. In 1968, *Rachel, Rachel*, directed by Paul Newman and starring Joanne Woodward, received four nominations, including Best Picture, due to the efforts of Warren Cowan, a leading press agent. Cowan used the basic strategies of getting free exposure for the artists in newspapers, magazines, and talk shows and, of course, advertisements in trade magazines. But he also set up private screenings for eight or ten "opinion-maker columnists, public relations men, and people who would get the word-of-mouth going." A big premiere for the movie was arranged in New York, with Newman and Woodward appearing on all the television shows. Moreover, the two stars reportedly spent all of Labor Day posing for the cover of *Life*, which was not "in their nature, but this movie was very special to them."[21] This extensive campaign would not have been effective, had not *Rachel, Rachel* been a good movie, enjoying critical acclaim; the New York Critics cited Woodward as best actress and Newman as best director of the year. But it also showed that ad campaigns are more necessary and more effective in the nomination than in the winning process: *Rachel, Rachel* was nominated but did not win any award.

Advertising still continues at present, but to a lesser extent. In 1982, for example, the six major studios reportedly spent about four million dollars between mid-December and mid-March on screenings, advertisements, and promotions, in their attempts to get nominations and awards.[22] And it is estimated that the studios of the five nominated films each spent about half a million dollars on advertisements.[23] Yet, in 1986, Universal (*Out of Africa*) and Warners (*The Color Purple*) each spent about $100,000 on trade paper advertisements, less than in previous years.[24]

These advertisements appeared in the two major trade journals, the *Hollywood Reporter and Daily Variety*, where a page can cost over three thousand dollars. An extensive ad campaign does not assure, of course, getting major nominations. Eighteen pages were bought for Bob Fosse's *Star 80* in *Daily Variety*, but it did not get a single nomination. And Twentieth Century-Fox bought many ads for *Heart Like a Wheel* and its star, Bonnie Badelia, but got only one nomination, for costume design. In 1984, *Silkwood* was advertised in fifty pages of the *Daily Variety*, *Yentl* in thirty-one, and *Terms of Endearment* in twenty-eight. *Terms of Endearment*, which won, did not need as much publicity as *Yentl* or *Silkwood*, because it opened to unanimously rave reviews and immediately became a box-office hit. It was also a much easier film to sell to the public—and to the Academy—than either *Yentl* or *Silkwood*. "Advertising insures that a movie will not be accidentally overlooked,"[25] one executive said, which was crucial in the case of *Yentl*, because it opened to lukewarm reviews; it received five minor nominations. As for *Silkwood*, it is hard to tell whether its five nominations were attributable to the campaign. Meryl Streep would have been nominated for Best Actress and Mike Nichols for Best Director without the campaign; but Cher, nominated for supporting award, possibly benefited more from the ads.

The ad campaigns are undoubtedly more important in getting nominations than in winning awards. There is a big question mark over the effectiveness of massive campaigns after the announcement of the nominations, though most studios engage in such campaigns. However, the free-lance system, with no contract players and studio stars, and the changing structure of the Academy membership, have often led to the unanticipated nominations of films and artists that in the big-studio era could never have been nominated. Pictures that have neither enjoyed critical acclaim nor a commercial popularity still have some chance to get nominated. Martin Ritt's *Cross Creek* in 1983 was panned by most reviewers and subsequently died quickly at the box office. Universal, which distributed the film, refused to share the advertising costs, though it is customary, and thus it could not be seen during the nominations. Its producer Robert Radnitz booked it at a Malibu theater and made up handbills for the members. With only six pages of advertisement in *Daily Variety, Cross Creek* garnered four nominations, two of which were for supporting players Rip Torn and Alfre Woodard.[26]

"The key to Academy Awards nominations is getting your picture seen," by as many voters as possible; "that's the justification for the advertising campaigns."[27] The studios therefore schedule many free screenings of films that have Oscar potential, and there are also free screenings by the Academy and the Guilds. The choice of films for these screenings and getting the members to see them thus become strategic issues, though the precise influence of these screenings on the films nominated is still unclear.

Societal Politics

External factors, such as the historical, political, and cultural settings in which films are made and viewed, have also influenced the types of films nominated and winning awards. Film artists, like other professionals (politicians, scientists), have been subject to both the disruptive and stimulative effects of their sociocultural surroundings.

World War II, for example, affected film artists by interrupting the progress of their careers. The war disrupted the careers of many established actors and directors, who were mobilized into the war effort, with some losing the popularity they had previously enjoyed. Clark Gable, "the king" of Hollywood in the 1930s, joined the Army Air Corps in 1942, rising in rank from lieutenant to major, and receiving the Distinguished Flying Cross and Air Medal for his bombing missions over Germany. Gable was absent from the screen for four years and his return, in *Adventure*, was trumpeted by MGM's publicity machine as "Gable's Back, and Garson's Got Him." But this as well as other postwar films failed and his popularity began to decline. The career momentum of Mickey Rooney, who had been America's biggest box-office star with the Andy Hardy series, was also severely interrupted by his military service, after which it plummeted.

But some actors actually benefited from the war, like Humphrey Bogart, who became a major star in the 1940s, after his appearance in *The Maltese Falcon* and particularly in *Casablanca*, the film that established him as hero. In other cases, the war delayed recognition that would have been accorded earlier. William Holden became a star with his very first film, as the boxer-violinist in *The Golden Boy* (1939). Then, mobilized to the army, he did not make any movies for three years; after the war his screen image ripened and his popularity rose, reaching a climax in 1950 with two films, *Born Yesterday* and *Sunset Boulevard.*

World War II had a quantitative as well as qualitative impact on the film industry, influencing both the subject matter and the style of the films produced. It is estimated that about one-third of Hollywood's ouput, five hundred out of seventeen hundred films, between 1942 and 1945. dealt directly or indirectly with the war.[28] These movies were more important as historical than as artistic phenomena, fulfilling, as critics Ken Jones and Arthur McLure have observed, a twofold goal: "to give unity of purpose for the war itself, and to give strength of purpose to the people on the home front."[29] Heavily propagandistic, they served as moral boosters and flag-wavers, dealing with timely issues that were of interest to most Americans at the time. In general, people enjoyed these films without applying the usual critical yardsticks.

All the award categories were influenced by the war, especially the major ones: Best Picture, the directorial, the four acting, and the writing awards. The male acting Oscars, as could be expected, were more determined by the war experience, because the war film has always been a typically masculine genre. Indeed, four of the Best Actors in the 1940s were chosen for roles in war movies: Gary Cooper in *Sergeant York*, James Cagney in *Yankee Doodle Dandy*, Paul Lukas in *Watch on the Rhine*, and Fredric March in *The Best Years of Our Lives.*

By contrast, there was only one Best Actress, Greer Garson in *Mrs. Miniver*, for a film about the war. Ironically, some of the female winners during the war were honored for playing traditional and stereotypical roles, like victimized or frightened wives—for example, Joan Fontaine in *Suspicion* and Ingrid Bergman in *Gaslight*. In the context of the times, these roles were reactionary, for during the war women began for the first time to participate actively in the economic and occupational structures. The only Oscar role that reflected the inner conflicts between domesticity and career, which many American women faced at the end of the war, was Joan Crawford's in *Mildred Pierce*, though, as was observed, at the end of this movie she was punished for having stepped into the male world and was relegated to her traditional role of housewife-mother.

Many films during the war were lavishly praised by critics and seen by the masses out of patriotism, rather than out of conviction for their artistic merits. Three films about, or related to, the war won Best Picture: *Mrs. Miniver* in 1942, *Casablanca* in 1943, and *The Best Years of Our Lives* in 1946. *Mrs. Miniver* was the least distinguished of the three, but it was nicely directed by William Wyler (who won an Oscar) and, more importantly, it at once reflected and reinforced the mood of the home front through its description of a "typical" British family during the Blitz. Some reviewers criticized its win on the ground that it was actually the war, not the film, that earned the Academy votes. Released in July 1942, *Mrs. Miniver* immediately became a blockbuster, and its six Oscars made it the most talked-about film of the year.

The timeliness of these films suited perfectly the mood of the nation. Hawks's *Sergeant York* reflected America's dominant attitude in July 1941, just months prior to its entry into the war. Its hero, Alvin York, starts as a conscientious objector and ends up committed to the war's cause, a transformation that articulated the feelings of millions of Americans who initially were reluctant to fight. And *Yankee Doodle Dandy* was released in May 1942, just as American soldiers departed to fight in Europe. "What could be more timely," one critic wrote, "than to have recalled for us the career of America's lustiest flag-waver?"[30]

Casablanca, the 1943 Oscar winner, was even timelier, for it was released after Casablanca had been chosen as the site of the Allied Forces Conference. The movie had tremendous charm due to its glorious cast, which, in addition to Humphrey Bogart, included Ingrid Bergman, Claude Rains, and Paul Henreid. And it was *the* movie that made Bogart an international star, crystalizing the immortal Bogart image as Rick Blain, the most famous café owner in film history. *Casablanca* was not a major box-office hit when originally released, but over the years it became a cult film. It was chosen as one of the ten Best American films of all time in a recent poll by the AFI. Wyler's *The Best Years of Our Lives* would have won awards in any year. Of the three aforementioned Oscar winners, it is the most interesting, though *Casablanca* is more entertaining. But it too cashed in on its timely release, dealing with the readjustment problems of many war veterans to civilian life. As was shown, the inspiration for this movie came from an article in *Time* magazine.

The number of nominations and awards bestowed on films about the war reflected quite accurately the changes and shifts in public opinion. In 1941, only one of the six major awards went to a war film—Gary Cooper in *Sergeant York*. In 1942, five out of the six awards were for war movies; the exception was Supporting Actor to Van Heflin in the crime melodrama *Johnny Eager*. In 1943 again, five of the six major Oscars were for such films; the exception was Ingrid Bergman in *Gaslight*. In 1944, two of the Best Picture nominees were politically relevant films: David O. Selznick's *Since You Went Away* and Twentieth Century-Fox's political biopicture *Wilson*.

Most of the writing awards in the 1940s were also given for war movies, including Emeric Pressburger for his original story, *The Invaders*; the four screenwriters of *Mrs. Miniver*; William Saroyan for his original story *The Human Comedy*; the three screenwriters of *Casablanca*; Lamar Trotti for his original screenplay *Wilson*; and Charles G. Booth, for the original script of *The House on 92nd Street* (1945), Henry Hathaway's film about the FBI's successful destruction of a spy ring in the US.

Note that after *The Best Years of Our Lives*, the war was quickly forgotten by Hollywood—at least, judging by the films nominated for Best Picture. In 1946, for example, the nominees included Olivier's *Henry V* and the melodrama *The Razor's Edge*, based on Somerset Maugham's book. In 1947, two religious comedies, *The Bishop's Wife*, and *Miracle on 34th Street*, and Lean's *Great Expectations*, were nominated; and in 1948, Olivier's *Hamlet*, Jean Negulesco's *Johnny Belinda*, and the ballet melodrama *The Red Shoes*.

The second historical era in which politics affected, in fact *impinged* on the operation of the Oscar Award, was in the early

1950s, during Senator Joseph McCarthy's second round of investigations in Hollywood; the first had been held in 1947. Most of the winning films in those years could be described as escapist or commercial entertainment. In sharp departure from the 1940s, in which the Oscar honored timely films about the war, just a few years later, Hollywood was so petrified by McCarthy that it went to the other extreme, honoring films that had nothing, or little, to do with surrounding political reality. For example, the 1950 nominees included tales about Hollywood (*Sunset Boulevard*), show business (*All About Eve*), a witty comedy (*Born Yesterday*), a family comedy about marriage and suburban life (*Father of the Bride*), and an adventure set in Africa's jungles (*King Solomon's Mines*).

The Oscar winners of 1951 and 1952 were even greater escapist entertainment, demonstrating the Academy's fear of voting for better films that were critical studies of the American Way of Life. MGM's musical, *An American in Paris*, featuring George Gershwin's celebrated score, won the 1951 award, competing against serious films, such as George Stevens's excellent *A Place in the Sun*, based on Theodore Dreiser's novel *An American Tragedy*; and Elia Kazan's powerful version of *A Streetcar Named Desire*. This win must have surprised MGM itself, for the next day it printed trade-paper ads showing Leo the Lion smirking coyly at an Oscar statuette, while the caption read: "Honestly, I was just standing in the sun waiting for a streetcar."[31]

The winner of the 1952 Best Picture, Cecil B. De Mille's circus adventure-melodrama, *The Greatest Show on Earth*, unaccountably won over such distinguished films as Fred Zinnemann's adult, psychological Western *High Noon* and John Ford's romantic and highly picturesque *The Quiet Man*. *High Noon* earned the largest number of nominations, seven, that year and was also cited by the New York Film Critics. There is evidence to suggest that *High Noon* lost for political rather than artistic reasons. The film has received great critical attention over the years, including political interpretations of its ideological contents. According to some critics, it was actually a symbolic allegory about American foreign policy during the Korean war. Marshal Kane (Cooper) wants peace, after cleaning up the town five years before (World War II), but reluctantly has to face new aggression (the Korean War). In this reading, the Quaker wife (Grace Kelly) stands in for the American pacifists and isolationists, though she too later realizes the importance of supporting her husband's cause. Thus *High Noon* propagated the idea that "war in certain given circumstances may be both moral and inevitable."[32]

And critic Philip French regards the film as a liberal statement, the archetypal Kennedy Western, contrasting it with *Rio Bravo*, which he considers the archetypal Barry Goldwater Western.[33] *High Noon* is accordingly seen as a parable about an existential man, Marshal Kane, who stands alone to defend his moral principles in the McCarthy era. The townsfolk, who refuse to help Cooper, deserting him one by one, are viewed as the American masses, afraid to defend their civil rights.

Whether or not these particular readings of *High Noon* are valid, one thing is clear, the film does deal with issues of civic responsibility, passive versus active involvement in public problems, and heroic behavior in political crises—all issues with explicitly political overtones in the early 1950s. Furthermore, the filmmakers responsible for *High Noon*, producer Stanley Kramer, director Fred Zinnemann, and particularly screenwriter Carl Foreman, were known for their liberal politics. In fact, this was Foreman's last film in America; he was then forced into exile to England. Cooper, known for his Republican, conservative leanings, was probably unaware at the time of the political message of his role, if, indeed, there was one. But some of his colleagues, like John Wayne, objected to the film's message, claiming that the rugged men of the West, who fought both nature and the Indians, would unite—not cower—in the face of four villains.[34] Further, in an 1971 interview, Wayne described *High Noon* as "the most un-American thing I've ever seen in my whole life," referring to "ole Coop putting the United States marshal's badge under his foot and stepping on it." He also boasted, "I'll never regret having helped run Foreman out of this country."[35]

The pessimistic, downbeat mood of Sydney Pollack's *They Shoot Horses, Don't They?* must have also worked against its inclusion in the 1969 Best Picture category, despite the fact that it was critically acclaimed and nominated for nine awards—though not Best Picture. Its omission among the five top contenders was conspicuous due to the fact that the film was nominated in many important categories, honoring three of its players with nominations: Jane Fonda in the lead, and Susannah York and Gig Young in the supporting classifications. Based on Horace McCoy's novel, set in the Depression, it describes a harrowing six-day marathon dance contest, stressing the fantasies, illusions, and madness of a group of young people in Los Angeles of the early thirties. The shabby locale and despair of the characters, most notably of Gloria (Jane Fonda), a suicidal, would-be actress, and another starlet (Susannah York) whose fantasy is to be the next Jean Harlow, must have depressed the Academy members, for they favored light-hearted fare, *Hello Dolly* and *Butch Cassidy and the Sundance Kid* as Best Picture nominees over Pollack's disturbing parable.

That Academy members, like other moviegoers, sometimes judge a film by the importance of its content and relevancy of its issues, was clear on other occasions. One recent example was the astonishing success of *Gandhi*, sweeping most of the 1982's Oscar awards. Cinematically, it was rather conventional, solemn biography of the noble political figure, lacking epic scope and visual imagination. The subject matter was genuinely epic, and it could have been a great movie had it been directed by a more subtle and inventive filmmaker, say David Lean. The figure of Gandhi was so inspirational and his preachings for antiviolent change so timely in the context of the 1980s, however, that most Academy members favored it over other nominees, such as Steven Spielberg's *E.T.*, or Sidney Lumet's *The Verdict*. Sydney Pollack's comedy *Tootsie* was excellent, but lacked the noble intent and "important" theme that *Gandhi* possessed. Vincent Canby described *Gandhi* as having "the air of an important news event, something that is required reading," yet faulting it for its earnestness: "All films about saintly men tend to look alike, even though the men themselves may be radically different."[36] But he understood the motivation of the Academy members: "To honor a film like *Gandhi*, a perfectly reverent if unexceptional film about an exceptional man, they are paying their dues to the race (human), certifying their instincts (good), and also the belief that movies about worthy subjects can make money."[37]

It is noteworthy that in this case the Academy's taste did not differ from the critics'. *Gandhi* opened to almost unanimously favorable reviews; the only dissenting voices among the major New York critics were Andrew Sarris and Pauline Kael. And it won the New York Film Critics, the National Board of Review, and the Golden Globe awards. However, unlike other years, in which there is a consensus among the critics' associations about the year's best, in 1982 there was sharp disagreement, with the Los Angeles Critics citing *E.T.*, and the National Society of Film Critics *Tootsie*.

The distinction between movie politics and societal politics is, in the final account, analytic rather than empirical, for the two political forces at times interweave in such a way as to become inseparable. The status of Orson Welles's masterpiece *Citizen Kane* in the American cinema deserves and has received more attention than this book can warrant, yet the reception of this classic by the Academy, by the film critics, and by the general public could serve as an illuminating example of the complex interplay between film, studio politics, and societal politics.

Contrary to popular notion, the merits of *Citizen Kane* were recognized at the time, though not as fully as they should have been. Apparently it was film columnist Louella Parsons who began spreading the rumor, upon seeing it in an advance preview, that its narrative was actually "a repulsive biography" of her employer, William Randolph Hearst (played by Orson Welles). Hearst accepted her view without seeing the film, but because there was nothing libelous about it all he could do was to demand RKO to shelve the movie and threaten to withdraw his support from Hollywood through his press empire.[38] There was some talk to scrap the movie, and its opening was postponed a number of times, until it finally got distribution in May 1941. RKO had tremendous problems convincing theaters to book the movie, and Hearst newspapers' boycott of every matter related to this studio did not help either. *Citizen Kane* received mostly good reviews in New York, though it failed commercially across the nation.

At nominations time, in January 1942, shortly after the United States had joined the Second World War, *Citizen Kane* was not overlooked by the industry. Rather, it was nominated for nine awards, including Best Picture, and three nominations for Orson Welles, as co-screenwriter (with Joseph L. Mankiewicz), director, and lead actor. But the cinematography, editing, music, sound, and art direction also received nominations. The competition for Best Picture was extremely intense that year, with *Citizen Kane* in contest with no less than nine other pictures: *Blossoms in the Dust* (four nominations), *Here Comes Mr. Jordan* (seven), *Hold Back the Dawn* (six), *How Green Was My Valley* (ten), *The Little Foxes* (nine), *The Maltese Falcon* (three), *One Foot in Heaven* (one), *Sergeant York* (eleven), and *Suspicion* (three). With so many good films in competition, it was inevitable that the important awards would be distributed among a small group of films and that some excellent films would not win any.

To the Academy's credit, the winning film, John Ford's *How Green Was My Valley*, which swept five awards, might not have been a landmark in the history of American film, but it is an excellent movie, with strong visual aspects in addition to an acceptable set of values and a more traditional morality than *Citizen Kane*. It is plausible to assume that Ford's movie was chosen for a variety of reasons: its ideology, cherishing the sacredness of the family (after all the country was at war), but also its aesthetic merits and high quality acting. *Citizen Kane*, by contrast, was dumped because of its downbeat, pessimistic message and Hearst's power in Hollywood. There is no doubt that *Citizen Kane*'s genuine cinematic merits were not recognized at the time, not just because of its dispute with Hearst, but also because they were so revolutionary and so far ahead of their times. Furthermore, Welles was extremely young, 26, and a newcomer in Hollywood; *Citizen Kane* was his very first movie.

Ironically, the film's most controversial aspect, its screenplay, was the only category honored by the Academy. At the same time, it is important to remember that William Wyler's *The Little Foxes* was another distinguished movie that lost in each of its nine nominated categories. And John Huston's directorial debut, *The Maltese Falcon*, another classic of its kind, also failed to win any award.

Politics and the Careers of Oscar Artists

The nature of film as a mass medium with great potential for political indoctrination and propaganda, and the great public exposure that film artists enjoy, onscreen and off, have often made them the first to be affected by changes in the country's political mood. The strategic position of the performing arts and media has always been recognized by the political elite, particularly in times of social change. The worst era for American film artists was undoubtedly during Senator Joseph McCarthy's political witch-hunting of Hollywood, when the careers of many Oscar artists were destroyed or hampered.

For example, Gale Sondergaard, the first Oscar supporting

winner (*Anthony Adverse*), was one of the earliest political casualties because of her marriage to director Herbert Biberman, who was suspected of Communist leanings and later became one of the "Hollywood Ten." Sondergaard was blacklisted at the peak of her career and subsequently did not work for two decades. When she appealed to the Screen Actors Guild for protection, its reply reportedly was: "All participants in the International Communist Party conspiracy against our nation should be exposed for what they are, enemies of our country and our form of government."[39] She emerged from forced retirement in 1965, in a one-woman show Off-Broadway, and later made several film comebacks, none too successful. In 1978, the Academy asked her as a gesture of reconciliation to be a presenter at Oscar's fiftieth anniversary show.

Another supporting winner, Anne Revere, for *National Velvet*, was also at the peak of her craft when she was blacklisted for taking the Fifth Amendment before the HUAC, on April 17, 1951. By that time, she had been in films for seventeen years with thirty-five films to her credit. Her last film before being blacklisted, *A Place in the Sun*, in which she played Montgomery Clift's mother, was allegedly severely cut, leaving in only a few of her scenes. Rumor has it that actor Larry Parks named her, along with others, as a member of the Communist Party. Revere was out of work for close to a decade, but like many others, she found roles in the Broadway theater, winning a Tony Award for Lillian Hellman's *Toys in the Attic*. Producer-director Otto Preminger, who helped many blacklisted artists, provided her a comeback part in the film *Tell Me That You Love Me Junie Moon* (1970); at age sixty-seven, she was too old to resume an active career.

Kim Hunter made a spectacular film debut in *A Streetcar Named Desire*, for which she won a supporting Oscar. However, shortly afterward her career was ruined when her name appeared in *Red Channels*, a Red-scare pamphlet. She too was unable to get any work in Hollywood or New York and was finally rescued by the producers of the television series *Omnibus*. Many artists feel that she was unjustly implicated.

Lee Grant also had an auspicious beginning in Hollywood, winning a supporting nomination for her first film, *Detective Story*, in which she played a shoplifter. She was married at the time to writer Arnold Manoff and was a close friend of actor J. Edward Bromberg, both of whom were suspect Communists. Grant did not get any work for ten years because she refused to cite her husband before the Committee. "The Committee wanted me to turn him in," she later recalled. "I simply wouldn't do it. No work was ever important enough to make me turn in my husband!"[40] Fortunately, she was still able to work in the theater; "movies and TV were closed to us, but not the theater." But "doing a play a year wouldn't support me, so I went to Herbert Berghoff and he set me up in a class." She taught drama for several years, during which her attorney worked hard to prove her innocence. Her name was indeed taken off a list with a mild apology from Washington DC. She claims she is not bitter for two reasons. First, "I was lucky, I was only thirty-two when it was over, but I still feel I have time to make up for." And second, "It was a fascinating war which fulfilled part of my life. I never would have believed it if I hadn't been part of it."[41]

Grant returned to films in an impressive role in *The Balcony* (1966), and has not stopped working since. She has been busy both as actress and director. In the 1970s, she won two more nominations, and a supporting Oscar for *Shampoo* in 1975. In her acceptance speech, she said: "I would like to thank the artistic community for sustaining me in my wins and losses, and sitting on the curb, whatever it was." It was greeted with huge applause.

Larry Parks's career was at its height in the 1940s, with a nomination for the title role of *The Jolson Story* (1946). But his career plummeted when he was forced to admit to past membership in the Communist Party. Officially he was never blacklisted, but Columbia Pictures did not renew his contract and other studios would not hire him. Very few actors arrived in Hollywood with the reputation of John Garfield, of the Group Theater fame. For his very first film, *Four Daughters*, he received a supporting nomination, and a few years later, a lead nomination for *Body and Soul*. However, in 1952 his career ended abruptly when he died of a heart attack the night before he was scheduled to appear before the Committee. Garfield was not accused of anything in particular, but was suspected of left-wing politics because of his membership in The Group Theater and some statements he made.

McCarthyism affected not just American, but foreign artists as well. For instance, Maurice Chevalier, who was extremely popular in the US in the 1930s, was refused reentry in 1951 for having signed a Communist-inspired document, "the Stockholm Appeal," which called for the banning of all nuclear weapons. French actress Simone Signoret also faced difficulties in getting film offers from Hollywood, despite many promises, because of her alleged politics. "Each time," she recalled, "there had been a vague offer of my participation in an American production made in France, negotiations had rapidly broken off."[42] Even in the late 1950s, despite assurance from American directors that times had changed, she held onto her belief that "McCarthy was not dead, even if the citizens of this country thought they had buried him."[43] Many offers fell through for what she describes as "Washingtonian reasons." When she was offered the lead in *Room at the Top*, her feeling was, "If I was going to lose Alice, I wanted to know immediately." Signoret feared that if Americans were involved, "there was no point in beginning to negotiate,"[44] but it was a British production and she not only got the part but also won an Oscar for it.

Producers, writers, and directors suffered from McCarthyism as much as performers, some even more. The "Hollywood Ten," a group of directors and screenwriters subpoenaed to appear before the HUAC in the fall of 1947, and cited for contempt of Congress because they refused to disclose their political affiliations, included: producer-director Herbert Biberman, director Edward Dmytryk, producer-writer Adrian Scott, and screenwriters Alvah Bessie, Lester Cole, Ring Lardner Jr., John Howard Lawson, Albert Matz, Samuel Ornitz, and Dalton Trumbo. They were all tried at the Federal Court in Washington DC in April 1948, and were given the maximum sentence of a year in jail and a fine of one thousand dollars. Blacklisted by the industry, some went abroad, others were forced into retirement, and still others wrote screenplays under pseudonyms.

Most of the "Hollywood Ten" were prominent film artists, with Oscar awards and nominations to their credit. Edward Dmytryk was nominated for the directorial award for *Crossfire*, which was also nominated for Best Picture. After his release from jail, he went into self-imposed exile in Europe. In 1951, however, he agreed to cooperate with the Committee and even became a "star witness" in its second round. His testimony incriminated several colleagues, but he himself was able to work, and his film version of Herman Wouk's *The Caine Mutiny*, was nominated for the 1954 Best Picture.

Robert Rossen, an Oscar-nominated director, was also blacklisted by the industry. In 1947, he was subpoenaed to appear before the Committee, but the hearings were suspended. He continued to work and his picture *All the King's Men* won the 1949 Oscar. Nominated, it is likely that he failed to win the directorial award because of politics; usually, there is a strong correlation between these two categories: the winner that year was Joseph L. Mankiewicz for *A Letter to Three Wives*. In the second round of hearings, however, Rossen was identified as a Communist by other witnesses, and his refusal to testify resulted in his being blacklisted. But like Dmytryk, two years later, he requested a second hearing, in which he admitted to his membership in the Communist Party and was subsequently able to work, though he decided never again to return to Hollywood. In 1961, Rossen scored his greatest success with *The Hustler*, nominated for nine awards, including Best Picture and Director, and winning two technical awards.

Rumor has it that director Jules Dassin was identified as a Communist by Edward Dmytryk, and forced into exile in Europe. Nonetheless, he was one of the few directors to have made good films abroad, including *Night and the City* in England, and *Rififi* in France. It is noteworthy that a major American company agreed to distribute *Rififi* on one of two conditions: that Dassin sign a declaration repenting his past and stating he was duped into subversive associations, or that his name be removed from the film as its writer-director. When he refused, the film was dropped and a small distributor picked it up. The negotiations with United Artists allegedly failed because of "hostile" public opinion. *He Who Must Die* also failed to get a major American distributor, and when the film was finally shown, only three showed up: Richard Brooks, Gene Kelly, and Walter Wanger.[45] It took over a decade for Dassin's reputation to be really restored, with the release of *Never on Sunday* in 1960, his greatest commercial success; it won him his first and only directorial nomination.

Among the blacklisted writers was Carl Foreman, whose screenplay for *High Noon* was nominated. Under public pressure, he left for England and worked there for years underground. He used the pseudonym Derek Frey for his screenplay for Joseph Losey's *The Sleeping Tiger*. But he was given no credit for *The Bridge on the River Kwai*, which won all major awards, including best screenplay to Pierre Boule, the author of the book, who had nothing to do with the screenplay.

Indeed, the Academy itself became a victim of McCarthy's polit-

And The Winner Is . . .

ical hysteria. On February 6, 1957, it decided to enact the following rule: "Any person who, before any duly constituted Federal legislative committee or body, shall have admitted that he is a member of the Communist party (and has not since publicly renounced the Party) or who shall have refused to answer whether or not he is, or was, a member of the Communist Party or shall have refused to respond to a subpoena to appear before such a committee or body, shall be ineligible for any Academy Award so long as he persists in such a refusal."

Screenwriters, more than any other talent group, were affected by this rule. Michael Wilson won the writing award with Harry Brown for *A Place in the Sun*, but refusing to answer charges of Communist affiliation, he found himself without work. In 1956, William Wyler's *Friendly Persuasion*, nominated for many awards, was released without giving any credit to Wilson's script, which he had written a decade before; the only writing credit mentioned was "from the book by Jessamyn West."

In the 1957 ceremonies an interesting incident occurred when the Best Story went to Robert Rich for *The Brave One*, but no writer claimed the award. The Writers Guild in the West acknowledged that "it knew nothing about the man," and that "he's as much of a mystery to us as he is to everybody else." The film's producer, Frank King also said he had no idea of his screenwriter's whereabouts, but added that he was a brilliant young writer whom he had met a few years ago in Germany, where he served as an American Army man.[46] To the embarrassment of the Academy, it later turned out that Rich was the pseudonym used by blacklisted writer Dalton Trumbo, one of the "Hollywood Ten." Trumbo got his long overdue Oscar in 1975, when producers Frank and Maurice King sent to the Academy an affidavit verifying that Rich was in fact Trumbo.[47]

The Defiant Ones was one of the most acclaimed films in 1958, earning nominations in most categories, including story and screenplay to Nathan E. Douglas and Harold Jacob Smith. But Douglas was the pseudonym of Ned Young, another blacklisted writer. The Academy, embarrassed at having to declare a member of a team ineligible, revoked its rule in January 1958, just weeks prior to the nomination process. The Board of Directors denied that the motive for revoking the 1957 rule was connected with *The Defiant Ones*. But it issued a statement calling the previous rule "unworkable and impractical to administer and enforce." According to the new regulations, the Academy would simply "honor achievements as presented." Dalton Trumbo hailed this decision, seeing in it the official end of the blacklist, but questioned how the industry could officially rescind a blacklist which it had never acknowledged.

The Use of the Oscar Show for Political Propaganda

Most artists believe that politics should be kept entirely out of the Academy Awards. In practice, however, this separation has been hard to achieve; film, like any art form, is potentially a political medium. The relationship between politics and the Oscar show involves a basic dilemma between the value of freedom of speech— should the winners be allowed to express their views openly in their acceptance speeches?—and the attempt to neutralize the Oscar show and isolate it from politics as much as possible. As was shown, movie politics and societal politics have always played some role in the nomination and in the winning processes. But the explicit use of the Oscar show for the propagation of personal causes has been a phenomenon of the 1970s.

Acceptance speeches with political overtones have been, at times, the most volatile aspects of the ceremonies because they were the least predictable; it is the only part of the show that is not—and cannot—be reheased in advance. The ceremonies' live audiences and the television viewers have come to expect such "explosive" incidents. The fact that John Wayne and Jane Fonda, two of the most politically oriented players, did not use the platform for political speeches was held in high regard by some, but it disappointed their fans, who expected them to take advantage of this unique opportunity.

Jane Fonda was highly praised for her performance in *They Shoot Horses, Don't They?* for which she won the New York Film Critics Award. However, many believed that her chances to win the Oscar were spoiled by her radical politics at the time: her visit to India, her support of the Black Panther Movement, and her fund-raising drives for reluctant GI and US Servicemen's Fund. There were other good performances in 1969, most notably Liza Minnelli's in *The Sterile Cuckoo*, but the opinion was that Fonda deserved the Oscar; the winner, however, was Maggie Smith in *The Prime of Miss Jean Brodie.*

Two years later, when Jane Fonda received her second nomination for *Klute*, the speculation was that she would either renounce her nomination or use the occasion to promote her politics. She had earlier sent a Vietnam veteran to accept her Golden Globe award from the Hollywood Foreign Press Association. For a while, she considered declining the prize, if she won, but on second thought decided to attend the ceremonies. "A woman who is much wiser than I am," she later explained, "said to me: 'You're a very subjective individual, an elite individual. The Oscar is what the working class relates to when it thinks of people in the movies.'" She was therefore persuaded that "It's important for those of us who speak out for social change to get that kind of acclaim."[48] When her name was announced winner, there was a mixture of cheers and boos. Contrary to everybody's expectations, Fonda gave a very restrained speech. "Thank you. And thank those of you who applauded," she said. "There's a lot I could say tonight. But this isn't the time or the place. So I'll just say thank you."

Shortly afterwards, she was unofficially blacklisted and did not work for several years in America. Earlier, she had, with actor Donald Sutherland, formed "the Anti-War Troupe" as part of her campaign against Vietnam; the troupe toured military camps in total defiance of the Pentagon. In July 1972 she went to North Vietnam, a move that put her career—and her very life—on the line. When she got back, she was called all kinds of names by her opponents: "a Commie slut," "Hanoi Jane," and "a traitor." Unintimidated, she cowrote and coproduced *F.T.A.* (*Free the Army*), a filmed version of the tour. She also campaigned, along with many other actors, for the Presidential election of Senator George McGovern. In 1973, she married Tom Hayden, the antiwar militant of the 1960s. Assisted with cinematographer Haskell Wexler, they codirected *Introduction to the Enemy*, a documentary of her visit to North Vietnam.

Her record as a screen actress at that time was rather poor, though not by choice. She appeared in Jean-Luc Godard's *Tout Va Bien* (*Everything's All Right*), a film about the student revolutions and strikes in 1968 Paris. Her commitment to socially relevant films was demonstrated by playing Nora, Ibsen's feminist heroine, in Joseph Losey's unimaginative 1973 *A Doll's House*. A cameo role

in the American-Soviet production *The Blue Bird* in 1975, was neither challenging nor rewarding.

For her American comeback, she chose a comedy, *Fun with Dick
and Jane* (1977), costarring George Segal. But the turning point of
her career was *Julia*, in which she was cast as playwright Lillian
Hellman, and which she said "means more to me than any movie
I've ever made."[49] When she was asked to cohost the 1977 Oscar
show, it was interpreted as a sign that Hollywood had "forgiven"
her. And in 1978, her second Oscar for *Coming Home* proved that
she had emerged triumphantly from her aborted career. Her successful comeback has been compared to that of Ingrid Bergman two
decades earlier, whose second Oscar for *Anastasia* was also some
kind of symbolic reconciliation. This comparison was made because both Fonda and Bergman were restored to respectability
while still young and attractive—in contrast to most blacklisted
artists, who had lost the most creative years of their lives and never
managed to restore their careers successfully.

In the late 1970s, Fonda's politics mellowed substantially and she
was gradually accepted as a mainstream actress and figure. Her
new causes were the ERA (now defunct), antinuclear war, rent
control, and other issues that are more accessible to and accepted
by the American public. She supports her husband's grass-roots organization, CED (Campaign for Economic Democracy), whose
goal is to curb the power of large corporations and monopolies.
Maturity in age, with second-time motherhood, have obviously
changed her, though she is still committed to film projects with
strong political overtones. Looking back on her past, she admits to
have been "a bit shrill," but also to have reached the conclusion that
"rallies and speeches aren't necessarily as effective as making one
hell of a good movie."[50] In the 1980s she has become a media star,
due to the enormous popularity of her workout books and videos.
Cohosting the 1986 Oscar show, she introduced Kermit the Frog,
an ironic commentary, certainly, on the fate of a previously radical
actress.

Charlie Chaplin, another political victim, was also forgiven by
the film industry and restored to legitimacy with an Honorary Oscar in 1972. Chaplin failed to win any award for *The Great Dictator*,
despite a brilliant performance in a distinguished film. Politics
probably had something to do with it. Chaplin was suspected of a
leftist bent during the war because he had made it public that he

was in favor of launching a second front in Europe to help the Russians. The subjects of *Modern Times* (1936), a satire on the impotence of the individual in the technological age, and *The Great Dictator*, a satire of Hitler and Fascism, also made him a political suspect; at the end of this film, he stepped out of character and made an impassioned speech for freedom. Needless to say, both films were made before the United States joined the war. And there was also talk about the fact that he never acquired an American citizenship, which made him all the more suspect. Public opinion started to turn against him after *The Great Dictator*, which was his last commercial hit in the US. His subsequent films, *Monsieur Verdoux* (1947) and *Limelight* (1952), failed dismally at the box office.

Some believe that Chaplin was persecuted because he refused to state publicly that he was disinterested in the Soviet Union; ironically enough, unlike many Americans, he had never visited Russia. Threatened with a subpoena to testify before the HUAC, he sent a wire: "I am not a Communist, neither have I ever joined any political party or organization in my life."[51] In 1952, when the Attorney General instructed the Immigration Authorities to deny him a re-entry visa, he vowed never again to return to the US. His friends found it ironic that he was suspected of leftist politics, for in his personal habits and life-style he represented to them "the height of wealthy conservatism."[52] This persecution occurred at a crucial time in his career.

Twenty years after he left, Chaplin returned to the US on a reconciliation tour. He was first honored by the Film Society of Lincoln Center, receiving an emotional standing ovation from his fans. It was just the beginning of what he himself described as a renaissance, a feeling of being born again. The Academy decided to confer on Chaplin an Honorary Oscar "for the incalculable effect he has had on making motion pictures, the art form of this century." These gestures proved that the New Hollywood, the younger generation of film artists, had really taken over from the old guard.

A year later, in 1973, a major political controversy erupted when Marlon Brando won Best Actor for *The Godfather*. Brando's contempt for the film industry and for Hollywood's glamour and crassness, was always a known fact. Arriving for his first film, *The Men*, he shocked the press when he stated that his only motive for being there was his lack of courage to reject the tremendous amounts of money he was offered to make films. But somehow people became used to his style, viewing it as part and parcel of his idiosyncratic personality. Brando was such a brilliant actor that he could get away with such statements. His derisive attitude toward Hollywood never damaged his career—in some ways it made him more popular and more mysterious.

Prior to *The Godfather*, Brando was nominated five times, the last time for *Sayonara*, which he reportedly made because he identified with its plea for racial peace and understanding. In the 1960s, looking for political and relevant movies, he made *Candy*, in which he played a guru, *Reflections in a Golden Eye*, as a homosexual military officer, and *The Countess from Hong Kong*, as an American diplomat. Most of these films failed, artistically and/or commercially. It was just when filmmakers and audiences began to describe him as a "has-been" that he delivered a brilliant comeback as Don Corleone in *The Godfather*, for which he had to take a screen test for the first time in his career. Paramount's executives were at first reluctant to give him the role, because they believed that he had lost his box-office power, but his test was reportedly so convincing that they could hardly recognize him.

His performance got rave reviews and many awards. But Brando rejected the Golden Globe and the Academy nomination (his sixth), sending them a telegram: "There is singular lack of honor in this country today." The award was also, according to critic Tony Thomas, an emotional gesture, "a sense of reaffirmation of an admittedly great, but wayward actor, who had become alienated by, or with Hollywood." But it was a strange gesture, for "it was a welcome home, extended to an actor, who in no way was concerned with being welcomed home."[53]

Applause greeted Brando's name when he was announced winner, upon which an Indian girl, Sacheen Littlefeather, walked to the podium and read a statement from the actor; the entire speech was later released to the press. Brando decided to voice his protest against the treatment of Indians, on and offscreen, through an Apache member of the Native American Affirmative Image Committee. "So, I, as a member of this profession," Brando wrote, "do not feel that I can as a citizen of the United States accept an award here tonight. I think awards in this country at this time are inapporiate to be received or given until the condition of the American Indian is drastically altered." And he concluded, "If we are not our

brother's keeper, at least let us not be his executioner." Brando's behavior was criticized by those who felt he should have at least refused the award in person; the explanation for his absence was that
he had been on his way to Wounded Knee, to support the Ogala La
Sioux's protest against racial discrimination. But his rejection of the
Oscar did not surprise those who knew him and, further, did not
meet with unanimous criticism.

The next "explosive" political incident occurred in the 1975 show
when Burt Schneider and Peter Davis were cited for their documentary, *Hearts and Minds*, an anti-Vietnam war film. Schneider
read in his acceptance speech a wire from a Viet Cong leader which
stated: "Please transmit to all our friends in America our recognition of all they have done on behalf of peace for the application of
the Paris Accords on Vietnam. These actions serve legitimate interests of the American people and the Vietnamese people." This bla-
tant propaganda, however, outraged many television viewers who
called the NBC network in anger. Consequently, Frank Sinatra,
one of the show's emcees, was asked by the Academy officials to
make the following statement: "We are not responsible for any political references made on this program tonight. And we are sorry
that they are made." It was the first time that the Academy has
taken an explicit stand as a body against political propaganda expressed on its platform.

After several ceremonies marked by political controversies, the
1976 Oscar show was relatively quiet and its proceedings smooth.
One journalist described it as "negatively notable, no protests, no
winners refusing awards, no political speeches, no surprises."[54]

But in the following show, another political casualty, playwright
Lillian Hellman, was restored to legitimacy. Her career was damaged in the 1950s, following a successful decade in Hollywood as a
screenwriter, adapting several of her Broadway plays to the screen,
such as *The Little Foxes*. Hellman was declared an uncooperative
witness after her refusal to testify before the Committee, sending
the now-famous and often quoted letter.

The invitation to participate in the show, as the presenter of the
writing awards, was yet another attempt of Hollywood's new generation to achieve reconciliation with the victims of the McCarthy
era. Following an emotional standing ovation, which caught her by
surprise, Hellman said: "My second reason for being here is per-

haps only important to me. I was once upon a time a respectable member of this community. Respectable didn't necessarily mean more than I took a daily bath when I was sober, didn't spit except when I meant to, and mispronounced a few words of fancy French. Then suddenly even before Senator Joseph McCarthy reached for that rusty, poisoned ax, I and many others were no longer acceptable to the owners of this industry. They confronted the wild charges of Joe McCarthy with a force and courage of a bowl of mashed potatoes." And she concluded: "But I have a mischievous pleasure in being restored to respectability, understanding full well the younger generation who asked me here tonight meant more by that invitation than my name or my history."

Warren Beatty, one of the show's cohosts, remarked cynically: "When I saw who was on this show tonight, Lillian Hellman, Norman Mailer, Jane Fonda, Donald Sutherland, I thought maybe the nicest thing to do was to say a few nice things about Reagan and Goldwater." Beatty, of course, did not know then that in two years Reagan would be elected the President of the United States.

The most controversial political incident took place in the 1978 ceremonies, when Vanessa Redgrave won the supporting award for *Julia*. Before the show began, hundreds of members of the Jewish Defense League (JDL) picketed outside the Music Center, protesting her involvement in *The Palestinians*, an anti-Zionist documentary. Redgrave had taken a strong anti-Israeli stand when she became an outspoken proponent of the Palestine Liberation Army (PLO). Neither the JDL signs, stating "Redgrave and Arafat: A Perfect Love Affair," and "Hell No to Vanessa Redgrave and the PLO," nor the PLO signs, "Vanessa: A Woman of Conscience and Courage," were seen by the television viewers; the police and special security officers managed to keep the two groups apart.

Redgrave's views have sharply divided the film industry over the issue of actors' participation in politics. Some Jewish producers, heavily represented in Hollywood, supported artists' rights to express freely their political views offscreen. The demands of the JDL from Twentieth Century-Fox, which produced *Julia*, never to hire Redgrave again and to repudiate officially her support of the PLO, were dismissed by the studio and by the Screen Actors Guild. The official reaction was: "While Fox as a company and the individuals who work there do not agree with Redgrave's political philosophy, we totally reject and we will not be blackmailed into supporting any policy of refusing to employ any person because of their political beliefs."[55]

Redgrave's performance in *Julia* was undoubtedly brilliant, and it followed three previously nominated roles, in *Morgan*, *Isadora*, and *Mary, Queen of Scots*, though she never won. Moreover, the competition in the supporting category was rather weak, with the other nominees being: Leslie Brown in *The Turning Point*, Quinn Cummings in *The Goodbye Girl*, Melinda Dillon in *Close Encounters of the Third Kind*, and Tuesday Weld in *Looking for Mr. Goodbar*.

The Academy officials expected Redgrave to make a political speech if she won. And they didn't mind when she spoke about the meaning of *Julia* to her: "I think Jane Fonda and I have done the best work of our lives and I think this was in part due to our director, Fred Zinnemann. And I also think it's in part because we believed in what we were expressing: two out of millions who gave their lives and were prepared to sacrifice everything in the fight against Fascist racist Nazi Germany." But then she proceeded into an impassioned political speech, replete with propagandistic statements: "You should be very proud that in the last few weeks you stood firm and you refused to be intimidated by the threats of a small bunch of Zionist hoodlums whose behavior is an insult to the stature of Jews all over the world and to their great and heroic record against fascism and oppression. I salute that record and I salute all of you for having stood firm and dealt the final blow against that period when Nixon and McCarthy launched a worldwide witch-hunt against those who tried to express in their lives and their work the truths that they believed in." And she concluded: "I salute you and I thank you, and I pledge to you that I'll continue to fight against anti-Semitism and Fascism."

Paddy Chayefsky, who presented the writing awards, chastised Redgrave. "I'm sick and tired," he said, "of people exploiting the occasion of the Academy Awards for the propagation of their own political propaganda." "Redgrave's win," he continued, "is not a pivotal moment in history, and doesn't require a proclamation." Charlton Heston, who had voted for her, reflected many people's opinion in the statement he made: "I thought it as much an error to interject what amounted to political commentary into her acceptance remarks as it was an error for people to oppose her nomination on political grounds."[56] Indeed, Redgrave's win surprised many and was interpreted as yet another sign of the "maturity" of the New Hollywood—it is unlikely that Redgrave would have won the award in the 1950s.

Redgrave's politics was at the center of another controversy a few months later, when she was cast as an Auschwitz concentration camp survivor in *Playing for Time*, Arthur Miller's television drama based on Fania Fenelon's memoirs of that era. This casting drew sharp protests from the Jewish community and the entertainment industry. Rabbi Marvin Hier, for example, said it was like "selecting Edgar Hoover to portray Martin Luther King," and Sammy Davis Jr. felt "It would be like me playing the head of the Ku Klux Klan." Dore Schary, former head of MGM production and honorary chairman of the Anti-Defamation League, issued a statement charging CBS with "a profound lack of sensitivity and understanding," calling the casting "a trick," and "a stunt."[57] In their defensive response, the show's producers and Miller said that other actresses, Barbra Streisand and Jane Fonda, were considered for the part and that Redgrave was the best actress available; some actresses reportedly turned the part down because they did not want to shave their heads. The producers reiterated their philosophy that performers should not be penalized for their personal views, and that it was a matter of principle not to involve politics in artistic decisions. Once again, Redgrave's performance was nothing short of brilliant, earning for it a well-deserved Emmy Award.

The intimate interplay between actors' politics and their careers was put again to test in 1982, when following a storm of protests from subscribers and musicians, the Boston Symphony Orchestra canceled its performances of Stravinsky's *Oedipus Rex*, which were to feature Vanessa Redgrave. She decided to sue them, and the case is still unresolved. Other than that, Redgrave's politics have not affected her ability to get work. She was recently cast in some highly desirable screen roles, including *The Bostonians*, as Olive Chancellor, a wealthy suffragette, for which she received a fifth Oscar nomination and the National Society of Film Critics Award, and David Hare's *Wetherby*, as the emotionally stifled teacher, for which she won another National Society Award. Andrew Sarris also singled out her work at the year's end, "I would have given the Oscar to Vanessa Redgrave for *Wetherby*, but I don't know if I would have waited around for her acceptance speech."[58]

The scandal of *Julia* was barely forgotten when another political controversy erupted in the 1979 ceremonies, caused by the nomination of two anti-Vietnam War films for Best Picture: Michael Cimino's *The Deer Hunter* and Hal Ashby's *Coming Home*, each garnering a large number of nominations. Unlike World War II, which saw the immediate production of war films, it took almost a decade for Hollywood filmmakers to risk producing movies about Vietnam. The only exception was John Wayne's *The Green Berets* in 1968, the first and only major film in favor of the American involvement in Vietnam. Both studios, Universal in the case of *The Deer Hunter* and United Artists in *Coming Home*, had serious fears that the public would not go to see them, though they felt good about their overall quality. *The Deer Hunter* opened to raves, and *Coming Home* to mixed reviews.

The Academy voters split the major awards between the two movies. *The Deer Hunter* won five: Best Picture, Director (Cimino), Supporting Actor (Christopher Walken), sound, and editing. And *Coming Home* won the two lead acting awards (Jane Fonda and Jon Voight) and original screenplay (Waldo Salt and Robert C. Jones, using Nancy Dowd's story). Ironically, John Wayne was chosen as the presenter of the Best Picture, though one could only speculate how he felt about handing it in to *The Deer Hunter*; the Duke kept his mouth shut!

During the ceremonies, there were mass demonstrations outside the auditorium, most against *The Deer Hunter*, but some in favor of *Coming Home*. Director Cimino was accused of violating historical truth and his artistic responsibility, though he claimed that his aim was to make a surrealistic, not realistic, picture. "My film has nothing to do with whether the war should or should not have been," he later said. "This film addresses itself to the question of the ordinary people of this country who journeyed from their homes to the darkness and back. How do you survive that?"[59]

"*The Deer Hunter* is a movie," Cimino explained. "It is not a newsreel. I was not trying to recreate reality."[60] But Cimino's explanations did not pacify his critics. On the night of the awards, the police arrested thirteen members of Vietnam Veterans Against the War who protested against the movie's "misinterpretation of reality." Another dissenting group, Hell We Won't Go Away Committee, denounced the film as "a racist attack on the Vietnamese people," citing the vicious violence, particularly the game of Russian roulette used by the Vietnamese in the narrative. "We didn't want the film to be honored blindly," said Linda Garrett, who formed the committee. "Even my progressive friends seemed blinded by the power of the film, by the emotional impact. They felt it was a great film despite its racism, despite its misinterpretation of history."[61] Other critics charged the film with portraying Americans as innocent victims and with eliminating any discussion of the war issues. Cimino was allegedly shocked by the demonstrations because he had intended the film to be an antiwar statement.

Further, the winners' speeches and off-camera remarks were seen as violation of the professional ethics of collegiality and courtesy. Jane Fonda charged that *The Deer Hunter* was racist and represented the Pentagon's view of Vietnam and, referring to the demonstrators as "my friends," described *Coming Home* as a "better picture." And winning the Oscar for playing a sensitive paraplegic war veteran, Jon Voight said in his acceptance remarks, "I accept this for every guy in a wheelchair."

International politics have entered into the Academy ceremonies through the nomination of foreign artists. In 1981, for example, the producer of the Best Animated Short, *The Fly*, was unable to obtain a visa to leave Hungary and attend the show. Instead, an official of the Hungarian Embassy in the US was authorized to represent him, which showed again how intricate the connection between politics and film art is.

The 1980s have been relatively quiet, so far as political scandals and upsets on the Oscar stage are concerned. Yet every year sees the nomination of explicitly political films and every ceremony includes some political remarks in the acceptance speeches. Moreover, one category, foreign films, has been particularly political as the most recent awards demonstrated. Four of the five nominees for the 1985 Best Foreign-Language Picture were explicitly political movies with strong ideological messages. The winner, the Argentinian *The Official Story*, is a disturbingly emotional drama about an upper-middle-class woman, a high-school history teacher, who begins to suspect that her adopted daughter is a child of one of the *desaparecidos*, the Argentinians who were abducted during the counterinsurgency of the juntas. And it competed against the Yugoslav *When Father Was Away on Business*, the Cannes Festival winner, a family tale set in Sarajevo in the early 1950s, when the country was torn between Marshal Tito's policies and the Stalinist Soviet Union. The other nominees were the Hungarian *Colonel Redl*, dealing with Alfred Redl, the powerful intelligence officer of the Austro-Hungarian Empire who, according to the movie, agrees to become a Russian agent to avoid disclosure of his homosexuality, then commits suicide; and *Angry Harvest*, a psychological drama about the relationship between a Jewish woman escaping the Nazis, and a devout Polish farmer in World War II. The fifth contender, the French comedy *Three Men and a Cradle*, was also political, though in the broad sense of this term, dealing with the changing definitions of gender roles.[62]

Many people seem to think that turning the annual Oscar show into an explicitly political platform will diminish the importance of the award and the event. However, it would be a mistake to think that there will be no more political controversies in the future. Whether the Academy likes it or not, the Oscar ceremonies are bound to have explosive political repercussions due to the potentially political nature of film as a mass, collective medium, and due to the event's extraordinary public exposure. What other public occasion provides a ready-made, attentive audience of one billion viewers?

Conclusion
The Oscar Award, Film, and
American Culture

The Oscar Award has changed the entire operation of the film industry through its pervasive influence on every aspect of it: the production companies, film artists and craftsmen, film critics, and filmgoers.

To begin with, the production companies now tend to release their prestigious and most important pictures in the late fall and early winter, particularly in the month of December. The pragmatic philosophy behind this idea is that these movies will be fresh in Academy members' minds by the time they receive the nomination ballots in January. Indeed, other things being equal, films released in December have better chances to be nominated than those released in any other month. Of the 45 films nominated for Best Picture in the 1980s, 18 (40 percent) were released in December, and 34 films between September and December. By contrast, only six of the 45 films opened between January and April, such as *Coal Miner's Daughter* in March; *Missing* in February; *Tender Mercies* in March; *Witness* in February; *Hannah and Her Sisters* in February; and *A Room with a View* in March. These pictures were released in the winter because their producers did not consider them to be "Oscar stuff," or serious contenders for Academy nominations. Indeed, *all five* nominees for the 1988 Best Picture were released in December! (*The Accidental Tourist, Dangerous Liaisons, Mississippi Burning, Rain Man,* and *Working Girl*).

By contrast, many films would have stood better chances to get nominations had they been released in more strategically fortuitous times. For example, Martin Scorsese's *King of Comedy*, and David Jones's *Betrayal*, both released in January 1983, would have featured more prominently in the nominations had they been released in the fall.[1] It is doubtful that *The King of Comedy* would have been more successful at the box office—it was a fiasco—or that it would have garnered a Best Picture nomination, but its three superb performances, by Robert De Niro, Jerry Lewis, and Sondra Bernhardt, would have had better chances to receive acting nominations, which none of them did. Similarly, the British film *Betrayal*, with screenplay by Harold Pinter from his noted play, also contained three superlative performances, by Ben Kingsley, Jeremy Irons, and Patricia Hodge, each of whom deserved, but did not earn, an acting nomination.

The release date of motion pictures was not always a crucial variable in the nominations. In the 1930s, only seven of the ninety-two nominated films (7.6 percent), and in the 1940s, ten (14 percent) of the seventy films premiered in December. The release date started to play a strategic role in the 1950s, when ten (20 percent) of the nominated films opened in December. But it was only in the 1960s that it became a *crucial* variable: sixteen (32 percent) of the nominated films in this decade, and thirteen (26 percent) in the 1970s were released in December, many around Christmas time. The "Awards Year" rule stipulates that films must play at least one week in Los Angeles prior to December 31.

However, one should not get the wrong conclusion that the film's release date counts more than its artistic merits, though it is definitely a contributing factor to the probability of getting nominated. Woody Allen, highly respected for his many talents, has shown complete disregard for the timing of his films' releases. All of his 1980s pictures were released in "the worst" season so far as Oscars are concerned, usually in February or March. Some critics feel that they would have garnered more nominations had they been released in November or December. It will be interesting to see how his latest, *Hannah and Her Sisters*, which received rave reviews upon its release in February, will feature in the 1987 Oscar nominations.

The Oscar's effect on the release date of motion pictures is yet another example of its many unanticipated consequences. Another displacement of goals in the award's operation has been its gradual acceptance as an *institutionalized* measure of film quality. The Oscar has become such an integral part of the film world that many professional critics are evaluating the various merits of films (acting, writing, direction) in terms of the Oscar. For better or for worse, the Oscar has become a legitimate yardstick of film excellence.

The use of Oscar as a measure in film reviews began in the 1950s. For instance, in 1958 one critic wrote in his review of David Niven's performance in *Separate Tables*: "I knew I was seeing a piece of acting worth an Oscar."[2] Niven did win Best Actor for this film.

And another critic was so overwhelmed with Liza Minnelli in *The Sterile Cuckoo* that he commented: "She does not play nineteen-year-old Pookie Adams, she is Pookie Adams, and you may mark your Oscar ballots right now."[3] Minnelli won her first Best Actress nomination for this role. *Variety*, the popular trade magazine, is known for using the Oscar and other "inside Hollywood" terms in its reviews. Thus, reviewing *Arthur*, it's critic noted that "John Gielgud gives a priceless performance, truly the kind that wins best supporting Oscars."[4] Gielgud won.

But critics use the Oscar not only for glowing praise. Pauline Kael, for example, did not like Gena Rowlands's performance in *A Woman Under the Influence*, noting that Rowlands is doing too much, "enough for half a dozen tours de force, a whole row of Oscars."[5] The Oscar has often been used as a derogatory concept, like in David Denby's review of *Places in the Heart*, which he did not like, because it was "too pious." "Parched and academic," wrote Denby, "the movie is too square for art—though it's perfectly designed for Oscars."[6] And he was right, at least as far as the prediction of Oscars was concerned; *Places of the Heart* was nominated for seven awards, including Best Picture.

The point is that film critics and audiences have incorporated the Oscar into their language and are making value judgments in terms of "Oscar-caliber" films and performances. Further, many are trying to predict, shortly after the films' release, what are their chances to get nominations and awards. In 1983, *The Big Chill* opened to rave reviews, with Richard Corliss writing in *Time*, "the eight star actors deserve one big Oscar."[7] Or Andrew Sarris stated in his review of *Twice in a Lifetime* (1985) that Amy Madigan "deserves an Oscar,"[8] Madigan was indeed nominated. That many critics are right in their predictions only shows that the parameters of what is an "Oscar caliber" film or performance are pretty well established.

The institutionalization of the Oscar as a legitimate symbol of success has also been reflected in its portrayal in films about Hollywood. *The Bad and the Beautiful* (1952), Vincente Minnelli's glossy melodrama, was one of the more successful "Hollywood on Hollywood" films. Using flashback as a device, its narrative consists of a series of recollections by a director (Barry Sullivan), a glamorous star (Lana Turner), a screenwriter (Dick Powell), and a studio executive (Walter Pidgeon) about a go-getting, ruthless producer (Kirk

Douglas), who is a winner of multiple Oscars. Providing a supposedly "inside" view of Hollywood, the film received special attention from the Academy, with five nominations and two awards, screenplay to Charles Schnee and supporting actress to Gloria Grahame.

Curiously, most of these "self-examination" movies have revealed an unflattering view of Hollywood and a disparaging attitude toward the Oscar. Joseph Levine's *The Oscar* (1966), based on Richard Sale's book, was a vulgar soap opera on the informal operations of the award. The film tells the story of a self-centered actor Frankie Fan (Stephen Boyd) who, waiting impatiently to be announced winner, recalls in a series of flashbacks his life: his abuse of his drama coach (Eleanor Parker) who launched his career, his marriage to a glamorous star (Elke Sommer) for publicity, his betrayal of an old friend (Milton Berle), and the extensive advertisement campaign to win the award. But his illusions are shattered when, much to his shock, another actor is chosen winner. *The Oscar* was the worst publicity Hollywood could devise for itself. Panned by all critics, it was also a fiasco at the box office. "Obviously the community doesn't need enemies so long as it has itself," wrote Bosley Crowther.[9] And other critics felt that "discriminating moviegoers perferred to watch the real thing—the Oscar cast—on television and hypothecate themselves as to the behind-the-scenes chaos involved."[10]

In recent years, the Oscar has been used on screen in humorous or cynical ways. Billy Wilder cast Henry Fonda with a good sense of irony in *Fedora* (1979), as the president of the Academy sent to a remote island to present an honorary Oscar to an aging but legendary film actress (Martha Keller), possibly standing in for Greta Garbo or Gloria Swanson. Fonda himself had not won an Oscar by 1979; he won in 1981. Blake Edwards also played a joke on Hollywood, casting his wife-actress Julie Andrews in *S.O.B.* (1980) as an actress who has won an Oscar for *Peter Pan* (i.e. *Mary Poppins*) and is now going out of her way, exposing her breasts, to change her previously wholesome screen image.

The ambivalence of film artists toward the Academy Award, its meaning and effects will probably continue. Film pioneer D. W. Griffith is reported to have said at the mention of the Academy of Motion Picture Arts and Sciences, "what art? what science?" And Alfred Hitchcock, who never won a competitive Oscar, described it as "a coveted annual prize whose previous year's winners nobody can ever remember."[11] Still, the fact remains that the Oscar has become, as producer Walter Mirisch said, "motion pictures' most effective ambassador" throughout the world. "The nickname stuck," Mirisch said while serving as president of the Academy, "and I have never been in any country in the world where the word Oscar has not entered the language."[12] Indeed, the word Oscar has entered into the most respectable dictionaries—what better proof of legitimization?

At present, the Oscar Award is more accepted by film artists as the ultimate symbol of achievement than ever before. Asked for his attitude toward the Oscar, William Hurt, the most recent winner, said, "If this was the way they chose to tell me that they liked my work, then I was going to accept it." "There are enough people that I now know and trust and admire and respect, who are members of that institution that I can't piss on it."[13] And the acceptance of the Oscar seems to be international. "In the French film industry," Simone Signoret observed, "there's always a smart guy who says before the umpteenth take of the same shot: 'Come on, let's do it again and we'll get the Oscar.'"[14]

The Preeminence of the Oscar in American Culture

But the Oscar has been much more than the most important and prestigious prize in the film world. The Oscar show is watched by one billion people, in and outside America, many of whom are not regular filmgoers, which extends the Oscar's popularity beyond the borders of the film world and beyond the borders of the US. Over the years the Oscar has become a preeminent symbol of American culture all over the world. Watching the annual show, the international viewers get a microcosm of American films, American television, and American culture. This international function contributes, explicitly and implicitly, to American ideological hegemony or cultural imperialism all over the world. The Oscar show serves as effective propaganda not just for American films, but for the American Way of Life.

Watching the annual ceremonies has become an obligatory ritual for many Americans, but the show has also been popular overseas. The clues to the issues of why the show's quality has had no impact on its popularity and why it has been beyond criticism seem to be in the cultural functions of the Oscar Award and the television show. The Oscar has functioned as a secular ritual in American culture, sharing many characteristics in common with religious rituals. The Oscar ceremonies are prescheduled, occurring every year at the same time. They are highly organized, following a strict set of rules and regulations; there are hundreds, not just ten "Academy commandments." The ceremonies are also collective, requiring the participation of a large public, live and via television. And most important of all, they reaffirm the central values in American dominant culture.

The Oscar Award has embodied such basic American orientations as democracy, equality, individualism, competitiveness, upward mobility, hard work, occupational achievement, and monetary success. The Oscar, like the cultural values it represents, highlights the inherent contradictions in achieving these values. These basic values are characterized by an inner dilemma between the cultural myth they embody and the corresponding reality. Each value exemplified by the Oscar can be stated as a dichotomy of opposite orientations: democracy-elitism, equality-discrimination, universalism-particularism, individualism-collectivism, competitiveness-collaboration, hard work-luck, and success-failure.

More than any other category, the acting awards have expressed the cultural contradictions inherent in the aforementioned values. For example, in no other profession has the conflict between the ideal of democracy and the reality of elitism been more apparent. Acting has been one of the most democratic of professions, with a broader social class base than any other. The choice of acting as a career has provided a channel for upward mobility for over half of the Oscar-nominated players, many of whom came from poor, uneducated families and from ethnic minorities. Acting is one of the most accessible professions, easily entered but also easily left. Entry requires less formal education and training than other lines of work; actual experience, "on the job" training, is far more important than educational diplomas and schooling.

Players' biographies are replete with rags-to-riches stories and the overnight-success syndrome, all myths that are still powerful in attracting new members into acting. One of the most startling success stories is exemplified by Sylvester Stallone. A product of a broken home, he grew up in New York's Hell's Kitchen, then in Silver Springs, Maryland, and then in Philadelphia.[15] After spending years at homes of foster parents, he was booted out of fourteen schools in eleven years. Stallone attended for a while the drama department of the University of Miami, where his instructors discouraged him from pursuing an acting career. He then tried his hand at a variety of jobs, the most glamorous of which was as usher at the Baronet Theater in New York. However, determined to become an actor, he managed to get some bit roles in films like *The Prisoner of Second Avenue*. When his career seemed to have reached a dead end, he decided to create his own opportunity and write a screenplay for himself. The result was *Rocky*, whose script he reportedly completed in three days, with a narrative that is similar to his own story: a down-and-out prizefighter rises to stardom against great odds. The rest is film history: *Rocky* won the 1976 Best Picture and established Stallone as the preeminent male star of his generation.

As well as being accessible, democratic, and a channel for upward mobility, acting is also one of the most stratified professions. The Oscar winners and nominees constitute a small elite, composed of the most accomplished actors who occupy the top positions of money, prestige, and power in the film world. The gap in rewards between this scarce elite and the rank-and-file members is immense. The supply of film artists has always surpassed the demand for them, which means that most of them are usually unemployed. By contrast, most Oscar winners go from one film project to another, and recently from the screen to the stage and vice versa. These career patterns attest to the operation of cumulative advantage, with the rich players becoming richer and the famous more famous, while the less successful players becoming progressively less famous and poorer.

The Oscar Award also exemplifies the contradiction between the values of hard work and luck as two determinants for successful careers. The Protestant ethic of hard work is still considered a legitimate avenue for achieving success. In acting, there is a strong emphasis on psychological motivation, ambition, self-discipline, physical energy, and work capacity as crucial requirements for success. Veteran actors, like John Wayne, rationalized their success by stressing the hard work of film acting, requiring physical rigors, irregular time schedules, long hours, and dire working conditions. And Walter Matthau was not joking when he described acting as "the hardest job known to mankind."[16]

But despite the emphasis on hard work, many players also realize that they have little control over their career opportunities, at times determined by luck or situational circumstances. Gary Cooper, a two-time Oscar winner, regarded acting as "just a job," which made him successful because he was "the right man at the right time." Cooper also differed from his colleagues in considering movie acting as "a pretty silly business for a man, because it takes less training, less ability, and less brains to be successful at it, than any other business I can think of."[17] The attitudes toward acting as a career, particularly of men, range from Jack Lemmon's "I have never lost a total passion to my work,"[18] and William Hurt's "I am proud to be an actor,"[19] to Marlon Brando's "acting has never been the dominant force in my life."[20] These differential attitudes have been manifest in the *subjective* meanings attached to the Oscar Award.

Still, most artists acknowledge the role of luck and accidental contingencies in their screen careers. Some became actors by accident, without ever making a conscious or deliberate occupational choice. James Stewart once summed up his career in this way: "If I hadn't been at some particular place at some particular time and some man hadn't happened to say so-and-so, and I hadn't answered this-and-that, I'd still be hunting a job in an architect's office."[21] Stewart majored in architecture at Princeton University, but never practiced. Another star, Bing Crosby, viewed his popularity as a series of lucky accidents, naming his autobiography, *Call Me Lucky*. "I'm not really an actor. I was just lucky," Clark Gable used to say. "If it hadn't been for people like Howard Strickling [MGM publicity man], I'd probably ended up a truck driver."[22] Luck also plays a considerable part in getting the Oscar-winning role. The Academy's history is replete with films made by artists neither intended nor originally cast in them. What would Jack Nicholson's career have been had Rip Torn not turned down the part of the dropout lawyer in *Easy Rider*, Nicholson's film break after ten years in Hollywood? Would this part have made Rip Torn a box-office star had he played it?

The conflict between individualism and collaboration is also demonstrated in the Oscar Award. Rugged, romantic individualism is most fully expressed in competitiveness and occupational achievement, and thousands of films have portrayed it onscreen. But romantic individualism also means rewarding artists for individual contributions in their respective expertise. At the same time, film is not only a complex, but also *collaborative* art form, though it is often hard to single out the relative contribution of each element (writing, direction, acting, cinematography, editing) to the success or failure of the final product—because they are intimately interdependent. However, the Oscar follows the primacy of individualism in American culture by honoring *individual* achievements.

Furthermore, it is almost impossible to define the elements of a good screen performance, though one knows a good performance when one sees one. Except for talent, individual performances depend on the support provided by the other players, on the way they are photographed, and on the manner in which they are edited. It is therefore not surprising that screen players often resent their lack of control over the final shape of their work—preferring to work in the theater, where they feel more directly responsible for their work. Ironically, more than other elements, it is acting that is blamed for the overall low quality of the film. But players are sometimes undeservedly praised when they appear in good or commercial films. When a film is good or powerful overall, every aspect of it seems to be good. Good films tend to overcome or overshadow mediocre, even bad, performances, but individual acting has a harder time overcoming an overall bad movie. This seems to be one of the inherent problems in evaluating films—the ability to distinguish the contribution of each element to the overall quality of the film. Good films tend to get nominations and awards in most categories, even in those that do not merit a nomination. By contrast, excellent individual contributions tend to be ignored or underestimated if they are involved in average or bad pictures.

Honoring individual achievements has been criticized in recent years because the structure of many films depends on ensemble acting, with a group of players complementing each other. As was mentioned, only Sam Shepard was nominated in *The Right Stuff*, and only Glenn Close in *The Big Chill*, two films cast with the best players in America and also films that relied heavily on ensemble acting. It is in such cases that other, less relevant factors, such as previous work, number of nominations, and popularity in Hollywood, begin to play a role in the nominations.

Some critics have proposed the establishment of a supplementary category for the best ensemble acting, honoring the *collective* achievements of a team of players. However, this is unlikely to happen for it is not only against the individualistic nature of film awards, but also against the value of individual competitiveness and achievement, highly cherished in American culture. "The comparatively striking feature of American culture," sociologist Robin Williams observed, "is its tendency to identify standards of excellence with competitive occupational achievement."[23] Yet the negative aspects of competition have also been apparent, as Slater noted: "The competitive life is a lonely one, and its satisfactions are very short-lived, for each race leads only to a new one."[24]

Finally, the Oscar Award has also functioned as an arena for conflict between universalism and particularism. Had the Oscar's reward system operated on completely matter-of-fact and rational principles, the *quality* of work would have been the sole criterion upon which artists' work would be evaluated. The universalistic ethos requires that artists producing high-quality work would be rewarded regardless of their ascribed statuses of age, gender, race, religion, or nationality. Such a reward system, however, is utopian: it does not exist. Indeed, one of the most important functions of the Oscar Award is to call the public's attention to the multiplicity of yardsticks and approaches in evaluating film art. Consequently, the more disagreement there is about the Oscars and the other film awards, the more critical and aware the movie public becomes of the problems in judging art quality in general.

What is amazing about the Oscar Award and its annual show is their *public* and *immediate* manifestations of these important cultural values. The Oscar audiences participate in the making or breaking of careers, in the rise and fall of artists, all of which is happening on their television sets before their own eyes. This international visibility contributes to the viability of the Oscar Award as an enduring and uniquely American symbol of achievement and success.

Appendices

Table 1: Awards in Six Categories by Year, 1927/8–1986

Year	Picture	Director	Actor	Actress	Supporting Actor	Supporting Actress
1927/8	Wings	Frank Borzage (Seventh Heaven) Lewis Milestone (Two Arabian Nights)	Emil Jannings (The Way of All Flesh; The Last Command)	Janet Gaynor (Seventh Heaven; Street Angel; Sunrise)		
1928/9	The Broadway Melody	Frank Lloyd (The Divine Lady)	Warner Baxter (In Old Arizona)	Mary Pickford (Coquette)		
1929/30	All Quiet on the Western Front	Lewis Milestone	George Arliss (Disraeli)	Norma Shearer (The Divorcee)		
1930/1	Cimarron	Norman Taurog (Skippy)	Lionel Barrymore (A Free Soul)	Marie Dressler (Min and Bill)		
1931/2	Grand Hotel	Frank Borzage (Bad Girl)	Fredric March (Dr. Jekyll and Mr. Hyde); Wallace Beery (The Champ)	Helen Hayes (The Sin of Madelon Claudet)		
1932/3	Cavalcade	Frank Lloyd	Charles Laughton (The Private Life of Henry VIII)	Katharine Hepburn (Morning Glory)		
1934	It Happened One Night	Frank Capra	Clark Gable	Claudette Colbert		

341

Table 1 (Continued)

Year	Picture	Director	Actor	Actress	Supporting Actor	Supporting Actress
1935	Mutiny on the Bounty	John Ford (The Informer)	Victor McLaglen (The Informer)	Bette Davis (Dangerous)		
1936	The Great Ziegfeld	Frank Capra (Mr. Deeds Goes to Town)	Paul Muni (The Story of Louis Pasteur)	Luise Rainer	Walter Brennan (Come and Get It)	Gale Sondergaard (Anthony Adverse)
1937	The Life of Emil Zola	Leo McCarey (The Awful Truth)	Spencer Tracy (Captains Courageous)	Luise Rainer (The Good Earth)	Joseph Schildkraut (The Life of Emil Zola)	Alice Brady (In Old Chicago)
1938	You Can't Take It With You	Frank Capra	Spencer Tracy (Boys Town)	Bette Davis (Jezebel)	Walter Brennan (Kentucky)	Fay Bainter (Jezebel)
1939	Gone with the Wind	Victor Fleming	Robert Donat (Goodbye Mr. Chips)	Vivien Leigh	Thomas Mitchell (Stagecoach)	Hattie McDaniel
1940	Rebecca	John Ford (The Grapes of Wrath)	James Stewart (The Philadelphia Story)	Ginger Rogers (Kitty Foyle)	Walter Brennan (The Westerner)	Jane Darwell (The Grapes of Wrath)
1941	How Green Was My Valley	John Ford	Gary Cooper (Sergeant York)	Joan Fontaine (Suspicion)	Donald Crisp	Mary Astor (The Great Lie)
1942	Mrs. Miniver	William Wyler	James Cagney (Yankee Doodle Dandy)	Greer Garson	Van Heflin (Johnny Eager)	Teresa Wright

Year	Picture	Director	Actor	Actress	Supporting Actor	Supporting Actress
1943	Casablanca	Michael Curtiz	Paul Lukas (*Watch on the Rhine*)	Jennifer Jones (*The Song of Bernadette*)	Charles Coburn (*The More the Merrier*)	Katina Paxinou (*For Whom the Bell Tolls*)
1944	Going My Way	Leo McCarey	Bing Crosby	Ingrid Bergman (*Gaslight*)	Barry Fitzgerald	Ethel Barrymore (*None But the Lonely Heart*)
1945	The Lost Weekend	Billy Wilder	Ray Milland	Joan Crawford (*Mildred Pierce*)	James Dunn (*A Tree Grows in Brooklyn*)	Anne Revere (*National Velvet*)
1946	The Best Years of Our Lives	William Wyler	Fredric March	Olivia De Havilland (*To Each His Own*)	Harold Russell	Anne Baxter (*The Razor's Edge*)
1947	Gentleman's Agreement	Elia Kazan	Ronald Colman (*A Double Life*)	Loretta Young (*The Farmer's Daughter*)	Edmund Gwenn (*Miracle on 34th Street*)	Celeste Holme
1948	Hamlet	John Huston (*The Treasure of the Sierra Madre*)	Laurence Olivier	Jane Wyman (*Johnny Belinda*)	Walter Huston (*The Treasure of the Sierra Madre*)	Claire Trevor (*Key Largo*)
1949	All the King's Men	Joseph L. Mankiewicz (*A Letter to Three Wives*)	Broderick Crawford	Olivia De Havilland (*The Heiress*)	Dean Jagger (*Twelve O'Clock High*)	Mercedes McCambridge
1950	All About Eve	Joseph L. Mankiewicz	Jose Ferrer (*Cyrano de Bergerac*)	Judy Holliday (*Born Yesterday*)	George Sanders	Josephine Hall (*Harvey*)

Table 1 (Continued)

Year	Picture	Director	Actor	Actress	Supporting Actor	Supporting Actress
1951	An American in Paris	George Stevens (A Place in the Sun)	Humphrey Bogart (The African Queen)	Vivien Leigh (A Streetcar Named Desire)	Karl Malden (Streetcar)	Kim Hunter (Streetcar)
1952	The Greatest Show on Earth	John Ford (The Quiet Man)	Gary Cooper (High Noon)	Shirley Booth (Come Back Little Sheba)	Anthony Quinn (Viva Zapata!)	Gloria Grahame (The Bad and the Beautiful)
1953	From Here to Eternity	Fred Zinnemann	William Holden (Stalag 17)	Audrey Hepburn (Roman Holiday)	Frank Sinatra	Donna Reed
1954	On the Waterfront	Elia Kazan	Marlon Brando	Grace Kelly (The Country Girl)	Edmond O'Brien (The Barefoot Contessa)	Eva Marie Saint
1955	Marty	Delbert Mann	Ernest Borgnine	Anna Magnani (The Rose Tattoo)	Jack Lemmon (Mister Roberts)	Jo Van Fleet (East of Eden)
1956	Around the World in 80 Days	George Stevens (Giant)	Yul Brynner (The King and I)	Ingrid Bergman (Anastasia)	Anthony Quinn (Lust for Life)	Dorothy Malone (Written on the Wind)
1957	The Bridge on the River Kwai	David Lean	Alec Guinness	Joanne Woodward (The Three Faces of Eve)	Red Buttons (Sayonara)	Miyoshi Umekil (Sayonara)
1958	Gigi	Vincente Minnelli	David Niven (Separate Tables)	Susan Hayward (I Want to Live!)	Burl Ives (The Big Country)	Wendy Hiller (Separate Tables)

Year	Film	Director	Best Actor	Best Actress	Best Supporting Actor	Best Supporting Actress
1959	*Ben-Hur*	William Wyler	Charlton Heston	Simone Signoret *(Room at the Top)*	Hugh Griffith	Shelley Winters *(The Diary of Anne Frank)*
1960	*The Apartment*	Billy Wilder	Burt Lancaster *(Elmer Gantry)*	Elizabeth Taylor *(Butterfield 8)*	Peter Ustinov *(Spartacus)*	Shirley Jones *(Elmer Gantry)*
1961	*West Side Story*	Robert Wise; Jerome Robbins	Maximilian Schell *(Judgment at Nuremberg)*	Sophia Loren *(Two Women)*	George Chakiris	Rita Moreno
1962	*Lawrence of Arabia*	David Lean	Gregory Peck *(To Kill a Mockingbird)*	Anne Bancroft *(The Miracle Worker)*	Ed Begley *(Sweet Bird of Youth)*	Patty Duke *(The Miracle Worker)*
1963	*Tom Jones*	Tony Richardson	Sidney Poitier *(Lilies of the Field)*	Patricia Neal *(Hud)*	Melvyn Douglas *(Hud)*	Margaret Rutherford *(The V.I.P.s)*
1964	*My Fair Lady*	George Cukor	Rex Harrison	Julie Andrews *(Mary Poppins)*	Peter Ustinov *(Topkapi)*	Lila Kedrova *(Zorba the Greek)*
1965	*The Sound of Music*	Robert Wise	Lee Marvin *(Cat Ballou)*	Julie Christie *(Darling)*	Martin Balsam *(A Thousand Clowns)*	Shelley Winters *(A Patch of Blue)*
1966	*A Man for All Seasons*	Fred Zinnemann	Paul Scofield	Elizabeth Taylor *(Who's Afraid of Virginia Woolf?)*	Walter Matthau *(The Fortune Cookie)*	Sandy Dennis *(Who's Afraid of Virginia Woolf?)*
1967	*In the Heat of the Night*	Mike Nichols *(The Graduate)*	Rod Steiger	Katharine Hepburn *(Guess Who's Coming to Dinner?)*	George Kennedy *(Cool Hand Luke)*	Estelle Parsons *(Bonnie and Clyde)*

Table 1 (Continued)

Year	Picture	Director	Actor	Actress	Supporting Actor	Supporting Actress
1968	*Oliver!*	Carol Reed	Cliff Robertson (*Charly*)	Katharine Hepburn (*The Lion in Winter*)	Jack Albertson (*The Subject Was Roses*)	Ruth Gordon (*Rosemary's Baby*)
1969	*Midnight Cowboy*	John Schlesinger	John Wayne (*True Grit*)	Maggie Smith (*The Prime of Miss Jean Brodie*)	Gig Young (*They Shoot Horses, Don't They?*)	Goldie Hawn (*Cactus Flower*)
1970	*Patton*	Franklin J. Schaffner	George C. Scott	Glenda Jackson (*Women in Love*)	John Mills (*Ryan's Daughter*)	Helen Hayes (*Airport*)
1971	*The French Connection*	William Friedkin	Gene Hackman	Jane Fonda (*Klute*)	Ben Johnson (*The Last Picture Show*)	Cloris Leachman (*The Last Picture Show*)
1972	*The Godfather*	Bob Fosse (*Cabaret*)	Marlon Brando	Liza Minnelli (*Cabaret*)	Joel Grey (*Cabaret*)	Eileen Heckart (*Butterflies Are Free*)
1973	*The Sting*	George Roy Hill	Jack Lemmon (*Save the Tiger*)	Glenda Jackson (*A Touch of Class*)	John Houseman (*The Paper Chase*)	Tatum O'Neal (*Paper Moon*)
1974	*The Godfather, Part Two*	Francis F. Coppola	Art Carney (*Harry and Tonto*)	Ellen Burstyn (*Alice Doesn't Live Here Anymore*)	Robert De Niro	Ingrid Bergman (*Murder on the Orient Express*)
1975	*One Flew Over the Cuckoo's Nest*	Milos Forman	Jack Nicholson	Louise Fletcher	George Burns (*The Sunshine Boys*)	Lee Grant (*Shampoo*)

Year	Picture	Director	Best Actor	Best Actress	Best Supporting Actor	Best Supporting Actress
1976	*Rocky*	John Avildsen	Peter Finch *(Network)*	Faye Dunaway *(Network)*	Jason Robards *(All the President's Men)*	Beatrice Straight *(Network)*
1977	*Annie Hall*	Woody Allen	Richard Dreyfuss *(The Goodbye Girl)*	Diane Keaton	Jason Robards *(Julia)*	Vanessa Redgrave *(Julia)*
1978	*The Deer Hunter*	Michael Cimino	Jon Voight *(Coming Home)*	Jane Fonda *(Coming Home)*	Christopher Walken	Maggie Smith *(California Suite)*
1979	*Kramer Vs. Kramer*	Robert Benton	Dustin Hoffman	Sally Field *(Norma Rae)*	Melvyn Douglas *(Being There)*	Meryl Streep
1980	*Ordinary People*	Robert Redford	Robert De Niro *(Raging Bull)*	Sissy Spacek *(Coal Miner's Daughter)*	Timothy Hutton	Mary Steenburgen *(Melvin and Howard)*
1981	*Chariots of Fire*	Warren Beatty *(Reds)*	Henry Fonda *(On Golden Pond)*	Katharine Hepburn *(On Golden Pond)*	John Gielgud *(Arthur)*	Maureen Stapleton *(Reds)*
1982	*Gandhi*	Richard Attenborough	Ben Kingsley	Meryl Streep *(Sophie's Choice)*	Louis Gossett *(An Officer and a Gentleman)*	Jessica Lange *(Tootsie)*
1983	*Terms of Endearment*	Richard Brooks	Robert Duvall *(Tender Mercies)*	Shirley MacLaine	Jack Nicholson	Linda Hunt *(The Year of Living Dangerously)*
1984	*Amadeus*	Milos Forman	F. Murray Abraham	Sally Field *(Places in the Heart)*	Hang S. Ngor *(The Killing Fields)*	Peggy Ashcroft *(A Passage to India)*
1985	*Out of Africa*	Sydney Pollack	William Hurt *(Kiss of the Spider Woman)*	Geraldine Page *(The Trip to Bountiful)*	Don Ameche *(Cocoon)*	Anjelica Huston *(Prizzi's Honor)*

Table 1 (Continued)

Year	Picture	Director	Actor	Actress	Supporting Actor	Supporting Actress
1986	*Platoon*	Oliver Stone	Paul Newman (*The Color of Money*)	Marlee Matlin (*Children of a Lesser God*)	Michael Caine (*Hannah and Her Sisters*)	Dianne Wiest (*Hannah and Her Sisters*)
1987	*The Last Emperor*	Bernardo Bertolucci	Michael Douglas (*Wall Street*)	Cher (*Moonstruck*)	Sean Connery (*The Untouchables*)	Olympia Dukakis (*Moonstruck*)
1988	*Rain Man*	Barry Levinson	Dustin Hoffman (*Rain Man*)	Jodie Foster (*The Accused*)	Kevin Kline (*A Fish Called Wanda*)	Geena Davis (*The Accidental Tourist*)

Table 2: *The Nationality of the Oscar Players (Given as a percentage)*

| | Winners | | | | | Losers | | | | | |
Nationality	Best Actors	Best Actresses	Supporting Actors	Supporting Actresses	All Winners	Best Actors	Best Actresses	Supporting Actors	Supporting Actresses	All Losers	All Players
American	70.2	79.6	72.0	85.4	76.4	66.7	71.6	81.7	79.5	76.2	76.3
British	22.8	15.9	18.0	8.3	16.6	26.2	15.9	10.6	14.4	15.7	16.0
Foreign	7.0	4.5	10.0	6.3	7.0	7.1	12.5	7.7	6.1	8.1	7.7
Total	100.0	100.0	100.0	100.0	100.0	100.0	100.0	100.0	100.0	100.0	100.0
	(57)	(44)	(50)	(48)	(199)	(84)	(88)	(142)	(132)	(446)	(645)

Table 3: *Best Picture Nominees by Genre (Given as a percentage)*

Genre	Nominees	Winners	All
Drama	46.1	41.0	45.2
Comedy	18.3	13.1	17.4
Historical	10.5	14.8	11.2
Musical	8.5	13.1	9.3
Action-Adventure	6.5	4.9	6.3
War	4.2	9.9	5.2
Suspense	3.6	1.6	3.2
Western	2.3	1.6	2.2
Total	100.0	100.0	100.0
	(306)	(61)	(367)

Table 4: *The Oscar-Winning Films by Number of Nominations and Commercial Appeal*

Year	Film	Nominations	Awards	Domestic Rentals*
1927/8	Wings	2	2	†
1928/9	Broadway Melody	3	1	3.00
1929/30	All Quiet On The Western Front	4	2	1.50
1930/1	Cimarron	6	3	2.00
1931/2	Grand Hotel	1	1	2.20
1932/3	Cavalcade	4	3	3.50
1934	It Happened One Night	5	5	†
1935	Mutiny on the Bounty	7	1	†
1936	The Great Ziegfeld	7	3	†
1937	The Life of Emil Zola	10	3	†
1938	You Can't Take It With You	7	2	†
1939	Gone with the Wind	11	8	76.70
1940	Rebecca	10	2	1.50
1941	How Green Was My Valley	10	5	2.80
1942	Mrs. Miniver	12	6	5.50
1943	Casablanca	8	3	3.70
1944	Going My Way	9	7	6.50
1945	The Lost Weekend	6	4	4.30
1946	Best Years of Our Lives	9	7	11.30
1947	A Gentleman's Agreement	8	3	3.90
1948	Hamlet	7	4	3.25
1949	All the King's Men	7	4	2.40

* in millions of dollars
† no data

Table 4 (Continued)

Year	Film	Nominations	Awards	Domestic Rentals
1950	All About Eve	14	6	2.90
1951	An American in Paris	8	6	4.50
1952	The Greatest Show on Earth	5	2	14.00
1953	From Here To Eternity	13	8	12.20
1954	On the Waterfront	11	8	4.50
1955	Marty	8	4	2.00
1956	Around the World in 80 Days	8	5	23.12
1957	The Bridge on the River Kwai	8	7	17.19
1958	Gigi	9	9	7.30
1959	Ben Hur	12	11	36.65
1960	The Apartment	10	5	6.65
1961	West Side Story	11	10	19.45
1962	Lawrence of Arabia	10	7	16.70
1963	Tom Jones	10	4	16.95
1964	My Fair Lady	12	8	12.00
1965	The Sound of Music	10	5	79.75
1966	A Man For All Seasons	8	6	12.75
1967	In the Heat of the Night	7	5	10.91
1968	Oliver!	11	6	16.80
1969	Midnight Cowboy	7	3	20.32
1970	Patton	10	7	28.10
1971	The French Connection	8	5	26.31
1972	The Godfather	10	3	86.27
1973	The Sting	10	7	78.20
1974	The Godfather, Part Two	11	6	30.67
1975	One Flew Over the Cuckoo's Nest	9	5	59.24
1976	Rocky	10	3	55.92
1977	Annie Hall	5	4	18.09
1978	The Deer Hunter	9	5	27.53
1979	Kramer vs. Kramer	9	5	60.00
1980	Ordinary People	6	4	23.12
1981	Chariots of Fire	7	4	30.60
1982	Gandhi	11	8	24.75
1983	Terms of Endearment	11	5	50.25
1984	Amadeus	11	8	22.82
1985	Out of Africa	11	7	43.10
1986	Platoon	8	4	69.74
1987	The Last Emperor	9	9	18.82
1988	Rain Man	8	4	43.60*

*(still running)

Table 5: *The Most Nominated Films, 1927–1989*

10 nominations: 27 movies

Year	Film	Nom.	A.W.
1937	*The Life of Emil Zola*	10	3
1939	*Mr. Smith Goes to Washington*	10	1
1940	*Rebecca*	10	2
1941	*How Green Was My Valley*	10	5
1943	*The Song of Bernadette*	10	4
1953	*Roman Holiday*	10	3
1956	*Giant*	10	1
1957	*Sayonara*	10	4
1960	*The Apartment*	10	5
1962	*Lawrence of Arabia*	10	7
1963	*Tom Jones*	10	4
1965	*Dr. Zhivago*	10	5
	The Sound of Music	10	5
1967	*Bonnie and Clyde*	10	2
	Guess Who's Coming to Dinner?	10	2
1969	*Anne of the Thousand Days*	10	1
1970	*Airport*	10	1
	Patton	10	7
1972	*Cabaret*	10	8
	The Godfather	10	3
1973	*The Exorcist*	10	2
	The Sting	10	7
1976	*Network*	10	4
	Rocky	10	3
1978	*Heaven Can Wait*	10	1
1981	*On Golden Pond*	10	3
1982	*Tootsie*	10	1

11 nominations: 18 movies

1939	*Gone with the Wind*	11	8
1941	*Sergeant York*	11	2
1942	*The Pride of the Yankees*	11	1
1950	*Sunset Boulevard*	11	3
1954	*On the Waterfront*	11	8
1961	*West Side Story*	11	10
1968	*Oliver!*	11	5
1974	*Chinatown*	11	1
	The Godfather, Part Two	11	6
1977	*Julia*	11	3
	Star Wars	11	7
	The Turning Point	11	0

Table 5 (Continued)

Year	Film	Nom.	A.W.
1982	*Gandhi*	11	8
1983	*Terms of Endearment*	11	5
1984	*Amadeus*	11	8
	A Passage to India	11	2
1985	*The Color Purple*	11	0
	Out of Africa	11	7

12 nominations: 6 movies

1942	*Mrs. Miniver*	12	6
1948	*Johnny Belinda*	12	1
1951	*A Streetcar Named Desire*	12	4
1959	*Ben-Hur*	12	11
1964	*My Fair Lady*	12	8
1981	*Reds*	12	3

13 nominations: 3 movies

1953	*From Here to Eternity*	13	8
1961	*Judgment at Nuremberg*	13	2
1964	*Mary Poppins*	13	5

14 nominations: 1 movie

1950	*All About Eve*	14	6

Notes

The notes indicate the author's name and year of publication if more than one work by that author is listed in the Selected Bibliography. For complete information of the notes' sources, see Selected Bibliography, p. 367.

Introduction

1. *New York Times*, April 17, 1983.
2. There have been several books on the Oscar Award, but none has addressed itself to the important concerns of this book. There have been pictorial books, such as Paul Michael's *The Academy Awards: A Pictoral History*, or the Associated Press's *Oscar: A Pictoral History of the Academy Awards*. Others have been brief historical accounts, such as Robert Osborne's *50 Golden Years of Oscar*, or Natalie Fredrick's *Hollywood and the Academy Awards*. There have also been reference books or statistical compilations, such as Richard Shale's *Academy Awards: An Ungar Reference Index*.
3. In the entire Academy history, only 608 players have been nominated in the four acting categories: 137 Best Actor, 129 Best Actress, 171 Supporting Actor, and 171 Supporting Actress nominees. In the analysis of careers, players nominated for both lead and supporting awards are counted once, as lead nominees. And players nominated in one category but winning in another, are also counted once, in the category in which they won. For example, Shelley Winters, nominated for a lead award, but winning two supporting Oscars, is included among the supporting actresses. And Meryl Streep, winning both lead and supporting awards, is included in the analysis of lead actresses.

Chapter One
The Academy and the Oscar Awards

1. This discussion draws on Shale, pp. 6-8.
2. Ibid., p. 6.

3. *Los Angeles Times*, September 30, 1932.
4. Ceplair and Englund, p. 18.
5. William B. DeMille, Academy Bulletin, May 1929.
6. Academy Bulletin, July-August 1930.
7. Academy Bulletin, June 1931.
8. *New York Herald Tribune*, October 9, 1933.
9. Capra, p. 187.
10. W.S. Van Dyke, chairman of the Academy's Reorganization Committee, quoted in Shale, p. 13.
11. Canby, *New York Times*, March 28, 1982.
12. Academy By-laws, 1943. The information and quotations about the procedures are taken from annual publications of the Academy's By-laws.
13. Class A were senior members of SAG, class B were junior members.
14. *American Cinematographer*, May 1977.
15. Some award categories, like Makeup, can consist of less than five nominees if there are not enough worthy achievements, but the vast majority contain five.
16. *McCalls'*, April 1962.
17. Academy Bulletin, May 1929.
18. Quoted in *New York Times*, March 28, 1982.
19. Academy Newsletter, 1940.
20. Academy Bulletin, 1929.
21. Academy Bulletin, 1935.
22. Ibid.
23. Academy Newsletter, 1943.
24. *New York Times*, March 30, 1949.
25. *New York Times*, March 31, 1949.
26. Ibid., April 1, 1949.
27. Ibid., April 3, 1949.
28. Ibid., April 1, 1949.
29. *Saturday Review*, April 16, 1949.
30. *New York Herald Tribune*, March 26, 1949.
31. *The Hollywood Reporter*, March 31, 1955.
32. Steinberg, pp. 176-7.
33. *New York Times*, April 15, 1984.
34. Ibid.
35. Michael Real in Mosco and Wasco, p. 171.
36. *New York Times*, April 11, 1984.

Chapter Two
The Preeminence of the Oscar

1. The following discussion is based on data in Steinberg (1980a) on various film awards.

2. *New York Times*, September 19, 1982.
3. Vincent Canby, *New York Times*, September 22, 1985.
4. *Village Voice*, February 25, 1986.
5. *New York Times*, March 29, 1981.
6. Linet (1980), p. 228.
7. *New York Times*, March 29, 1981.
8. Aljean Harmetz, *New York Times*, April 8, 1984.
9. Mel Gussow, *New York Times*, May 29, 1983.
10. Stephen Holden, *New York Times*, February 20, 1982.
11. *Variety*, October 1, 1980.

Chapter Three
The Nomination System

1. Because there is wide distribution of ages among the winners, the median age is a better and more accurate statistical measure than the average age. The median age points the age at which half of the group received their first nomination.
2. Katz, p. 1123.
3. *New York Times*, March 29, 1957.
4. *Variety*, October 23, 1957.
5. Faulkner (1979), p. 276.
6. *Current Biography*, September 1975.

Chapter Four
The Oscar as International Award

1. Academy Bulletin, 1929.
2. Ibid.
3. See Table 3 for the nationalities of the nominated players.
4. Ibid.
5. *Los Angeles Examiner*, March 9, 1940.
6. *New York Times*, April 30, 1948.
7. Tony Awards Show, June 3, 1982.
8. Michael Reeves, *On Cable*, December 1982.
9. See Jarvie (1978) for a discussion of the decline of provincialism in American culture and the demographic changes of the movie-going public in the 1960s.
10. Emanuel Levy, "Popular Taste in the American Cinema." Paper presented at the annual meetings of the American Sociological Association, New York, August 1986.
11. *The Hollywood Reporter*, April 1965.
12. *New York Times*, March 4, 1984.
13. Walker, p. 3.

Chapter Five
The Winning Process

1. Garson Kanin in Peary, p. 114.
2. Herbert Ross in Peary, p. 88.
3. McCambridge, p. 133.
4. Bergman and Burgess, p. 398.
5. Ibid., p. 399.
6. Hotchner (1979), p. 144.
7. Faulkner (1979), p. 250.
8. Ibid., p. 273.
9. Stanley Kramer in Peary, p. 517.
10. These statistics are based on a 1983 survey, *Cable Guide*, March 5, 1984.
11. Each of these romantic teams made several movies together; those mentioned in brackets are examples of their best-known collaborations.
12. Levy, Emanuel, "The Democratic Elite: America's Movie Stars," *Qualitative Sociology*, October 1987.
13. *Current Biography*, December 1966.
14. Rex Reed, *New York Times*, October 16, 1966.
15. Fontaine, p. 146.

Chapter Six
The Oscar-Winning Films

1. The 352 films consist of 58 Oscar-winning and 294 Oscar-nominated pictures. Comparison between these two groups demonstrates to what extent the winning films have been similar or different from those nominated.
2. The genre of biopictures is used here in its broadest sense to include all films inspired by real-life individuals or events, regardless of their historical accuracy or specific artistic form.
3. Other notable biopictures made by Warners, not nominated for Oscars, included *Alexander Hamilton* (1931), *Voltaire* (1933), and *Juarez* (1939).
4. Jacobs, p. 527.
5. Each of the 352 Oscar-nominated films is classified according to its dominant genre, though in actuality many films are hybrids and cross several genres. See Table 3 for the genre of all winning and nominated films.
6. The two other Oscar-winning pictures that received only one award are: *The Broadway Melody* and *Mutiny on the Bounty*. See Table 4 for the number of nominations and awards of each winning film.

7. The domestic rentals are based on *Variety*'s annual tabulations, in which films are ranked according to rentals paid to their distributors in the United States and Canada. They do not include rentals in foreign movie markets and should not be confused with the films' box-office receipts.

8. The number of male and female winning roles is not identical because in the first year Janet Gaynor won for three different roles and Emil Jannings for two, and there has been two ties in each category. The unit of analysis here is not the performer, but the Oscar-winning role.

9. Otis Ferguson, "The Life of Emil Zola," *New Republic*, August 18, 1937.

10. Howard Barnes, *The New York Herald Tribune*, November 12, 1947.

11. The third and last black player to win an Oscar was Louis Gossett Jr., as supporting actor in *An Officer and a Gentleman* in 1982. The number of black players nominated for acting awards has also been very small: 19 (3 percent) out of the 608 nominees.

12. From 1932 to the present, only three black players have appeared on the Motion Picture Herald Poll, which ranks the 10 box-office stars of the year. They were: Sidney Poitier in 1968, Richard Pryor in 1982, and Eddie Murphy in 1983.

13. *The Nation*, December 14, 1946.

14. *New York Times*, April 4, 1954.

15. See Biskind for an interesting ideological reading of this film along these lines.

16. *The New York Times*, December 3, 1945.

17. Ibid., November 20, 1975.

18. Ibid., October 29, 1941.

19. Dwight MacDonald, quoted in Halliwell, p. 48.

20. *The Saturday Review*, June 11, 1960.

21. *The Apartment* grossed in domestic rentals about 6.6 million dollars and was the least commercially successful of the Oscar-winning films in the 1960s. See discussion in Chapter Eleven.

22. *People*, March 26, 1984.

Chapter Seven
The Oscar-Winning Films: Other Genres

1. Fox's musical, *Sunny Side Up*, starring Janet Gaynor and Charles Farrell, was the most popular film in 1929.

2. Gable, quoted in *Current Biography*, May 1945.

3. Butler, p. 173.

4. *Newsweek*, August 31, 1942.

5. *The New York Times*, September 2, 1942.

6. Butler, p. 217.

7. Monaco (1979), pp. 105, 147-8.

8. *The New York Times*, March 6, 1970.

9. Several films have been hybrids, borrowing elements from the mystery-suspense, but were not typical genre movies. For example, *The Thin Man* is classified here as a comedy rather than a mystery, and Billy Wilder's *Witness for the Prosecution* and Otto Preminger's *Anatomy of a Murder* are described as courtroom dramas rather than murder mysteries.

10. Quoted in Libby, p. 176.

11. They included: Walter Huston and Maria Ouspenskaya in *Dodsworth*; Laurence Olivier and Geraldine Fitzgerald in *Wuthering Heights*; Bette Davis and James Stephenson in *The Letter*; Bette Davis, Patricia Collinge, and Teresa Wright in *The Little Foxes*; Eleanor Parker and Lee Grant in *Detective Story*; Anthony Perkins in *Friendly Persuasion*; Fay Bainter in *The Children's Hour*; and Samantha Eggar in *The Collector*.

12. Katz, p. 1251.

13. *The New York Times*, September 20, 1986.

14. Dialogue on Film, *American Film*, January-February 1986.

15. Oscar Barnes's interview with Zinnemann, *The New York Times*, August 9, 1964.

16. Dialogue on Film, ibid., 1986.

17. Spotto, pp. 20, 22.

18. *American Film*, October 1986.

Chapter Eight
The Oscar-Winning Roles

1. This chapter is based on the analysis of 221 Oscar-winning roles in the four acting categories, consisting of: 60 Best Actor, 61 Best Actress, 50 Supporting Actor, and 50 Supporting Actress roles. The categories are not equal because lead roles were given from the first year, but supporting from 1936 on, and there have been two ties in each of the lead categories. Moreover, in the first year, Emil Jannings won for two roles and Janet Gaynor for three. The unit of analysis is the *role*, not the performer.

2. Most studies have examined the portrayal of women in television (Tuchman, et al.). The few books on the depiction of women in film (Haskell; Mellen, 1977) have provided excellent insights, but were not very systematic in their research methods and not very methodic in their selection of films. This examination avoids the problem of

selective data by examining the *entire* population, not a sample, of Oscar roles.

3. See Gans, and also Maltby, for a discussion of the relationship, real and imagined, between filmmakers and their audiences.

4. The age of all screen characters was divided into four subcategories: adolescent (less than 18 years of age), young (from 19 to 35), middle-aged (from 36 to 55), and old (more than 56).

5. For example, 21 percent of the Supporting Actor, but only 12 percent of the Best Actor roles, have been young.

6. Mellen (1977), pp. 71-85.

7. *Time*, January 27, 1975.

8. Katz, p. 142.

9. *New York Times*, May 30, 1942.

10. Sarris, *Village Voice*, August 21, 1969.

11. Haskell, p. 18.

12. Ibid., p. 243.

13. Levy shows that half of American movie stars have not completed high school education.

14. Interview with Sidney Skolsky, *New York Post*, July 10, 1960.

15. See Schur for an explanation of this theory.

16. Monaco (1979), p. 289.

17. Klapp (1963), p. 11.

18. Tuchman, p. 5.

19. Haskell (1974), p. 160; Rose in Pirie (1981), p. 232.

20. The notion of culture lag is based on sociologist Ogburn's theory of social change (1922), which distinguishes between material and non-material culture. Ogburn claimed that because technological innovations are more rapidly accepted than new ideas or values, there is usually a culture lag during which the nonmaterial elements lag behind the material ones.

21. For example, in 1973, women constituted 51 percent of the population and about 40 percent of the labor force, but only 26 percent of the characters portrayed on television were female (Tuchman et al., pp. 7, 10). Various studies have found that prime-time television programs have contained more men than women, and men have been shown as dominant, competent, and authoritative, and in diverse occupational roles. Women, by contrast, have been shown in limited number of occupations and depicted as less competent and less authoritative (Gornick and Morgan, 1973; Miles, 1975).

22. Studies dealing with the portrayal of gender on television have documented that males have outnumbered females in every type of program. Because of its research design, examining four award categories, with equal number of male and female roles, this study does

not deal with the paucity of women's roles in American film, a fact which has been documented by Monaco (1979, pp. 91-8) and others.

Chapter Nine
The Oscar as a Reward System

1. *New York Times*, March 29, 1981.
2. Quoted in Hotchner (1976), p. 183.
3. Diane Waldman in Peary, p. 301.
4. Bergman and Burgess, p. 405.
5. Winters, p. 364.
6. Ibid., pp. 308-9.
7. Vermilye and Ricci (1976), p. 28.
8. Hirsch, p. 113.
9. Quoted in Stevenson, p. 63.
10. Smith, p. 102.
11. Windeler (1974), p. 289.

Chapter Ten
The Meanings of the Oscar Award

1. Stevenson, p. 63.
2. Quoted in Shale, p. vii.
3. Academy Bulletin, May 16, 1929.
4. Ibid.
5. Academy Bulletin, August 11, 1930.
6. *People*, March 26, 1979.
7. *The Courier-Journal and Times*, Louisville, Kentucky, February 18, 1973.
8. *New York Post*, September 1, 1973.
9. Milland, p. 221.
10. Ibid., p. 222.
11. Ibid., p. 225.
12. Ibid., p. 223.
13. Ibid., p. 225.
14. Cagney, p. 107.
15. McCambridge, p. 134.
16. Stevenson, p. 63.
17. Annette Insdorf, *New York Times*, September 19, 1982.
18. Ibid.
19. Hotchner (1979), p. 147.
20. Ibid., p. 155.
21. *New York Times*, September 18, 1983.

22. Faulkner (1979), p. 73.
23. *New York Daily News*, August 30, 1982.
24. Linet, p. 106.
25. Ibid., p. 230.
26. *New York Times*, April 1, 1984.
27. *New York Times*, April 26, 1970.
28. Heston, p. 91.
29. *New York Times*, March 26, 1985.
30. Winters, p. 376.
31. Ibid., p. 271.
32. Fontaine, p. 147.
33. Milland, p. 227.
34. McCambridge, p. 134.
35. Ustinov, p. 327.
36. Bacall, p. 196.
37. Hyams, p. 156.
38. Benchley, p. 199.
39. *New York Times*, March 21, 1952.
40. Benchley, p. 199.
41. Bacall, p. 196.
42. Cottrell, p. 134.
43. Tomkies (1971), p. 118.
44. Ibid.
45. Haddad-Garcia, p. 151.
46. Ibid., p. 52.
47. Quoted in Capra, p. 188.
48. *Time*, March 8, 1971.
49. *Variety*, March 3, 1971.
50. *New York Daily News*, "Parade," October 27, 1985.
51. Pickard (1979), p. 122.
52. *New York Daily News*, April 16, 1971.
53. Essoe, p. 39.
54. Brode, p. 218.
55. Higham, pp. 50-51.
56. Schildkraut, p. 215.
57. Ibid., p. 216.
58. Thomas, pp. 3-4.
59. Ibid., p. 5.
60. Ibid., p. 6.
61. Bergman and Burgess, p. 422.
62. Hotchner (1979), p. 151.
63. Ibid.
64. Milland, p. 226.
65. Ibid., p. 227.

66. *New York Times*, April 26, 1970.
67. Fontaine, pp. 145-6.
68. Ibid., p. 146.
69. Broderick Crawford File, AMPAS Library.
70. Signoret, p. 253.
71. Ibid., p. 263.
72. McCambridge, p. 134.
73. Heston, p. 91.
74. Freedland (1980), p. 177.
75. Poitier, pp. 252-3.
76. Ibid., p. 253.
77. Mills, p. 263.
78. Ibid., p. 264.
79. *American Cinematographer*, May 1977.
80. Janet Gaynor File, AMPAS Library.
81. *The Providence Sunday Journal*, September 27, 1968.
82. Harrison, pp. 217-8.
83. *The Hollywood Reporter*, April 8, 1959.
84. McCambridge, pp. 133-4.
85. Bergman and Burgess, p. 543.
86. Tierney and Herskowitz, p. 140.
87. Fontaine, pp. 130-1.
88. Russell and Chase, p. 142.
89. Ibid., p. 160.
90. Swanson, pp. 488-9.
91. Winters, pp. 372-3.
92. Capra, p. 153.
93. Ibid., p. 154.
94. Frank, p. 388.
95. Ibid., p. 389.
96. Ibid., p. 395.
97. Linet, p. 205.
98. *The Sunday News*, October 1, 1972.
99. Walker, p. 214.
100. Ibid., p. 248.
101. Kelley, p. 273.
102. Ibid., p. 259.
103. Ibid., p. 260.

Chapter Eleven
The Multiple Effects of the Oscar

1. For a theoretical formulation of cumulative advantage in science, see Cole and Cole (1973), Merton (1973), Zuckerman (1977). The

theory has been mostly applied to science, but not to other social institutions.

2. The figures are based on *Variety*'s annual compilations of box-office champion movies in terms of rentals paid to their distributors in the U.S. and Canada. These figures include the rentals of a film up to date, but they don't take into account the inflation factor. Thus, the rentals of *The Best Years of Our Lives*, 11 million dollars, are equivalent of at least 80 million at present.

3. Craig Pettigrew, *Box Office*, March 3, 1980.

4. *Reds*'s domestic rentals were 21 million dollars, but its budget is estimated at over 35 million dollars. A movie is considered profitable if its domestic rentals are twice as much as its costs. For a description of *Reds*'s performance, see Harmetz, *New York Times*, March 28, 1982.

5. Aljean Harmetz, *New York Times*, March 13, 1983.

6. Marcia Chambers, *New York Times*, March 25, 1986.

7. Sally Bedell Smith, *New York Times*, February 8, 1984.

8. McCambridge, p. 134.

9. Robert Lindsay, *New York Times*, March 28, 1982.

10. Capra, p. 144.

11. Fontaine, p. 146.

12. McCambridge, p. 134.

13. Ibid., p. 135.

14. *Playboy*, May 1971.

15. Ibid.

16. Heston, p. 92.

17. Burns, p. 178.

18. *On Cable*, December 1982.

19. Milland, p. 225.

20. McCambridge, p. 134.

21. About one-fifth of male and female Oscar winners have also received a Tony Award, but twice as many actresses (18 percent) as actors (9 percent) have been nominated for a Tony.

22. Zec, p. 21.

23. *New York Post*, November 1939, Luise Rainer File, New York Public Library.

24. *Newsweek*, April 15, 1963.

25. Vermilye, p. 9

26. John Russell Taylor, Review of *Once Upon a Time in America*, *The London Times*, quoted in Springer (1970), p. 261.

27. Pickford, pp. 151-2.

28. *Current Biography*, June 1941.

29. *New York Times*, Sunday Magazine, July 12, 1981.

30. Interview with Linda Gross in Peary, p. 397.

31. Ibid., p. 400.

32. Swanson, p. 489.
33. *Current Biography*, April 1981.
34. *Current Biography*, October 1978.
35. Steven Grant in Peary, pp. 348-50.
36. *Current Biography*, December 1955.
37. Michael Ritchie in Peary, p. 365.
38. *Current Biography*, July 1972.
39. Katz, p. 789.
40. Fontaine, p. 146.
41. McCambridge, p. 134.
42. Hyams, p. 157.
43. *On Cable*, December 1982.
44. Fontaine, p. 132.
45. Capra, p. 172.

Chapter Twelve
Politics and the Oscar Award

1. Academy Bulletin, September 1930.
2. Ibid.
3. Quoted in Leslie Raddatz, *TV Guide*, April 8, 1972.
4. *Hollywood Reporter*, March 31, 1951.
5. Capra, p. 116.
6. Ibid., p. 117.
7. This count is based on the producing studio, not the distribution company. Thus, independent producer Goldwyn made *The Best Years of Our Lives*, but it was released through RKO, and Selznick's *Gone with the Wind* and *Rebecca* were distributed by MGM and United Artists respectively. *Hamlet* was produced by the Rank studio and distributed in America by Universal-International.
8. Thomas (1978), p. 138.
9. Ibid., pp. 138-9.
10. Sheila Graham, *New York World-Telegram and Sun*, April 16, 1966.
11. Dick Kleiner, *New York World-Telegram and Sun*, February 18, 1965.
12. Joe Hyams, *New York Herald Tribune*, February 26, 1961.
13. *Newsweek*, October 31, 1960.
14. Quoted in Essoe (1981), p. 35.
15. *Los Angeles Times*, March 30, 1961.
16. *Los Angeles Mirror*, March 7, 1961.
17. *Daily Variety*, March 21, 1961.
18. *The Hollywood Reporter*, April 10, 1962.
19. Booklet sent to Academy members concerning advertisement, 1961, Academy Awards File, AMPAS Library.

20. Murray Schumach, *New York Times*, December 4, 1961.
21. *New York Times*, April 14, 1969.
22. Harmetz, *New York Times*, March 28, 1982.
23. Ibid., April 8, 1984.
24. Ibid., March 18, 1986.
25. Ibid., April 8, 1984.
26. Ibid.
27. Ibid., March 18, 1986.
28. Jowett, pp. 317-18.
29. Jones and McClure, p. 15.
30. McGilligan, p. 159.
31. *New York Times*, March 30, 1952.
32. The Swedish critics Gunnar Oldin and Harry Schein are quoted in French, p. 35.
33. Ibid., p. 34.
34. Quoted in Nachbar, p. 27.
35. *Playboy*, May 1971.
36. *New York Times*, March 13, 1983.
37. Ibid., April 17, 1983.
38. Jewell, pp. 140-41.
39. Quoted in Sally Ogle Davis, "Battling It Out in Hollywood," *New York Times*, Sunday magazine, April 25, 1982.
40. *Daily News*, February 7, 1977.
41. Ibid.
42. Signoret, p. 253.
43. Ibid., p. 255.
44. Ibid., p. 257.
45. Mercouri, pp. 129-31.
46. *New York Times*, March 29, 1957.
47. Ceplair and Englund, pp. 418-19.
48. Haddad-Garcia, p. 62.
49. Ibid., p. 67.
50. Ibid., p. 68.
51. Chaplin, p. 449.
52. Manvell, p. 34.
53. Thomas (1973), p. 246.
54. *Films in Review*, April 1977.
55. Quoted in *New York Times*, February 1, 1978.
56. *New York Herald Tribune*, April 5, 1978.
57. Richard F. Shepard, *New York Times*, August 8, 1979.
58. *Village Voice*, February 25, 1986.
59. *Current Biography*, January 1981.
60. Edmunds and Mimura, p. 242.

61. *Current Biography*, January 1981.
62. Cinemas of foreign countries are probably more explicitly and directly political than their American counterpart. But the nomination of political films also has to do with the regulations of this particular category. Films are sent for consideration by the equivalent academies of foreign countries, and are then narrowed down to five by a committee. Members are required to prove that they have seen all five nominees before voting, which means that a very small part of the electorate participates in the selection of foreign films.

Conclusion

1. Vincent Canby, *The New York Times*, March 4, 1984.
2. Anthony Carthew, *Daily Herald*, quoted in Garrett (1975), p. 151.
3. Clifford A. Ridley, *National Observer*, October 27, 1969.
4. *Variety*, July 15, 1981.
5. *New Yorker*, December 9, 1974.
6. *New York*, October 1, 1984.
7. *Time*, September 12, 1983.
8. *Village Voice*, October 29, 1985.
9. *New York Times*, March 5, 1966.
10. Parish and Pitts, p. 275.
11. Quoted in Leonard Lyons, *New York Post*, April 12, 1969.
12. *American Cinematography*, May 1977.
13. *American Film*, July-August 1986.
14. Signoret, p. 253.
15. *Current Biography*, October 1977.
16. Ibid., June 1966.
17. Arce, p. 134.
18. *New York Times*, Sunday magazine, July 12, 1981.
19. Acceptance speech, Oscar ceremonies, March 2, 1986.
20. Thomas (1973), p. 24.
21. *Current Biography*, April 1941.
22. Essoe (1970), p. 39.
23. Williams, p. 480.
24. Slater, p. 6.

Selected Bibliography

Adams, John G. *Without Precedent: The Story of the Death of McCarthyism.* N.Y.: Norton, 1983.

Aherne, Brian. *A Proper Job.* Boston: Houghton Mifflin Co., 1969.

Arce, Hector. *Gary Cooper: An Intimate Biography.* N.Y.: Morrow, 1979.

Arden, Eve. *Three Faces of Eve.* N.Y.: St. Martin's, 1985.

Astor, Mary. *A Life on Film.* N.Y.: Delacorte, 1971.

Austin, Bruce. *The Film Audience.* Metuchen, N.J.: Scarecrow, 1973.

Bacall, Lauren. *Lauren Bacall by Myself.* N.Y.: Knopf, 1979.

Baker, Carroll. *Baby Doll.* N.Y.: Arbor House, 1983.

Barrymore, Ethel. *Memories.* N.Y.: Harper, 1955.

Baxter, Anne. *Intermission.* N.Y.: Putnam's, 1976.

Becker, Howard S. *Art Worlds.* Berkeley: University of California Press, 1982.

Benchley, Nathaniel. *Humphrey Bogart.* Boston: Little, Brown, 1975.

Bergman, Andrew. *We're in the Money: Depression America and Its Movies.* N.Y.: New York University Press, 1971.

Bergman, Ingrid and Alan Burgess. *Ingrid Bergman: My Story.* N.Y.: Delacorte, 1980.

Biskind, Peter. *Seeing Is Believing.* N.Y.: Pantheon, 1983.

Bogdanovich, Peter. *Pieces of Time.* N.Y.: Arbor House, 1973.

Bosworth, Patricia. *Montgomery Clift.* N.Y.: Harcourt Brace Jovanovich, 1978.

Braun, Eric. *Deborah Kerr.* London: W.H. Allen, 1977.

Brode, Douglas. *The Films of Dustin Hoffman.* Secaucus, N.J.: Citadel, 1983.

Burns, George. *The Third Time Around.* N.Y.: Putnam, 1980.

Butler, Ivan. *Cinema in Britain.* Cranbury, N.J.: A. S. Barnes, 1973.

Cagney, James. *Cagney by Cagney.* N.Y.: Doubleday, 1976.

Capra, Frank. *The Name Above the Title.* N.Y.: Macmillan, 1971.

Carey, Gary. *All the Stars in Heaven.* N.Y.: Dutton, 1981.

Ceplair, Larry and Steven Englund. *The Inquisition in Hollywood.* N.Y.: Doubleday, 1980.

Chaplin, Charles. *My Autobiography*. N.Y.: Simon and Schuster, 1964.

Cole, Jonathan and Stephen Cole. *Social Stratification in Science*. Chicago: University of Chicago Press, 1973.

Cole, Lester. *Hollywood Red: The Autobiography of Lester Cole*. Palo Alto, California: Ramparts, 1981.

Colman, Juliet Benita. *Ronald Colman*. N.Y.: Morrow, 1975.

Cooper, Jackie. *Please Don't Shoot My Dog: The Autobiography of Jackie Cooper*. N.Y.: Morrow, 1981.

Cottrell, John and Fergus Cashin. *Richard Burton: Very Close Up*. Englewood Cliffs, N.J.: Prentice-Hall, 1972.

Crowther, Bosley. *Hollywood Rajah: The Life and Times of Louis B. Mayer*. N.Y.: Holt, 1960.

Curtis, James. *Between Flops: A Biography of Preston Sturges*. N.Y.: Harcourt Brace Jovanovich, 1982.

De Mille, Cecil B. *Autobiography*. Englewood Cliffs, N.J.: Prentice-Hall, 1959.

Edwards, Anne. *Vivien Leigh*. N.Y.: Simon and Schuster, 1977.

Edmunds, I.G. and Reiko Mimura. *The Oscar Directors*. London: Tantivy, 1980.

Essoe, Gabe. *The Films of Clark Gable*. Secaucus, N.J.: Citadel, 1970.

──────. *The Book of Movie Lists*. Westport, Connecticut: Arlington, 1981.

Faulkner, Robert. *Hollywood Studio Musicians*. Chicago: Aldine, 1970.

Faulkner, Trader. *Peter Finch: A Biography*. London: Angus and Robertson, 1979.

Finch, Christopher. *Rainbow: The Stormy Life of Judy Garland*. N.Y.: Ballantine, 1975.

Fontaine, Joan. *No Bed of Roses*. N.Y.: Morrow, 1978.

Frank, Gerold. *Judy*. N.Y.: Harper & Row, 1975.

Fredrick, Nathalie. *Hollywood and the Academy Awards*. L.A.: Award Publications, 1968.

Freedland, Michael. *Gregory Peck*. N.Y.: Morrow, 1980.

French, Brandon. *On the Verge of Revolt: Women in American Films of the Fifties*. N.Y.: Ungar, 1978.

French, Philip. *Westerns*. N.Y.: Viking, 1974.

Gans, Herbert. *Popular Culture and High Culture*. N.Y.: Basic Books, 1975.

Garrett, Gerald. *The Films of David Niven*. Secaucus, N.J.: Citadel, 1976.

Gordon, Ruth. *My Side*. N.Y.: Harper & Row, 1976.

Gornich, V. and B. Morgan. *Women in Sexist Society: Studies in Power and Powerlessness*. N.Y.: Basic Books, 1971.

Guinness, Alec. *Blessings in Disguise*. N.Y.: Knopf, 1986.

Gussow, Mel. *Don't Say Yes Until I Finish Talking: A Biography of Darryl F. Zanuck*. N.Y.: Doubleday.

Haddad-Garcia, George. *The Films of Jane Fonda*. Secaucus, N.J.: Citadel, 1981.

Halliwell, David. *Halliwell's Film Guide*. N.Y.: Scribner's, 1983.

Harrison, Rex. *Rex: An Autobiography*. N.Y.: Morrow, 1975.

Haskell, Molly. *From Reverence to Rape: The Treatment of Women in the Movies*. N.Y.: Holt, Rinehart and Winston, 1974.

Heston, Charlton. *The Actor's Life*. N.Y.: Dutton, 1978.

Higham, Charles. *Charles Laughton*. N.Y.: Doubleday, 1976.

Hirsch, Foster. *Elizabeth Taylor*. N.Y.: Galahad, 1973.

Hotchner, A.E. *Doris Day: Her Own Story*. N.Y.: Morrow, 1976.

————. *Sophia: Living and Loving*. N.Y.: Morrow, 1979.

Hyams, Joe. *Bogart and Bacall*. N.Y.: David McKay, 1975.

Jacobs, Lewis. *The Rise of the American Film*. N.Y.: Teachers College Press, 1968.

Jarvie, I. C. *Movies and Society*. N.Y.: Basic Books, 1971.

————. *Movies as Social Criticism*. Metuchen, N.J.: Scarecrow, 1978.

Jewell, Richard. *The RKO Story*. N.Y.: Arlington, 1982.

Jones, Ken and Arthur McClure. *Hollywood at War*. N.Y.: A. S. Barnes, 1973.

Jowett, Garth. *Film: The Democratic Art*. Boston: Little, Brown, 1976.

Katz, Ephraim. *The Film Encyclopedia*. N.Y.: Crowell, 1979.

Kelley, Kitty. *Elizabeth Taylor: The Last Star*. N.Y.: Simon and Schuster, 1981.

Klapp, Orrin. *Heroes, Villains, and Fools*. Englewood Cliffs, N.J.: Prentice-Hall, 1963.

————. *Symbolic Leaders*. Chicago: Aldine, 1964.

Koch, Howard. *As Time Goes By*. N.Y.: Harcourt Brace and Jovanovich, 1978.

Larkin, Rochelle. *Hail Columbia*. N.Y.: Arlington, 1975.

Levy, Emanuel. *John Wayne: Prophet of the American Way of Life*. Metuchen, N.J.: Scarecrow, 1987.

Libby, Bill. *They Didn't Win the Oscars*. Westport, Connecticut: Arlington, 1980.

Linet, Beverly. *Susan Hayward*. N.Y.: Atheneum, 1980.

McCambridge, Mercedes. *The Quality of Mercy*. N.Y.: Times Books, 1981.

McCarthy, Clifford. *Bogey: The Films of Humphrey Bogart*. Secaucus, N.J.: Citadel, 1965.

McGilligan, Patrick. *Cagney: The Actor as Auteur*. N.Y.: Barnes, 1975.

Maltby, Richard. *Harmless Entertainment*. Metuchen, N.J.: Scarecrow, 1983.

Manvell, Roger. *Chaplin*. Boston: Little, Brown, 1974.

Mast, Gerald. *Howard Hawks, Storyteller*. N.Y.: Oxford University Press, 1982.

Mellen, Joan. *Women and their Sexuality in the New Film.* N.Y.: Horizon, 1973.

——. *Big Bad Wolves: Masculinity in the American Film.* N.Y.: Pantheon, 1977.

Mercouri, Melina. *I Was Born Greek.* N.Y.: Doubleday, 1971.

Merton, Robert K. *The Sociology of Science.* Chicago: University of Chicago Press, 1973.

Michael, Paul. *The Academy Awards: A Pictorial History.* Indianapolis: Bobbs-Merrill, 1964.

Miles, B. *Channeling Children: Sex Stereotyping on Prime Time TV.* Princeton, N.J.: Women on Words and Images, 1975.

Milland, Ray. *Wide-Eyed in Babylon.* N.Y.: Morrow, 1974.

Mills, John. *Up in the Clouds, Gentlemen Please.* N.Y.: Ticknor and Fields, 1981.

Monaco, James. *American Film Now.* N.Y.: New American Library, 1979.

Monaco, Paul. *Cinema and Society.* N.Y.: Elsevier, 1976.

Mosco, Vincent and Janet Wasko, ed. *Popular Culture and Media Events.* Norwood, N.J.: Ablex, 1985.

Nachbar, Jack, ed. *Focus on the Western.* Englewood Cliffs, N.J.: Prentice-Hall, 1974.

Osborne, Robert. *Fifty Golden Years of Oscar.* L.A.: ESE, 1979.

Parish, James R. and Michael R. Pitts. *Hollywood on Hollywood.* Metuchen, N.J.: Scarecrow, 1978.

Peary, Danny, ed. *Close-Up: The Movie Star Book.* N.Y.: Galahad, 1978.

Pickard, Roy. *Hollywood Gold.* N.Y.: Toplinger, 1979.

Pickford, Mary. *Sunshine and Shadow.* N.Y.: Doubleday, 1955.

Pirie, David. *Anatomy of the Movies.* N.Y.: Macmillan, 1981.

Poitier, Sidney. *This Life.* N.Y.: Knopf, 1980.

Robinson, David. *Chaplin: His Life and Art.* N.Y.: McGraw-Hill, 1985.

Rosen, Marjorie. *Popcorn Venus.* N.Y.: Coward, McCann, and Geoghegan, 1973.

Russell, Rosalind and Chris Chase. *Life Is Not a Banquet.* N.Y.: Random House, 1977.

Sarris, Andrew. *The American Cinema: Directors and Directions 1929-1968.* N.Y.: Dutton, 1968.

——. *The John Ford Movie Mystery.* Bloomington, Indiana: Indiana University Press, 1975.

——. *Politics and Cinema.* N.Y.: Columbia University Press, 1979.

Schary, Dore. *Heyday: An Autobiography.* Boston: Little, Brown, 1970.

Scherle, Victor and William Turner Levy. *The Films of Frank Capra.* Secaucus, N.J.: Citadel, 1977.

Schildkraut, Joseph. *My Father and I.* N.Y.: Viking, 1959.

Schur, Edwin. *Labeling Women Deviant.* Philadelphia: Temple University Press, 1984.

Shale, Richard. *Academy Awards*. N.Y.: Ungar, 1978.

Signoret, Simone. *Nostalgia Isn't What It Used to Be*. N.Y.: Harper & Row, 1978.

Slater, Philip E. *The Pursuit of Loneliness*. Boston: Beacon, 1970.

Smith, Henry Nash. *Virgin Land: The American West as Symbol and Myth*. N.Y.: Vintage, 1950.

Spotto, Donald. *Stanley Kramer Film Maker*. N.Y.: Putnam, 1978.

Springer, John. *The Fondas*. Secaucus, N.J.: Citadel, 1970.

Steinberg, Cobbett. *Reel Facts*. N.Y.: Facts on File, 1980.

———. *TV Facts*. N.Y.: Facts on File, 1980.

Stevenson, Isabelle, ed. *The Tony Award*. N.Y.: Crown, 1980.

Stine, Whitney. *Mother Goddam: The Story of the Career of Bette Davis*. N.Y.: Hawthorne, 1974.

Swanson, Gloria. *Swanson on Swanson*. N.Y.: Random House, 1980.

Thomas, Bob. *Joan Crawford*. N.Y.: Simon and Schuster, 1978.

Thomas, Tony. *The Films of Marlon Brando*. Secaucus, N.J.: Citadel, 1973.

Thompson, Charles. *Bing: An Authorized Biography*. N.Y.: David McKay, 1975.

Tierney, Gene and Mickey Herskowitz. *Self-Portrait*. N.Y.: Wyden, 1979.

Tomkies, Mike. *Duke: The Story of John Wayne*. Chicago: Henry Regnery, 1971.

Tornabene, Lyn. *Long Live the King*. N.Y.: Simon and Schuster, 1976.

Tuchman, Gaye, Arlene Kaplan Daniels, and James Benet, eds. *Hearth and Home: Images of Women in the Mass Media*. N.Y.: Free Press, 1978.

Ustinov, Peter. *Dear Me*. Boston: Little, Brown, 1977.

Vermilye, Jerry. *Cary Grant*. N.Y.: Galahad, 1973.

———, and Mark Ricci. *The Films of Elizabeth Taylor*. Secaucus, N.J.: Citadel, 1976.

Walker, Alexander. *Peter Sellers*. London: Weidenfeld and Nicholson, 1981.

Weiss, Elizabeth, ed. *The Movie Star*. N.Y.: Viking, 1981.

Williams, Robin M. *American Society*. N.Y.: Knopf, 1970.

Windeler, Robert. *Sweetheart: The Story of Mary Pickford*. Boston: G.K. Hall, 1974.

———. *Julie Andrews*. N.Y.: St. Martin's, 1983.

Winters, Shelley. *Shelley*. N.Y.: Morrow, 1980.

Zec, Donald and Anthony Fowles. *Barbra*. N.Y.: St. Martin's, 1981.

Zuckerman, Harriet. *Scientific Elite*. N.Y.: Free Press, 1977.

Index

Abe Lincoln in Illinois, 97, 101
Abraham, F. Murray, 106
Academy of Motion Picture Arts and Sciences (AMPAS), 1–29
Acting Branch, 5–8
Action-adventure films, 167–71
Adjani, Isabelle, 51
Adventures of Robin Hood, The, 169
African Queen, The, 189–90
Agee, James, 132
Aimee, Anouk, 93
Airplane, 170
Airport, 97, 108, 170–71
Alamo, The, 160, 298–300
Aleandro, Norma, 91
Alda, Alan, 26
Alexander, Jane, 54, 100, 140
Alexander's Ragtime Band, 152
Alfie, 78
Alice Doesn't Live Here Anymore, 97, 204
All About Eve, 61, 102, 125, 192, 210, 260
Allen, Woody, 143, 179, 330
Allgood, Sara, 137
All of Me, 150
All Quiet on the Western Front, 163
All That Jazz, 93, 121, 155
All the King's Men, 99, 102, 132
All the President's Men, 139
All This and Heaven Too, 124
Amadeus, 80, 106, 155
Amarcord, 90

Ameche, Don, 52, 97
America, America, 143
American Graffiti, 147,
American in Paris, An, 153, 155, 307
American Theater Wing, 43
Anastasia, 215–16
Anatomy of Murder, 130
Anderson, Judith, 172
Anderson, Lindsay, 83
Anderson, Maxwell, 163
Anderson, Michael, 78, 168
Andrews, Julie, 84, 98, 154, 281–82, 332
Angels with Dirty Faces, 39, 189
Angry Harvest, 263, 328
Anna Christie, 295
Anne of the Thousand Days, 161
Ann-Margret, 70, 203
Annie Hall, 143–44, 171, 179, 261
Anthony Adverse, 99
Antoinette Perry (Tony) Awards, 31, 42–45
Apartment, The, 93, 142, 150, 261, 296, 300
Apocalypse Now, 93, 166
Arkin, Alan, 54, 220
Arliss, George, 16, 52, 81, 100
Arnold, Edward, 142
Around the World in 80 Days, 78, 168, 260
Arrangement, The, 182
Arrowsmith, 125
Arthur, 331

Arthur, Jean, 142, 145, 211
Ashby, Hal, 326
Ashcroft, Peggy, 63, 81, 97
Astaire, Fred, 33, 156, 171, 223, 292
Astor, Mary, 58
Atlantic City, 118, 262
Attenborough, Richard, 32, 79
Auer, Mischa, 220
Auntie Mame, 59, 100, 146
Awful Truth, The, 128, 145, 149

Baby Doll, 195
Bacall, Lauren, 112
Bad and the Beautiful, The, 198, 331
Bad Day at Black Rock, 188
Badelia, Bonnie, 302
Badham, Mary, 50
Bad Seed, The, 100
Bainter, Fay, 60
Baker, Carroll, 195
Ballard, Lucien, 113
Ball of Fire, 127
Bancroft, Anne, 100, 270, 271
Bannen, Ian, 104
Barnes, George, 172
Barrault, Marie Christine, 87
Barry Lyndon, 79, 162
Barrymore, Drew, 116
Barrymore, Ethel, 116, 129
Barrymore, John, 116, 125
Barrymore, Lionel, 116, 125, 142
Barthelmess, Richard, 15
Baryshnikov, Mikhail, 55
Bates, Alan, 147
Battleground, 132
Baum, Vicki, 125
Baxter, Anne, 61, 125, 192, 194
Baxter, Warner, 102, 174
Beatty, Warren, 131, 145, 162, 323
Beaver, Louise, 129
Becket, 160
Beery, Wallace, 41, 107, 125, 188

Behind the Mask, 115
Being There, 93
Bells of St. Mary's, The, 136, 212, 215
Ben-Hur, 153, 159–60, 210
Benny, Jack, 25
Benton, Robert, 139
Bergman, Ingmar, 85, 90–91
Bergman, Ingrid, 102, 136, 215–16, 235, 244–45, 253, 297, 305
Berkeley, Reginald, 137
Berlin Film Festival, 35
Bernhardt, Sondra, 329
Bernstein, Carl, 139
Best Years of Our Lives, The, 55, 131–32, 260, 305–6
Betrayal, 329–30
Biberman, Herbert, 312
Bidwell, Charles, 298
Big Chill, The, 71, 331, 337
Big Country, The, 175
Biopictures, 119–22
Birdman of Alcatraz, The, 118
Black Orpheus, 263
Blair, Betsy, 61, 138
Blair, Linda, 50
Blossoms in the Dust, 126
Blue Thunder, 84
Bogart, Humphrey, 112, 134, 189–90, 238–39, 285, 304
Bonnie and Clyde, 131, 134
Boone, Pat, 6
Boot, Das, 88
Booth, Charles G., 306
Booth, Shirley, 51, 100, 273
Borgnine, Ernest, 103, 138, 188
Born Yesterday, 100, 146
Borzage, Frank, 16
Boston Symphony Orchestra, 325
Bostonians, The, 221, 325
Bound for Glory, 138
Boyer, Charles, 86, 124
Boys' Town, 187

Brackett, Charles, 293
Brando, Marlon, 63, 99, 102, 106, 133–34, 135, 188, 264–65, 320–22, 336
Brave One, The, 316
Brazil, 38
Breakfast Club, The, 7
Breaking Away, 140
Brennan, Walter, 108, 175, 270
Brickman, Marshall, 144
Bridge on the River Kwai, The, 52, 78, 165, 260
Brief Encounter, 77
Bringing Up Baby, 149
Broadway Melody, The, 151–52
Broadway Melody of 1936, The, 152
Brook, James, 144
Brooks, Mel, 79
Brooks, Richard, 128
Brown, Joe E. 41
Brown, Harry, 316
Browne, Leslie, 55, 324
Brynner, Yul, 100, 252
Burke, Billie, 74
Burns, Cathy, 55
Burns, George, 52, 97, 148, 268
Burstyn, Ellen, 52, 204, 270, 274
Burton, Richard, 57, 62, 84, 100, 106, 117, 239
Bus Stop, 70
Butch Cassidy and the Sundance Kid, 143
Butterfield 8, 193, 198, 296
Butterflies Are Free, 148
Byington, Spring, 142

Cabaret, 115, 135, 155
Cacoyannis, Michael, 147
Cactus Flower, 99
Caesar and Cleopatra, 77
Cagney, James, 2, 3, 33, 39, 189, 233, 304
Caine, Michael, 40, 53, 70, 84, 89

Caine Mutiny, The, 134
Camille, 295
Canby, Vincent, 7, 26, 38, 40, 84–85, 136–37, 171, 211–12, 309
Candy, 321
Cannes Film Festival, 34–35, 36, 61, 79, 87, 89, 91–93, 138, 327
Capra, Frank, 4, 9, 33, 101, 128, 141, 266, 287, 292
Captain Blood, 169
Cardiff, Jack, 83
Carnal Knowledge, 88
Carney, Art, 52, 105, 187
Caron, Leslie, 153
Carson, Johnny, 26, 27, 29
Carter, Jimmy, 139
Casablanca, 86, 189, 305–6
Cass, Peggy, 100
Cat Ballou, 174
Cat on a Hot Tin Roof, 123, 196
Cats, 80,
Cavalcade, 137, 260
Chambers, John, 15
Champ, The, 107, 125, 188
Champion, 88
Champlin, Charles, 38
Channing, Carol, 55
Chaplin, Charles, 15, 109, 145, 148, 223, 319–20
Chariots of Fire, 79, 120, 138, 171, 263, 301
Chase, Chevy, 41
Chayefsky, Paddy, 103, 104, 138, 324
Cher, 302
Chevalier, Maurice, 16, 223, 313
Children of a Lesser God, 45
Children's Hour, The, 64
Chinatown, 173
Christie, Julie, 81, 175, 265
Chronicle of the Burning Years, 93
Cilento, Diana, 83, 143
Cimarron, 173, 260

Cimino, Michael, 166, 326–27
Cinderella Liberty, 282
Circus, The, 148
Citadel, The, 222
Citizen Kane, 138, 293, 310–11
City Lights, 148
Clayburgh, Jill, 147
Clayton, Jack, 83
Cleopatra (1934), 159
Cleopatra (1963), 72, 143, 160, 301
Clift, Montgomery, 54, 132–33, 295
Clockwork Orange, A, 79
Close Encounters of the Third Kind, 324
Close, Glenn, 55, 71, 337
Coal Miner's Daughter, 121, 140, 155, 182, 329
Cobb, Irving S., 25
Cobb, Lee J., 134, 283
Coburn, Charles, 86, 145
Cocoon, 97
Cohan, George M., 189
Cohn, Harry, 292
Cohn, Sammy, 146
Colbert, Claudette, 101, 129, 141, 251, 264
Collinge, Patricia, 55
Colman, Ronald, 226
Colonel Redl, 327
Columbia Pictures, 62, 78, 141, 291
Come Back Little Sheba, 100, 117
Comédie Francaise, 51
Coming Home, 104, 166, 206, 326
Connery, Sean, 83
Conti, Tom, 84
Conversation, The, 173
Cooper, Gary, 4, 69, 101, 170, 182, 187, 215, 304, 308, 336
Cooper, Gladys, 86
Cooper, Jackie, 50, 188
Coppola, Carmine, 114

Coppola, Francis Ford, 114, 135, 166
Coquette, 127, 280
Corey, Wendell, 241
Corman, Avery, 140
Cornell, Katharine, 124
Cortesa, Valentina, 193, 253
Costa-Gavras, 85
Countess from Hong Kong, The, 321
Country Girl, The, 134
Courtenay, Tom, 8, 40, 84, 101
Cousin, Cousine, 87
Coward, Noel, 76, 137
Crain, Jeanne, 129
Cravenne, Georges, 32
Crawford, Broderick, 81, 132, 246–47
Crawford, Joan, 41, 51, 102, 125, 199, 214, 244, 296–97, 305
Cries and Whispers, 85, 90
Crisp, Donald, 81, 137
Crosby, Bing, 26, 60, 134, 142, 187, 212, 251, 336
Cross Creek, 303
Crossfire, 123, 128–29
Crowther, Bosley, 23, 132, 136, 137, 164, 332
Cruel Sea, The, 78
Cukor, George, 103, 106, 125, 146, 153, 155
Cummings, Quinn, 50, 324
Curtis, Tony, 130
Curtiz, Michael, 106
Cyrano De Bergerac, 101

Dangerous, 127, 192, 221
Danton, 88
Dark at the Top of the Stairs, 70
Dark Victory, 124
Darling, 78
Darwell, Jane, 280
Dassin, Jules, 87, 148, 315
David Di Donatello Award, 32

Davies, Marion, 285

Davis, Bette, 9, 17, 33, 60, 61, 69, 101, 102, 118, 124, 125, 126, 127, 192, 195, 196, 210, 219, 221, 236, 295

Davis, Judy, 63

Davis, Peter, 322

Davis, Sammy, Jr., 325

Day, Doris, 57, 112, 189, 213

Day for Night, 88, 193

Days of Wine and Roses, 150, 281

Dead End, 128

Dean, James, 110

Deer Hunter, The, 261, 326–27

Defiant Ones, The, 129, 316

De Havilland, Olivia, 112, 116, 127, 136, 196, 215, 253

De Mille, Cecil B., 159, 167

De Mille, William, 231

Denby, David, 331

De Niro, Robert, 84, 122, 188, 329

Dépardieu, Gérard, 88

Dern, Bruce, 206, 282–83

De Sica, Vittorio, 85

De Wilde, Brandon, 50

Diary of a Mad Housewife, 69

Diary of Anne Frank, The, 83

Dillon, Melinda, 324

Directors Branch, 5, 7–8

Dirty Harry, 139

Disraeli, 100

Divorce Italian Style, 89

Dix, Richard, 173

Dmytryk, Edward, 128, 314

Doctor Dolittle, 155, 301

Doctor Strangelove, 146

Doctor Zhivago, 159

Dodsworth, 101

Dog Day Afternoon, 121

Dolce Vita, La, 87, 89–90

Donat, Robert, 76, 222, 295

Double Indemnity, 142, 173, 293

Douglas, Kirk, 69, 93

Douglas, Michael, 41, 136

Douriff, Brad, 55

Dowd, Nancy, 326

Dr. Jekyll and Mr. Hyde, 107

Drake, William A., 125

Dresser, The, 8, 40, 80, 101, 262

Dresser, Louise, 16

Dressler, Marie, 41, 97, 127, 225–26, 267

Dreyfus, Alfred, 128

Dreyfuss, Richard, 97, 105, 213

Duel in the Sun, 58, 175

Duke, Patty, 50, 100, 136

Dunaway, Faye, 105, 200, 265

Dunne, Irene, 6, 145, 173

Durbin, Deanna, 50, 293

Durning, Charles, 147

Duvall, Robert, 84, 106

Eagles, Jeanne, 124

Earthquake, 170

East of Eden, 99, 110, 194

Eastwood, Clint, 41, 139

Educating Rita, 40, 150

Edwards, Blake, 332

81/2, 90

Elephant Man, The, 15, 45, 79, 122, 262

Elmer Gantry, 118, 194, 300

Emigrants, The, 85

Emmy Award, 31, 32, 42, 45, 325

Equus, 100

E.T., 116, 309–10

Evans, Edith, 52, 83, 143

Exorcist, The, 64, 70, 261

Face to Face, 91

Falk, Peter, 298

Fallen Idol, The, 90, 172

Fanny and Alexander, 88, 91

Fairbanks, Douglas, Sr., 294

Farewell My Lovely, 282

Farmer's Daughter, The, 102, 127

Farrell, Charles, 41, 112
Father Takes a Wife, 58
Fedora, 332
Fellini, Federico, 85, 87, 90
Fenelon, Fania, 325
Ferber, Edna, 173
Ferrer, Jose, 101, 253
Fiddler on the Roof, 101, 155
Field, Rachel, 124
Field, Sally, 62, 206, 207, 221, 237
Fielding, Henry, 143
Finch, Peter, 56, 63, 103, 109, 235
Finney, Albert, 8, 70, 84, 143
First Blood, 167
Firth, Peter, 100
Fitzgerald, Barry, 60, 142
Fletcher, Louise, 99, 136, 200, 253, 277
Fly, The, 327
Flynn, Errol, 112, 169
Fonda, Henry, 33, 97, 104, 114, 115, 129, 145, 188, 226–27, 275, 332
Fonda, Jane, 26, 114, 193, 206, 240, 308–9, 325, 326–27
Fontaine, Joan, 70, 105, 116, 172, 237, 246, 266–67, 285, 304
Fontanne, Lynn, 100, 116
Foote, Horton, 130
Ford, Glenn, 104
Ford, Harrison, 41, 57, 84
Ford, John, 33, 109, 137, 174, 240, 259, 311
Foreign Correspondent, 172
Foreman, Carl, 307–8, 315
Forman, Milos, 80, 136
Fortune Cookie, The, 78
Forty Second Street, 137, 152
Fosse, Bob, 121, 155, 274
Four Daughters, 69, 82
Fox, Michael J., 41
Fox Studios, 20, 137

Frances, 60, 201
Franciosa, Anthony, 54, 101
Free Soul, A, 116
French Connection, The, 135, 168–69
French, Philip, 308
Friedkin, William, 168
Friendly Persuasion, 316
From Here to Eternity, 102, 117, 132, 188, 194, 280
Funny Girl, 99, 107, 182

Gable, Clark, 41, 101, 141, 157, 169, 295, 303–4, 336
Gandhi, 32, 79, 99, 106, 120, 309–10
Garbo, Greta, 16, 41, 92, 125, 145, 295
Garfield, John, 55, 65, 128, 313
Garland, Judy, 50, 102, 114, 201, 295–96
Garr, Terry, 147
Garson, Greer, 59–60, 69, 112, 126, 249, 280, 293, 297, 305
Gaslight, 70, 173, 142, 305–6
Gaynor, Janet, 16, 20, 41, 73, 97, 112, 198, 201, 249
Gazzo, Michael V., 55
Gelbart, Larry, 147
Gentleman's Agreement, A, 77, 123, 128–29, 293
Georgy Girl, 83, 115
Giannini, Giancarlo, 86–87
Gibbons, Cedric, 17
Gilliam, Terry, 38
Giant, 110
Gielgud, John, 81, 92, 331
Gigi, 114, 123, 153, 261
Gish, Lillian, 33, 58, 175, 224
Give 'Em Hell Harry, 101
Gleason, Jackie, 62
Goddard, Jean Luc, 48
The Godfather, 79, 135, 188, 320–21

The Godfather, Part II, 67, 70, 135, 188

Going My Way, 76, 142, 187, 212

Golden Globe Awards, 39–40, 89, 150, 321

Golden Palm (Palme d'Or), 34, 36, 93, 138

Goldwyn, Samuel, 131, 291, 294

Gone with the Wind, 13, 15, 76, 116, 195, 295

Goodbye Girl, The, 97, 105, 143, 324

Goodbye Mr. Chips, 76, 126

Good Earth, The, 158, 198

Gordon, Ruth, 97

Goulding, Edmund, 125

Graduate, The, 54, 147, 190

Grahame, Gloria, 198, 332

Grammy Award, 31, 42, 44–46

Grand Hotel, 125

Grand Illusion, 85, 90

Grant, Cary, 102, 145, 149–50, 217, 245, 279

Grant, Lee, 55, 312–13

Granville, Bonita, 50

Grapes of Wrath, The, 137, 280

Great Dictator, The, 145, 148, 319–20

Great Expectations, 77, 129

Great McGinty, The, 148

Great Waltz, The, 55

Great White Hope, The, 100

Great Ziegfeld, The, 59, 120, 152, 182

Greatest Show on Earth, The, 167, 307

Green Berets, The, 326

Greenberg, Jerry, 168

Greene, Graham, 172

Greenstreet, Sidney, 55, 283

Grey, Joel, 234

Greystoke: The Legend of Tarzan, 110

Griffith, D.W., 58, 332

Griffith, Hugh, 81, 240

Guardsman, The, 100, 117

Guess Who's Coming to Dinner?, 100, 130, 147

Guest, Judith, 140

Guinness, Alec, 78, 165, 171, 252

Guns of Navarone, The, 165

Gwenn, Edmund, 81, 251

Hackman, Gene, 168–69, 252, 284

Hadjidakis, Manos, 87

Hail the Conquering Hero, 149

Hall, Grayson, 196

Haller, Ernest, 15

Hamlet, 22, 23, 77, 157, 260

Hannah and Her Sisters, 144, 330

Hardy, Oliver, 149

Hare, David, 115, 325

Harlowe, Jean, 145

Harris, Julie, 54

Harris, Richard, 70

Harrison, Rex, 56, 84, 100, 154, 250

Harry and Tonto, 105, 187

Hart, Moss, 128, 141

Harvey, 148

Harvey, Laurence, 70

Haskell, Molly, 191

Hathaway, Henry, 170, 306

Hatful of Rain, A, 101

Hawn, Goldie, 99

Hawks, Howard, 56, 127, 189, 225

Hayakawa, Sessue, 52

Hayes, Helen, 34, 97, 108, 127, 170–71

Hays, Will H., 39

Hayward, Susan, 39, 106, 235, 273, 276–77

Head, Edith, 25, 125

Hearst, William Randolph, 310–11

Heart Like a Wheel, 302

Hearts and Minds, 322
Heaven Can Wait (1943), 145
Heaven Can Wait (1978), 145
Hecht, Harold, 293
Heckart, Eileen, 148
Hedda, 203
Heflin, Van, 306
Heiress, The, 116, 132, 196
Hellman, Lillian, 50, 99, 124, 322–23
Hello, Dolly!, 155, 301
Henry V, 76, 157
Henry, Justin, 50, 140
Hepburn, Audrey, 84, 85, 146, 148, 153, 250, 267, 274, 295
Hepburn, Katharine, 52, 100, 107, 108, 110, 112, 118, 126, 127, 131, 193, 196, 197, 218–19, 242, 292
Here Comes Mr. Jordan, 145
Herlihy, James Leo, 135
Herrick, Margaret, 17
Hersholt, Jean, 22
Heston, Charlton, 81, 160, 210, 236, 247–48, 267, 325
He Who Must Die, 315
Hickey, William, 41
Hier, Marvin, 325
High Noon, 187, 307–8
High Sierra, 189
Hill, George Roy, 143
Hiller, Wendy, 66, 76, 81, 118
Hirsch, Judd, 140
His Girl Friday, 149
Historical epics, 156–63
Hitchcock, Alfred, 33, 172, 225, 332–33
Hitler, Adolph, 320
Hobson, Laura Z., 128
Hodge, Patricia, 330
Hoffman, Dustin, 54, 70, 106, 134, 140, 147, 206, 242–43, 253, 265
Hold Back the Dawn, 116, 293

Holden, William, 126, 133, 134, 295, 304
Holliday, Judy, 61, 100, 146, 150
Hollywood Foreign Press Association, 52–53
Holm, Celeste, 128
Home of the Brave, 129
Hondo, 175
Hope, Bob, 26
Hospital, The, 241
Houghton, Katharine, 131
House on 92nd Street, The, 306
Housman, John, 97
Howard, Leslie, 76
How Green Was My Valley, 137–38, 293, 311
How the West Was Won, 143
Hudson, Hugh, 79
Hudson, Rock, 112
Hughes, John, 7
Hull, Josephine, 148
Human Comedy, The, 164,
Hungary, 327
Hunter, Kim, 99, 312
Hurt, John, 122
Hurt, William, 106, 333, 336
Hustler, The, 78, 300, 315
Huston, Anjelica, 41, 54, 114
Huston, John, 23, 44, 113
Huston, Walter, 101, 113
Hutton, Timothy, 97, 140

I am a Fugitive from a Chain Gang, 137
Imitation of Life, 129
Indiana Jones and the Temple of Doom, 57
Informer, The, 259–60
In Old Arizona, 102
In Old Chicago, 128
Inside Daisy Clover, 98
In the Heat of the Night, 82, 123, 130–31, 187

Intruder in the Dust, 129
Invaders, The, 76, 164
In Which We Serve, 76, 164
Irons, Jeremy, 330
Isadora, 324
Island Alive, 294
It Happened One Night, 101, 141, 263, 292
It Should Happen to You, 150
Ivanhoe, 159
I Want to Live!, 39

Jackson, Charles, 135
Jackson, Glenda, 81, 148
James Bond movies, 83
Jannings, Emil, 15, 73, 86
Jaws, 46, 137, 170–71
Jewison, Norman, 131
Jezebel, 60, 124, 195, 198
Joffe, Roland, 80
Johnny Belinda, 23, 136, 197
Johnny Eager, 306
Jones, David, 329
Jones, James Earl, 100, 113
Jones, Jennifer, 112, 277, 285, 297
Jones, Robert C., 326
Jones, Shirley, 194, 297–98
Joplin, Scott, 143
Judgment at Nuremberg, 56, 115, 118, 123
Julia, 115, 199, 323–24
Julius Caesar, 133

Kael, Pauline, 133, 309, 331
Kagemusha, 93
Kaminska, Ida, 52, 86
Kanin, Garson, 98, 146
Kantor, MacKinlay, 131
Karate Kid, The, 7
Kaufman, Boris, 133
Kaufman, George S., 141
Kazan, Elia, 99, 128, 129, 130, 133–34

Keaton, Buster, 149
Keaton, Diane, 85, 143–44, 162
Kedrova, Lila, 84, 86
Kelly, Gene, 153
Kelly, Grace, 134, 187, 296
Kelly, Nancy, 100
Kempson, Rachel, 115
Kennedy, Arthur, 84
Kennedy Center Awards, 44–45
Kent, Sidney, 20
Kerr, Deborah, 92, 132, 182, 196, 280
Kerr, Walter, 26
Kesey, Ken, 136
Key Largo, 194
Keys of the Kingdom, The, 87
Killing Fields, The, 80
King and I, The, 100, 123
King, Frank, 316
King, Martin Luther, Jr., 28
King of Comedy, The, 329
King Solomon's Mines, 170
Kingsley, Ben, 99, 106, 234–35, 330
Kiss of Death, 70
Kiss of the Spider Woman, 106, 262, 294
Kitty Foyle, 156, 209
Kline, Kevin, 89
Klute, 193
Knight, Shirley, 55, 196
Koch, Howard, 231
Korda, Alexander, 23, 75, 76, 113
Korjus, Miliza, 55
Kramer, Stanley, 56, 110, 129, 147, 225
Kramer Vs. Kramer, 109, 123, 139–40, 190, 205–6, 219
Krasker, Robert, 172
Kubrick, Stanley, 79, 146, 162

La Cava, Gregory, 126, 128
La Motta, Jack, 122

Ladies of Leisure, 292
Lady for a Night, 67, 292
Ladykillers, 78
Lady Sings the Blues, 69
Lancaster, Burt, 117, 118, 132, 250, 295, 300
Lanchester, Elsa, 117
Lange, Jessica, 60, 69, 147, 201, 207
Lansbury, Angela, 55
Lassaly, Walter, 143
Last Emperor, The, 80, 120, 162, 179
Last Summer, 70
Laurel, Stan, 149
Laurie, Piper, 62
Laughton, Charles, 81, 117, 144, 157, 244
Lavender Hill Mob, The, 78
Lawrence of Arabia, 78, 103, 120, 159
Lean, David, 76, 78, 106, 129, 159, 176, 178
Leads, Andrea, 126
Leap into Void, 93
Lee, Harper, 130
Le Gallienne, Eva, 52
Leigh, Vivien, 76, 99, 195, 249
LeMaire, Charles, 125
Lemmon, Jack, 62, 68, 108, 142, 145, 150, 281, 336
Lenny, 79, 121
Lenya, Lotte, 196
LeRoy, Mervyn, 126
Letter, The, 124
Letter to Three Wives, A, 132
Levine, Joseph, 332
Lewis, Jerry, 329
Libeled Lady, 145
Lifeboat, 172
Life of Emile Zola, The, 120, 128, 189
Lilies of the Field, 130, 143
Limelight, 110
Lion in Winter, The, 78, 107, 161

Lithgow, John, 221
Little Foxes, The, 101, 124, 138, 311
Little Women, 137
Litvak, Anatole, 23, 102, 136
Lives of a Bengal Lancer, The, 169–70
Lloyd, Frank, 157
Lloyd, Harold, 149
Lombard, Carole, 58
Loneliness of the Long Distance Runner, The, 83
Longest Day, The, 165
Lonely Hearts, 70
Look Back in Anger, 82
Looking for Mr. Goodbar, 324
Loos, Anita, 126
Loren, Sophia, 86, 103, 234, 238, 245, 277–78
Los Angeles Film Critics Association, 37–38
Lost Horizon, 128
Lost Weekend, The, 135–36, 293
Love, Bessie, 152
Love Me or Leave Me, 189
Lubitsch, Ernst, 107, 125, 145, 292
Lucas, George, 73, 147
Lukas, Paul, 99, 199, 304
Lumet, Sidney, 104, 121, 129
Lunt, Alfred, 116
Lynch, David, 79

McCabe and Mrs. Miller, 175
McCambridge, Mercedes, 99, 102, 132, 233–34, 237, 247, 253, 264, 266, 272
McCarey, Leo, 128, 142, 144–45
McCarthy, Joseph, 83, 134, 307, 314, 322–23
McCormack, Patty, 100
McCoy, Horace, 309
McCrea, Joel, 145
McDaniel, Hattie, 130
McGraw, Ali, 213

McGuire, Dorothy, 128
MacLaine, Shirley, 97, 105, 106, 142, 144, 236, 296
McNamara, Maggie, 54, 100
McQueen, Steve, 165, 218
Madame Curie, 127
Madigan, Amy, 331
Magnani, Anna, 51, 56, 61, 86, 89, 103, 198
Magnificent Ambersons, The, 59, 196, 293
Malden, Karl, 99, 134
Malone, Dorothy, 61, 194
Maltese Falcon, The, 173, 189, 283, 311
Man for All Seasons, A, 78, 101, 120, 161, 261
Manhattan, 144
Mankiewicz, Joseph L., 109, 125, 315
Mann, Delbert, 138
March, Fredric, 4, 34, 107, 108, 132, 251, 267, 274, 304
Marie Antoinette, 70
Marie-Louise, 88
Martin, Steve, 150
Marty, 103, 123, 138–39, 188
Marvin, Lee, 81, 148, 174, 218, 252
Marx, Groucho, 299
Mary Poppins, 99, 146, 154, 222
Mary, Queen of Scots, 324
Mason, James, 65, 77, 102
Mason, Marsha, 70, 282
Massey, Raymond, 101
Mastroianni, Marcello, 86, 87, 88, 89
Matthau, Walter, 62, 148, 284, 336
Maugham, W. Somerset, 124
May, Elaine, 7
Mayer, Louis B., 1, 19, 279, 290
Mazurski, Paul, 147

Mean Streets, 139
Member of the Wedding, The, 100
Men, The, 320
Menges, Chris, 80
Mercouri, Melina, 87
Meredith, Burgess, 52
Metro-Goldwyn-Mayer (MGM), 1, 2, 17, 19, 125, 126, 290–94
Midler, Bette, 54
Midnight Cowboy, 78, 134–35, 190, 282
Midnight Express, 79
Mildred Pierce, 102, 199, 305
Miles, Sylvia, 282
Milestone, Lewis, 16
Milford, Penelope, 232
Milland, Ray, 81, 135, 232–33, 237, 246, 273, 281
Miller, Arthur, 137, 325
Miller, Jason, 55
Mills, John, 52, 81, 248–49
Min and Bill, 97, 127
Mineo, Sal, 50, 299
Minnelli, Liza, 115, 156, 331
Minnelli, Vincente, 114, 155, 331
Miracle Worker, The, 100, 136
Mirisch, Walter, 333
Missing, 86, 124, 328
Mission, The, 36
Mister Roberts, 108, 145
Mitchell, Thomas, 175
Mitchum, Robert, 129
Modern Times, 148, 320
Mon Oncle d'Amerique, 88
Monaco, James, 168
Monsieur Vincent, 85
Montgomery, Robert, 145
Moody, Ron, 101
Moon Is Blue, The, 100
Moore, Mary Tyler, 52, 140
Moorehead, Agnes, 59, 196
More the Merrier, The, 145

Moreno, Rita, 248, 280–81
Morgan, 115, 324
Morley, Robert, 55
Morning Glory, 98, 127, 193
Mourning Becomes Electra, 59, 115
Mr. Skeffington, 86
Mr. Smith Goes to Washington, 86
Mrs. Miniver, 102, 126, 164, 297, 305
Muni, Paul, 4, 54, 112, 120, 128, 189
Murder Inc., 298
Murphy, Brianne, 7
Murphy, Eddie, 41
Murray, Don, 55
Musical films, 151–56
Mutiny on the Bounty (1935), 157
My Cousin Rachel, 72
My Fair Lady, 100, 153–54, 222
My Sister Eileen, 127

National Association of Theater Owners, 41
National Industry Recovery Act, 3
National Society of Film Critics, 37, 325
Natural, The, 71
Negulesco, Jean, 23
Nelson, Harmon Oscar, 17
Nelson, Ralph, 130
Network, 104, 105, 200
Never on Sunday, 87
Newman, Paul, 100, 106, 117, 143, 224, 301–2
New York Drama Critics Award, 45
New York Film Critics Circle, 37, 39, 60, 91–93, 110, 118, 130, 133, 136, 138, 139
New York Film Festival, 34–36
Ngor, Haing S., 80
Nicholas and Alexandra, 161
Nicholas Nickleby, 80

Nichols, Dudley, 240
Nichols, Mike, 54, 70, 117, 147
Nicholson, Jack, 41, 104, 106, 136, 144, 251, 336
Nielsen ratings, 26, 46
Night and the City, 315
Night of the Iguana, The, 196
Night of the Shooting Stars, The, 32
Nights of Cabiria, The, 90
Ninotchka, 295
Niven, David, 118, 252, 330
Nobel Prize, 13, 26, 44, 290
None but the Lonely Heart, 116, 149
Norma Rae, 79, 121, 206
Norris, Chuck, 41
North, E. H., 166
Notorious, 86
Now Voyager, 196
Nugent, Frank S., 189
Nuit de Varenne, La, 88

Oberon, Merle, 113
O'Connor, John, 28
Odets, Clifford, 134
Oedipus Rex, 325
Of Human Bondage, 9, 295
Official Story, The, 88, 327
O'Hara, John, 193
Oliver!, 78–79, 90, 101
Olivier, Laurence, 68, 76, 77, 106, 158
O'Neal, Ryan, 188, 265
O'Neal, Tatum, 50, 97, 188
O'Neill, Eugene, 115
One Flew Over the Cuckoo's Nest, 99, 136–37, 171, 200, 261
One Night of Love, 152
On Golden Pond, 97, 114, 123, 140, 188, 263
On the Waterfront, 99, 102
Open City, 88
Ordinary People, 97, 123, 140
Orion, 294

Osborne, John, 143
Oscar, The, 332
O'Toole, Peter, 84, 103, 106
Our Town, 54
Ouspenskaya, Maria, 55
Out of Africa, 114, 120, 162–63

Pacino, Al, 84
Page, Geraldine, 52, 101, 105–6, 175, 192, 227
Palm Beach Story, The, 149
Paper Chase, The, 97
Paper Moon, 97, 188
Papillon, 190
Paramount, 291
Parker, Alan, 79
Parks, Larry, 313
Parsons, Louella, 76, 252
Passage to India, A, 80, 97
Patch of Blue, A, 83
Patton, 165–66, 171, 182
Pawnbroker, The, 82
Paxinou, Katina, 86
Paxton, John, 128
Peck, Gregory, 29, 69, 106, 128, 130, 146, 248
Penn, Arthur, 131
Penny Serenade, 149
Perrine, Valerie, 63
Persona, 90
Peterson, Wolfgang, 88
Peyton Place, 70
Philadelphia Story, The, 101, 102, 145
Piaf, 80
Piccoli, Michel, 93
Pickford, Mary, 98, 127, 225, 280, 294
Pidgeon, Walter, 112
Pillow Talk, 57, 73
Pinky, 129
Pinter, Harold, 330
Place in the Sun, A, 83, 307

Places in the Heart, 140, 207, 221, 331
Planet of the Apes, 15
Platoon, 163, 166
Players Directory, The, 22
Playing for Time, 325
Pocketful of Miracles, 298
Poitier, Sidney, 129, 130, 187, 248, 268
Polanski, Roman, 79, 162
Pollack, Sydney, 106, 114, 147, 162, 309
Pollyanna, 280
Poseiden Adventure, The, 83, 170–71
Powell, Michael, 76, 77
Preminger, Otto, 130
Pressburger, Emeric, 23, 76, 306
Preston, Robert, 52, 221
Price, Waterhouse and Company, 13, 27
Pride of the Yankees, The, 60
Private Life of Henry VIII, The, 75, 137
Prizzi's Honor, 114, 263
Public Enemy, The, 189,
Pulitzer Prize, 45, 130, 132
Puzo, Mario, 135
Pygmalion, 75, 83

Quiet Man, The, 307
Quinn, Anthony, 85, 146, 253
Quo Vadis?, 121, 159

Rachel, Rachel, 117, 196, 301–2
Radnitz, Robert, 303
Raging Bull, 122
Ragtime, 70
Raiders of the Lost Ark, 57, 79, 84, 171
Rain Man, 140, 329
Rainer, Luise, 59, 86, 155, 278–79, 295
Rainmaker, The, 118, 197
Rains, Claude, 68–69
Raintree County, 58

Rambo, 167
Rank, J. Arthur, 77
Rasch, Raymond, 109
Razor's Edge, The, 77, 194
RCA Victor, 24
Reagan, Ronald, 20, 29
Real Thing, The, 80
Rear Window, 172
Rebecca, 104, 172
Rebel Without a Cause, 64
Redford, Robert, 139, 140, 143, 213
Redgrave, Colin, 115
Redgrave, Lynn, 70, 115
Redgrave, Michael, 115, 218
Redgrave, Vanessa, 81, 115, 199, 221, 323–25
Redman, Joyce, 83, 143
Red River, 57
Reds, 79, 162, 261
Red Shoes, The, 22, 23, 77
Reed, Carol, 78, 90, 106, 155, 172
Reed, Donna, 194
Reflections in a Golden Eye, 321
Reisz, Karel, 83
Remarque, Eric Maria, 163
Remick, Lee, 130
Rennahan, Ray, 15
Renoir, Jean, 90, 225
Resurrection, 67
Revere, Anne, 312
Richardson, Joely, 116
Richardson, Natasha, 116
Richardson, Ralph, 92, 110, 218
Richardson, Tony, 142–43
Rififi, 315
Right Stuff, The, 171, 337
Riskin, Robert, 141
Ritt, Martin, 131, 206
Ritter, Thelma, 118
River, The, 207
RKO, 131, 292
Robe, The, 121, 133

Robertson, Cliff, 81
Robinson, Edward G., 211, 224
Robson, May, 52
Rocky, 67, 138–39, 213–14, 335
Rogers, Ginger, 81, 156, 209
Rogers, Henry, 296
Rogers, Will, 25, 41
Rollins, Howard, Jr., 55
Roman Holiday, 133, 146
Roman Spring of Mrs. Stone, The, 196
Romeo and Juliet (1968), 161
Room at the Top, 83, 199
Rooney, Mickey, 50, 112, 224, 304
Roosevelt, Franklin D., 3, 4, 20
Rose, The, 69
Rose Tattoo, The, 56, 118, 123, 198
Rosemary's Baby, 98
Ross, Diana, 54
Ross, Herbert, 100
Rossen, Robert, 314–15
Rotta, Nino, 114
Roud, Richard, 35
Rowlands, Gena, 52, 331
Ruggles of Red Gap, 144
Rules of the Game, The, 90
Russell, Harold, 55
Russell, Larry, 109
Russell, Rosalind, 59, 84, 85, 100, 127, 146, 224, 297
Rutherford, Margaret, 81, 83
Ryan, Robert, 129
Ryan's Daughter, 67

Sadie Thompson, 58
Saint, Eva Marie, 134, 251
Sale, Richard, 332
Salt, Waldo, 134, 326
Sanders, George, 125
San Francisco, 86, 169
Sands of Iwo Jima, 57
Sand Pebbles, The, 165, 301
Sarandon, Susan, 63

Sargent, Alvin, 140
Sarris, Andrew, 38, 137, 190, 290, 309, 325, 331
Satyricon, 90
Saturday Night and Sunday Morning, 83
Save the Tiger, 108, 150
Scarface (1932), 189
Schaffner, Franklin J., 166
Schanberg, Sydney, 80
Schary, Dore, 231, 325
Scheider, Roy, 84
Schell, Maria, 56
Schell, Maximilian, 56, 86
Schildkraut, Joseph, 128, 244
Schisgal, Murray, 147
Schlesinger, John, 104, 134
Schnee, Charles, 332
Schneider, Burt, 322
Schulberg, Budd, 134
Scofield, Paul, 62, 101
Scorsese, Martin, 36, 122, 234, 329
Scott, George C., 62, 104, 166, 182, 240–42, 273, 300
Scott, Martha, 54
Screen Actors Guild (SAG), 3–5, 10, 323
Search, The, 68
Searchers, The, 174
Seaton, George, 10
Sellers, Peter, 84, 93, 146
Selznick, David O. 266, 285, 289–90, 294
Separate Tables, 118, 196, 330
Sergeant York, 101, 121, 182, 305
Seven Beauties, 87
Seven Brides for Seven Brothers, 134
Seven Faces of Dr. Lao, 15
Seventh Heaven, 97
Seventh Seal, The, 90
Seventh Veil, The, 77
Shane, 133, 174
Shanghai Express, 125

Shaw, George Bernard, 76
Shaw, Robert, 143
Shearer, Norma, 16, 41, 102, 294, 295
She Done Him Wrong, 144
Shepard, Sam, 337
Sherwood, Robert, 131
Shire, Talia, 114
Shoeshine, 85
Shop on Main Street, The, 86
Signoret, Simone, 199, 247, 314, 333
Silkwood, 302
Simon, Neil, 148
Sin of Madelon Claudet, The, 108, 127
Sinatra, Frank, 102, 268, 322
Since You Went Away, 142, 306
Sister Kenny, 127
Sixteen Candles, 7
Skippy, 50
Skolsky, Sidney, 17
Smith, Maggie, 81, 89, 192
Snake Pit, The, 23, 102, 136
Snodgress, Carrie, 54,
S.O.B., 332
Soldier's Story, A, 131
Some Came Running, 296
Some Like It Hot, 150
Sondergaard, Gale, 99, 311–12
Sons and Lovers, 93, 300
Sophie's Choice, 109, 263
Sorry, Wrong Number, 117
Sounder, 123
Sound of Music, 154–55
Southerner, The, 90
Spacek, Sissy, 85, 121, 156, 207
Spellbound, 136, 172
Spiegel, Sam, 293
Spielberg, Steven, 73, 137
Stagecoach, 57, 174, 175
Stage Door, 126
Stalag 17, 133

Stallone, Sylvester, 41, 104, 138–39, 167, 334–35
Stamp, Terence, 55
Stanley, George, 17
Stanwyck, Barbara, 117, 127, 224
Stapleton, Maureen, 55, 106, 171
Star, The, 192
Star 80, 302
Star Is Born, A (1937), 126, 201
Star is Born, A (1954), 102, 115, 201
Star Wars, 57, 84, 144, 171
Steiger, Rod, 65, 103, 131, 187, 251
Stella Dallas, 127
Sterile Cuckoo, The, 115, 331
Sternberg, Josef von, 125
Stevens, George, 78, 133, 145
Stewart, James, 33, 102, 112, 118, 130, 142, 145, 148, 218, 222, 250, 336
Sting, The, 143, 261–62
Story of Adele H., The, 51
Story of Louis Pasteur, The, 120, 189
Strada, La, 90
Straight, Beatrice, 249
Strasberg, Lee, 52
Straw Dogs, 190
Streep, Meryl, 41, 60, 62, 69, 80, 109, 140, 162, 205, 220, 268–69, 275–76, 285–86
Street Angel, 97
Streetcar Named Desire, A, 99, 123, 195, 197, 307
Streisand, Barbra, 40, 100, 107, 156, 252, 275, 325
Stroheim, Erich von, 52
Sturges, Preston, 148–49
Styne, Jules, 146, 217
Suddenly Last Summer, 196
Sullavan, Margaret, 112
Sullivan's Travels, 149
Summer and Smoke, 196
Sunday Bloody Sunday, 104

Sunrise, 97, 198
Sunset Boulevard, 52, 126, 192
The Sunshine Boys, 97, 148
Suspense films, 171–73
Suspicion, 116
Sutherland, Donald, 140
Swanson, Gloria, 16, 58, 126, 192
Sweet Bird of Youth, 100, 192

Tandy, Jessica, 99
Taradash, Daniel, 133
Taviani, Paolo and Vittorio, 32
Taxi Driver, 139
Taylor, John Russell, 279
Taylor, Elizabeth, 58, 69, 106, 117, 193, 196, 216–17
Ten Commandments, The, 121, 159
Tender Mercies, 140, 262, 329
Terms of Endearment, 97, 104, 140, 144, 171, 302
Tesitch, Steve, 140
Tess, 79, 162
Thalberg, Irving G., 102, 294
That Hamilton Woman, 76
There's One Born Every Minute, 58
These Three, 50
They Shoot Horses, Don't They?, 308–9
Thief of Bagdad, The, 76
Thin Man, The, 144
Third Man, The, 78, 90
This Sporting Life, 83
Thoroughly Modern Millie, 70
Three Coins in the Fountain, 134, 146
Three Men and a Cradle, 328
Three Smart Girls, 50
Through a Glass Darkly, 90
Tierney, Gene, 296
Tiger Makes Out, The, 54
Todd, Michael, 78, 293
To Each His Own, 116, 127
To Kill a Mockingbird, 64, 130
Toland, Gregg, 14, 132

Tom Jones, 67, 78, 142–43
Tommy, 203
Tone, Franchot, 157
Tootsie, 60, 309–10
Topkapi, 148
Topol, 86, 101
Thompson, Ernest, 114
Three Smart Girls, 64
Toland, Gregg, 14
Tootsie, 147
Torn, Rip, 303, 336
Towering Inferno, The, 170–71
Tracy, Spencer, 67, 68, 108, 110, 112, 169, 187, 220
Trader Horn, 169
Treasure of the Sierra Madre, The, 113
Trespasser, The, 58
Trevor, Claire, 194
Trip to Bountiful, The, 97, 105, 263
Tri-Star, 294
Troell, Jan, 85
Trotti, Lamar, 306
True Grit, 174, 240
Truffaut, Francois, 48, 65
Truman, Harry S., 20
Trumbo, Dalton, 316
Turner, Kathleen, 41
Turning Point, The, 55, 144, 262, 324
Tuttle, William, 15
Twelve Angry Men, 123, 129
Twelve O'Clock High, 132
Twentieth Century-Fox, 61, 291–93, 300–1, 323
Twice in a Lifetime, 331
Two Women, 103
Tyson, Cicely, 232

Ullmann, Liv, 85, 92
Umberto D, 88
Umeki, Miyoshi, 86
United Artists, 293–94
Universal, 38, 50

Universal-International, 61
Unmarried Woman, An, 147
Ustinov, Peter, 81, 148, 238

Vagabond, 34
Valenti, Jack, 27
Valiant, The, 68
Van Fleet, Jo, 99, 194
Varda, Agnes, 34
Varsi, Diana, 55
Venice Film Festival, 33–34
Verdict, The, 83
Verne, Jules, 168
Victor/Victoria, 67
Vidor, King, 74, 125, 127, 225
Vietnam War, 326–27
Virgin Spring, The, 90
Viva Villa!, 157
Voight, Jon, 70, 104, 134, 326

Wajda, Andrzei, 48, 88
Wake Island, 164
Wald, Jerry, 296
Walken, Christopher, 326
Walsh, Raoul, 102
Walters, Julie, 40, 150
War films, 163–67
Ward, Mary Jane, 136
Warner Brothers, 2, 291–94
Warren, Robert Penn, 132
Watch on the Rhine, 99, 199
Waters, Ethel, 129
Waterston, Sam, 80
Watkin, David, 163
Watson, Lucille, 99
Wayne, John, 57, 174, 217–18, 226, 239–40, 252, 267, 298–99, 308, 326, 335
Weill, Claudia, 7
Weir, Peter, 73
Weld, Tuesday, 58
Welles, Orson, 33, 293, 310–11
Werner, Oskar, 86

Wertmuller, Lina, 87
West, Jessamyn, 316
West, Mae, 144
Western films, 173–75
Westerner, The, 175
West Side Story, 153
Wetherby, 116, 325
Whatever Happened to Baby Jane?, 192
When Father Was Away on Business, 327
White Banners, 60
White Heat, 189
Whitmore, James, 101
Who's Afraid of Virginia Woolf?, 117
Widmark, Richard, 55
Wilde, Jack, 50
Wilder, Billy, 33, 117, 125–26, 142, 150, 236–37, 293, 332
Wilder, Thornton, 69
Williams, Robin (actor), 26–27
Williams, Robin (sociologist), 338
Williams, Tennessee, 56, 99, 123, 195–96
Wills, Chill, 299
Wilson, 142, 306
Wilson, Michael, 316
Winfield, Paul, 232
Winger, Debra, 144
Wings, 163, 292
Winters, Shelley, 62, 66, 171, 216, 235, 237, 238, 250
Wise, Robert, 153–54, 165
Witness, 57, 329
Witness for the Prosecution, 117
Wiz, The, 45
Wizard of Oz, The, 51
Woman Under the Influence, A, 331

Wood, Natalie, 58, 97
Wood, Sam, 126
Woodard, Alfre, 303
Woodward, Bob, 139
Woodward, Joanne, 117, 136, 196, 250, 267, 301–2
World According to Garp, The, 326
Wright, Teresa, 55, 297
Writers Branch, 5
Writers Guild of America, 22, 316
Written on the Wind, 61, 194
Wuthering Heights, 15
Wyler, William, 33, 106, 124, 128, 132, 175, 176–77
Wyman, Jane, 84, 136, 251, 269–70
Wynyard, Diana, 137

Yankee Doodle Dandy, 305
Yates, Peter, 140
Year of the Quiet Sun, 34
Yentl, 40, 302
York, Susannah, 308–9
You Can't Take It With You, 141
Young, Gig, 236, 246, 283
Young, Loretta, 58, 102, 127, 220, 235
Young Lions, The, 56

Z, 85–86, 123
Zaentz, Saul, 136
Zanuck, Darryl, 102
Zanussi, Krzystof, 34
Zeffirelli, Franco, 161
Zinnemann, Fred, 106, 132–33, 161, 176–78, 280
Zorba the Greek, 147
Zukor, Adolph, 292